## NEGOTIATING COPYRIGHT IN THE AMERICAN THEATRE: 1856–1951

Drawing on fascinating archival discoveries from the past two centuries, Brent Salter shows how copyright has been negotiated in the American theatre. Who controls the space between authors and audiences? Does copyright law actually protect playwrights and help them make a living? At the center of these negotiations are mediating businesses with extraordinary power that rapidly evolved from the mid-nineteenth to mid-twentieth centuries: agents, publishers, producers, labor associations, administrators, accountants, lawyers, government bureaucrats, and film studio executives. As these mediators asserted authority over creativity, writers organized in response, through collective minimum contracts, informal guild expectations, and professional norms, to protect their presumed rights as authors. This institutional, relational, legal, and business history of the entertainment history in America illuminates both the historical context and the present law. An innovative new kind of intellectual property history, the book maps the relations between the different players from the ground up.

Brent Salter is a Postdoctoral Fellow at the Stanford Center for Law and History, Stanford Law School. His research focuses on legal and business histories of creative communities, intellectual property history, histories of labor organization in creative industries, contemporary and historical issues in arts policy.

CAMBRIDGE INTELLECTUAL PROPERTY AND INFORMATION LAW

As its economic potential has rapidly expanded, intellectual property has become a subject of front-rank legal importance. Cambridge Intellectual Property and Information Law is a series of monograph studies of major current issues in intellectual property. Each volume contains a mix of international, European, comparative and national law, making this a highly significant series for practitioners, judges and academic researchers in many countries.



A list of books in the series can be found at the end of this volume.

# Negotiating Copyright in the American Theatre: 1856–1951

**BRENT SALTER**
Stanford Law School

CAMBRIDGE
UNIVERSITY PRESS

**CAMBRIDGE**
**UNIVERSITY PRESS**

University Printing House, Cambridge CB2 8BS, United Kingdom

One Liberty Plaza, 20th Floor, New York, NY 10006, USA

477 Williamstown Road, Port Melbourne, VIC 3207, Australia

314–321, 3rd Floor, Plot 3, Splendor Forum, Jasola District Centre, New Delhi – 110025, India

103 Penang Road, #05–06/07, Visioncrest Commercial, Singapore 238467

Cambridge University Press is part of the University of Cambridge.

It furthers the University's mission by disseminating knowledge in the pursuit of education, learning, and research at the highest international levels of excellence.

www.cambridge.org
Information on this title: www.cambridge.org/9781108484756
DOI: 10.1017/9781108676182



First published 2022

*A catalogue record for this publication is available from the British Library.*

*Library of Congress Cataloging-in-Publication Data*
NAMES: Salter, Brent, author.
TITLE: Negotiating copyright in the American theatre : 1856–1951 / Brent Salter, Stanford Law School.
DESCRIPTION: New York : Cambridge University Press, 2021. | Series: Cambridge intellectual property and information law | Includes bibliographical references and index.
IDENTIFIERS: LCCN 2021024862 (print) | LCCN 2021024863 (ebook) | ISBN 9781108484756 (hardback) | ISBN 9781108676182 (ebook)
SUBJECTS: LCSH: Copyright – Performing rights – United States – History. | Copyright – Drama – United States – History. | Theater – Law and legislation – United States – History.
CLASSIFICATION: LCC KF3030.2 .S25 2021 (print) | LCC KF3030.2 (ebook) | DDC 346.73/0482–dc23
LC record available at https://lccn.loc.gov/2021024862
LC ebook record available at https://lccn.loc.gov/2021024863

ISBN 978-1-108-48475-6 Hardback

# Contents

# Figures

# Tables

# Acknowledgments

This book sits on a shelf (or some digital repository) because of support from generous communities and people across the world. I started to first think about this project in Australia as I was working at institutions including Opera Australia and the Sydney Theatre Company. I am grateful for conversations I had with Australian theatre practitioners that helped sow the seeds of this project including Rob Brookman, Ben Winspear, Jo Dyer, David Berthold, Rachel Healy, John Frost, Tom Wright, Gale Edwards, Tommy Murphy, Brendan Cowell, and Alana Valentine. I am also the fortunate beneficiary of encouragement from Australian scholars including Isabella Alexander, Shaunnagh Dorsett, Lisa Ford, Nicole Graham, Alex Reilly, and Simon Rice. In particular, I want to thank three Australian mentors: Katherine Biber, Bruce Kercher, and Kathy Bowrey. The profound influence that Kathy, Katherine, and Bruce have had on my scholarship is hopefully evident in the pages that follow and will continue to inform my work throughout my career.

At Yale, I was humbled to receive incredible support for my research across the campus. The Graduate Programs Office at Yale Law School has created a doctoral program that provides an extraordinary degree of flexibility to grow as a teacher and scholar. Special thanks in particular to Maria Dino, Gordon Silverstein, and Allegra di Bonaventura. The library system across Yale – especially the librarians and archivists – met my numerous questions with skill, promptness, patience, and good cheer, often sending me down paths that I never would have contemplated. Thank you all for supporting my work, especially Melissa Barton and Susan Brady at Beinecke Rare Book and Manuscript Library. Legal scholars and historians at Yale have shaped the ways I will think about interdisciplinary scholarship and teaching. I am grateful for support from Claire Priest, James Whitman, and George Priest. The theatre community at Yale – and in particular the faculty and students at Yale School of Drama, and the theatre students and faculty at Yale College – welcomed me throughout my time in New Haven. I want to thank Marc Robinson, Catherine Sheehy, Joseph Roach, and James Bundy for their support. In the spring of 2019

I taught a seminar at Yale College on legal and business histories of the American Theatre. The talented students in the seminar that informed my thinking on many issues explored in this book include Brantley Butcher, Jake Gluckman, Shannon Linder, Scott Feiner, Aidan O'Connor, Simon Rabinowitz, Charlie Romano, Ryan Seffinger, and Adam Wassilchalk.

I want to particularly thank Amy Kapczynski (Yale Law), John Witt (Yale Law/History), and Jean-Christophe Agnew (Yale History/American Studies) who served on my dissertation panel at Yale. They are all incredible scholars who have always supported my career and curiosities at the crossroads of law, history, and the arts. My supervisor Nicholas Parrillo (Yale Law/History) and Joan Channick (Yale School of Drama) are the kind of mentors I aspire to be when I am hopefully in a similar position. I owe both Nick and Joan my deepest gratitude for their continuing support and wisdom. At Stanford, I have had the privilege to work with an extraordinary group of legal historians and legal scholars whose research I admire including Rabia Belt, Greg Ablavsky, Lawrence Friedman, Paul Goldstein, Rowan Dorin, and Robert Gordon. Amalia Kessler and Bernadette Meyler are incomparable scholars and mentors to whom I owe my deepest thanks for all things both great and small. Amalia and Bernie are models for inclusivity and for how I hope to live my life as a scholar, teacher, and colleague.

The project, and ongoing scholarship, has also benefited from the invaluable guidance of many legal scholars, historians, and theatre scholars. I give particular thanks to the brilliant and generous Jose Bellido, Catherine Fisk, Christopher Sprigman, Steven Wilf, and Derek Miller.

This project has taken me to archives across the United States. I thank the many librarians, staff, and archivists at institutions and sites including Amherst College Archives and Special Collections, Beinecke Library at Yale, Harvard Theatre Collection-Houghton Library, Library of Congress, National Archives and Records Administration (New York and Philadelphia), New York Public Library for the Performing Arts, Special Collections Research Center Southern Illinois University Carbondale, George Mason University Historical and Special Collections, and Harvard Law School Library. I was very fortunate to have access to private collections that were critical for this research including The Shubert Archive in New York and the private collections of the Dramatists Guild of America. I am incredibly grateful to The Shubert Archive's Mark Swartz, Maryann Chach, Sylvia Wang, and Helice Koffler. I also extend my deep gratitude to Ralph Sevush and Tina Fallon at the Dramatists Guild for their ongoing support of my research and also their commitment to the preservation of the archival memory of the American theatre. Likewise, I would like to thank Abbie Van Nostrand and Amy Marsh at Samuel French for supporting the preservation of theatre archival material and in particular the role they have played in the preservation of the important Samuel French collection housed at Amherst College. A special thanks also to George Penny and George Middleton for allowing me to use the sketch by Austin Strong (Start of Part II). For permissions, I would also like to thank Houghton Library, Harvard (Chapter 8), Playbill (Chapter 7), Special Collections Research Center, and Southern Illinois University Carbondale (Chapter 3). Other images in the book are in the public domain. Thank you to Mark Swartz at The Shubert Archive for permission to use the cover image "J.J. Shubert in his office at 39th Street & Broadway, c. 1909."

The project would not exist without the generous financial and in-kind support of Stanford Law School; a Humanities and Methodology Teaching Fellowship (Yale University); Kauffman Program in Law, Economics, and Entrepreneurship Fellowship (Yale Law School); Special Research Fellowship (Yale School of Drama); Houghton Library Fellowship (Harvard University); Harvard/Cambridge Center for History and Economics, History Project Grant; Legal History Fellowship (Yale Law School); Beinecke Fellowship (Yale University); Research Fellowship (New York Public Library); Oscar M. Ruebhausen Grant (Yale Law School); and Yale Law School Doctoral Scholarship. These institutions have also supported my broader agenda of surrounding projects including Brent Salter: "The Ordinary Authors of the Bureau of New Plays: Copyright and Reallocating Authority in the American Theatre (1936–1949)," *Cardozo Arts & Entertainment Law Journal* 39 no. 1 (2021); Brent Salter and Catherine Fisk: "Assumptions and Fragilities of Labor Relations in the American Theatre," *Ohio State Law Journal* 83 (2022); "Copyright, Crisis, and Welfare in the Federal Theatre Project (1935–1939)" (article under preparation at the time of publication of the book).

My thanks to Lionel Bently, the series editor at Cambridge University Press and Matt Gallaway and his diligent team at CUP, especially Chloe Quinn and Jadyn Fauconier-Herry. A special thank you to Paula Clarke Bain (indexing) and Helen Kitto (copy editing) for their thoughtful and thorough contribution to the book.

To Elizabeth, Arabella, and Oscar: for your love and encouragement, this book is for you.

# Introduction

This book is a historical account about the negotiation of creativity in the American theatre. It is a history of how the American theatre organized its relationships and how stakeholders, and in particular dramatists, responded to these developments. The book examines how copyright law has interacted with the American theatre in dynamic and counterintuitive ways, helping to facilitate theatrical production between authors of original copyright works and audiences. But copyright plays only a supporting role in the much larger theatrical economy. This is a history of how the industry was shaped by the evolution of mediating businesses and the practices they established which copyright has mostly accommodated. The growth in mediating businesses, and responses to these developments, has accompanied enduring uncertainties about the authority dramatists are often assumed to have over the work they create.

Scholarship on the relationship between law and the American theatre devotes considerable energy to the intellectual property rights that creative stakeholders are assumed to control as either text-based writer authors of original works, or aspire to control as nonwriter collaborators.[1] Since 1856, the United States federal statutory copyright framework has continued to appear to expand the protections of the author dramatist. The author of the text – usually the playwright – is assumed to enjoy the exclusive initial rights to the dramatic work. The text-based authorship narrative in the American theatre did not find voice through legal pronouncement alone. Throughout most of the twentieth century, and beyond, the resilient trade association Dramatists Guild has nurtured the cause of playwrights, composers, lyricists, and librettists, successfully negotiating minimum standards for these groups with other stakeholders in the industry.

[1] I use the expressions creative collaborator or creative stakeholder as a way to identify artistic stakeholders involved in the production process that fall into two subgroups including, but not necessarily limited to: (1) "writer" creative collaborators (including playwrights, composers, lyricists, and librettists); and (2) "nonwriter" creative collaborators including dramaturgs, designers, stage directors, and actors (whose creative contribution is not text-based). I distinguish these two subgroups of creative stakeholders from other stakeholders – including, but not limited to – publishers, playbrokers, lawyers, accountants, producers, union, guild and labor associations, that mediate the production process.

Former President of the American Dramatists Guild John Weidman claims that "as long as anyone can remember the community of artists and businessmen who make theatre have shared a common set of assumptions about how a play or a musical makes its way from the page to the stage."[2] At the core of these common assumptions is the historical prioritization of a text-based independent-contracting model of organization. So copyright has protected the work of dramatists as independent contractors, and the playwrights have realized many of these protections through successful and sustained maintenance and enhancement of minimum standards in the form of a basic uniform agreement that has evolved over the last century.[3]

A common narrative in contemporary legal scholarship that explores the relationship between copyright law and the theatre goes something like as follows. The United States Copyright Act of 1976, or its equivalent in many common law jurisdictions, protects dramatic works,[4] distinguishable from literary works because they are performed. The literature will often acknowledge that a key element of copyright law is that it incorporates works of authors "fixed in any tangible medium of expression."[5] Because of the fixation requirement, a framework that prioritizes the contribution of the dramatist emerges. The text-based framework has endured despite theatre's inherently collaborative and ephemeral nature and despite the notable absence of terms including "dramatist" or "playwright" in copyright codes. There are often attempts to imagine what the law could look like that incorporates the contributions of nonwriter creative collaborators such as directors, dramaturgs, or actors.[6] The commentary

[2] John Weidman, "Protecting the American Playwright: The Seventh Annual Media and Society Lecture," *Brooklyn Law Review* 72 (2007): 640.

[3] The broad protections playwrights are assumed to enjoy have been described as an "anomaly," "exceptional," and "a unique power." The playwright's authority is assumed to exist at the intersection of statutory law and "industry custom and practice … protected through contractual relationships." *See* Carol Kaplan, "Once More unto the Breach," *Vanderbilt Journal of Entertainment and Technology Law* 16, no. 2 (2014): 303; Shane Valenzi, "A Rollicking Band of Pirates: Licensing the Exclusive Right of Public Performance in the Theatre Industry," *Vanderbilt Journal of Entertainment and Technology Law* 14, no. 3 (2012): 778. *See also* Jessica Litman, "The Invention of Common Law Play Right," *Berkeley Technology Law Journal* 25 (2010): 1425 and analysis below in Chapter 1, however, who maps the tension between the "author-centric rhetoric" and whether the development of the common law play right was ever an author's right: (1424–1425). Litman also acknowledges how dramatists secured "exceptional author's rights through collective action that was not tied to any statute or judicial decision" (at 1425).

[4] *See* 17 U.S.C., § 102(a)(3) "Works of authorship include the following categories: … dramatic works, including any accompanying music."

[5] 17 U.S.C., § 102(a).

[6] Michael Carroll makes the following distinction between "writer" and "nonwriter" collaborators: "Even though producers, directors, and performers may qualify as 'authors' of their contributions under copyright law, this Article treats this group collectively as 'performers' to focus on the mutually dependent relationship between the writers of source works and those who render them in performance." *See* Michael Carroll, "Copyright's Creative Hierarchy in the Performing Arts," *Vanderbilt Journal Entertainment & Technology Law* 14, no. 4 (2012): 804.

will often consider whether[7] it is possible to fix stage directions in a tangible medium of expression,[8] or whether nonwriter contributions meet the threshold of originality.[9] The literature also considers whether, or when, a contribution is a joint work,[10] derivative work,[11] or work-made-for-hire.[12] What often follows is

7 For examples of the many treatments, *see* Talia Yellin, "New Directions for Copyright: The Property Rights of Stage Directors," *Columbia-VLA Journal of Law & the Arts* 24, no. 3 (2001): 317; Richard Amada, "Elvis Karaoke Shakespeare and the Search for a Copyrightable Stage Directions," *Arizona Law Review* 43, no. 3 (2001): 677; Beth Freemal, "Theatre, Stage Directions & (and) Copyright Law," *Chicago-Kent Law Review* 71, no. 3 (1996): 1017; Jennifer J. Maxwell, "Making a Federal Case for Copyrighting Stage Directions: Einhorn v. Mergatroyd Productions," *John Marshall Review of Intellectual Property Law* 7, no. 2 (Winter 2008): 393; Margit Livingston, "Inspiration or Imitation: Copyright Protection for Stage Directions," *Boston College Law Review* 50, no. 2 (March 2009): 427; Deana S. Stein, "Every Move That She Makes: Copyright Protection for Stage Directions and the Fictional Character Standard," *Cardozo Law Review* 34, no. 4 (April 2013): 1571; Jessica Talati, "Copyrighting Stage Directions & the Constitutional Mandate to Promote the Progress of Science," *Northwestern Journal of Technology and Intellectual Property* 7, no. 2 (Spring 2009): 241; Susan Keller, "Collaboration in Theater: Problems and Copyright Solutions," *UCLA Law Review* 33, no. 3 (February 1986): 891; Douglas M. Nevin, "No Business Like Show Business: Copyright Law, the Theatre Industry, and the Dilemma of Rewarding Collaboration," *Emory Law Journal* 53, no. 3 (Summer 2004): 1533; Pedro Jose F. Bernardo, "Transformative Adaptation, Performance, and Fair Use of Literary and Dramatic Works: Delineating the Rights of Playwrights and Adapters," *Ateneo Law Journal* 53, no. 3 (2008): 582. For an interesting paper outside of the property lens *see generally* David Leichtman, "Most Unhappy Collaborators: An Argument against the Recognition of Property Ownership in Stage Directions," *Columbia-VLA Journal of Law & the Arts* 20, no. 4 (1996): 683.

8 *See* 17 U.S.C., § 102(a).

9 *See* 17 U.S.C., § 102(a): "Copyright protection subsists, in accordance with this title, in original works of authorship. . ."

10 *See* Copyright Act of 1976, § 101. There is an expansive literature on the application of joint works to theatre, especially with respect to *Thomson v. Larson*, 147 F.3d 195 (2nd Cir. 1998) (involved a nonprofit theatre that workshopped new plays where a dramaturg Lynn Thomson developed a work with writer Jonathan Larson). To name just a few articles that examine joint works and the case: Matthew Rimmer, "Heretic: Copyright Law and Dramatic Works," *Queensland University of Technology Law and Justice Journal* 2, no. 1 (2002): 137–141; Jane C. Lee, "Upstaging the Playwright: The Joint Authorship Entanglement between Dramaturgs and Playwrights," *Loyola of Los Angeles Entertainment Law Journal* 19, no. 1 (1998): 75; "Recent Cases," *Harvard Law Review* 112, no. 4 (February 1999): 964; Nevin, "No Business Like Show Business," 1533; Mary LaFrance, "Authorship, Dominance, and the Captive Collaborator: Preserving the Rights of Joint Authors," *Emory Law Journal* 50, no. 1 (Winter 2001): 193; Jennifer Womack, "Big Shop of Horrors: Ownership in Theatrical Design," *Fordham Intellectual Property, Media & Entertainment Law Journal* 18, no. 1 (Autumn 2007): 225; Paulette S. Fox, "Preserving the Collaborative Spirit of American Theater: The Need for a Joint Authorship Default Rule in Light of the Rent Decision's Unanswered Question," *Cardozo Arts & Entertainment Law Journal* 19, no. 3 (2001): 497; Faye Buckalew, "Joint Authorship in the Second Circuit: A Critique of the Law in the Second Circuit Following Childress v. Taylor and as Exemplified in Thomson v. Larson," *Brooklyn Law Review* 64, no. 2 (1998): 545; Roberta Rosenthal Kwall, "Author-Stories: Narrative's Implications for Moral Rights and Copyright's Joint Authorship Doctrine," *Southern California Law Review* 75, no. 1 (November 2001): 1 (Kwall's illuminating work focuses more on issues of moral rights); Carrie Ryan Gallia, "To Fix or Not to Fix: Copyright's Fixation Requirement and the Rights of Theatrical Collaborators," *Minnesota Law Review* 92, no. 1 (November2007): 231. *See also* Shyamkrishna Balganesh, "Unplanned Coauthorship," *Virginia Law Review* 100, no. 8 (December 2014): 1683.

11 *See* 17 U.S.C., § 101. *See also* 17 U.S.C., § 106(2): Under the Copyright Act, a copyright owner has the exclusive right "to prepare derivative works based upon the copyrighted work."

12 *See* 17 U.S.C., § 201(b).

an examination of the limits of copyright: fair use;[13] merger doctrine;[14] and *Scenes a Faire*;[15] or, for example, whether a new work is distinctly delineated.[16] Finally, there may be a consideration of options outside of copyright including breach of contract, false representation, or unfair competition,[17] unjust enrichment, and misappropriation law.[18]

Following the exploration of potential options what is left but to decide other appropriate legislative and judicial responses. It could be a statutory licensing scheme,[19] or an amalgamated system incorporating doctrines of joint authorship and derivative works.[20] It is more likely there will be a more general, and very reasonable, plea to broaden judicial interpretation for instances of novel contributions.[21]

Unquestionably, there are authors of successful works who have achieved critical acclaim and reaped extraordinary economic benefits through industry royalty structures.[22] But as obvious as it is to state that the history of the American theatre includes incredible stories of success, it is just as undeniable to acknowledge the multitude of tales of playwright subordination. Todd London and his coauthors in

13 *See* 17 U.S.C., § 107.

14 When there is only one or a limited number of ways to express an idea, copyright law will not protect merger between the expression and the idea. *See Morrissey* v. *Proctor & Gamble Company*, 379 F.2d 675, 678–679 (1 Cir. 1967); *Aliotti* v. *R. Dakin & Co.*, 831 F.2d 898, 901 (9th Cir.1987).

15 The circumstance where there is no other way to express an idea except by using particular elements and in such instances the elements are referred to as *Scenes a Faire. See, for example*, *Atari, Inc.* v. *N. Am. Phillips Consumer Elecs. Corp.*, 672 F.2d 607, 616 (7th Cir. 1982); *Murray Hill Publications, Inc.* v. *Twentieth Century Fox Film Corp.*, 361 F.3d 312, 319–320 (6th Cir. 2004); *Zambito* v. *Paramount Pictures Corp.*, 613 F. Supp. 1107, 1111–1112 (E.D.N.Y 1985); 788 F.2d 2 (2d Cir. 1985); *Schwartz* v. *Universal Pictures Co.* 85 F. Supp. 270(S.D. Cal. 1949). *See also* Maxwell, "Making a Federal Case," 393.

16 *See Nichols* v. *Universal Pictures Corporation*, 45 F.2d 119 (2d Cir. 1930); *see* Stein, "Every Move that She Makes," 1593–1607 (particularly 1597–1600).

17 *See generally* Yellin, "New Directions for Copyright," 317–347 (particularly 344–345).

18 *See* Livingston, "Inspiration of Imitation," 469–479.

19 *See* Carroll, "Copyright's Creative Hierarchy," 810–827.

20 *See* Nevin, "No Business Like Show Business," 1560–1569.

21 A broader understanding might read like the following: "Ultimately, a director who creates a truly novel staging of a classic or new play should be able to sue successfully a later director for copyright infringement if the later director closely copies the most striking features of the original director's staging. That result is consistent with copyright doctrine and policies, which seek to encourage creation of artistic works while allowing second comers to be inspired by earlier efforts, and with the theatre's long tradition as both an individual and collaborative art." (Livingston, "Inspiration of Imitation," 487.) Or maybe: "This comment advocates for the copyright protection of stage directions that fulfill the requirements of the Copyright Act and proposes that copyrighting stage directions will not devastate the rights of playwrights because fair use and *scenes a faire* will limit the protection granted to stage directions, thereby ensuring the promotion and advancement of the arts" (Maxwell, "Making a Federal Case," 393 (abstract)).

22 Philip Boroff, for example, reports that *Hamilton* "composer-lyricist-librettist and actor" Lin Manuel Miranda "amassed $12.7 million in author royalties and profit participation from the Broadway production in the 12 months ending in July 2017." *See* Philip Boroff "'Hamilton' Pays Miranda & Seller Tens of Millions a Year," *Broadway Journal*, April 26, 2018, http://broadwayjournal.com/hamilton-pays-miranda-seller-tens-of-millions-a-year/.

*Outrageous Fortune: The Life and Times of the New American Play*, expose the many impossible economic challenges confronting the American dramatist.[23] The theatre literature also charts a less certain and more fragile economic and artistic history for the American playwright. That history often suggests the professional experience of the American dramatist is one of economic marginalization, isolation, and considerable compromise rather than authority.[24]

What we are left with is a standoff between dueling, and equally legitimate, tales of oppression – an unedifying struggle between creative claimants over legal recognition of intellectual property rights they are assumed to possess or think they ought to possess. For many dramatists, as writer Peter Stone reminds us, copyright is often conceived as a "birthright" that starts with a blank page and is only rewarded after the production is realized on the stage.[25] The dramatists also describe themselves as "property owners" under the law "who license the use of their property."[26] Copyright serves as the necessary legal shield against infringement and is an instrument used for compensating creation. In contrast, for nonwriter collaborators, and scholars that champion their cause, copyright protection is an aspirational normative project about what a rights framework ought to be. Courts and legislators should be able to find ways within the law to acknowledge the inherently collaborative nature of how theatre is created.

—

The standoff between writer and nonwriter collaborators, therefore, is an ongoing theme in the legal history of the American theatre – the intellectual property rights that stakeholders either possess or aspire to possess. But another way to think about

23 *See* Todd London with Ben Pesner and Zannie G. Voss, *Outrageous Fortune: The Life and Times of the New American Play* (New York: TDF, 2009). *See also* Todd London: Keynote Speech *American Dramatists Guild Annual Conference*, Washington DC, June 10, 2011 (available on YouTube: www.youtube.com/watch?v=5E_l-ZlevR8).

24 *See generally* Todd London et al., *Outrageous Fortune*. *See also*, a far from exhaustive list: Percy MacKaye, *Epoch: The Life of Steele MacKaye, Genius of the Theatre* (New York: Boni and Liveright, 1927: 2 vols.); George Middleton, *These Things Are Mine: The Autobiography of a Journeyman Playwright* (New York: The Macmillan Company, 1947); Thomas Kitts, *The Theatrical Life of George Henry Boker* (New York: P. Lang, 1994); Arthur Hornblow, *A History of the Theatre in America: From Its Beginnings to the Present time* (Vol. 2, Philadelphia, PA: J. B. Lippincotte and Co., 1919); Clement Foust, *The Life and Dramatic Works of Robert Montgomery Bird* (New York: The Knickerbocker Press, 1919); Howard Teichmann, *George S Kaufman: An Intimate Portrait* (New York: Atheneum, 1972); John Gassner (ed.) in association with Mollie Gassner, *Best Plays of the Early American Theatre: 1787–1911* (Mineola, NY: Dover Publications, [2000], c.1967); Cecile Rukgaber, *The Theatrical Syndicate and Its Effects upon the American Theatre* (MA Thesis, University of Wyoming, 1955). Jack Poggi's analysis is limited to economic matters with a cursory consideration of legal issues: Jack Poggi, *Theatre in America: The Impact of Economic Forces, 1870–1967* (Ithaca, NY: Cornell University Press, 1968).

25 Sandra Salmans, "Why Investors in Broadway Hits Are Often Losers," *New York Times*, November 22, 1981, 129, 138.

26 *See* Dramatists Guild of America, "Authors Should Maintain a Legal Right to Their Work," www.dramatistsguild.com/no-union (and *see* full quote in Epilogue).

the history of economic and artistic control over theatrical creation is to reconstruct the dynamic path that the production process has to undergo to eventually be realized in front of an audience in a performance space. How does the industry organize its relationships in this space of transformation and who controls this space?

If the central inquiry is to explain the historical structure of the industry, we can also begin to think about copyright's relationship with the author of the original work in the context of the larger production process. For example, vesting the author with initial control over copyright is a practical place to begin transforming a work into a final production on the stage. Initial copyright control serves the role of an administrative adjunct for production to commence. And the author or authors could be anyone, but the point is that it is a practical and reliable place to begin to organize production in the larger theatrical economy where the common goal among all stakeholders is eventual staging. Copyright, in the context of the broader structure of the industry, can also be framed as an instrument that helps move the evolving work from one stage of the process to the next in the space between the author and the audience.[27]

Copyright understood as one tool within a larger bag that helps facilitate the process of production in the American theatre takes on different characteristics to that of competing creative claimants seeking to define the intellectual property rights that they possess, do not possess, or aspire to possess. The author's control over copyright is understood in relational terms with other stakeholders. The author subject's initial control over copyright is an offering to the production process – it undergoes constant dynamic renegotiation within the larger organizational space between the author and the audience. In the ongoing relationship between stakeholders, the triumvirate of authorship, ownership, and control coexist only in form at an initial static point in time; a starting point from which to renegotiate control as

[27] Carys Craig, for example, explores authorship as a "dialogical process," where the works of an author "must be understood in their social context, and her acquired rights must be examined in relation to her audience and other members of her communicative communities." *See* Carys Craig, *Copyright, Communication and Culture: Towards a Relational Theory of Copyright Law* (Cheltenham UK: Edward Elgar, 2011), 54. *See also* Rebecca Curtin's work on the private ordering and commercial practices between authors and publishers prior to the Statute of Anne which helps explain practices after the enactment of the Statute of Anne: Rebecca Schoff Curtin, "The Transactional Origins of Authors' Copyright," *Columbia Journal of Law & the Arts* 40, no. 2 (2016): 175. My work also owes much to the earlier relational contracts literature. Stewart Macaulay, "Non-Contractual Relations in Business: A Preliminary Study," *American Sociological Review* 28 (1963): 55. *See also* Lisa Bernstein, "Opting out of the Legal System: Extralegal Contractual Relations in the Diamond Industry," *Journal of Legal Studies* 21, no. 1 (1992): 115; David Campbell and Donald Harris, "Flexibility in Long-Term Contractual Relationships: The Role of Co-operation," *Journal of Law and Society* 20, no. 2 (1993): 166. On the hidden and often unfettered power of stronger parties to dictate the terms of industry practice *see also* Stewart Macaulay, "Lawyers and Consumer Protection Laws," *Law & Society Review* 14, no. 1 (1979): 115. (As also discussed in Robert Gordon, "Is the World of Contracting Relations One of Spontaneous Order or Pervasive State Action? Stewart Macaulay Scrambles the Public-Private Distinction," in *Revisiting the Contracts Scholarship of Stewart Macaulay*, ed. Jean Braucher, John Kidwell, and William Whitford (Oxford, UK and Portland, OR: Hart Publishing, 2013), 49.)

the work transforms into a performance. The initial allocation of rights to the author must inevitably cede to the larger institutional structures of the theatrical economy. As a necessary consequence, stakeholders other than creative writer and nonwriter collaborators – that establish and control the institutional structures in the space between authors and audiences – assert extraordinary influence over both economic and artistic dimensions of the production process.

The text of the play is originally a blueprint. That is, the play is active and requires the collaboration of others to be fully experienced as culture and to generate income for those associated. It is only by the transformation of the original physical text into the performance that, for the most part, copyright income is generated. Control over the intangible theatrical right in the text and performance of that text has no inherent economic or artistic value in itself until exploited in a material place and time. A rights discourse engages in conversations about whether dramatists or other creative collaborator contributions such as stage directors, actors, dramaturgs, or designers are valued both economically and artistically, and consequently, there is an inevitable preoccupation with the rights that claimants should or should not possess. But these preoccupations divert attention away from the ongoing collective managerial contributions working within larger industry structures that establish how creation is realized. Who are the actual stakeholders – and what organizational structures do they create – that control how theatrical production is realized on the stage? How do creators like playwrights respond as a group to these structures?

—

Mediating stakeholders who controlled the transformation of the theatrical work from the playwright's manuscript to the theatrical stage shaped the structure of the industry from the mid-nineteenth to mid-twentieth centuries. Further, copyright law developed in ways that accommodated these mediating interests.[28] The mediating stakeholders evolved in different forms: for-profit, nonprofit, and government projects.[29] The stakeholders included playbrokers and transnational publishers, and the commercial impresarios emerging in the 1890s that formed booking businesses. They included trade associations such as the playwrights' association Dramatists Guild and government agencies created during the New Deal period. These mediating stakeholders and the institutional structures they developed also informed practices in the second half of the twentieth century and continue to influence practices to this day.

I call these stakeholders mediators as they do not only facilitate the process of production from page to the stage but transform the work into the material

[28] *See* discussion of the legal developments in Chapter 1.

[29] The nonprofit and government discussions in this book are not analyzed in detail, but form part of my larger research agenda and are to be published in separate article-length studies: *See* Brent Salter, "The Ordinary Authors of the Bureau Of New Plays: Copyright and Reallocating Authority in the American Theatre (1936–1949)," *Cardozo Arts & Entertainment Law Journal* 39 no. 1 (2021); "Copyright, Crisis, and Welfare in the Federal Theatre Project (1935–1939)" (article under preparation).

performance.[30] The ability to transform the original script is how mediators assert economic and artistic influence over theatrical creation. Thus, when I speak to the notion of control over production in the American theatre, I am referring to how stakeholders who have the resources and capabilities to turn an intangible right into a production on the stage negotiate that transformation process in the space between authors and audiences.

The resources and capabilities essential for production that mediators possess – of which copyright is only one part – exist in various forms. For example, staging involves control over rehearsal prompt scripts, dramaturgical notes, advance royalty notices, theatrical programs, material correspondence in the form of letters and memos, and theatrical contracts. Realization of the production involves control over theatre real properties in which to present the theatrical work, and, for example, control over the physical printing of the play. The realization of the theatrical work requires control over physical material such as sets and costumes. Staging the production involves control over administrative processes including business organization, media strategies, controlling transportation routes, accounting procedures, and controlling communication networks between internal stakeholders that mediate the movement of creativity daily between authors and audiences.[31] Realizing the

30 Thus, understanding the space between author and audience where the work transforms to the stage requires more than an investigation of the human agent alone as the source of authority over creativity. This requires a move away from viewing the process through the prism of the theatrical stakeholder as a cultural intermediary toward mediation. Bruno Latour's departure from the intermediary is his rejection of compartmentalized human agency and its different categories in which there is someone "inter." Mediators are things that transform the connecting points they mediate while intermediaries are just human carriers of information/opportunities – "transport[ing] meaning or force without transformation." Bruno Latour, *Reassembling the Social: An introduction to Actor-Network Theory* (New York: Oxford University Press, 2005), 39. Theatre scholar Marlis Schweitzer examines the "assemblage of objects that accelerated the transnational movement of theatrical commodities," at the turn of the nineteenth century. Schweitzer, also drawing on Latour, is interested in "moments of disturbance or rupture, when managerial dependency on machines or other objects became all-too visible." *See* Marlis Schweitzer, *Transatlantic Broadway: The Infrastructural Politics of Global Performance* (Houndmills, Basingstoke, Hampshire, UK; New York: Palgrave Macmillan, 2015), 17.

31 I use the expression movement to capture the fluid negotiations that shape authority structures between stakeholders in practice. And movement also embodies the ephemerality of the art form itself. There is a rich more recent body of theatre literature that scrutinizes histories of theatrical management and processes of production in the space between authors and audiences. Marlis Schweitzer describes this work as pushing back against "the anti-commercial bias in theatre scholarship, emphasizing the value of attending to economics and the practicalities of business decisions." *See* Marlis Schweitzer, "Aggressive, Beleaguered, Commercial, Defiant: Marc Klaw and Abraham Erlanger," in *The Palgrave Handbook of Musical Theatre Producers*, eds. Laura McDonald and William Everett (New York: Palgrave Macmillan US: Imprint: Palgrave Macmillan, 2017), 60. *See also*, for example, Schweitzer, *Transatlantic Broadway*; Nic Leonhardt, "Transatlantic Theatrical Traces: Oceanic Trade Routes and Globe-Trotting Amusement Explorers," *The Passing Show* 30 (2013/2014): 2; Nic Leonhardt and Stanca Scholz-Cionca: "Circulation, Theatre Mobility and Its Professionalization in the Nineteenth Century," in *A Cultural History of Theatre in the Age of Empire (1800–1920)*, ed. Peter W. Marx (London: Bloomsbury, 2017); James Harding and John Rouse, *Not the Other Avant-garde: The Transnational Foundations of Avant-garde Performance* (Ann Arbor:

production also involves a process of forming personal relationships and networks of trust. A well-placed reliable source of quality product in a theatrical economy where one's word was their bond, and finance, depended on who thought well of you. The historically specific nature of the relationship matters to the reading of the dynamics in the industry. Creation has distinctive historical forms that generate different kinds of interpersonal and normative demands that theatrical stakeholders both include and exclude.[32]

Steven Wilf writes of the need "to turn to a deeper understanding of how historical actors have sought to recast the contours of intellectual property law."[33] I aim to understand the practices of various stakeholders in the theatre community both known and relatively unknown.[34] Historical actors do not only include creative

University of Michigan Press, 2006); Christin Essin and Marlis Schweitzer, "Communities of Production: A Materialist Reading with an Offstage View," in *A Cultural History of Theatre in the Modern Age*, ed. Kim Solga (London, UK; New York: Bloomsbury, 2017); David Savran, *A Queer Sort of Materialism: Recontextualizing American Theatre* (Ann Arbor: The University of Michigan Press, 2003); Mark Hodin, "The Disavowal of Ethnicity: Legitimate Theatre and the Social Construction of Literary Value in Turn-of-the-Century America," *Theatre Journal* 52 (2000): 219; Tracy C. Davis, *The Economics of the British Stage: 1800–1914* (Cambridge, UK; New York: Cambridge University Press, 2000); David Savran, *Highbrow/Lowdown: Theater, Jazz, and the Making of the New Middle Class* (Ann Arbor: The University of Michigan Press, 2009); Peter A. Davis, "The Syndicate/Shubert War," in *Inventing Times Square: Commerce and Culture at the Crossroads of the World*, ed. William R. Taylor (New York: Russell Sage Foundation, 1991); Michael Schwartz, *Broadway and Corporate Capitalism: The Rise of the Professional-Managerial Class, 1900–1920* (New York: Palgrave Macmillan, 2009); Lisa Surwillo, *Stages of Property: Copyrighting Theatre in Spain* (Toronto: University of Toronto Press, 2007); Mattie Burkert, *Speculative Enterprise: Public Theaters and Financial Markets in London, 1688–1763* (Charlottesville: University of Virginia Press, 2021). And *see* Derek Miller's ongoing research of the history of Broadway and the American theatre: *See, for example*, Derek Miller, "Average Broadway," *Theatre Journal* 68, no. 4 (December 2016): 529; Derek Miller, *Copyright and the Value of Performance, 1770–1911* (Cambridge, UK: Cambridge University Press, 2018).

32 I am grateful for discussions with Kathy Bowrey on this point. This book, and ongoing research, also hopes to engage with scholarship on anthropologies of bureaucracy in private, nonprofit, and state-based organizations and through the prism of law, history, and creativity. *See* Kathy Bowrey, *Copyright, Creativity, Big Media and Cultural Value Incorporating the Author* (Abingdon, UK; New York: Routledge Books, 2021). *See* Chihab El Khachab, "Current Trends in the Anthropology of Bureaucracy – A Report," https://allegralaboratory.net/current-trends-in-the-anthropology-of-bureaucracy-a-report/. And such work also owes a great debt to the long line of scholarship on bureaucracy influenced by Max Weber, *Economy and Society: An Outline of Interpretive Sociology* (Berkeley: University of California Press, 1978) (edited by Guenther Roth and Claus Wittich; translators, Ephraim Fischoff et al.).

33 Steven Wilf, "Copyright and Social Movements in Late Nineteenth-Century America," *Theoretical Inquiries in Law* 12, no. 1 (January 2011): 123.

34 This project is influenced by a broader legal history literature that interrogates histories of the ordinary, and histories of the local. For example, in Lisa Ford's close reading of law and frontier settlements in Georgia and New South Wales, the author argues that the legal conflicts of the 1830s reflected uncertainties about which rules governed the land and indigenous people and settlers on the peripheries of these settlements. Laura Edwards' extensive archival research of post-revolutionary records from the Carolinas explores the differences between state laws that protected the rights of legally recognized individuals, and local laws, built around maintaining the "peace" and social order.

collaborators. Actors that engage in theatrical creation include administrators, accountants, lawyers, and government agents. Other actors include playbrokers, publishers, play reporters, and film studio executives. By framing control over production through the lens of these alternative mediating stakeholders, the histories of other actors also emerge. The legal histories of extraordinary women engaged in shaping theatrical business and legal practices go largely untold, as do the histories of minority groups,[35] and ordinary authors without the omnipotent reputation of an O'Neill, Miller, Williams, or Bernard Shaw.[36]

I, therefore, turn to how a variety of mediating actors control the production process in the space between the author and audience by how they establish and consolidate personal relationships, by how they interact with their surrounding resources essential for production, and by how they establish administrative processes. Copyright is only one part that combines with these many other dimensions of the larger project involved in realizing theatre creation. By the term realize, I refer to the ability to turn the intangible right into the material performance on stage. Stakeholders able to realize the production are also in a better position to design internal contracting procedures, define and establish relationships of use with other stakeholders, restructure legal strategies around areas of law outside of copyright, and are also in a better position to take advantage of a copyright framework that, for the most part, has accommodated mediating interests. Stakeholders removed from

It is in the minutiae of everyday interactions between actors – the reconstruction of "a previously unknown historical world" – that the complexity of the issues surrounding copyright control can begin to be explored. *See* Lisa Ford, *Settler Sovereignty Jurisdiction and Indigenous People in America and Australia, 1788–1836* (Cambridge, MA: Harvard University Press, 2010); Laura Edwards, *The People and Their Peace: Legal Culture and the Transformation of Inequality in the Post-Revolutionary South* (Chapel Hill: University of North Carolina Press, 2009). *See also* John Witt's biographical organization in *Patriots and Cosmopolitans: Hidden Histories of American Law* (Cambridge, MA: Harvard University Press, 2007). *See also* Karen Tani's brilliant grand and localized history of the welfare state in twentieth-century America: Karen Tani, *States of Dependency: Welfare, Rights, and American Governance, 1935–1972* (New York: Cambridge University Press, 2016).

35 For an illuminating study on the intersection of race, copyright, and the history of American performance communities, *see*: Anthea Kraut, *Choreographing Copyright: Race, Gender, and Intellectual Property Rights in American Dance* (New York: Oxford University Press, 2016). *See also* among the exciting and expanding literature: Caroline Joan Picart, *Critical Race Theory and Copyright in American Dance: Whiteness as Status Property* (New York: Palgrave Macmillan, 2013); Olufunmilayo Arewa, "Copyright on Catfish Row: Musical Borrowing, Porgy and Bess, and Unfair Use," *Rutgers Law Journal* 37, no. 2 (2006): 277; K. J. Greene, "Intellectual Property at the Intersection of Race and Gender: Lady Sings The Blues," *Journal of Gender, Social Policy & The Law* 16, no. 3 (2008): 365; Matthew Morrison, "Race, Blacksound, and the (Re)Making of Musicological Discourse," *Journal of the American Musicological Society* 72, no. 3 (2019): 781.

36 The scope of this book does not examine some of these histories in detail, but they are explored at greater length in ongoing research, particularly with respect to the Federal Theatre Project and the noncommercial theatres of the first half of the twentieth century. *See* Salter, "The Ordinary Authors of the Bureau Of New Plays" and "Copyright, Crisis, and Welfare in the Federal Theatre Project."

realizing the material production, like dramatists, require legal and organizational responses that enable them to negotiate effectively with sources of mediating power.

—

Theatrical mediating stakeholders in this book, and accompanying projects,[37] shaped industry practices through ongoing micro negotiations and interactions. There is always a risk in examining the micro experience in terms of broader ramifications. The individual case study moment may simply be an anomaly when situated next to larger empirical trends or legal and industry reforms. Specific and seemingly benign stories of everyday interactions that survive in the archive must also be read in the context of the creator of the archive. For example, to what extent do the stories that survive in the records of a private company archive reveal a "complete" history of that organization? What do archives leave out? In recovering the stories from the archives I am acutely aware that there will inevitably be gaps and gaps are possibly a consequence of what has survived the vagaries of time, what material an organization chooses to preserve, and just as importantly what material I choose to tell this history.[38] But what individual moments can capture are histories of the ordinary, and untidy histories of contradiction and compromise within the broader structure of the industry. Who benefited from legal and industry reforms and how were reforms interpreted in daily industry operations and interactions?

An examination of daily interactions shows how creators' responded to the development of mediating structures, and how labor and competition law in these ongoing negotiations has played a central role in shaping the legal history of the industry. The Dramatists Guild is an association, not a trade union. The playwright is an independent contractor, not an employee. Dramatists may be members of a trade association group, but ultimately they negotiate as individuals with other mediating stakeholders about a specific production.[39] Playwrights often justify their independent-contracting status through the understandable lens of the personal relationship they have with their work. For many dramatists, copyright,

37 *See* Salter, "The Ordinary Authors of the Bureau Of New Plays" and "Copyright, Crisis, and Welfare in the Federal Theatre Project."; Brent Salter and Catherine Fisk, "Assumptions and Fragilities of Labor Relations in the American Theatre," *Ohio State Law Journal* 83 (forthcoming 2022).

38 And this is not necessarily suggesting an intention to omit specific material based on what that material says about the history of the organization or individual. Records may not survive for many reasons including, for example, the lack of both space and funding to store archival resources.

39 However, Dramatists Guild members "who are having their work produced on Broadway are required by [Guild] bylaws to use the [Approved Production Contract] to license their rights to producers, and then have those contracts reviewed and certified by the Guild." So when producers agree to the terms of the Guild contract for Broadway and first class productions, the agreement will go through a certification process. In addition, "If an APC is not certified by the Guild, it automatically terminates, so the writer is not bound to its substandard terms. A DG member can only license their work without a certified APC by withdrawing from the Guild." *See* Dramatists Guild of America, "First Class and Broadway," www.dramatistsguild.com/broadway.

independent-contracting status, and authorship are intimately connected. Current President of the Dramatists Guild Doug Wright alludes to these justifications when he writes, "copyright guarantees us only one thing, one ephemeral, fleeting, but indispensable thing: our singularity as artists."[40] It is the "innate worth of an individual author's voice." Copyright allows the dramatist to be the "CEO of … [their] own imagination" which distinguishes the theatrical author from employee writers in other mediums such as television or film, for example.[41] An attack on the dramatic author's voice offends the playwright's "ancestral home," the theatre.[42] The Dramatists Guild emphasizes the relationship between copyright, control, and authorship in a 2020 statement titled "Authors should maintain the Legal Rights to their Work."[43]

> [T]he Guild still believes in the primacy of copyright. *Your work truly belongs to you.* You have the exclusive right to control where, how and by whom it is presented. We've spelled this all out, and more, in The Dramatists Bill of Rights. We feel so strongly about this principle that we've sacrificed the benefits of unionization available to conventional employees, like our Writers Guild colleagues in film and television, our fellow theatrical collaborators in the Society of Directors and Choreographers and the United Scenic Artists union, and the United Scenic Artists union.

In response, mediators have consistently claimed that if playwrights are independent contractors, joined together as members of a trade association rather than a union, their Guild is not entitled to an exemption from competition law.[44] Producers have invoked this argument in ongoing negotiations with the dramatists over the last century.

Another reason to explore daily stakeholder interactions is to highlight how positions were not belligerent. Stakeholders in this history, for the most part, were driven by shared goals in a deeply collaborative art form: to have the work ultimately produced for an audience. Observing daily interactions provides insights into how stakeholders work toward reasonable compromises behind the scenes to advance the larger goal of realizing the production.[45] Todd London identifies the importance of

40 *See* Doug Wright, "Playwrights and Copyright," *Columbia Journal of Law & the Arts* 38, no. 3 (2015): 304.

41 Wright, "Playwrights and Copyright," 304.

42 *See* Jesse Green, "Exit, Pursued by a Lawyer," *New York Times*, January 29, 2006.

43 *See* Dramatists Guild of America, "Authors Should Maintain a Legal Right to Their Work," www.dramatistsguild.com/no-union.

44 The Guild writes further in response to why members can't "own our copyrights and still be a union" in its recently release statement: "after surviving two anti-trust lawsuits, dramatists are viewed by the law as property owners who license the use of their property, rather than employees entitled to collectively bargain for the conditions of their labor." *See* Dramatists Guild of America, "Authors Should Maintain a Legal Right to Their Work."

45 I am grateful for discussions with Ralph Sevush of the Dramatists Guild on this point.

"the depth and duration of [the] relationship – between artists and institutions."[46] The desire for community is often lost in the scholarship dominated by histories of well-known almighty playwrights, or estates of playwrights, alleged to wield their copyright swords against all those who dare to question the dramatists' authority at law.

But observing daily reasonable interactions also shows how influence over the production process is established incrementally over time – how power imbalances hide behind the veil of seemingly reasonable exchanges that evolve in local and ongoing negotiations. Thus, this is a story about seemingly innocuous, but consequential, moments of negotiation which occur during daily administrative interactions required to transform an author's words into a theatrical production. The negotiations explored are illustrative rather than exhaustive. It is the inherent normality of ongoing negotiations between stakeholders, and responses to industry structures, which reveal how control over the production process undergoes constant moments of revision and compromise. Mediators who have structured the industry became adept at working with both copyright and other areas of law to navigate the processes of production. State and federal copyright law, employment law, union and association minimum contracts, informal guild expectations, and professional norms all guide how theatre-makers interact with the more nebulous space of theatre creation.[47]

Of course, transforming the work into a realized production through a mediator is of potential benefit to all. Creators, like dramatists, do not necessarily have an understanding of the "pulse" of the market,[48] or lack access to producers.[49] A broker, for example, can streamline matching a play with a producer so the writer can get on with the business of writing plays. But streamlining alone is not the guiding principle in these complicated interactions. The transformation of the work involves more than a process of streamlining. Streamlining suggests there is an inevitable natural trajectory in the creation process involving the licensing of the dramatic author's intellectual property rights. But if you think about the transaction as interpersonal and relational in constructing the path for artistic and economic realization, there is nothing natural or inevitable here. The focus is not about extracting opportunities from an author's intangible property but reconstructing the author's initial intangible right by creating the conditions for the realization of the final production on the stage in the larger industry structure that exists between author and audience. Mediating stakeholders who have shaped these conditions

[46] *See* London et al., *Outrageous Fortune*, 279.

[47] I am grateful for discussions with Derek Miller on many of these issues.

[48] Arthur E. Krows, *Play Production in America* (New York: H. Holt and Company, 1916), 2.

[49] *See* Alfred Bernheim, *The Business of the Theatre* (New York: Actor's Equity Assoc., 1932), 114 (and generally 113–117).

engage in ongoing negotiations with creative collaborators defining the extent, and limits, of creator access to the industry.

—

This history proceeds in two parts. Part I explains how a variety of stakeholders who controlled the process of transforming the theatrical work from the playwright's manuscript to the theatrical stage designed industry structures from the mid-nineteenth to early-twentieth centuries. The stakeholders included playwright agents and publishers who flooded the American theatrical market with foreign works. The stakeholders also included the commercial theatrical producers that controlled theatre houses and theatrical attractions across the country. Reliance on mediation becomes more noticeable throughout the second half of the nineteenth century as the industry continues to centralize around a small group of theatrical impresarios including the Theatrical Syndicate. I start Part I by examining legal developments of the mid-nineteenth century in the context of an evolving theatrical mediating industry. Mediators established practices around the circulation of unpublished manuscripts rather than published compositions as required under federal copyright law. Mediating stakeholders used the federal registration process selectively to achieve particular goals. Stakeholders used the common law incrementally and strategically to advance positions that furthered mediating interests. The legal framework appears to expand the rights of dramatic authors. But courts and legislators were developing a flexible copyright framework that provided theatrical mediators the space to fortify their control over the production process.[50]

Part II examines how American playwrights responded to mediators of the theatrical economy. The dramatists' choice to bargain collectively as members of a trade association has created complications which the industry has struggled to have clarified legally to this day: whether the Guild and its independent-contracting dramatists are subject to, or exempt from, competition law.

[50] *See* Shyamkrishna Balganesh and Taisu Zhang, "Legal Internalism in Modern Histories of Copyright," *Harvard Law Review* 134 (2021): 1066 (Review Essay). The authors argue that the interdisciplinary turn in histories of copyright overlooks the role of legal internalism in copyright's evolution and how copyright "has always been understood as a creation of the law." (abstract) Importantly, the authors do not view legal internalism as an "orthodox approach with its myopic focus on purely legal sources." Instead of drawing binary lines, the authors argue that "copyright's legal internalism is capable of melding with the myriad external (nonlegal) sources that the interdisciplinary turn in the field has embraced. This internalist approach thereby allows for a richer, more nuanced, yet *legally grounded* historical narrative of copyright." (1130)

PART I

# Mediating the American Theatre

# 1

# Copyright and the Facilitation of Theatrical Production

If copyright is framed as just one of the many tools used to facilitate production in the larger theatrical economy, it is also possible to envision copyright law's development outside the prism of dramatist-centric expansion narratives. As scholars including Oren Bracha and Catherine Fisk have shown, author rhetoric lives throughout the decisions of courts in the second half of the nineteenth century.[1] Developments in the law suggest a more fluid framework than one that prioritized the rights of author dramatists, however. There was broad space within the law to accommodate theatrical mediators and the industry structures they created.

Assumptions about the priority of the author at law are understandable. For the American dramatist, expansions in federal statutory copyright law over the last two centuries give the appearance of a series of extraordinary triumphs. The first major revision to United States copyright law in 1831, following the 1790 Act,[2] extended authors' copyright protection from fourteen years to twenty-eight years with the option to renew the privilege for another fourteen years.[3] In 1856, an amendment for the first time secured authors' performance rights in dramatic compositions.[4] In 1870, Congress extended to authors the right to translate and dramatize "their own works" and centralized the registration process in the hands of the Library of Congress.[5] The 1891 reforms expanded copyright protections beyond United States citizens or residents to foreign authors. The reforms were reciprocal so the same privileges extended to US

[1] *See* Oren Bracha, *Owning Ideas: The Intellectual Origins of American Intellectual Property: 1790–1909* (New York: Cambridge University Press, 2016); Oren Bracha, "The Ideology of Authorship Revisited: Authors, Markets, and Liberal Values in Early American Copyright," *Yale Law Journal* 118, no. 2 (2008): 186. Catherine Fisk, *Working Knowledge: Employee Innovation and the Rise of Corporate Intellectual Property, 1800–1930* (Chapel Hill: University of North Carolina Press, 2009).

[2] Act of May 31, 1790, ch. 15, 1 Stat. 124.

[3] Act of February 3, 1831, ch. 16, §§ 1–2, 4 Stat. 436, 436–437.

[4] Act of August 18, 1856, ch. 169, 11 Stat. 138.

[5] Act of July 8, 1870, ch. 230, §§ 86, 85, 90–91, 16 Stat. 198, 212, 213. With respect to dramatic compositions at §86: "and in the case of a dramatic composition, of publicly performing or representing it, or causing it to be performed or represented by others."

authors in foreign countries.[6] In 1897, following these earliest reforms, a public performance right in musical works was added for the first time as were criminal penalties for the unlawful performance and representation of works – reforms in part driven by advocacy on behalf of dramatists as a response to deep concerns about rampant piracy.[7] In 1909,[8] and over the next five years,[9] federal copyright legislation underwent a major overhaul to, among other things, acknowledge the rapid advancement in new technologies such as film.[10] The 1909 Act extended copyright protections to twenty-eight years plus a renewal period of twenty-eight years,[11] and allowed authors to register copyright in an unpublished script but also retain the right to pursue infringement claims "at common law or in equity."[12]

The 1976 Act expanded the protections of the author into a new space. No longer encumbered by a system that required proactive registration, copyright protection was now automatic for authors who reduced their work to "fixed in any tangible medium of expression."[13] The Act extended the term of protection to "the life of the author and fifty years after the author's death,"[14] as well as the scope of protection. For example, the author could now license or assign any part of the exclusive right that they owned.[15] The struggles and triumphs of

6 *See* Act of March 3, 1891, ch. 565, §§3,13, 26 Stat. 1106, 1107, 1110.

7 *See* Act of January 6, 1897, ch. 4, 29 Stat. 481. Where the penalty was defined as any person who publicly performed or represented a dramatic composition without consent "...shall be liable for damages therefor, such damages in all cases to be assessed at such sum, not less than one hundred dollars for the first and fifty dollars for every subsequent performance, as to the court shall appear to be just..." *See* the extensive coverage in the *New York Dramatic Mirror* in the wake of piracy leading up to the reforms including references cited in the notes of Chapter 3.

8 Act of March 4, 1909, ch. 320, 35 Stat. 1075.

9 *See* Act of August 24, 1912, ch. 356, 37 Stat. 488; *see also*, Act of March 28, 1914, ch. 47, 38 Stat. 311.

10 Act of August 24, 1912, ch. 356, §5(l), 37 Stat. 488, 488 ("Motion-picture photoplays").

11 Act of March 4, 1909, ch. 320, §§ 23, 24, 35 Stat. 1075, 1080, 1081. Previously in the 1870 Act it was twenty-eight years plus a renewal of fourteen years: Act of July 8, 1870, ch. 230, §§87, 88.

12 *See* Act of March 4, 1909, ch. 320, §§ 2, 11, 35 Stat. 1075, 1076, 1078. On development on the common law in the United States more generally *see* the important work of Zvi S. Rosen, "Common-Law Copyright," *University of Cincinnati Law Review* 85, no. 4 (2018): 1055. There is an expansive literature on the history of common law copyright, whether copyright is perpetual or limited by statute, and the seminal case of *Donaldson* v. *Becket* (1774) 4 Burr. 2408. *See* Ronan Deazley, *On the Origin of the Right to Copy: Charting the Movement of Copyright Law in Eighteenth Century Britain, 1695–1775* (Oxford; Portland, OR: Hart Pub., 2004); Mark Rose, *Authors and Owners: The Invention of Copyright* (Cambridge, MA: Harvard University Press, 1993). And on the rejection of common law copyright after publication in the United States *see Wheaton* v. *Peters* (1834) 33 U.S. 591.

13 *See* Copyright Act of 1976, Pub. L. No. 94–553, § 102, 90 Stat. 2541, 2544–45 (effective in 1978). But you did have to register, for example, as a prerequisite for an infringement suit and to pursue certain remedies for infringement (§§ 411–412).

14 *See* Copyright Act of 1976, §302(a). And, of course, was followed by further extensions in the years to come.

15 *See* Copyright Act of 1976, §201 d (2). Regarding the divisibility of copyright into subsidiary streams of revenue and the exclusivity arrangements that have been controlled by mediating publishers, *see* Shane Valenzi, "A Rollicking Band of Pirates: Licensing the Exclusive Right of Public Performance in the Theatre Industry," *Vanderbilt Journal of Entertainment and Technology Law* 14, no. 3 (2012): 778.

copyright's expansion have been the subject of commentary, and most tell the stories of the American dramatists' attempts to reform the law to advance American drama.[16]

Sitting within the folds of this period of expansion lived an alternative legal history, however.[17] First, this is not a history of authors alone. Federal copyright law protects authors or owners of works (who were not necessarily the same), authors or proprietors, authors or assigns, or similar derivations.[18] Thus, this is a history of relationships between authors and "others" and the negotiation of copyright control between these stakeholders.[19] Further, federal copyright protection required a proactive

16 *See generally* Thomas Walsh, *Playwrights and Power: The Making of the Dramatists Guild* (Hanover, NH: Smith and Kraus, 2016). On the dramatists struggles to advance internal practices that better served the playwright, *see* George Middleton, *These Things Are Mine: The Autobiography of a Journeyman Playwright* (New York: The Macmillan Company, 1947). Harrison Fiske, editor of the *Dramatic Mirror* from 1879 onwards, embarked on a longer-term crusade to advance the federal legislative cause of dramatists (*see* notes in Chapter 3 with respect to 1897 reforms in particular). On specific drama-centric legislative reform movements *see, for example*, on 1856 amendments: Oren Bracha, "Commentary on the U.S. Copyright Act Amendment 1856," in Lionel Bently and Martin Kretschmer, eds., *Primary Sources on Copyright (1450–1900)* (Cambridge, UK: Arts and Humanities Research Council, 2008) available online at www.copyrighthistory.org. *See also* Richard Fawkes, *Dion Boucicault: A Biography* (London; New York: Quartet Books, [1981] c1979), 90–92; Robert Hogan, *Dion Boucicault* (New York: Twayne Publishers, Inc. 1969), 103–106; Thomas Kitts, *The Theatrical Life of George Henry Boker* (New York: Peter Lang, 1994), 116–119; Edward Bradley, *George Henry Boker, Poet and Patriot* (Philadelphia, University of Pennsylvania Press; London, H. Milford, Oxford University Press, 1927), 120–122; Alfred Bernheim, *The Business of the Theatre* (New York: Actor's Equity Assoc., 1932), 21–23.

17 *See* Jessica Litman who examines doctrinal developments of the nineteenth century, particularly in the common law, in enlightening detail. In particular, Jessica Litman, "The Invention of Common Law Play Right," *Berkeley Technology Law Journal* 25 (2010): 1381; Jessica Litman, "What Notice Did," *Boston University Law Review* 96, no. 3 (2016): 717.

18 *See* 17 U.S.C., §201(a) where copyright in a work "vests initially in the author or authors of the work"; and "[t]he ownership of a copyright may be transferred in whole or in part" (§201(d)(1)) including "any subdivision of any of the rights" (§201(d)(2)). Further, the "legal or beneficial owner of an exclusive right under a copyright" is able to "institute an action for any infringement of that particular right" (§501(b)).

19 *See, for example*, the protection of the author or assign (or other) throughout the history of developments in federal copyright law: 1790 Act, §1: "or their executors, administrators, or assigns"; 1830 Act, §1: "and the executors, administrators, or legal assigns of such person or persons"; 1856 Act: "shall be deemed and taken to confer upon the said author or proprietor, his heirs or assigns"; 1870 Act, §86: "and his executors, administrators, or assigns, shall, upon complying with the provisions of this act, have the sole liberty of printing, reprinting, publishing, completing, copying, executing, finishing, and vending the same; and in the case of a dramatic composition, of publicly performing or representing it, or. causing it to be performed or represented by others"; 1891 Act, §1 (amending §4592), "and the executors, administrators, or assigns of any such person shall"; 1897 Act (amending §4966): "Any person publicly performing or representing any dramatic or musical composition for which a copyright has been obtained, without the consent of the proprietor of said dramatic or musical composition, or his heirs or assigns"; 1909 Act: §8: "That the author or proprietor of any work made the subject of copyright by this Act, or his executors, administrators, or assigns, shall have copyright for such work under the conditions and for the terms specified in this Act"; 1909 Act, §2: "That nothing in this Act shall be construed to annul or limit the right of the author or proprietor of an unpublished work, at common law or in equity, to prevent the copying, publication, or use of' such unpublished work without his consent, and to obtain damages therefor."

registration process throughout the nineteenth and most of the twentieth century up until the major reforms of 1976. Proactive registration required certain skill sets, an understanding of legal processes, and access to resources. The gateway for statutory protection in the text and associated performance rights, particularly in the period before the 1909 reforms, was filing of the title, publication and delivery, and copyright notice on each copy of the work.[20] In 1909, federal statutory protection no longer required publication or registration of title but retained the notice requirement until 1978.[21] Jessica Litman observes, "[f]or 176 years of United States copyright history ... accurate copyright notice was essential to securing a copyright in almost all works."[22]

Federal copyright law after 1909 also protected unpublished scripts: "works of an author of which copies are not reproduced for sale" which included "a dramatic or musical composition."[23] Coupled with the technical conditions of registration was an evolving statutory framework – including the 1909 Act and the period beyond 1976 – that required all assignments to be in writing.[24] The 1909 Act also distinguished between the sale of the material object and transfer of the copyright in that object: "copyright is distinct from the property in the material object copyrighted, and the sale or conveyance, by gift or otherwise, of the material object shall not of itself constitute a transfer of the copyright, nor shall the assignment of the copyright constitute a transfer of the title to the material object".[25]

Catherine Fisk's arresting research on the evolution of the work-for-hire doctrine in the second half of the nineteenth century also shows how employer/employee copyright relationships were transformed.[26] By tracing the development of case law in the second half of the nineteenth century, of which several critical cases involved theatre practice,[27]

20 *See, for example,* Act of May 31, 1790, ch. 15, §§ 1, 3–4, 1 Stat. 124, 124–125 (and note a); Act of April 29, 1802, ch. 36, §1, 2 Stat. 171, 171 (adding notice requirements in 1802 initially in "one or more" newspapers and by 1830 "inserted" in "every edition published"); Act of February 3, 1831, ch. 16, §§ 4–5, 4 Stat. 436, 437. The 1891 Act which first secured protections for foreign authors also required clear registration processes: Act of March 3, 1891, ch. 565, § 3, 26 Stat. 1106, 1107–1108 (including printing in the United States, not overseas).

21 Although you still could follow the pre 1909 standards of deposit and publication, it was now not a necessary requirement. *See* Act of March 4, 1909, ch. 320, §§ 9, 11, 12, 35 Stat. 1075, 1077–1078. Section 9 preserves the notice requirement; section 11 secures the new protection for unpublished works – works "not reproduced for sale" – with deposit of one complete copy; section 12 provides for the formal protection to be perfected by deposit of two copies once published (thus, the order changes from previous Acts: publication and then deposit). In 1988, the Berne Convention Implementation Act ended the notice requirement altogether: Berne Convention Implementation Act of 1988, Pub. L. No. 100–568, § 7, 102 Stat. 2853, 2857–59.

22 *See* Litman, "What Notice Did," 718.

23 *See* Act of March 4, 1909, ch. 320, §11, 35 Stat. 1075, 1078.

24 *See* Act of March 4, 1909, ch. 320, §42, 35 Stat. 1075, 1084. *See also* earlier major statutory reforms that specified writing requirement: 1831 Act: §§ 6–7; 1870 Act: §89. *See also* Copyright Act of 1976, §204(a).

25 *See* Act of March 4, 1909, ch. 320, §41, 35 Stat. 1075, 1084.

26 Fisk, *Working Knowledge.*

27 *See* the key turning point case of *Keene* v. *Wheatley*, 14 F. Cas. 180 (C.C.E.D. Pa. 1861) where an equitable basis for the judgment was that employers had a right to the intellectual property produced by their employees (articulated through an implied intent) that can be contrasted with the earlier *The*

Fisk examines how a default rule of employer ownership over an employee's intellectual property gradually emerges.[28] Indeed, Fisk and Oren Bracha (in separate work) introduce several vital prompts about emerging authority structures in the nineteenth century that speak to this book.[29] In the progressively liberal market, Bracha writes, the notion of the romantic author becomes subsumed into "increasingly large and concentrated workshops controlled and ran by entrepreneurs."[30] Assignment in this environment, for Bracha, is taken for granted. The evolving framework allowed for the actual "ownership and management" of copyright by entrepreneurs.[31] Fisk also gestures to this point – the connection between authors and copyright had become "attenuated and mediated by corporations."[32] The creative efforts of the author dissolve into the larger collaborative project – the workshop – of the corporation, which exploits creation across multiple adapted mediums. These developments in the courts eventually find voice in the 1909 Copyright Act: "the word 'author' shall include an employer in the case of a work made for hire."[33]

Thus, these added layers of copyright's history present several complications for the individual author's expansionist narrative. It is a history about authors and owners and the two may or may not be the same. For the author (or owner) to secure protections and benefits under federal copyright law required proactive steps. Until 1909, these steps included compliance with a registration process and written assignment if the author wanted to exploit or protect the copyright in the work. After 1909, the author could follow the same process. Alternatively, the author could secure copyright registration for an unpublished script but still had to meet notice conditions and explicit writing requirements for assignment in the copyright that was not presumed to transfer with the material object work.

*Octoroon* case of *Roberts* v. *Myers*, 20 F. Cas. 898 (C.C.D. Mass. 1860) where an express assignment had to be made for transferal of copyright to be complete. Compare these cases to the later decision of *MacKaye* v. *Mallory and Anor* (1881) 6 F. 743; *MacKaye* v. *Mallory*, *Mallory* v. *MacKaye*, 12 F. 328 (C. C. S.D.N.Y. 1882). MacKaye countersued seeking an injunction. Despite the onerous contractual conditions placed on the playwright a valid assignment was held to have taken place. Beyond this, the assignment included the transferal of any attribution in the original work. MacKaye's widow successfully revived the litigation in 1897 receiving a royalty payment of $138: *MacKaye* v. *Mallory*, 79 F. 1,1 (2d Cir, 1897); *MacKaye* v. *Mallory* 80 F. 256 (C.C. S.D.N.Y. 1897) (*see also* Chapter 3).

28 Oren Bracha also charts the evolution of the work-for-hire doctrine from express contracts, to equitable right, to an implied intent to eventually a per se right which is ultimately articulated in legislation: 35 Stat. 1075 (1909). *See* Oren Bracha, "The Ideology of Authorship Revisited: Authors, Markets, and Liberal Values in Early American Copyright," *Yale Law Journal* 118 (2008): 186, 248–264.

29 Jessica Litman also observes how both Fisk and Bracha "suggest that the work made for hire doctrine arose in part because of the increasing appreciation of corporate personhood." *See* Litman, "What Notice Did," 735 (note 97).

30 Bracha, *Owning Ideas*, 93.

31 Bracha, *Owning Ideas*, 127.

32 Fisk, *Working Knowledge*, 2

33 Act of March 4, 1909, ch. 320, §62, 35 Stat. 1075, 1088. So there was not a specific definition of what constituted a work made for hire beyond description of what it included.

But how easy was it for playwrights to meet the proactive conditions for federal copyright protection for either published or unpublished scripts? The Library of Congress estimated in 1918, among a total collection of approximately 60,000 dramatic composition titles, "in more than 20,000 cases, while the title has been recorded, no copies have been received."[34] Not only was the registration process for many titles incomplete,[35] but compositions recorded as published were sometimes not published, or were published at a much later date.[36] Therefore, the accuracy of the record itself is questionable.[37] Further, the requirements of having to publish a dramatic composition before 1909 hardly fell within the skill set, or available resources, of the American dramatist. It was the publisher in the larger theatrical economy – who possessed the relevant competencies and material resources – that housed and published plays and unpublished manuscripts.[38] It was the theatrical producer with the networks and resources that could transform published or unpublished scripts into final productions and exploit theatrical works into subsidiary mediums.

The failure to deliver published plays to perfect federal copyright protection draws attention to a more critical contradiction between the formalities of the federal copyright registration system and how the industry produced theatre and structured its relationships. The statutory framework evolved on the assumption that the industry published its dramatic compositions. In nineteenth-and early-twentieth-century theatre practice, nothing could be further from the truth.[39] The American

34 *See* Library of Congress Copyright Office, *Dramatic Compositions Copyrighted in the United States: 1870–1916*: Vol 1. A–N (Washington, DC: Government Printing Office, 1918), (1).

35 *See, for example*, *Roberts* v. *Myers*, 20 F. Cas. 898, 899 (C.C.D. Mass. 1860) where Dion Boucicault had registered the title of the play *The Octoroon* but not delivered the scripts. The Court in this instance seemed unconcerned that registration was not perfected. Litman claims that in later cases, however, the courts were more insistent on perfecting titles. For example, in the second instance of *The Octoroon* case in 1862, the court found that although the registration was not perfected there was a claim in common law: *Boucicault* v. *Fox*, 3 F. Cas. 977 (C.C.S.D.N.Y. 1862). In *Boucicault* v. *Hart*, 3 F. Cas. 983 (C.C.S.D.N.Y. 1875) the court is acknowledging a shift toward the need to perfect registration: *see* Litman, "The Invention of the Common Law Play Right," 1405. *See also Koppel* v. *Downing*, 11 App. D.C. 93 (1897); *Carillo* v. *Shook*, 5 F. Cas, 68 (C.C.S.D.N.Y. 1876).

36 *See, for example*, the proceedings involving the French play A *Celebrated Case*, as examined in Chapter 2 and corresponding court records: U.S. Circuit Court of Maryland. Equity Case Files, 1801–1911 (PH-369; NAID 563016). Case 276A, "Sheridan Shook and Albert M. Palmer, Copartners doing business under the name Shook & Palmer v. William J. Gilmore." Filed Feb. 28, 1878, The National Archives at Philadelphia.

37 The comprehensive record of over 60,000 dramatic compositions registered with the Copyright Registration Office and published in their 1918 record in two volumes is in need of closer investigation on issues including how many of these registrations might have been never perfected, and who were the parties registering the work (publisher, producers, playwrights, or other parties), and for example, how many titles were registered that were illegally copied titles. I begin to consider some of these issues in Chapter 3 in relation to Alexander Byers. *See* the important ongoing research on common law copyright and registration by Zvi Rosen: Zvi Rosen and Richard Schwinn, "An Empirical Study of 225 Years of Copyright Registrations," *Tulane Law Review* 94 (2020): 1003; Zvi Rosen, "Common-law Copyright," *University of Cincinnati Law Review* 85 (2018): 1055.

38 *See* Litman, "What Notice Did," 734–735.

39 *See, for example*, Barrett H. Clark, ed., *America's Lost Plays*: Vol 1 (Princeton, Princeton University Press, 1940–1942), v–vi cited in Litman, "The Invention of the Common Law Play Right," 1384.

theatrical economy, through theatrical mediators, traded in the business of unpublished manuscripts, and more importantly, the performance rights attached to unpublished manuscripts. And what emerges is an alternative legal system in the state courts mainly concerned with establishing the rules about common law performance rights attached to unpublished manuscripts.[40] It was the state courts – despite the authorship rhetoric throughout decisions from the period – developing common law jurisprudence that accommodated copyright narratives beyond the rights of dramatist authors. In the second half of the nineteenth century, until the 1909 legislative reforms, state law about unpublished scripts did not necessarily apply across state borders.[41] Plays performed in one state and printed and sold in other states were often found to fall outside the jurisdiction of the state of the initial performance.[42] Further, the rule that it was not unlawful to reproduce a performance from memory – despite the protests of influential copyright scholar Eaton Drone and gradual developments in the courts[43] – lingered and remained unsettled throughout much of the second half of the nineteenth century.[44] There was little motivation for potential mediating copyists to stop reproducing successful works in one state and exploiting them across the country at undercut prices.

The 1909 Act aimed to remedy many of these gaps. First, the process for federal copyright registration changed. Before 1909, an applicant filed for registration and then subsequently published. The 1909 Act required an author or owner to first publish and provide notice, and afterward file and deposit

40 For a detailed examination of the development of performance rights in the United States *see* Litman, "The Invention of the Common Law Play Right," and Rosen, "Common-law Copyright," 1062 who writes: "The common-law performance right grew organically out of the statutory copyright laws in place as courts struggled to determine where publication and infringement has occurred, partially out of necessity." And it was after the 1856 Act where you start to see an increase in theatre-related common law copyright litigation.

41 I am grateful for comments by an anonymous reviewer on this issue.

42 In 1909, when authors or proprietors were able to register unpublished works, this nineteenth century out-of-state practice effectively ended. Look, however, at cases like *Palmer* v. *DeWitt*, 47 N.Y. 532 (1872), to be discussed, that sided with the proprietor but was an intra-state case.

43 *See* Eaton Drone, "Refutation of the Theory that the Right to Use a Play May be Acquired by Means of Memory," in *A Treatise on The Law of Property in Intellectual Productions in Great Britain and the United States* (Boston, MA: Little Brown, 1879), 566–576. Drone collapsed the distinction between it being unlawful to copy a work from stenography but lawful to do so from memory. *See also* commentary by Derek Miller, *Copyright and the Value of Performance, 1770–1911* (Cambridge, UK: Cambridge University Press, 2018), 156–171 on the distinction and treatment by Drone. For Drone, it was "clear, both on principle and authority, that the property in a manuscript play is not injuriously affected by authorized public representation, unless by the operation of some statute" (at 574). *See also* Litman, "The Invention of the Common Law Play Right," 1410–1416.

44 *See* Litman, "The Invention of the Common Law Play Right," 1408 citing the persistence of the rule in federal court cases (for example *Shook* v. *Rankin*, 21 F. Cas. 1337 (C.C.D. Minn. 1875)) as well as state courts. Litman writes (at note 167): "The durability of the rule supports an inference that many 19th century courts continued to view copyright as conferring rights related to making and distributing material objects rather than rights in intangible works of authorship." However, this rule was changing by the end of the 1870s. On the development of the law around the memory cases *see* Miller, *Copyright and the Value of Performance*, 156–171 and Chapter 2.

copies.[45] An author or owner under the 1909 Act, as discussed, could alternatively secure federal copyright protection for an unpublished work thus opening the opportunity to sue under federal law for an infringement against an unpublished script across the country.[46] There were now more, and arguably easier, ways for owners – which included manager and publisher mediating stakeholders – to register their work.

Another development in the law concerning unpublished plays – which evolved before the 1909 Act and persisted after the reforms – essentially divested dramatists of any claim they may have been able to make under state or federal copyright law.[47] Courts adopted a parol transfer rule that operated under the presumption that mediators, like publishers or producers, had acquired the author's copyright before it was published or performed, despite limited or no evidence – such as written evidence – to support the acquisition.[48] And, as Jessica Litman notes, the parol transfer rule concerning unpublished works persisted into the twentieth century.[49]

45 Act of March 4, 1909, ch. 320, §§ 9 and 12, 35 Stat. 1075, 1077–1078. Of course, this is if the applicant wanted to get protection through publication. *See* registration with respect to §11: "That copyright may also be had of the works of an author of which copies are not reproduced for sale." But if you did publish: "the privilege of registration of copyright secured hereunder shall not exempt the copyright proprietor from the deposit of copies under sections twelve and thirteen of this Act where the work is later reproduced in copies for sale."

46 Act of March 4, 1909, ch. 320, §11, 35 Stat. 1075, 1078.

47 I am grateful for an anonymous reviewer drawing my attention to this point. *See also*, Jane C. Ginsburg, "'With Untired Spirits and Formal Constancy': Berne Compatibility of Formal Declaratory Measures to Enhance Copyright Title-Searching," *Berkeley Technology Law Journal* 28 (2013): 1583.

48 *See here* Litman, "What Notice Did," 732–734, 739–740. On the operation of the parol transfer *see Pulte* v. *Derby*, 20 F. Cas. 51,52 (C.C.D. Ohio 1852) (author failure to assign copyright did not undermine the validity of the transfer because at the time of agreement author had not recorded copyright protection); *Parton* v. *Prang*, 18 F. Cas. 1273, 1278 (C.C.D. Mass. 1872); *Callaghan* v. *Myers* 128 U.S. 617, 658 (1888). Drone also concluded that "The owner's rights, either in whole or in part, in an unpublished play, may be transferred by parol." Drone, *Treatise on The Law of Property in Intellectual Productions*, 581 and *see also* Drone at 104 citing cases including *Palmer* v. *De Witt*, 47 NY 538: "This property in a manuscript, is not distinguishable from other personal property. It is governed by the same rules of transfer and succession, and is protected by the same process, and has the benefit of all the remedies accorded to other property so far as applicable." *See* Drone, again, at 104 (and note 3): "While there has been much discussion as to the necessity of a writing in assigning statutory copyright, it has never been disputed, and is well settled, that the literary property in an unpublished work may be transferred by word of mouth" (citing: *Turner* v. *Robinson*, 10 Ir. Ch. 121, 510; *Little* v. *Gould*, 2 Blatchf. 165, 362; *Lawrence* v. *Dana*, 2 Am. L. T. R. n.s. 402; *Palmer* v. *De Witt*, 47 NY 538; *Parton* v. *Prang*, 3 Cliff 537 (in treatise the citation differs from reported citation above)). Litman (at 733–734), however, also suggests recourse for authors could come in the form of an equitable claim (citing, inter alia, *Lawrence* v. *Dana*, 15 F. Cas. 26, 53–55 (1869) (note different citation to Drone at note 89)).

49 *See* Litman, "What Notice Did," 738 (at note 119) who cites *Houghton Mifflin Co.* v. *Stackpole Sons, Inc.*, 104 F.2d 306, 311 (2d Cir. 1939); *Gerlach-Barklow Co.* v. *Morris & Bendien, Inc.*, 23 F.2d 159 (2d Cir. 1927); *Grant* v. *Kellogg Co.*, 58 F. Supp. 48 (S.D.N.Y. 1944). And the reasoning of *Parton* v. *Pang* is still adopted: "Ownership of an unpublished composition presumptively includes all the rights which the common law recognized therein, among them being the privilege of publication and of securing a statutory copyright.": *Gerlach-Barklow Co.*, 23 F.2d at 161 (citing *Parton* v. *Prang*, 18 F. Cas. 1273 (C.

The operation of the parol transfer provides a moment to consider where authors' rights in unpublished works and associated performance rights are situated in the larger collaborative endeavor of live theatrical creation. Dramatists write plays because they want their work performed. The divestment of the dramatist represents the important initial offering to the production process. It is inevitable that if the shared goal of all stakeholders is eventual performance, the initial authorship rights of the dramatist will always be an accessory to the production priorities of mediating stakeholders who have the resources and networks to realize the work on the stage.

The expressions "author … or assigns" and "author … or legal assigns," or derivation, in copyright law, situates the author and "other" such as assignee, licensee, in a conversation about the transformation of the work from the author to the audience. There is an original creation, and that creation transforms into a final realized production on the stage through theatrical mediating stakeholders with the resources and networks to facilitate this transformation process. The "or" in the American theatre represents the crucial first stage that connects the dramatic author with dramatic performance. Author divestment in initial intellectual property rights is essential if the goal is production. Divestment will inevitability require the author to compromise their initial rights and submit to the process.

To summarize, federal copyright's development up to 1976 appears to secure expansive protections for American dramatists. Federal copyright protection until 1909, however, developed on the foundations of registering published scripts. The industry, in contrast, established its practices based on unpublished manuscripts. Thus, an alternative legal history developed at common law, mostly in the state courts, around unpublished scripts and the performance rights attached to these scripts. The text and performance of that text were intimately connected. After 1909, although the author or owner could register and protect their unpublished manuscripts under federal copyright law, the theatre industry often continued to bypass federal courts to pursue state common law claims.[50]

Developments in the courts regarding the performance rights attached to unpublished scripts also appear to point toward prioritizing the protection of the American author. The common law "play right" – Eaton Drone's 1879 natural rights-based theory that secured performance rights in an author's unpublished manuscript and associated rights – emerged in the courts using similar author-centric rhetoric. But a feature of common law developments before, and appearing to continue after the 1909 Act, was the persistence of a parol transfer. The transfer presumed that producers or publishers had acquired the author's copyright before publishing or

C.D. Mass. 1872) as well as Drone, *Treatise on The Law of Property in Intellectual Productions*, 239; *Turner* v. *Robinson*, 10 Ir. Ch. 121). The rule persisted despite the 1909 Act providing a clear distinction between transferring the object and assignment of the copyright: Act of March 4, 1909, ch. 320, § 41, 35 Stat. 1075, 1084.

50 *See* Litman, "The Invention of the Common Law Play Right," 1384 (and accompanying references at note 20). And the new 1909 Act provided this option as well: *see* Act of March 4, 1909, ch. 320, § 2, 35 Stat. 1075, 1076.

performing the work, even when no evidence supported it.[51] Jessica Litman observes that theatre copyright litigation in the period before 1909 in particular, "was asserted almost exclusively by and on behalf of the theatre managers and publishers who claimed to be the playwright's assigns."[52] So the parties were asserting their rights as assignees or licensees of the playwright, and also employing the rhetoric of authorship despite the absence of the playwright from the proceedings.

The American theatre industry moderated its engagement with the federal copyright system up until 1976. Owners did not always perfect their federal copyright registration by failing to deliver scripts to the Copyright Office (either intentionally or out of ignorance of the law) and deferred to the courts seeking common law "play right" claims. Thus, until 1976, many dramatic works did not enjoy federal copyright protection at all. Stakeholders other than playwrights pursued an alternative path in the courts concerning control over unpublished manuscripts and the performance rights attached to these scripts.[53]

After 1976, federal copyright protections subsist in works of authorship as long as the author reduces the work to a material form.[54] Again, this critical moment appears to represent another expansion in the protections of the American dramatist under federal copyright law. It is the dramatist collaborator that reduces the work to a fixed medium of expression in what is an inherently ephemeral art form. But with new fixed requirements for authorship also follows new authorial claims. The nonwriter collaborator, such as the theatrical director that works in the ephemeral space, now has the opportunity to make clearer claims to authorship by showing how they can fix their creative contribution in a tangible medium of expression. Post-1976 cases in the broader entertainment industry also suggest assumptions about authority over the transferal of copyright without a formally executed transfer endure. Publishers continue to assume that they own the copyright in works that they publish whether or not the author has executed or signed a transfer.[55] And in the space between authors and audiences, new influential stakeholders enter the industry next to traditional theatrical mediating businesses including private investors, conglomerated brokerage houses, and technology companies.

The absence of the playwright from many of the legal proceedings leads Litman to question how one can "miss important information when we take author's rights language at face value, without asking ourselves who is speaking the language and what, exactly, he or she seeks to accomplish."[56] What is required "involve[s] our taking a painstaking look at the way that authors and copyright owners structure their

51 *See* Litman, "What Notice Did," 739–740.

52 Litman, "The Invention of the Common Law Play Right," 1424.

53 I am grateful for helpful feedback from anonymous reviewers who highlighted some of these longer-term developments.

54 Noting again registration is necessary under 17 U.S.C. § 411(a) in order to institute "civil infringement actions." Further, registration is a "prerequisite to pursue certain remedies for infringement" (§ 412).

55 *See* Litman, "What Notice Did," 741 (and note 138).

56 Litman, "The Invention of the Common Law Play Right," 1424.

interactions, to figure out where, if anywhere, an intervention might be effective."[57] This book responds to these provocations, exploring through the archive how the American theatre established organizational structures and negotiated its relationships. The doctrinal developments at the federal and state level are in conversation with these histories of industry organization. Despite whatever authorship rhetoric was being used by the courts – and despite advocates advancing legislative reform based on protections for authors – copyright provided considerable accommodations for mediating interests and the industry structures they created.[58] The dramatists responded to an industry structured around mediators, and a copyright framework that has accommodated mediating interests, by organizing as a group under the umbrella of a trade association. And as the Dramatists Guild trade association evolved in response to mediating businesses, areas of law outside of copyright altogether began to play a critical role in shaping control structures over theatrical production.

57 Jessica Litman, "What We Don't See When We See Copyright As Property," *Cambridge Law Journal* 77, no. 3 (2018): 556. *See also* Jessica Litman, "Copyright and Property-Think," Thirteenth Annual International Intellectual Property Lecture, Emmanuel College, Cambridge University, March 13, 2018. The video is available at https://sms.cam.ac.uk/media/2700035. Litman speaks about the necessity, in a contemporary context, to explore the copyright "ecosystem carefully and from the inside in order to understand the reasons that it has persistently given creators short thrift."

58 The 1856 Act and 1897 Act, as will be discussed in the next two chapters, were author-driven causes. There was extensive newspaper coverage around the claims of dramatists in industry publications like the *New York Dramatic Mirror*.

# 2

# The Publisher's Unpublished Empire

In 1856, following years of agitation in the American playwriting community, previous failed attempts at legislative reform,[1] and reform in Britain,[2] an amendment to the United States Copyright Act provided authors or proprietors a public performance right in their original dramatic works.[3] The 1856 revision was the first of several legislative movements in the second half of the nineteenth century aimed to validate the authorial ambitions of the American playwright, secure their economic interests, and encourage the expansion of American drama.

Reform also sought to remedy the oppressive practices that compromised the limited statutory control American dramatists had over their work in the first half of the nineteenth century. Although the first American copyright statutes protected the author's right to publish and distribute textual copies of their work, the dramatist had no federal protection against an unauthorized performance.[4] Under this restricted statutory regime, theatrical mediators, including the owners of theatres across the country, compensated authors in the form of, for example, limited outright

[1] *See* in particular the failed Ingersoll Bill: H.R. 9 (Ingersoll Bill) (United States) January 3, 1844. On the failure of the Bill and the later development of the public performance right for a musical composition *see* Zvi S. Rosen, "The Twilight of the Opera Pirates: A Prehistory of the Exclusive Right of Public Performance for Musical Compositions," *Cardozo Arts & Entertainment Law Journal* 24, no. 3 (2007): 1157. On the history of the long struggle to achieve better statutory protection for American playwrights *see* Clement Foust, *The Life and Dramatic Works of Robert Montgomery Bird* (New York: The Knickerbocker Press, 1919); Edward Bradley, *George Henry Boker, Poet and Patriot* (Philadelphia, University of Pennsylvania Press; London, H. Milford, Oxford University Press, 1927); Thomas Kitts, *The Theatrical Life of George Henry Boker* (New York: P Lang, 1994); George Middleton, *The Dramatists Guild: What It Is and Does, How It Happened and Why* (New York: Dramatists Guild of the Authors' League of America, 1959); George Middleton, *These Things Are Mine: The Autobiography of a Journeyman Playwright* (New York: The Macmillan Company, 1947).

[2] *See* Dramatic Literary Property Act (1833) 3 & 4 Will.4, c.15; Copyright Law Amendment Act (1842) 5 & 6 Vict., c.45.

[3] Act of August 18, 1856, 11 Stat. 138.

[4] The first Federal Copyright Act was enacted in 1790: Act of May 31, 1790, ch. 15, 1 Stat. 124, "An Act for the Encouragement of Learning, by securing copies of maps, charts, and books, to the authors and proprietors of such copies, during the times therein mentioned." It extended protection to the authors of published works or to the assigns of their copyright, as well as to authors of unpublished and future works.

payments, benefit performances, or through prize competitions. Dramatists often had negligible control over the artistic development of their work. Many American dramatists played the role of mere scribe having to adapt the work at the last minute to meet the changing needs of the owner of the theatre.[5]

Recent studies have provided detailed accounts of the lobbying process in the years before the 1856 revisions to the Federal Copyright Act.[6] Oren Bracha suggests the most striking feature of the passage of the successful 1856 amendment – driven by the efforts of dramatists George Henry Boker,[7] Dion Boucicault,[8] and New York Senator William Henry Seward[9] – was the general ambivalence toward its success or failure.[10] In correspondence between playwright Robert Montgomery Bird and Boker,[11] Bird wrote the "dramatic interest" is "so utterly insignificant that members of Congress cannot be expected to trouble themselves, or even think about the bill".[12]

5 On the oppressive conditions for playwrights in the first half of the nineteenth century *see* Middleton, *These Things Are Mine*; Kitts, *The Theatrical Life of George Henry Boker*; Arthur Hornblow, *A History of the Theatre in America: From its Beginnings to the Present Time* (Vol. 2, Philadelphia, PA: J. B. Lippincotte and Co., 1919); Foust, *The Life and Dramatic Works of Robert Montgomery Bird*; Howard Teichmann, *George S Kaufman: An Intimate Portrait* (New York: Atheneum, 1972); John Gassner, ed., in association with Mollie Gassner, *Best Plays of the Early American Theatre: 1787–1911* (Mineola, NY: Dover Publications, [2000] 1967); Cecile Rukgaber, *The Theatrical Syndicate and Its Effects upon the American Theatre* (MA Thesis, University of Wyoming, 1955). For a general overview of developments in the industry in the nineteenth century *see* Elizabeth Wollman, *A Critical Companion to the American Stage Musical* (London; New York: Bloomsbury Methuen Drama, 2017), Chapters 1–2.

6 On this history *see* Oren Bracha, "Commentary on the U.S. Copyright Act Amendment 1856," in Lionel Bently and Martin Kretschmer, eds., *Primary Sources on Copyright (1450–1900)* (Arts and Humanities Research Council, Cambridge University, 2008), www.copyrighthistory.org/cam/tools/request/showRecord.php?id=record_us_1856.

7 On Boker's involvement *see* Bradley, *George Henry Boker, Poet and Patriot*, 120–122; Kitts, *The Theatrical Life of George Henry Boker*, 116–119.

8 On Boucicault's involvement, *see* Dion Boucicault, "Leaves from a Dramatist's Diary," *North American Review* 149 (1889): 228; Richard Fawkes, *Dion Boucicault: A Biography* (London; New York: Quartet Books, [1981] 1979), 90–92; Robert Hogan, *Dion Boucicault* (New York: Twayne Publishers, Inc., 1969), 103–106.

9 Boker and Seward appear to be the key figures behind the drive toward reform. Judge Robert Conrad is also referred to as being involved in its drafting: *Daily Evening Bulletin*, September 2, 1856, 4. As an Irishman, Dion Boucicault expressed reluctance, in public, in playing an active role in the reform movement. In 1856 he wrote: "It would … seem both grasping and ungrateful to press a claim for more. With the deepest interest in all that concerns the welfare of this country, I beg to disclaim any active interference in her legislative conduct." *See Daily National Intelligencer*, May 19, 1856, 3.

10 *See* Bracha, "Commentary on the U.S. Copyright Act Amendment 1856."

11 *See generally* letter Bird to Boker, January 31, 1853, reprinted in Foust, *The Life and Dramatic Works of Robert Montgomery Bird*, 147–150. Bird writes at 148: "Nobody knows or cares anything about the measure; but on the other hand, nobody that I know of makes any objection to it. There is absolutely no opposing interest. Neither managers nor actors have any interests against it; nor have publishers or readers … Some advantages would result from it to all. The theatres would have more new plays to produce – the publishers more copy to print – the public more books to read. The immediate advantage to writers would be not unimportant to them pecuniarily – though no one would be taxed in consequence".

12 Bird to Boker, January 31, 1853, reprinted in Foust, *The Life and Dramatic Works of Robert Montgomery Bird*, 148.

Following, but not replicating, the structure of the 1833[13] and 1842[14] amendments in Britain, the Bill provided any copyright[15]

> granted under the laws of the United States to the author or proprietor of any dramatic composition, designed or suited for public representation, shall be deemed and taken to confer upon the said author or proprietor, his heirs or assigns, along with the sole right to print and publish the said composition, the sole right also to act, perform, or represent the same, or cause it to be acted, performed, or represented, on any stage or public place during the whole period for which the copyright is obtained…

The press, for the most part, viewed the amendment as an opportunity to solve significant inadequacies in the copyright framework as it applied to American dramatists,[16] and an opportunity for new American drama to flourish.[17] Despite some cynicism about the potential for the revision to advance the cause of

13 *See* Dramatic Literary Property Act (1833) 3 & 4 Will.4, c.15.

14 *See* Copyright Law Amendment Act (1842) 5 & 6 Vict., c.45.

15 *See* Act of August 18, 1856, 11 Stat. 138. It applied when all the requirements for copyright protection were satisfied such as registration on a county by county or state by state basis, and publication. In 1870, Congress allowed registration of works at the Library of Congress. The 1870 Act (16 Stat. 198) also granted authors the right to dramatize and translate their own material. Oren Bracha neatly summarizes the 1856 bill's passage (notes omitted): "The bill was introduced on April 10th, 1856 by Senator Seward. It was passed by Senate on July 16th after a short discussion in which the chair of the Judiciary Committee Senator James Bayard stated 'the only value of a copyright to a dramatic author really is to protect the representation of his production in theatres.' The House passed the bill on August 16th, and signed it into law two days later." Bracha, "Commentary on the U.S. Copyright Act Amendment 1856."

16 Bracha identifies many of these reports (*see* notes 31–42) in Bracha, "Commentary on the U.S. Copyright Act Amendment 1856": which I expand on here. *See, for example*, in the *New York Daily Times*: "Common equity requires that the dramatist should have the same protection for his property as the button maker. Why is it that the author who writes successful novels should have it in his power to make a fortune, while the one whose bent leads him to produce successful plays should be unrewarded?": "Dramatic Copyright," *New York Daily Times*, June 24, 1856, 4. The American dramatist has been described as: "a kind of vagabonds to whom the law accords no protection in the exclusive enjoyment of their productions": "The Rights of Lecturers," *New York Daily Times*, October 31, 1855, 4; and who "are treated in a manner more shameful than any authors have been treated since the days of Grub-street hacks; that their emoluments are wholly insufficient for the demands of their most reasonable wants; that their works are 'pirated' on both sides of the Atlantic, and that the interposition of the strong arm of the government in their behalf is a necessity which will no longer bear concealment": "Copyright in a New Phase," *American Publishers' Circular and Literary Gazette*, June 28, 1856, 373. In the *New York Daily Tribune*, August 26, 1856, 4: "Let us have the decency to give the man who is doing more for the world than ten times ten thousand flytraps or puffed volumes of nonsense an equal chance of what is rightfully his." Indeed, the press called for the swift passing of the bill: "We call on the members of the House to show an equal consideration for the high interests involved by passing this bill before the end of the present session, otherwise it will lie with the dust accumulating on it, in that department with the awful words 'unfinished business' are inscribed as gloomily prophetic as the terrible legend that DANTE beheld written above the gates of the Inferno": "Dramatic Copyright," *New York Daily Times*, August 1, 1856, 4.

17 "We are glad to see that the prospects for a lucrative season at all the houses are exceedingly good, and that the new dramatic copyright has encouraged several writers of eminence to enter the field of dramatic authorship." *See New York Herald*, November 8, 1856, 4.

American drama,[18] newspapers began reporting lawsuits against infringers in the immediate months following the enactment.[19] Indeed, conditions for some dramatists improved dramatically after the 1856 amendment. Bronson Howard emerged as one of America's first professional playwrights by the end of the nineteenth century. Popular dramatists such as Clyde Fitch were commanding royalties as high as 10 percent of the gross ticket takings. Augustus Thomas and Charles Klein were making extraordinary amounts for writing successful single plays.[20] And other new dramatic voices including Martha Morton, Frances Hodgson Burnett, William Vaughan Moody, and Langdon Mitchell were forging successful careers in the theatre. Jack Poggi writes among those "that became millionaires by writing plays around the turn of the century were George Ade, Avery Hopwood, Owen Davis, and Winchell Smith."[21]

The success of these playwrights is situated next to an alternative history of an industry evolving around the interests of rapidly expanding publishing entrepreneurs, however. Transnational industry practices developed by Samuel French in London and his son Thomas Henry (T. H.) French in the United States – known as French and Son – enabled a market in foreign works kept in unpublished manuscript form to flourish in the decades after 1856.[22] French and his associates established expansive authority over European plays – becoming "the agent of many foreign authors and practically became their representative in America"[23] – despite a federal copyright legal framework in the United States that provided no statutory legal protection for foreign

[18] For a more cautious view of the first registrations and impact of the reforms, *see* "Plays and Playwrights," *New York Daily Times*, September 9, 1856, 4.

[19] One of the first copyright registrations "[t]he first dramatic copyright" under the amendment was taken out in Philadelphia for a five-act comedy by Thomas Elliott titled *Law and Fashion*. *See Charleston Courier*, September 19, 1856, 2. There are reports that Dion Boucicault was commencing litigation in Boston under the new law in October/November 1856 for alleged infringement against his original work *Violet, or the Life of an Actress*. *See The Daily Picayune*, October 8, 1856, 2; *see also Boston Evening Transcript*, November 24, 1856, 4; *New York Herald*, December 1, 1856, 5 (citing the *Evening Gazette*, Boston as the "first [arrest] under the new Dramatic Copyright Law"). The *New Daily Times* was also reporting registrations in early September: *see* "Plays and Playwrights," *New York Daily Times*, September 9, 1856, 4.

[20] Jack Poggi writes that Thomas received $175,000 in royalties for *Arizona* and Klein $300,000 for *Lion and the Mouse*. *See* Jack Poggi, *Theatre in America: The Impact of Economic Forces: 1870–1967* (Ithaca, NY: Cornell University Press, 1968), 249.

[21] Poggi, *Theatre in America*, 249. Poggi's emphasis here on the success of male playwrights overlooks the important contribution, and successes, of women writers. *See* Amelia Howe Kritzer, ed., *Plays by Early American Women, 1775–1850* (Ann Arbor: University of Michigan Press, 1995); Brenda Murphy, ed., *The Cambridge Companion to American Women Playwrights* (Cambridge, UK; New York: Cambridge University Press, 1999); Sherry Engle, *New Women Dramatists in America, 1890–1920* (New York: Palgrave Macmillan, 2007).

[22] *See* important ongoing work on "trade courtesy" in the nineteenth century by Robert Spoo, that speaks to the industry publishing arrangements. In particular, Robert Spoo, *Without Copyrights: Piracy, Publishing, and the Public Domain* (New York: Oxford University Press, 2013), 13–64.

[23] *See* "Obituary Notes: Samuel French," *Publishers Weekly*, April 16, 1898 [No. 1368], 689.

dramatists until 1891.[24] A population of 199 productions[25] of Broadway plays or musicals[26] produced between the seasons 1870–1 and 1880–1 gives some insight into the extent of foreign production during this period.[27] The population shows the influence of English drama and dramatists on Broadway, but also the significant number of authors from France who had their work produced in America.[28] Twenty-four percent of authors in the population are from the United States, English authors (37 percent), French (21 percent), and Irish authors (12 percent). Thus, 76 percent of authors in the population hailed from a European country of origin. A review of the nationality of authors in Samuel French's restricted catalogue of contracts before 1900, housed at Amherst College, also reveals the substantial number of works from Britain and France.[29]

24 Act of March 3, 1891, ch. 565, 26 Stat. 1106. The Act, for the first time in the United States, provided copyright protections for foreigners as long as they complied with the registration requirements including, more controversially, the manufacture of the work in the United States.

25 The raw data used to construct this population was extracted from the *Internet Broadway Database* (IBDB), an online database of Broadway productions from the 1800s to the present day produced by The Broadway League: The Broadway League in association with Theatre Development Fund and New York State, "Internet Broadway Database," www.ibdb.com/about. In terms of method, IBDB compiles its material in the following manner: "Information found in IBDB is derived primarily from theatre programs (in most cases from a production opening night). Supplemental information was taken from newspaper and magazine reports, theatrical text books, interviews with theatre professionals, and League archives." It must be noted that IBDB provides a far from exhaustive archive of productions from each season, particularly before 1900. So, for example, the 199 productions that make up the population of this study does not represent all the productions on Broadway for the 1870–81 period. A sample of 199 is large enough to at least provide an impression of the influence of foreign authors on Broadway for the 1870–81 period. The actual number of productions that I extracted for the study was larger: 239 productions. The forty productions not included in the sample did not identify a writer in IBDB and I was unable to identify the author from external sources. I identify the 1870s in this sample because it was a particularly active time for the French and Son business in developing its business models and many of the cases discussed in the chapter emerge in this decade.

26 Broadly defined into these two categories, but in a spreadsheet on file I provide more specific details about genre.

27 The 199 productions include original productions, revivals, and often multiple productions of the one play staged over different seasons.

28 Country of origin of the dramatist was used as the basis for making comparisons. For consistency and accuracy purposes, this was the way I could best make comparisons between groups. The following must be noted. I have, for example, categorized the author Dion Boucicault as Irish, but much of Boucicault's career was spent in the United States, and indeed, Boucicault is often attributed as a chief agitator for copyright reform in the United States and a key participant in the 1856 movement. Country of origin (place of birth) was where I could find consistent data across the authors and thus this is how the authors have been categorized. Further, for this small sample here I define author as including dramatic author of the play, author of the libretto or book, and I also include the author of the English adaptation where provided. The criteria I have used to identify an author, or multiple authors, for consistency purposes, is based on IBDB's identification under the category of writer when I extracted data between the seasons 1870–1 to 1880–1.

29 I am grateful to The Archives & Special Collections at Amherst College and Samuel French for providing me access to the restricted collection of Samuel French contracts, and the unpublished catalogue. Because the catalogue at the point of writing is not available to the public, I will not provide a specific breakdown of the number of contracts in the restricted collection that engage the work of

The rhetoric surrounding the encouragement of the American dramatist also sat uncomfortably with other developments in the broader organizational structure of the theatre business. The American theatre moved toward an increasingly centralized system throughout the second half of the nineteenth century.[30] Theatre creation was evolving around a combination system where theatrical mediators toured entire companies along specific railroad circuits producing a high volume of foreign plays.[31] These circuits had centralized brokering headquarters in large cities and particularly in New York.

The rise of the combinations in the latter half of the nineteenth century has received considerable attention in the theatre literature. The history examined in this chapter is about how publishing mediators in the immediate years following the 1856 amendments, who have received less archival attention, controlled the theatrical production process. The chapter is about how these mediators established organizational structures and practices to transform textual works into ephemeral performances in the space between foreign authors and American audiences. And as new mediators began to shape the way that works transformed between the author and audience, American playwrights also began the long process of seeking to define how they would respond to industry mediating structures as a group. In the 1870s, there were calls for the formation of an association "such as existing in Paris and London." But no such organization of any consequence came into existence until Bronson Howard's American Dramatists Club of 1891 and, more importantly, the Dramatists Guild of 1919.[32]

French and Son created authority structures over the production process by accumulating physical chattels, bundling theatrical services, and efficiently organizing retail spaces. The publisher consolidated power by implementing processes to administer these chattels and spaces, and by exploiting dual citizenry. French and

foreign authors. The collection is substantial and based on an approximation, many of the contracts involve foreign works up to 1900.

30 *See generally* Alfred Bernheim, *The Business of the Theatre* (New York: The Actors' Equity Association, 1932), particularly 34–50.

31 *See* Bernheim, *The Business of the Theatre*, 59 (citing Walter P. Eaton who explains how the Syndicate could provide "foreign authors long and profitable tours" because they controlled the touring European market across the United States). Eaton continued: "It followed, also, that native authors depended too largely for a hearing on the judgments of a few ignorant men, and that the ambitious actor or the small manager with a new, untried play, unless it seemed to their mercenary standards sure of popular success, or unless the actor or manager was willing to come to their terms, had no chance at all." Bernheim also describes the combination businesses: "Combination companies, instead of being localized as were the stock companies, are organized in a producing center, generally New York City, where they remain while they can attract profitable audiences, after which they visit the available theatres throughout the county." *See* Bernheim, *The Business of the Theatre*, 26.

32 *See* Bracha, "Commentary on the U.S. Copyright Act Amendment 1856" who cites: "Dramatic Copyright," *New York Daily Times*, January 19, 1856, 4. *See* "Dramatic and Musical Matters," *New York Herald*, August 25, 1856, 1: writing as early as 1856 about collective organization: "We presume that the next step will be the formation of a Dramatic Authors' Society, to decide upon the terms to be made with managers for the representation of original pieces. Congress has done all that it can for the authors; now let them do something for themselves."

Son also developed transatlantic licensing systems by establishing a network of exclusive relationships with stakeholders, controlling the movement of unpublished foreign manuscripts, and most importantly, controlling the rights to perform these works. The publisher established relationships with the leading British and French Societies and formed intimate connections with Broadway producers which allowed for the transferal of theatrical material across the Atlantic to the American stage. French and Son, and its associates, turned to the law when their industry-created mediating structure came under threat. The legal strategy aimed to test whether an American dramatist's common law rights over the performance of an unpublished manuscript extended to the work of a foreign author controlled by American mediating stakeholders.

## I. AUTHORITY, PLATES, AND THE PHYSICAL SPACE

### A. *Securing Control over Printing Plates*

The Samuel French publishing business was established in 1830 and rapidly expanded over the next two decades.[33] In the mid-1850s, the American theatrical entrepreneur started publishing plays, including his *French's American Drama*, but soon moved into the lucrative business of buying the plates used to print plays.[34] French purchased "every set" of printing plates he could find and within a short time established a "virtual monopoly" over theatrical printing in New York.[35] As early as 1856, French was advertising that he had 100,000 plays on hand – a number which, as the Samuel French organization itself states, "should be taken guardedly." French was perhaps prone, like his successor Wentworth Hogg, "of adding the occasional zero for affect."[36]

French first went to London in 1859 where he formed a close relationship with the theatrical publisher Thomas Hailes Lacy who started in the profession as a playwright, actor, and manager.[37] Lacy was publishing plays as early as

33 The Thomas Hailes Lacy arm of the business, before it was taken over by French, started in 1830. For several years French acted as a theatrical agent and claimed he was publishing in the 1840s. *See* Samuel French Company, *Truly Yours: One Hundred and Fifty Years of Play Publishing and Service to the Theatre* (New York: Samuel French Company, 1980), 1 in "Truly Yours," Samuel French Theatre Collection [Box 23, Samuel French History Publications], Amherst College Archives and Special Collections, Amherst College Library [hereafter, Samuel French Collection]. French first came to New York to start publishing plays in 1835: *see* "Obituary Notes: Samuel French," 689.

34 *See* "Truly Yours," Samuel French Theatre Collection, 1.

35 Two of his first series were *French's Standard Drama* and *French's Minor Drama*. *See* Samuel French Company, "Truly Yours," Samuel French Theatre Collection, 1.

36 "Truly Yours," Samuel French Theatre Collection, 1. The majority of these plays were reprints, but French did publish American plays including George Aiken's adaptation of *Uncle Tom's Cabin* and Dion Boucicault's *The Poor of New York*. *Uncle Tom's Cabin* was published by French in 1858 and Dion Boucicault's *The Poor of New York* (also known as the Streets of New York) was published in 1857. Much of his early expansion was built on the back of the encouragement of amateur theatre providing not only plays but also costumes, technical equipment, and props.

37 *See* "Obituary: Thomas Hailes Lacy," *The Publishers' Circular*, Vol. 36, August 16, 1873, 565.

1830[38] and began concentrating on his publishing affairs more over the next decade. Lacy, like French, expanded his business in a short period by acquiring the plates of popular works from his publishing predecessors – "Duncombe, Webster, Oxberry, and Cumberland all came into his grasp."[39]

A prosperous transatlantic partnership followed for more than a decade, with French eventually taking over Lacy's London business in 1872 for £5000.[40] With business interests in London and New York, French had an advantage over other publishers because he had the physical space to store theatrical material across the Atlantic, a monopoly over the plates to print plays, and the capability to administer the material in multiple jurisdictions. Samuel French, operating in England, acquired the American rights to many English and continental plays. The publisher also later transferred the "sole and exclusive" control over this foreign content to his son T. H. French, who was running the New York arm of the business after 1872.[41]

### B. *The Consolidation of Control through the Physical Space*

French and Son controlled the transatlantic movement of theatrical material by how it organized and operated its physical repositories. It was through these physical hubs that theatrical material was housed, accounted for, and publicized across the Atlantic. The two pictures below (Figures 2.1 and 2.2) of the London office space show how the physical division of space French created was in conversation with the prevailing transatlantic statutory and common law copyright regimes.[42] French also used the space to bundle theatrical services and expand control over the theatrical process beyond the dramatic work itself.

In the public "view of the interior," Figure 2.1, the customer could purchase the printed and published version of works registered and protected under the copyright statute. French, as described in an interview, crosses the room, and swings open "a wide, sliding door of iron, let into the wall" revealing a "great recess, or cupboard," which French describes as "his safe."[43] In the safe is the labor of his authors not

38 "Truly Yours," Samuel French Theatre Collection, 5.

39 "Truly Yours," Samuel French Theatre Collection, 5.

40 Memorandum of Agreement between Thomas Hailes Lacy and Samuel French, March 19, 1872, extracted in "Truly Yours," in Samuel French Theatre Collection (agreement reproduced in inside front and back cover of "Truly Yours," and *see* page 9).

41 Memorandum of Agreement between Thomas Hailes Lacy and Samuel French, March 19, 1872, "Truly Yours," Samuel French Theatre Collection.

42 *See* "Interview with Samuel French," in Samuel French Company, *Truly Yours: One Hundred and Fifty Years of Play Publishing and Service to the Theatre* (New York: Samuel French Company, 1980), 18; "A Chat with Mr Samuel French," *The Sketch* 10, June 19, 1895, 434.

43 *See* "Interview with Samuel French," in "Truly Yours," Samuel French Theatre Collection, 18. Images are at 18, 21 in "Truly Yours," Samuel French Theatre Collection [Box 23]. Note: the authors of "Truly Yours" state that the extract of the interview was first published in *The Sketch*, July 19, 1875. *The Sketch*, however, did not start publishing until 1893. The actual original citation and full article can be found at "A Chat with Mr Samuel French," *The Sketch* 10, June 19, 1895, 434. I have

FIGURE 2.1 View of the interior

realized in print – French's manuscript collection of over 2000 works that dwarf the published, and publicly displayed, offerings – "which the rights are protected only by the equity law of stage rights."[44]

Thus, the publisher divided the business space into published works controlled under the statutory laws of copyright, on public display, and the much larger

reproduced Figures 2.1 and 2.2 from an original copy of *The Penny Pictorial Magazine*, January 10, 1901, 301.

44 "Interview with Samuel French," in "Truly Yours," Samuel French Theatre Collection, 18; "A Chat with Mr Samuel French," *The Sketch* 10, June 19, 1895, 434.

collection protected under the common law – the unpublished manuscripts, hidden from public view in the "safe." The separation between published works and manuscripts also represented a distinction between the formal, public, and ornamental features of the business, and the informal, hidden but substantive aspects. The real engine behind French's publishing enterprise was trading in performance rights attached to manuscripts of foreign works, not glossy published plays offered as a dedication to the public. The French manuscript properties act as a private library. Access to this private collection relates to agreements that rely on the symbolic value of common law copyright: proto rights that anticipate the creation of an enforceable exclusive intangible right in advance of the legal machinery to influence the arrangement.

The physical space was divided further into the higher floors which included stock scenery, makeup, costumes and wigs, lighting, and other technical equipment. In the cellar, Figure 2.2, was French's "real storehouse – my bank,"[45] of stereotyped plates with which Lacy and French originally consolidated their monopoly over the transatlantic dramatic publishing industry. The cellar also held a reservoir of plays "of the Elizabethan age cheek by jowl with modern farcical comedies."[46]

Staging and other related theatre paraphernalia provided important leverage to sweeten the interest of potential licensees to fall into line with exclusive intellectual property control. The production capabilities offered by French were essential to value creation for the titles and hard to duplicate from scratch. No theatre owner had ready access to replace this amalgam of expertise. Only actor/stock companies could do it on their own, and these were the production houses displaced by this new entrepreneurial market model established by French. The publisher controlled the intangible right and the theatrical staging material needed to realize that right on stage.

The "physical" dramatic content (scripts both published and unpublished) and theatrical staging ephemera were in constant dialogue with the administrative, accounting, and publicity documents of the business. French's *Catalogue of Dramatic Pieces*, 1875,[47] lists plays, the number of acts, the genre,[48] the name of the author, and whether it was a published play or in manuscript form (designated by "MS"). The annotations provide, "One and two act pieces at 5s per act; three four and five act pieces, at 3s 6d. per act."[49] Other pamphlets include "elaborat[e]" notes and instructions about types of staging and lighting, summaries of plots, and intricate

45 "Interview with Samuel French," in "Truly Yours," Samuel French Theatre Collection, 18; "A Chat with Mr Samuel French," *The Sketch* 10, June 19, 1895, 434.

46 "Interview with Samuel French," in "Truly Yours," Samuel French Theatre Collection, 18; "A Chat with Mr Samuel French," *The Sketch* 10, June 19, 1895, 434.

47 *See* "Catalogue of Dramatic Pieces" (London: Samuel French Publisher, 1875) in Samuel French Theatre Collection [Box 23, Samuel French Catalogue of Dramatic Pieces].

48 The collection included dramas, plays, comedies, opera, operettas, musicals, farces, comic, burlesque works, extravaganzas, and pantomimes: "Catalogue of Dramatic Pieces," Samuel French Theatre Collection, 3.

49 *See* "Catalogue of Dramatic Pieces," Samuel French Theatre Collection, 3.

FIGURE 2.2 The cellars and vaults

details about costumes and scales of fees for performances.[50] French provided the amateur or professional theatre practitioner a one-stop catalogue with convenient prompts to purchase not only scripts but all of the relevant surrounding staging and equipment as determined by French and Son rather than the original author.

50 *See* descriptions in "Interview with Samuel French," in "Truly Yours," Samuel French Theatre Collection, 18; "A Chat with Mr Samuel French," *The Sketch* 10, June 19, 1895, 434. The French collection also includes detailed tariff rates for Samuel French plays around the same period: *see* "Dramatic Authors Society, Provincial Tariff," 3rd Issue, December 31, 1879, 30 in Samuel French Theatre Collection [Box 17, Press Books and Copyright Certificates]. Where the tariffs (royalties/performance) are determined on the basis of the class of theatre and the particular proprietor of the material. Samuel French's proprietary over plays is considerably larger than anyone else in the tariff booklet. To give an example, for the play *Black Domino* authored by T E Wilks, a drama in three acts (D3), for a first class theatre the rate is 15/-, second class 10/6, third class 7/6, fourth 5 /-, and the amateur rate is 15 /-.

And the transferal of works throughout the transatlantic theatrical economy operated under a precise system that accounted for the stock on hand and value of the stock. The organization kept journals of all contractors,[51] and stock books included exhaustive details about different genres currently in stock, as well as total takings and value of the stock on hand.[52]

Thus, the French and Son business controlled the movement of works between the author and audience through the housing and administration of the material assets of the business. The author writes the play and French secures the physical manuscript. The publisher either keeps the work in manuscript form, hoping to secure protections to perform the script under the common law, or publishes the work under the protection of statutory copyright law. The provision of staging – advertised through a catalogue system – is essential to value-creation because the intangible property has to generate income through exploitation over a limited term in material space. There is limited value in the unpublished (and presumably less familiar) script per se or an intangible right per se. What is the actual value of the limited right to use the script for a set time if the user cannot efficiently stage it for the term of the agreement? Intangible rights of this sort need to be made material to generate income. Expertise and control over chattel staging property are the ways to facilitate the exploitation of the work over time and space without requiring additional investment by the licensee. The rights are leverage for controlling not just exploitation of the performance rights to the dramatic work but leverage into control of the means of staging the particular work. Through that dynamic, French can make these intangible rights feasible or valuable even when the license is for a limited time.[53]

And it is French who determines what staging is relevant for a particular play, as outlined in his catalogues, and the price for the staging equipment and the printed text – whether that be acting additions or published versions. It is French, rather than the author, who presumably writes the abstracts of the plays and determines the genres in which they fit. Thus, the mediation process not only removes the author from the financial benefits of mediation that surround the script itself, but also from control over the artistic parameters of the work. The author is removed from the value creation process because they are not well placed to create value. Author theory assumes the artist makes something of value. That is not the case in the Samuel French organizational structure. Value comes from the practices of

51 *See, for example*, "1862 Contractors Book," in Samuel French Theatre Collection [Box 25, Miscellaneous Business Records, Newspaper Clippings, Contracts, and Event Documentation].

52 *See* "Samuel French Stock Book," July 1, 1864, in Samuel French Theatre Collection [Box 5, Account Books]. To give an example of the stock on hand and its value for the entry on July 1, 1866, "Plays Standard Drama" has a value of $3,865.05 (US Office) and there is a number in the left column "7,7301" which could be the number of copies which seems high. However, it could be correct given that a further column attributes their value at 5c a copy so 5c x 77301 does equal $3,865.05 – the value attributed to the stock of standard drama.

53 I am indebted to Kathy Bowrey for conversations on these issues.

transforming words into acts on a stage, and these practices change the artistic parameters and relevance of authorial contributions.

## II. LICENSING THE TRANSATLANTIC MOVEMENT OF INTELLECTUAL CREATION

### A. *Sole and Exclusive*

The establishment of physical spaces that housed theatrical material provided the necessary infrastructure for control over creation in the industry. The licensing system that French developed was the vehicle through which French moved works across the Atlantic. Following the 1856 copyright revisions, French built a contracting system by acquiring the publishing rights of foreign authors as well as securing the performance rights in Britain and North America. Thus, French could potentially exploit two streams of revenue: the rights in the performance of the work and the rights in the eventual published text. But it was the rights attached to the performance of the script that was the source of greatest profit and contention. To exploit these rights, French and his associates moved with agility between legal and industry-based frameworks. The group used legislation to its advantage across multiple jurisdictions and appealed to the common law when the statutory regime did not protect its interests. At the same time, the publisher continued to develop and refine industry contracting models.

The publisher's control over the flow of theatrical creation from the continent to the United States also required a legal and literal transformation of the work through the London office: the legal transformation from one jurisdiction to another and the literal translation of the work from a foreign language to English. France and Britain entered into an international convention in 1852 which gave foreign authors the right to prevent the unauthorized translation of their works in Britain,[54] but at the same time did not constrain the prevention of "fair Imitations or Adaptions to the *English* stage."[55]

In response to the invitation to develop a "fair" industry-based licensing system, Lacy and French settled on a scheme that involved sole and exclusive control over the foreign translated work in Britain and North America. French described the system in an interview.[56] The foreign author would write the play, produce it in their own country, and then find a "speculator," such as Samuel French. The speculator and author agreed to terms for the sole and exclusive right to perform the work in

54 *See* International Copyright Act, 1852, 15 & 16 Vict., c.12.

55 International Copyright Act, 1852, 15 & 16 Vict., c.12, section 6; *see also* "The Rights of Dramatists: How Foreign Plays Find a Market," *New York Times*, September 30, 1878, in Samuel French Theatre Collection [Box 17, Press Books and Copyright Certificates].

56 "The Rights of Dramatists," Samuel French Theatre Collection.

Britain. The play was translated and produced in Britain, and then Samuel French extended the sole and exclusive agreement to cover the United States.[57]

Samuel French, therefore, secured control over English versions of European-based works by exclusivity agreements. The Dramatic Authors' Society in England enhanced French's control over the movement of theatrical works into the United States by granting the publisher sole and exclusive agency in the United States.[58] And Samuel French used his geographic base in England and his American citizenry to his advantage in transatlantic transactions. He controlled the English translation throughout the continent and England, and, as an American citizen, entered into contracts and commenced legal proceedings in the United States.[59]

### B. *The Manuscript and Its Performance*

A central tenet of the French agreement with foreign authors was that the foreign author initially printed, but did not publish, the work. In England, French requested the author to translate and print an English version of the play. The author then transferred the title to the English purchaser (Samuel French) within three months at which time the title, not the script itself, was registerable at Stationers' Hall.[60] French could alternatively protect the licensed work under statutory law in Britain by performing the unpublished script.[61]

Keeping the work in manuscript form was even more critical when transferring it to the United States. The publisher Samuel French continued to emphasize this point to the press, claiming "a play must not be published; manuscript is sacred."[62]

57 And this occurred in the decades before the international copyright reforms of the 1891 United States Chace Act. On the history of the use of the copyright "performance" to best exploit and control the work across the Atlantic *see* Derek Miller, "Performative Performances: A History and Theory of the 'Copyright Performance'," *Theatre Journal* 64, no. 2 (2012): 161.

58 *See* "The Rights of Dramatists," Samuel French Theatre Collection; *see* the contract: "Dramatic Authors Society of England and Thomas Henry French, October 1878" in Samuel French Theatre Collection [Restricted Contracts Collection].

59 And also using the US citizenry of French's mediating affiliates in America.

60 *See* "The Rights of Dramatists: How Foreign Plays Find a Market," Samuel French Theatre Collection. The important point here is that one could register but not have to deposit in the United Kingdom in order to avoid copying by competitors.

61 After 1842 (Copyright Law Amendment Act, 1842, 5 & 6 Vict., c.45) as Derek Miller has examined, statutory protection in Britain could alternatively be established through publication by way of performance. Therefore, in order to control the work in Britain, French kept the script in manuscript form so a physical copy could not be taken and produced by competitors, but also attained British statutory copyright protection through publication by way of performance. Publication by performance was not provided for under the 1856 US copyright amendments. *See* Derek Miller, "Performative Performances," 161–177 and also Derek Miller, *Copyright and the Value of Performance, 1770–1911* (Cambridge, UK: Cambridge University Press, 2018). *See also* Catherine Seville, *Literary Copyright Reform in Early Victorian England: The Framing of the 1842 Copyright Act* (Cambridge, UK; New York: Cambridge University Press, 1999).

62 *See* "The Rights of Dramatists: How Foreign Plays Find a Market," Samuel French Theatre Collection.

Federal statutory registration in the United States, unlike Britain, eventually required publication of the script. The script, once registered, was easily accessible by competitors. French and Son insisted on not publishing scripts so it could exploit the performance rights attached to the work and shield the play from piracy. By keeping the play in manuscript form, French and Son believed they could closely monitor its physical circulation. Thus, French circulated a limited number of scripts to a close network of trusted producers engaged in exclusivity deals.[63]

The terms that foreign authors were able to negotiate with Samuel French varied based on experience and success in Europe. At the higher end of the scale, regarding the outright sale of foreign rights to Samuel French, the payments were extraordinary – up to £15,000, French claimed.[64] For the adaptation of the French play *A Celebrated Case*, the authors received as much as US$10,000.[65]

These agreements were the exception, however. Samuel French asserted considerable influence over the royalty terms, contractual control over the physical manuscript, and the performance rights attached to the work. For example, the British authors of the play *Queen's Evidence* granted French exclusive control to the performance of the work in the United States on the terms of US$15 royalty per performance.[66] A condition for the exclusivity grant was that the work "shall not be printed, published or dedicated to the public, for a period of ten years from the date hereof."[67] Thus, the authors could not exploit the work in a published form for ten years, and Samuel French and Son had exclusive control over the performance of the work for this extended period.

63 As will be examined further in this chapter and Chapter 3, sometimes scripts were registered and never perfected – that is, the published scripts were not deposited but the registration record states that the registration has been perfected. This was a significant issue with respect to dramatic works between 1870 and 1916.

64 As noted, the French Organization has suggested, Hogg and French both were perhaps prone to exaggerate numbers, and French, it is claimed, was not always good with dates: *see* "Truly Yours," 1.

65 In an interview with French, September 1878, the publisher is quoted as having paid "several thousand dollars" for *A Celebrated Case*. In the same article French states that he paid the English author "Over $5,000" for *Our Boys*: *see* "The Rights of Dramatists," Samuel French Theatre Collection. The papers around the time of the litigation with W Gilmore in Baltimore specifically note the amount of $10,000 for *A Celebrated Case*. *See, for example*, "Foreign Authors' Rights in Plays," *The Spirit of the Times*, February 2, 1878, 718; "A Wonderful Memory: A Remarkable Instance of Memorizing A Celebrated Case," *San Francisco Chronicle*, September 22, 1878, 7 (from the *New York Sun*, September 5); "Fights for Foreign Plays," *New York Sun*, January 27, 1878, in Samuel French Theatre Collection [Box 17, Press Books and Copyright Certificates]. The exclusive rights agreement itself (in French) between the authors of *A Celebrated Case* and Samuel French does not specify the amount: "Contract: Adolphe D'Ennery and Eugene Cormon and Samuel French, 1877/78" in Samuel French Theatre Collection [Restricted Contracts Collection Library]. In terms of other examples, French also claimed to pay Victorien Sardou $5,000 for *Ferreol*: "Wars of the Theatres: Disputed Rights in Foreign Plays," *New York Daily Tribune*, March 2, 1878, 2.

66 *See* contract: "George Bonqueit and Henry Peitit and Samuel French, October 1878" in Samuel French Theatre Collection [Restricted Contracts Collection].

67 *See* contract for *Queen's Evidence*: "George Bonqueit and Henry Peitit and Samuel French, October 1878" in Samuel French Theatre Collection [Restricted Contracts Collection].

In other contracts, these royalty rates changed depending on jurisdiction or city.[68] The 1890 standard agreement for the exploitation of the play *Doctor Bill* in the United States, provides a more realistic profile of the contractual arrangements between the publisher and authors/adapters. The writers' received an upfront advance payment of US$250. For the payment, French secured the American rights. French's only contractual obligation was to promote the play and to secure the best terms for fees and royalties. The contract also provided that French retain one-third of all net profits.[69]

Some of the most profitable deals that French and Son made involved production agreements with American managers to stage foreign translated works. T. H. French was not only at the helm of the French and Son publishing business in the United States, but by the end of the 1870s was in a close, often volatile,[70] although financially rewarding, relationship with Broadway managers Sheridan Shook and A. M. Palmer.[71] The most popular works from Europe including *Diplomacy*, *The Two Orphans*, *Agnes*, *The Danicheffs*, *Pink Dominos*, and *A Celebrated Case*, moved through this narrow passage. The works traveled from the authorial pages of playwrights in Europe through French the elder in London and his son T. H. French in the United States. The partnership of A. M. Palmer and Sheridan Shook then produced the work on the Broadway stage at the Union Square Theatre. T. H. French observed in 1879 that it was in the "speculation" of works from France where the firm made its "principal gains."[72]

68 *See, for example*, the contract for *Dan'l Druce* (written by W. S. Gilbert) where the nightly rates varied between Canada (US$15/night) and US cities which varied between US$25 and US$30. Contract: "Samuel French and Sons and Henry Jarett and AM Palmer in French, March 1876" in Samuel French Theatre Collection [Restricted Contracts Collection]. This is the contract between the publisher who has the exclusive license from the foreign author and the theatre producer (sub-licensee). It can be assumed that this royalty is paid back to the author. The publisher and theatre manager usually share a portion of the profits, the original author receives an upfront payment and likely an ongoing royalty.

69 Extracted in "Truly Yours," Samuel French Theatre Collection, 10–11. *See also* contract: "Samuel French and George Alexander and Hamilton Aide," in Samuel French Theatre Collection [Box 24, Business Records] (note: original author was Albert Carre) and George Alexander was the manager.

70 *See, for example*, Thomas Henry writing to his father stating that Palmer and Shook were "very hard people to deal with": "T. H. French to Samuel French," April 13, 1878, in Samuel French Theatre Collection [Box 19, Letter Book]. It was however a lucrative partnership. T. H. French and A. M. Palmer eventually went into partnership over the Madison Square Theatre: *see* "Co-partnership agreement – A. M. Palmer and T. H. French, November 1885" in Samuel French Theatre Collection [Restricted Contracts Collection]. And there are examples throughout the contracts collection between the publishers and managers involving individual licensing deals to produce plays in the United Sates at the Union Square and on tour: contract for *Danicheff* (March 10, 1876), contract for *Pink Dominos* (August 9, 1877).

71 *See* article: "French and Son: Something of the Great Dramatic Publishers of the World. A Chat with T. H. French on the Past and Coming Successes of the American Stage, June 10, 1879" in Samuel French Theatre Collection [Box 17, Press Books and Copyright Certificates].

72 *See* Article: "French and Son: Something of the Great Dramatic Publishers of the World," Samuel French Theatre Collection.

The French organization entered into long-term contractual relationships with theatrical managers on Broadway to produce foreign works of which the original author had limited to no connection to the terms of these deals. The conditions in the publisher/producer agreements often provided French and Son access to the net profits of the shows Palmer and Shook managed. For example, the contract between French and Shook/Palmer for *Pink Dominos*, based on the French work *Les Dominos Roses* by Alfred Hennequin and Alfred Delacour, provided that the parties divide the profits "equally"[73] and the publishers would not be responsible for any losses.[74] It is not clear what royalties or percentage of profits were accountable to the original authors, but it is possible, based on similar agreements, the author royalty was about US$15 a performance. The contract for the English adaptation of the French work *Danicheff* provided an outright payment from Shook and Palmer to French and Son of "one thousand dollars in gold" to cover the first twenty-five performances. The author royalty rate was US$25 per performance after these first performances in New York, and variable amounts in other American cities.[75] In agreements with other producers, there was sometimes a small outright payment upfront for the license to perform the work, but in most instances, the standard agreement was a nominal royalty rate per performance.[76]

Thus, Samuel French in London and T. H. French in New York developed an efficient way to secure control over the English translations of the most successful foreign works in England and the United States. The system involved a combination of control over the physical stock kept in manuscript form to avoid piracy and the development of a "sole and exclusive" licensing scheme that exploited the performance rights through close relationships with a small network of Broadway theatrical managers.

## C. *Turning Practice into Law*

French believed he was offering foreign authors protections that legislation could not provide. The publisher was benefitting "his own house," but he also felt he was a "benefactor to authors":[77]

73 *See* contract: "Samuel French/Thomas H. French and Sheridan Shook/A. M. Palmer, August 1877" in Samuel French Theatre Collection [Restricted Contracts Collection], (Clause V).

74 "Samuel French/Thomas H. French and Sheridan Shook/A. M. Palmer," in Samuel French Theatre Collection [Restricted Contracts Collection], (Clause VII).

75 *See* contract: "Sheridan Shook/A. M. Palmer and Samuel French and Son, March 1876" in Samuel French Theatre Collection [Restricted Contracts Collection] (and less for matinees). *See also* US Counsel General Letter, March 10, 1876, in Samuel French Theatre Collection [Restricted Contracts Collection] (which confirms that this amount goes to original authors).

76 *See, for example*, contract in relation to *Gascon*: "T. H. French and Edward Arnoh, 1876" in Samuel French Theatre Collection [Restricted Contracts Collection] ("surrender" script for US$200 and US$10 or US$5 per performance depending on the city).

77 "The Rights of Dramatists," Samuel French Theatre Collection. Referring to suits commenced which will be discussed below in Section III.

> [S]ince we have taken this business up we have done for the author what he couldn't do for himself, we have worked and protected his property in a business way.

There is no question that the publisher provided authors with access to broader distribution, modernized the sale and licensing of printed copies and public performances, and administered the payment of royalties in a timelier fashion.[78] Samuel French also felt that his ability to protect authors through licensing schemes and the courts was a form of security for foreign authors that did not previously exist. French stated to the *New York Times* in 1878: "By this success [protection of *A Celebrated Case* as discussed below in Section III] we and others are enabled to make handsome offers to French authors for other plays."[79]

Sections of the press, and notably the *Dramatic News*, were somewhat more skeptical about French's motivations. In an 1878 *Dramatic News* article titled "French and Son Monopolists," the journal criticized T. H. French's methods in the United States, claiming he had established a "sole and exclusive right" in his contracts where no right existed in federal copyright law. French resorted to a "Pandora's box of lawsuits, injunctions, and cross-fire affidavits" to assert his contractual rights.[80] The *Dramatic News* claimed that the French publishing operation traded in dramatic works like other speculators "dealt in pork, or grain, or felt hats." The business also was "absolutely ignorant of the prevailing style," simply engaging in selling short – "in other words, to find an immediate customer among the credulous and simple people of the American stage."[81] It was an exclusive right French asserted serving no more than an opportunity to further mediating ambitions over foreign works.

The response to such claims from French's supporters was one of bewilderment. For example, one commentator wrote that "[t]he great offense" of the publisher and his associates was that they had introduced an "equitable arrangement of acquiring and paying for the right to produce foreign plays in the United States." And despite an environment of extensive copying of actual performances, the publisher's model apparently "made piracy [of foreign works] impossible".[82]

The *Dramatic News*'s claim that French and Son was primarily motivated by personal interest had merit, however. In March 1878, Congress introduced a Bill, sponsored by Sheridan Shook, where "Henry French help[ed] to pay what expenses

78 "Truly Yours," Samuel French Theatre Collection, 12–13.

79 *See* "The Rights of Dramatists," Samuel French Theatre Collection.

80 "French and Son, Monopolists," *New York Dramatic News*, (circa 1878) in Samuel French Theatre Collection [Box 17, Press Books and Copyright Certificates].

81 "French and Son, Monopolists," Samuel French Theatre Collection.

82 *See* "Unnamed Press Clipping," Samuel French Theatre Collection. [Box 17, Press Books and Copyright Certificates], (bottom right of page 3 of press clippings).

may be necessary to push it through,"[83] titled, A *Bill for the better protection of acting-plays and literature.*[84] The Bill provided:[85]

> [T]he law of copyright shall cover and protect *managers*, actors and other citizens of the United States who shall procure through purchase the right to a play, be it farce, comedy, tragedy, drama, or spectacular representation, from a foreign author, for the purpose of playing or publishing the same in the United States.

Samuel French, who already had significant control over works entering the country from France, wanted to strengthen his authority through legislative intervention. The response to the Bill was scathing despite some claims that authors believed it represented their best interests.[86] *The Library Table* suggested that the one virtue of the "clumsily and carelessly worded" Bill was its shortness, and it had "no chance of passing" thus deserved no further discussion.[87] The *Library Table* also claimed that the only stakeholder who objected to international copyright protection was the American publisher. International copyright protection would open the market to foreign publishers that French controlled through his sole and exclusive licensing system.[88] The *Dramatic News* claimed the Bill would "merely subserve" the "private fortunes" of French, Palmer, and Shook. The better form of legislative response, the paper argued, was international copyright law which would provide comprehensive and transparent protection for foreign authors in the United States and American authors in foreign jurisdictions.[89]

83 *See* "The New Proprietary Right Bill," *New York Dramatic News*, (circa 1878) in Samuel French Theatre Collection [Box 17, Press Books and Copyright Certificates].

84 *See Congressional Record Containing the Proceedings and Debates of the Forty-Fifth Congress, Second Session* (Vol VII), 1882. The Bill was introduced in the House of Representatives on March 19, 1878, by Mr. Joseph Blackburn (Ky.) (H.R. 3975) was read a first and second time and sent to the Committee on the Library. *See also* Journal of the Senate of the United States of America being the Second Session of the Forty-Fifth Congress, 307 where the Bill was read for the first and second time by unanimous consent (S. 943) on March 19, 1878, by Mr. Blaine and sent to the Committee on the Library. *See also* "Congressional Topics," *New York Times*, March 27, 1878, 1 (reports that on March 26 the Bill was pending before the Joint Committee on the Library for the Better Protection of acting plays and dramatic literature.)

85 *See* H.R. 3975, 45th Cong. 2D Session (1878). Emphasis added on managers (the category which French would fall under) and the Bill also reported in "The New Proprietary Right Bill," Samuel French Theatre Collection. *See also* The *Library Table*, Vol. 4, April 27, 1878, 221.

86 *See, for example*, Don Platt, "Protection for Play Writers," *The Washington Post*, April 2, 1878, who wrote that he prepared the Bill at the request of the American Authors' Dramatic Association and if passed would in fact assist American authors by opening up the market to greater competition and indeed restrict the power of the speculators like French. In response to Platt's letter to the editor, copyright lawyer E. Gilmore called the Bill a "delusion and a snare" which would benefit "a certain New York dramatic firm": *see* E Gilmore, "Protecting Dramatic Authors," *The Washington Post*, April 4, 1878.

87 *See The Library Table*, 221.

88 *The Library Table*, 221. *See also* "The Big Metropolis," *The Washington Post*, April 1, 1878, where the correspondent writes that the new bill was "for the sole benefit of a rich firm of theatrical speculators."

89 *See* "Kill It," *New York Dramatic News* (circa 1878) in Samuel French Theatre Collection [Box 17, Press Books and Copyright Certificates]. (This is possibly a continuation of the article "The New

Commentators also started to observe how proposed reforms that favored foreign works potentially discouraged new American dramatic voices. The *Spirit of the Times* conceded in 1878:

> It is a notorious fact that American dramatic authors receive very little encouragement for the writing of original pieces. This system of favoring Parisian plays is disastrous to native talent. A writer has no chance. Managers actually refuse to read American plays, because they are in the habit of producing French works after their success has been established in Paris. The Union Square Theatre has usually given at the least six foreign plays to one American.[90]

Thus, there was a belief the failed Bill was "framed solely in the interest"[91] of publishers and managers. French and his associates had to explore other ways to maintain the control they had established over foreign works in the United States when there was a threat to their industry-based licensing system. The American courts became a critical forum for French and his associates to push their claims.

## III. AUTHORITY, THE UNPUBLISHED MANUSCRIPT, AND THE COMMON LAW

### A. *The Authorial Rights of Samuel French and His Associates*

For stakeholders who challenged the growing Samuel French business structure, the central issue for clarification was whether the publisher and his producing associates had any rights to assert in the American courts. French was not an author, foreign authors he represented had no federal statutory legal standing in the United States, and the publisher was insistent that his works remain in an unpublished form to avoid piracy in a jurisdiction where printing and publication was a requirement for federal statutory copyright protection.

Despite these complications, the burgeoning French and Son publishing business, and its close producing associates Sheridan Shook and Albert Palmer, saw opportunities to solidify their mediating authority by testing the boundaries of the common law. Adopting a litigation strategy highlighted the contradictions between

Proprietary Right Bill" or an editorial.) No date is given in the archive copy of the article, but it is likely to have been published in March or April of 1878 given the Bill was introduced in March of 1878. Protecting foreign authors against theatrical piracy became a broader moral issue, filtering into political and even religious discourse in the second half of the nineteenth century. In 1887 Reverend Dr. Henry Van Dyke uttered to his congregation: "Our country professes to be founded on justice and the desire to secure to every man his natural right, and yet it refuses to recognize this right of intellectual property within its own borders, if the owner be a citizen of another country. The effect of this policy upon the moral sense of the nation must be just the same as that produced upon the moral sense of the boy if his father told him, 'My son, it is a sin to steal a pin, but it is not a sin to steal a book from an Englishman.'" *See* "Copyright," *New York Dramatic Mirror*, January 14, 1888, 6.

90 *See* "Foreign Authors' Rights in Plays," *The Spirit of the Times*, February 2, 1878, 718.

91 "Kill It," Samuel French Theatre Collection.

a legal system built on authorship rhetoric appearing to advance American drama and the stakeholders the system benefited. It was the publishers and managers who were asserting the natural, authorial, common law rights of foreign authors in courts rather than the authors themselves, as was the case in many of the other common law theatre cases from the period.[92] In the absence of a statutory solution that would have allowed "managers" to assert the rights of foreign authors – as Shook and T. H. French unsuccessfully sought to enact – the publisher and managers used the courts to further the "sole and exclusive" control they had built through their industry contracting models.

Another aspect of the litigation strategy was that French and Son asserted rights in common law claims over manuscripts even though their core business was supposed to be the publication of plays. It was more prudent for French and Son to keep their plays in manuscript form to ward off copying of the performance. Keeping the work in a manuscript form also strengthened the legal argument at common law under what would become the Eaton Drone "playright" theory even before Drone was associated with the concept of a play right.[93] At the same time, French had another incentive to keep the work of foreign authors in manuscript form as it allowed him to negotiate long-term exclusive control over scripts with the original foreign author. As shown, this arrangement could be as long as ten years of exclusive control.

In a series of cases in the 1870s, the triumvirate of French and Son, Palmer, and Shook sat at the helm of a litigation strategy to protect the work of foreign dramatic authors and their unpublished manuscripts in the United States. And the French play *Une Cause Celibre* (A *Celebrated Case*) became an important vehicle to advance the authority of the producing and publishing mediators.

### B. *Accommodating Mediators in the Courts*

A *Celebrated Case*, written by the French playwrights Adolphe D'Ennery and Eugene Cormon, came to the attention of French and Son in the immediate years after Samuel took control over Lacy's publishing business in London. In 1877, Samuel French acquired the sole and exclusive right to produce the English translation of the work in Britain and the United States for $10,000.[94] French later transferred the exclusive rights to present the play to Shook and

92 *See* Litman, "The Invention of the Common Law Play Right," 1424.

93 Eaton S. Drone, *A Treatise on The Law of Property in Intellectual Productions in Great Britain and the United States* (Boston, MA: Little Brown, 1879). Drone's common law "play right" extended the author's common law right in the manuscript to the performance of the unpublished manuscript.

94 *See* agreement for *A Celebrated Case* (in French): Adolphe D'Ennery and Eugene Cormon and Samuel French in Samuel French Theatre Collection [Restricted Contracts Collection]. *See also* "Fights for Foreign Plays," Samuel French Theatre Collection. (As discussed above in the notes it is likely that this is the amount as reported on multiple occasions in the press.) In return they would receive a share of receipts with no mention of whether the authors receive a royalty or a percentage of the share, but possible a royalty on each performance based on similar agreements from the period and the success the authors and publishers had previously with *Two Orphans*.

Palmer.[95] In return, French and Son would "get a share of the receipts" for the initial run in New York and later seasons throughout the country.[96]

The movement of *A Celebrated Case* across the Atlantic followed the classic Samuel French contracting model in action reaping considerable financial rewards for the publishers and producers through close-knit networks. The play about a French soldier wrongly accused and executed for allegedly murdering his wife was an extraordinary success,[97] opening at the Union Square under the management of Shook and Palmer in January 1878 and running for 111 performances,[98] followed by tours throughout the country.[99] With the success of a play in the second half of the nineteenth century, no matter what control and monitoring mechanisms were in place, inevitable instances of copying the performance followed and *A Celebrated Case* was no exception.[100]

In late January 1878, the New York papers ran stories suggesting that Dion Boucicault and Lester Wallack were "painting scenes and distributing the cast for a play almost identical in plot and incident with D'Ennery and Cormon's *Celebrated Case*".[101] The Boucicualt production was a source of considerable concern for both

95 *See* "Testimony," U.S. Circuit Court of Maryland. Equity Case Files, 1801–1911 (PH-369; NAID 563016). Case 276A, "Sheridan Shook and Albert M. Palmer, Copartners doing business under the name Shook & Palmer, v. William J. Gilmore." Filed February 28, 1878, The National Archives at Philadelphia. The case was concluded quickly (by March 6 or 7, 1878) but there are a number of filings. These include: Filings, February 28–end of case, circa 60 pp. including complaint, order, and transcript. This document consists of about thirty pages. With respect to the transfer "on or about the 19th day of December 1877, the said firm of Samuel French and Samuel French and Son, in consideration of a large sum of money to them paid by your [complainants], duly sold assigned transferred and delivered unto your [complainant] the aforesaid manuscript and all the right, title and interest in and to the same, and all rights thereto, therein and thereunder in North America". I am grateful to Gail Farr, Archives Specialist NARA at Philadelphia, for her invaluable assistance in helping recover this case record.

96 *See* "Fights for Foreign Plays," Samuel French Theatre Collection.

97 *See* the eventual published version (acting addition) of *A Celebrated Case* in Samuel French Theatre Collection [Box 58, Manuscripts].

98 Its original run at the Union Square Theatre was from January 23 to May 11, 1878. *See* The Broadway League in association with Theatre Development Fund and New York State, "Internet Broadway Database," www.ibdb.com.

99 On the success of the show *see* T. H. French to Samuel French writing at the end of January 1878 suggesting that the production was still packed in and doing well: "T. H. French to Samuel French," January 28, 1878, in Samuel French Theatre Collection [Box 19, Letter Book]. *See also* mentions of the production: "T. H. French to Leo Copper Esq," September 21, 1878, in Samuel French Theatre Collection [Box 19, Letter Book]; "T. H. French to F. Williams," February 14, 1878, in Samuel French Theatre Collection [Box 19, Letter Book] (success in Boston); "T. H. French to Samuel French," May 18, 1878, in Samuel French Theatre Collection [Box 19, Letter Book] (doing well in Brooklyn); "T. H. French to Samuel French," June 12, 1878, in Samuel French Theatre Collection [Box 19, Letter Book] (has "made them all so much money"); and "T. H. French to Leo Copper," August 29, 1878, in Samuel French Theatre Collection [Box 19, Letter Book] (discussing how successful the play has been by the numbers, and "[t]his firm will make over $20,000 on the play.").

100 *See* "T. H. French to Samuel French," February 19, 1878, in Samuel French Theatre Collection [Box 19, Letter Book] (discussing "the thieves" in relation to *A Celebrated Case*).

101 *See* "Manager Palmer's Play: Dispute about 'A Celebrated Case'," *New York Times*, January 20, 1878, 2.

T. H. French and Samuel.[102] In response, the Wallack Theatre claimed that they had simply reconstructed a similar work from newspaper reports published in England and France.[103] Boucicault and Wallack paused production.[104] Reports in the *Spirit of the Times*, however, soon surfaced questioning whether the associates at Union Square had any claim to legal authority over the play. It was reported Boucicault "boldly declare[d] that there is no protection for the translated works of foreigners,"[105] and there was no law that could "prevent Mr Boucicault, or any other man, from translating or imitating it, and disposing of it where they please."[106] The *Spirit of the Times* also alleged that Boucicault, one of the architects of the 1856 amendments and champions of dramatic authors,[107] would make good use of the law's limitations:[108]

> by pirating, with the aid of scissors, and his really astonishing powers of adaption any successful French play that may be brought out here, notwithstanding the large sums paid to authors and the supposed copyright laws, which practically do not exist.

But Shook, Palmer, and French were determined to find alternative solutions to secure their sole and exclusive contractual rights over foreign unpublished works through the common law. D'Ennery and Cormon's successful English translation *Two Orphans* was the subject of the curious proceedings in *Shook* v. *Rankin* (1875).[109] The plaintiff producer claimed he had the copyright assigned to him, and a copyright certificate that appeared to establish an assignment had taken place.[110] The copyright registration here seems deficient, as noted by Jessica Litman.[111] The copyright for *Two Orphans* is registered under the author

102 *See, for example*, "Thomas Edwards to Samuel French," January 15, 1878, in Samuel French Theatre Collection [Box 19, Letter Book] (Edwards writes that "I am afraid that Mr. Wallack is going to give us some trouble"); "T. H. French to Samuel French," January 22, 1878, in Samuel French Theatre Collection [Box 19, Letter Book] (referring to Wallack "threatening to do the play" and "that old devil Boucicault"). *See also* "T. H. French to J. C. Williamson," January 23, 1878, in Samuel French Theatre Collection [Box 19, Letter Book] suggesting that because of "the rascality of Wallack and Boucicault" they have had to produce the show ahead of time.

103 *See also* on the proceedings which appear to be based on a larger fight between the Fifth Avenue Theatre and A. M. Palmer: "Boucicault's Intrigues: Managing Wallack and the Fifth Avenue Surreptitiously," *New York Daily Tribune*, January 22, 1878, 2; "A Dramatists Methods," *New York Times*, January 22, 1878, 8; "Foreign Authors' Rights in Plays," 718.

104 *See* "Manager Palmer's Play," 2.

105 "Foreign Authors' Rights in Plays," 718.

106 "Foreign Authors' Rights in Plays," 718.

107 Oren Bracha however suggests that the key agitators for reform were George Henry Boker and New York Senator William Henry Seward. *See* Oren Bracha, "Commentary on the U.S. Copyright Act Amendment 1856."

108 *See* "Foreign Authors' Rights in Plays," 718.

109 21 F. Cas. 1337 (Circuit Court, D. Minnesota).

110 21 F. Cas. 1337, 1338.

111 *See* Litman, "The Invention of the Common Law Play Right," n 172 (1409–1410). The court in this instance stated that the plaintiff having made a prima facie case, "Now, there is no question if all these

N. H. Jackson and the plaintiff is the producer, Shook. Litman suggests "neither defendants nor the court appears to have raised the issue of invalidity due to the failure of the registrant to publish and deposit copies."[112] Thus, with what was possibly a defective registration, Shook established a prima facie case under federal copyright law. The case was subject to no other proceedings and neither was the validity of the registration. Shook, therefore, appears to keep the play in manuscript form, avoid the potential ravages of piracy, and, at the same time, commences proceedings in the federal courts.[113]

Around the same period, Shook pursued a similar claim against Rankin in Illinois.[114] Here, the Court granted an injunction against the performers to not use "the whole or any part" of the translator's copyrighted play.[115] The Court, however, also held that this did not enjoin the group from using another English translation of *Two Orphans.*[116] In another case *French* v. *Conelly* (1875),[117] the New York Superior Court granted a preliminary injunction, applying the earlier New York decision of *Palmer* v. *De Witt,*[118] finding, "that the property of an author, or his assignees, in an unpublished MS., is protected and governed in its use, enjoyment and transfer, the same as other personal property."[119] *French* v. *Conelly* also went against the grain of earlier state common law memory cases, addressed below, with the Court finding that despite the defendant committing the work to memory:[120]

allegations are true, and if it shall be established on the final hearing in this cause that the copy-right was legal and valid, that the complainants would be entitled to an injunction": 21 F. Cas. 1337, 1338.

112 Litman, "The Invention of the Common Law Play Right," n 172 (1409–1410). *See* Record #47738 © N. Hart Jackson, United States; 1875: 983, Feb. 1 ; 2c. Feb. 1." in Library of Congress Copyright Office, ed., *Dramatic Compositions Copyrighted in the United States: 1870–1916 (O–Z)* (Washington, DC: Government Printing Office, 1918): 308. The record does note "2c," that is, two copies have apparently been deposited. But Samuel French in an interview suggests that *Two Orphans* was not published until later after its successful run when it became "common property." It is possible that *Two Orphans* was published after the 1875 proceedings: *see* "Wars of the Theatres: Disputed Rights in Foreign Plays," *New York Tribune*, March 2, 1878.

113 The issue of whether it was not copyright infringement to reproduce a script from memory was also sustained. In this instance, the defendant was found to have not committed the script to memory and thus could not rely on the exception (21 F. Cas. 1337, 1339).

114 *See Shook* v. *Rankin*, 21 F. Cas. 1335 (1875) (Circuit Court, N.D. Illinois).

115 *Shook* v. *Rankin*, 21 F. Cas. 1335, 1337 (1875).

116 *Shook* v. *Rankin*, 21 F. Cas. 1335, 1337 (1875).

117 1 N.Y. Weekly Digest 196 (NY Superior Court 1875).

118 *Palmer* v. *De Witt*, 47 N.Y. 532 (1872). In this case a Henry D. Palmer had an injunction successfully reinstated where the defendant printed and published a British play in which Palmer had been assigned the exclusive rights to perform and publish in the United States. The court held the assignee Palmer had the legal and equitable rights in the manuscript with respect to the transfer. The rights of the foreign author in this instance could be relinquished by contractual agreement: *Palmer* v. *De Witt*, 47 N.Y. 532, 543 (1872).

119 1 N.Y. Weekly Digest 196, 197. This case also involved Adolphe D'Ennery as author of an adaption which was translated (Jules Verne's *Around the World in Eighty Days*).

120 1 N.Y. Weekly Digest 196, 197.

> it would seem to better accord with justice and good morals, that the carrying away in the memory, or in the stenographic notes of a spectator, of the contents of a play, unauthorized by the owner, is an infringement of his proprietary rights.

The 1872 proceedings in *Palmer* v. *De Witt* established important foundations for the authority that publishers like French could assert over foreign unpublished works in state common law courts. The issue for the Court in *Palmer* was whether the assignee of a foreign unpublished manuscript could restrain the defendant publisher from printing the unpublished manuscript. The Court's answer was definitive, upholding the right of the assignee "as the sole proprietor of the right to print and publish the work within the United States."[121] Writing specifically on the foreign author and their assigns, the Court found that the "alienage of the author is no obstacle to him or his assignee in proceeding in our courts for a violation, or to prevent a violation of his rights of property in his unpublished works."[122]

So French, Palmer, and Shook had some success in the courts protecting their contractually negotiated exclusive American rights over English translations of foreign manuscripts (although mostly in the context of a right to publish). The successful litigation also caused potential copyists to pause before mounting productions. French and Son warned managers attached to the Boucicault production that litigation may soon follow. In response, the Boucicault production shut down.

In February 1878, however, French and Son received notice that W. J. Gilmore, lessee of the Holiday Street Theatre in Baltimore, had mounted a production of *A Celebrated Case*.[123] Gilmore "surreptitiously secur[ed] a copy of the play" by apparently gaining the confidence of Shook and Palmer when he was in New York.[124] The licensed production controlled by Shook and Palmer had played to crowded audiences in New York and Boston.[125] Shook and Palmer began proceedings in the city Circuit Court in February, but the matter moved to the Federal Circuit on procedural grounds. Shook and Palmer were residents of New York and Gilmore a resident of Maryland.[126] Sources, including court transcripts of record

121 *Palmer* v. *De Witt*, 47 N.Y. 532, 544 (1872). Note this is a different Palmer in this case – a Henry Palmer as opposed to Albert Marshall Palmer, Manager of the Union Square Theatre in the 1870s.

122 *Palmer* v. *De Witt*, 47 N.Y. 532, 540 (1872). It would also be a position that Drone would emphasize: *see* Drone, *Treatise on The Law of Property in Intellectual Productions*, 106, 581.

123 *See* "T. H. French to Samuel French," February [15/21], 1878 in Samuel French Theatre Collection [Box 19, Letter Book] where T. H. writes to his father that they are going to commence litigation in Baltimore to stop "a man named Gilmore"); "T. H. French to Samuel French," February 27, 1878, in Samuel French Theatre Collection [Box 19, Letter Book] (T. H. writing that they are about to commence proceedings against Gilmore). *See also* "T. H. French to Samuel French," March 2, 1878, in Samuel French Theatre Collection [Box 19, Letter Book] (T. H. suggesting that the lawsuit in Baltimore is receiving plenty of coverage in the press and provides details about the suit).

124 *See* "Wars of the Theatres," 2.

125 *See* "Testimony," US Circuit Court of Maryland (press clipping extracts). By early March the production played to "crowded houses at Ford's Opera House" in Baltimore: *see* "A Celebrated Case," *New York Sun*, March 7, 1878.

126 *See* US Circuit Court of Maryland. Equity Case Files, 1801–1911 (PH-369; NAID 563016). Case 276A, "Sheridan Shook and Albert M. Palmer, Co-partners doing business under the name Shook &

and Samuel French himself, suggest that the play had never been published in either French or the subsequent English translation.[127] That said, the Library of Congress Dramatic Composition Record contains an entry for the work in January 1878 registered to Shook and Palmer. And indeed, the registration also gives the impression that the process is complete as two copies appear in the registration record.[128]

The contradiction between the copyright record and court transcript highlights the possible inaccuracies that abound in the Library of Congress registration records for dramatic compositions. Alternatively, the contradiction could suggest that the courts were willing to believe that the work was never published without verifying its publication status, or just simply willing to hear the matter as a common law claim in a federal court as appears to be the case in this instance.[129]

The plaintiffs, as expected, framed their complaint on the proprietary nature of the work, the exclusivity of the contractual relationship, and the work's intimate connection to the original authors as it was still in manuscript form – "it is as much

Palmer v. William J. Gilmore." Filed February 28, 1878, The National Archives at Philadelphia. In the prior preliminary proceedings as outlined in the archive record the plaintiff was enjoined from performing the work and a bond for damages was posted. The US Court was going to hear a motion for an injunction but a panel could not be formed, the parties sought hearing in the state court, that held it did not have jurisdiction to hear the matter. *See also* "Wars of the Theatres," 2; "Celebrated Case," *New York Sun*, March 7, 1878: "The suit was begun in the City Circuit Court about ten days ago, but was afterward removed to the United States Circuit Court under an act of Congress, the complainants being citizens of another State."

127 *See* "Testimony," US Circuit Court of Maryland, "neither the said drama in the French language ... nor the aforesaid translation thereof ... has ever been published by [the authors, French or Shook and Palmer] ... but the said drama in the French language, and the said translation thereof ... have always been, and are now in manuscript unpublished." *See also* "Wars of the Theatres: Disputed Rights in Foreign Plays," *New York Tribune*, March 2, 1878, where it notes: "The play has never been printed; It is as much private property as any play can be"; "A Wonderful Memory: A Remarkable Instance of Memorizing A Celebrated Case," *San Francisco Chronicle*, September 22, 1878, 7 (from the *New York Sun*, September 5); "A Celebrated Case," *Chicago Daily Tribune*, August 27, 1878.

128 *See* Record #6562 "© Sheridan Shook and A. M. Palmer, New York; 1878; 844, Jan. 18; 2c. Jan. 18." Recorded as "a play and dramatic composition in 6 acts" in Dramatic Compositions Copyrighted in the United States: 1870–1916 (A-N), ed. Library of Congress Copyright Office (Washington, DC: Government Printing Office, 1918): at p. 308. A later record #6561 "a drama in a prologue and 4 acts, by D'Ennery and Cormon. Philadelphia, 1894." © Penn pub. co., Philadelphia; 1S94 : 28468, July 7; 2c. Aug. 2. And the virtual card record confirms the 1878 registration: Celebrated Case, Record number 844, 1878, (Drama/Comp), S Shook and A M Palmer (Time-Period: 1870–1897; Drawer Label: CAV-CHAM; Card No: 0318). There is a further curious record below this: 1876, "D'Ennery and Cormon" [the authors] registered under a G. Munro. The original card was accessed from The United States Copyright Office, Virtual Card Catalogue, https://vcc.copyright.gov/browse.

129 All options were possibly on the table in this evolving and contested legal terrain but it appears the court was considering this work as an unpublished manuscript. It also must be noted that the registration record is January 18, 1878, and the proceedings concluded by March 7–8, 1878. Act of July 8, 1870, ch. 230, § 90, 16 Stat. 198, 218 required "within ten days from the publication ... deposit in the mail two copies of such copyright book or other article." But this still does not account for the record stating that two copies have been deposited, "2c," in the registration record on the January 18 date. Further, just because the record states copies have been deposited does not mean physical copies were actually deposited – an ongoing issue with respect to dramatic compositions.

private property as any play can be."[130] Thus, as the assignees claimed to have attained private property from the original authors of the work, they demanded their rights over the unpublished manuscript "be respected" throughout the country as had been the case in New York.[131]

The defendant's response was vague and anecdotal. The Holliday Street Theatre claimed compliance "with all the requirements of the law," perhaps because of the lack of protection for foreign authors.[132] The defendant also claimed that the resounding success of the production at the Holliday Street Theatre, staged at "a reduced admission," was the only reason why the plaintiff started proceedings: "if this was not a *superior* adaptation there would have been no opposition to its production"; "if the cast was not a *superior* one, and the stage mountings and setting done in a superior style, there would have been no opposition to its protection".[133]

The decision was an emphatic victory for the plaintiffs. Judge William Giles held that Shook and Palmer were entitled to relief and the defendants were "perpetually enjoined" from performing the play and using the title *Une Cause Celibre* or *A Celebrated Case*.[134] His Honor held that the plaintiffs, by assignment from Samuel French, were "exclusively entitled" to the unpublished manuscript of the dramatic work and had "the exclusive right" to represent the English translation of the work in North America.[135] Thus, the contracting model that French perfected had now also weathered considerable judicial scrutiny despite the absence of statutory protections for foreign authors.

The case received extensive coverage in the press both immediately before and after the judgment,[136] with Samuel and T. H. French in particular feeling vindicated for the substantial investment in time and money they had made in their stable of foreign works.[137] T. H. French, head of the largest publisher of plays in the United States, once again emphasized the importance of victory in the courts as part of

130 *See* "Wars of the Theatres," 2; "Testimony," US Circuit Court of Maryland.

131 *See* "Wars of the Theatres," 2; *see also* "Testimony," US Circuit Court of Maryland; D'Ennery and Cormon had assigned sole and exclusive rights in the English translation of the work in England and the United States to French, and French assigned the right to produce the work to Shook and Palmer.

132 One can only speculate given the defendant did not expand on his reasoning for how he complied with the law.

133 *See* "Affidavit of Charles Ford (item 3 press clipping)," US Circuit Court of Maryland.

134 "Final Decree of Judge William F. Giles, 6 March 1878," US Circuit Court of Maryland.

135 The Court also ordered costs for the complainants. "Final Decree of Judge William F Giles, 6 March 1878," US Circuit Court of Maryland.

136 *See, for example*, before the proceedings: "A Celebrated Case in Baltimore," *New York Times*, March 2, 1878; "Wars of the Theatres," 2. After the proceedings *see, for example*, "A Celebrated Case," *New York Sun*, March 7, 1878; "The Litigation at an End," *Cincinnati Inquirer*, March 7, 1878; "A Celebrated Case," *New York Times*, March 7, 1878. *See also* "T. H. French to Samuel French," March 2, 1878, in Samuel French Theatre Collection [Box 19, Letter Book] (T. H. suggesting that the lawsuit in Baltimore is receiving plenty of coverage in the press).

137 *See, for example*, "T. H. French to C. Gardiner," March 6, 1878, in Samuel French Theatre Collection [Box 19, Letter Book] (T. H. writing "we have won on every point in Baltimore"); "T. H. French to John Free Esq," March 8, 1878, in Samuel French Theatre Collection [Box 19, Letter Book] (T. H. writing that he heard "Gilmore is sick"); Samuel French Organization to

a broader agenda: secure control over unpublished foreign works and the organization will maintain its control over the movement of plays across the American theatre industry and the performance rights attached to those scripts. T. H. French's statement to the press in the days before the final decree was hardly a call to arms for American dramatists:

> For several years I have bought nearly all the successful French plays that have been introduced into this country. France is the fountain head of dramatic literature; it has the best writers, and we might as well acknowledge the truth. I wish we could get as good plays in England and in this country, but we can't do it.[138]

In the months that followed, other stakeholders continued to push back and challenge the decision in Maryland. In August 1878, Shook and Palmer sought injunctive relief against two men G. B. French (no relation) and Edward Byron to restrain them from playing *A Celebrated Case* in Boston.[139] In their defense, the two men claimed that although the work was assigned to an American citizen (Samuel French) "in the absence of an international copyright law they could not obtain any exclusive title or property in a foreign production".[140] Further, testing the boundaries of the memory/material transcribing distinction – the issue of whether it was legal to perform a work recalled from memory[141] – the defendants submitted evidence that they visited the Union Square Theatre "four or five times" to commit the work to memory without help from stenographic or photographic aids. In this case, the Massachusetts Supreme Court ultimately agreed with the defendants and dissolved the injunction. The Court found Byron had committed the play to memory. As reported in the papers, without statutory copyright protection, "an uncopyrighted play, once acted publicly, is open to anybody who wishes to use it," as long as it is not taken down in material form.[142] Although the case appeared to fall in line with many of the earlier memory cases,[143] it sits at odds with the consistently

Mr. Baridge, March 8, 1878, in Samuel French Theatre Collection [Box 19, Letter Book] (writing about the victory and buoyed to stop other productions of *A Celebrated Case*); "T. H. French to A. M. Palmer," March 8, 1878, in Samuel French Theatre Collection [Box 19, Letter Book] (writing about how unfair it was to play *A Celebrated Case* all over the country and that you and me received nothing – which may be a reference to the actions of piracy which would now hopefully be halted in light of the case); and "T. H. French to Samuel French," March 8, 1878, in Samuel French Theatre Collection [Box 19, Letter Book] (T. H. French writing to his father with "glorious news to communicate" regarding the litigation in Baltimore).

138 *See* "Wars of the Theatres," 2.

139 *See* "A Celebrated Case: Hearing in Supreme Court Reserved," *Boston Daily Globe*, August 28, 1878; "Hearing on Injunction before Chief Justice Gray Yesterday," *Boston Daily Globe*, August 27, 1878.

140 "A Celebrated Case," *Boston Daily Globe*, August 28, 1878.

141 The development of the memory doctrine is explored in illuminating detail by Derek Miller, *Copyright and the Value of Performance, 1770–1911* (Cambridge, UK: Cambridge University Press, 2018), Ch 3.

142 *See* "A Wonderful Memory: A Remarkable Instance of Memorizing A Celebrated Case," *San Francisco Chronicle*, September 22, 1878, 7 (from the *New York Sun*, September 5).

143 *See Keene* v. *Kimball* 82 Mass. (16 Gray) 545 (1860).

successful exclusive rights claims made by Palmer, Shook, and the French organization.

But the case is interesting for its timing as much as its result. The 1878 Boston *A Celebrated Case* proceedings concluded a year before the publication of Eaton Drone's work on the natural rights theory of the common law play right – extending rights in the unpublished manuscript to the performance of the unpublished manuscript – which immediately began to win favor with the courts in the latter half of the nineteenth century.[144] Indeed, within four years of the *A Celebrated Case*, a decision in the same jurisdiction of Massachusetts, *Tompkins* v. *Halleck*, came to a very different result.[145] In this case,[146] where the play was still unpublished, and thus "not a complete dedication to the public,"[147] later performances either obtained "by memory or by stenograph are alike injurious."[148] The *Tompkins* decision in Massachusetts represented a shift away from many memory cases to that point, overruling the decision of *Keene* v. *Kimball*.[149] The case also reflected the success of a longer legal strategy undertaken by influential mediating stakeholders including French, Shook, and Palmer to protect exclusive rights of foreign works in American courts.

Around the same time as the *A Celebrated Case* litigation in Boston, Samuel and T. H. also commenced proceedings against Thomas Maguire from San Francisco to enjoin the defendant from staging an unpublished translated adaptation of Victorien Sardou's *Diplomacy*.[150] French had a license to publish and perform the work, and the defendant producer was alleged to have staged the piece in a San Francisco venue. *Diplomacy*, like *A Celebrated Case*, was a popular foreign work in high demand,[151] and the French Organization anxiously waited for news on the outcome of the litigation toward the end of August 1878.[152] The New York Supreme Court's decision in *French* v. *Maguire*[153] confirmed the position of earlier

144 *See* Litman, "The Invention of the Common Law Play Right," 1381 and Drone, *Treatise on The Law of Property in Intellectual Productions*.

145 133 Mass. 32 (1882).

146 *See also* Litman, "The Invention of the Common Law Play Right," 1412–1413.

147 133 Mass. 32 (1882), 43–44.

148 133 Mass. 32 (1882), 43–44. Here we see the collapsing of the distinction between unlawful copying through stenography and lawful copying by memory as articulated by Eaton Drone: Drone, *Treatise on The Law of Property*, 571–572.

149 82 Mass. (16 Gray) 545 (1860). But, of course, not a shift in memory cases across other jurisdictions.

150 *French* v. *Maguire*, 55 How. Pr. 471 (N.Y. Sup. Ct. 1878). T. H. French prewarned of the likeliness that *Diplomacy* would be pirated. In an interview with the *New York Tribune* in March 1878, French said "I haven't the slightest doubt that, if it is successful, two or three other managers will produce it in defiance of the law." *See* "Wars of the Theatres," 2.

151 *See* "T. H. French to R. M. Field," February 16, 1878, in Samuel French Theatre Collection [Box 19, Letter Book] (T. H. writing that Sardou's *Diplomacy* would be negotiated on the same terms as the highly successful *Une Cause Celebere*.)

152 Thomas Edwards would send regular notices to Samuel French throughout July and August about whether there was any news on the outcome of the case: (Various Correspondence T. Edwards to Samuel French in July/August 1878, in Samuel French Theatre Collection [Box 19, Letter Book]).

153 55 How. Pr. 471 (N.Y. Sup. Ct. 1878).

decisions,[154] using authorship rhetoric for the benefit of the publishers, by holding that the "author" continued to enjoy protections over their unpublished manuscript. Unlike the legal landscape in Britain, performance did not constitute publication and thus an offering to the public. And although the observer could appropriate as "much as his memory may be capable of retaining," the Court also held that "it will not allow the hearer and observer to appropriate and use the entire composition, with its incidental stage accompaniments. That right still remains in the author and his assignee."[155] The *French* v. *Maguire* decision for French and his associates helped erase whatever uncertainty may have arisen after the Boston *A Celebrated Case* proceedings.[156] And French could now proceed with even more confidence given the prevailing influence of the Drone-based natural rights common law play right developments.

—

The 1856 Act splintered the two major legislative revisions of 1831 and 1870 which, in form, spoke to furthering the protections of American dramatists. But both the 1831 and 1856 Acts made protections available to authors or their assigns.[157] The 1856 Act also extended protections in performance rights to the "author or proprietor."[158] At the same time, federal copyright protection was available only to United States residents or citizens. The benefits of dual citizenship in the United States and Britain soon became abundantly clear. Transatlantic mediating stakeholders with citizenship in the United States could use the courts to advance common law claims. American stakeholders could also exploit the inconsistent application of the federal copyright statutory registration process that became centralized at the Library of Congress after 1870.[159] American stakeholders registered foreign titles under their own name giving the impression that there was a valid, and perfected, registration tied to a United States proprietor. Yet the registration process was often not perfected as producers were reluctant to deposit copies of published works. And under the evolving parol transfer, any sale of a script from author to the publisher complimented presumed assignment in all rights associated with the work. The intention of the parties was not subject to strict scrutiny. It was presumed there was a legal transfer, and the transferal of ownership presumed to subsist in the American owner-publisher.

154 Including reference to *Palmer* v. *De Witt*, 1 N.Y. Weekly Digest 196 (N.Y. Sup. Ct. 1875) (at 479–480).

155 55 How. Pr. 471, 479 (N.Y. Sup. Ct. 1878).

156 After the decision, T. H. French was keen to remind any producers of the potential ramifications of producing the work. T. H. French wrote to R. M. Field in Boston about the *Maguire* decision and added that if the work was used "I will be compelled to pursue all legal remedies to prevent it and hold you for all damages." *See* "T. H. French to R. M. Field," August 23, 1878, Samuel French Theatre Collection.

157 Or proprietors. *See, for example*, Act of February 3, 1831, ch. 16, 4 Stat. 436 §§ 1, 3, 4, 9; Act of July 8, 1870, ch. 230, 16 Stat. 198 §§ 22, 53, 54, 86, 91, 101, 102.

158 Act of August 18, 1856, ch 169, 11 Stat. 138 (1856).

159 Act of July 8, 1870, ch.230, §§85, 91.

Samuel French and his associates developed an effective legal strategy in the courts to secure broad control over foreign works in the United States that complemented internal contracting practices. French secured sole and exclusive contractual control over the foreign unpublished manuscript in the United States and transferred this exclusive right to a small network of American producers (while also retaining an ongoing interest in the work on Broadway and tours throughout the country). As the script remained in an unpublished form, it allowed publishers to advance their common law claims with respect to foreign manuscripts in state courts (and sometimes federal courts). The evolving common law play right doctrine, eventually promoted by Eaton Drone at the end of the 1870s, was appearing to be more sympathetic toward foreign authors in form but mainly Samuel French and his associates in substance. For Drone, the common law made "no distinction between a native and a foreigner."[160] And perhaps even more importantly for French, according to Drone, was that protections at common law which extended to an "alien friend" also included "him or his assignee."[161]

Protection under the statutory regime required the registration of the title, notice, and publication of the work. In contrast, French established his publishing empire by keeping most of his lucrative foreign scripts in manuscript form. The choice to not register many scripts in the Samuel French collection served several purposes: the avoidance of rampant copying of scripts and their performance, the scourge of the theatrical industry, and also the potential to protect the unpublished manuscript under the common law. The publishing entrepreneurs forged their business success on the back of an organizational model of inherent contradictions. French and Son ran a play-publishing business that derived extraordinary profits and influence from not publishing plays. The company claimed foreign authors had common law rights in state courts when no rights existed in federal statutory law. But the publisher and his associates, on occasions, also moved strategically between state and federal courts, capitalizing on an infant centralized registration system, to advance federal claims.

The lack of statutory rights for foreign authors did not slow down the operation of the rapidly expanding French publishing empire. In 1891, foreign authors were finally granted statutory protection under the Chace amendments.[162] Anecdotal accounts imply that the 1891 international copyright revisions sometimes may have exacerbated the distinctions between foreign and American dramatists.[163]

160 *See* Drone, *Treatise on The Law of Property in Intellectual Productions*, at 581 and 106 citing cases including *Jeffreys* v. *Boosey*, 4 H. L. C. 815; *Keene* v. *Wheatley*, 9 Am. Law Reg. 33; *Crowe* v. *Aiken*, 2 Biss. 208; *Palmer* v. *DeWitt*, 47 N.Y. 532.

161 *See* Drone, *Treatise on The Law of Property in Intellectual Productions*, 106 citing *Palmer* v. *DeWitt*, 47 N.Y. 532.

162 Act of March 3, 1891, ch. 565, 26 Stat. 1106.

163 And exacerbated the distinctions despite the stricter requirements of the manufacturing clause which required particular foreign works imported to the United States to be manufactured in the United States. The Act of March 3, 1891, ch. 565, 26 Stat. 1106, §3 specifically refers to the following categories: "That in the case of a book, photograph, chromo, or lithograph, the two copies of the

Playwright George Middleton suggested that in 1893 American actress Kathryn Kidder paid French author Victorien Sardou US$2,500 advances and 20 percent of takings on nightly box offices that exceeded US$5,000 for the American rights to *Madame Sans-Gene*. In comparison, Owen Davis, one of the most financially successful American playwrights of the same period, would take about 8 percent of the "company share" – which equated to about 60 percent of the weekly receipts (US$125–US$250 a week). For Middleton, "royalties paid to French dramatists were far beyond those any American dramatist could command."[164] When Samuel French passed away in 1898, the *Publishers Weekly* wrote that "[m]ost of the European plays which previous to the last ten or fifteen years made notable success in this country were brought here by Samuel French."[165]

French and Son did have a stable of American works, which continued to grow toward the end of the nineteenth century and the first half of the twentieth century. The organization encouraged the amateur theatre movement, the "little theatres," and the regional theatres throughout the twentieth century to become the expansive business it is today and champion of new American works.[166] But the most striking organizational feature of the industry that emerged in the immediate decades following the 1856 amendments was the consolidation of control in the hands of theatrical managers building centralized brokerage businesses out of major American cities, and publishing entrepreneurs like Samuel French structuring how unpublished foreign works moved throughout the American theatrical economy. Controlling intangible rights in scripts and associated performance rights were functional tools used for transforming works. But control over the intangible right was ultimately reliant on factors including who controlled physical spaces, how stakeholders administered these spaces, and control over the development of customary licensing practices. Mediators like Samuel French shaped the production process in the theatrical economy by bundling a range of services and connecting with a sophisticated network of stakeholders across the industry that allowed for the broad distribution of works between authors and audiences.

same required to be delivered or deposited as above shall be printed from type set within the limits of the United States, or from plates made therefrom, or from negatives, or drawings on stone made within the limits of the United States, or from transfers made therefrom." On the manufacturing clause, *see* Miller, *Copyright and the Value of Performance*, Ch. 4, especially at 232–233 in consideration of *Hervieu* v. *Ogilvie*, 169 F. 978 (1909) which excluded printed dramatic compositions as being classified as a book under the manufacturing clause.

164 Middleton, *These Things Are Mine*, 312. As previously noted, Owen Davis was a very financially successful dramatist.

165 "Obituary Notes: Samuel French," 689.

166 *See* Samuel French website, "History," www.samuelfrench.com/resources/history/, also discussed in "Truly Yours," Samuel French Theatre Collection.

# 3

# The Enduring "Piratical" Pursuits of Alexander Byers

As Samuel French was building an empire in the United States on the back of foreign dramatists, another group of enterprising publishers established lucrative mediating businesses in alternative markets. Alexander Byers, commonly known as one of America's most successful theatrical thieves, mediated the movement of theatrical creation between authors and audiences by developing business models outside and within formal legal frameworks for over three decades.[1] Studying the ascendancy of Samuel French and his associates is instructive for understanding how mediating power over the production process was asserted through order and methodical organization. Byers' methods of mediation are an equally compelling study of the state of nature.

Theatrical Renaissance man Steele MacKaye possessed astonishing talents.[2] He was an actor, playwright,[3] manager, and patented a remarkable array of inventions that revolutionized the American theatre in the late-nineteenth century.[4] MacKaye's

1 The expansive coverage of Byers' business activities in the *New York Dramatic Mirror* labels the publisher in a variety of provocative ways including "pirate," or "play pirate," one of the "play thieves," a "play stealer," "notorious," "bogus," "audacious," "pestiferous," "dishonest," part of a "gang" of pirates, and his activities in Chicago as the "hub" of piracy.

2 MacKaye's name was James Morrison Steele MacKaye. The main archival collection pertaining to his legal records are housed at Dartmouth: MacKaye Family papers, 1751–1998, Manuscript ML-5, Rauner Special Collections Library, Dartmouth [hereafter MacKaye Family papers]. Percy MacKaye, Steele MacKaye's son, has written a widely cited work on Steele MacKaye: Percy MacKaye, *Epoch: The Life of Steele MacKaye, Genius of the Theatre, in Relation to His Times & Contemporaries* (2 Vols.: New York: Boni and Liveright, 1927).

3 MacKaye wrote about thirty plays throughout his career, but without question his most celebrated work was *Hazel Kirke* written in 1878–9 (and premiered in 1880). Other major works included *Money Mad (Through the Dark)* and *Paul Kauvar (Anarchy)*.

4 Steele MacKaye's inventions between 1879 and 1893 included: the Double Stage, Ventilation Devices, Indirect Lighting Devices, Overstage Orchestra, Fireproof Devices for Scenery, Air-cooling and Purifying Devices, Playbills and Tickets, Elevator Stage for Orchestra, Folding Chair, Luxauleator (curtain of light), Nebulator (cloud creator), Proscenium Adjustor, Wave Maker, Sliding Stage, Telescopic Stage, Floating Stage, 13 Devices for Illuminating and Coloring the Stage and Scenery, 40 Apparatus for Producing Increased Realism in Stage Effects, Spectatorium (a large stadium for live events that was never completed), Scenitorium. *See* "Inventions and Legal Papers: List of Inventions," Box 9.5, MacKaye Family papers.

production of *Hazel Kirke*, which opened at Madison Square Theatre in February 1880,[5] accentuated his precocious artistic and commercial abilities. Reverend Dr. George Mallory and his brother Marshall rebuilt Madison Square for MacKaye to stage "[w]holesome [p]lays," like *Hazel Kirke*, featuring American performers and new American dramatic voices.[6] The Madison Square Theatre included MacKaye's "double stage" invention that could be raised and lowered, expanding and reducing the size of the performance area as well as allowing for quicker changes in scenes.[7] MacKaye's play *Hazel Kirke* was also a box-office phenomenon, celebrated in the popular theatrical press in 1881 as "the most successful play ever produced," having the "longest run on record in America,"[8] and eventually touring multiple productions across the country under an innovative organizational booking model.[9]

Steele MacKaye never benefited from the financial riches that inevitably followed the success of his play, however. MacKaye was an employee of the Mallory brothers and did not have a legal interest in *Hazel Kirke*.[10] The oppressive employment contract between producer Marshall Mallory and Steele MacKaye, which MacKaye would dispute for years, had the writer surrender all control and future royalties to his dramatic works in return for a

5 *Hazel Kirke* opened on February 4, 1880 and was "withdrawn" after 486 consecutive performances on May 31, 1881. *See* Arthur H. Quinn, ed., *Representative American Plays* (New York: The Century Co., 1922), 498. Copies of the scripts are in the MacKaye collection: "Hazel Kirke Typescript taped to Paper," 1880, Box 14, MacKaye Family papers.

6 *See* "Rev. G.S. Mallory's Death: … Wholesome Plays Only Presented," *New York Times*, March 3, 1897, 12. Extensive documentation in relation to the play including MacKaye's dispute with the Mallory brothers can be found at: "Hazel Kirke," Box 14.4–14.5, MacKaye Family papers.

7 *See* "New Stage Inventions of Steele MacKaye," "Inventions and Legal Papers: …," Box 9.7, MacKaye Family papers.

8 *See* "Poster: The Madison Square Theatre Company: Hazel Kirke," The Jay T. Last Collection of Graphic Arts and Social History, Huntington Digital Library: https://hdl.huntington.org/digital/collection/p16003coll4/id/2378/rec/1. The *New York Dramatic Mirror* celebrated the increasing popularity of the play, *see* "The Week at the Theatres: Hazel Kirke," *New York Dramatic Mirror*, June 19, 1880, 7; "The American Dramatist at Home and Abroad," *New York Dramatic Mirror*, September 25, 1880, 6; "An Undeserved Rebuke to Metropolitan Managers," *New York Dramatic Mirror*, October 23, 1880, 6; "Metropolitan Success and their Lessons to Managers," *New York Dramatic Mirror*, February 26, 1881, 6.

9 These booking systems were under the management of the Frohman brothers as well as Marc (occasionally spelt Mark) Klaw and Abe Erlanger who would go on to become the central partners of the Theatrical Syndicate formed in 1896.

10 In *MacKaye* v. *Mallory*, MacKaye had no copyright interest in a work where there had been a contractual assignment of rights from employee creator to employer Marshall Mallory. *See MacKaye* v. *Mallory*, 6 F. 743 (1881); *MacKaye* v. *Mallory*, 12 F. 328 (C.C. S.D.N.Y. 1882). MacKaye countersued seeking an injunction. On the dispute *see* MacKaye, *Epoch: The Life of Steele MacKaye*, Vol. 1, Chap. 13 "The Shadow of a Contract"; Catherine Fisk, *Working Knowledge: Employee Innovation and the Rise of Corporate Intellectual Property, 1800–1930* (Chapel Hill: University of North Carolina Press, 2009), 154–158. The first summons and complaint in the dispute: NY Common Pleas: Steele MacKaye against Marshall Mallory and George Mallory, January 5, 1881, Box 8, MacKaye Family papers.

modest annual fee.[11] And because of the assignment, the original creator abandoned any right to attribution in his work.[12]

The legal dispute between Mallory and MacKaye, not resolved until 1897 after MacKaye's death,[13] represented a defining moment in the nineteenth-century doctrinal shift concerning employer/employee copyright relationships.[14] But the owners of *Hazel Kirke* were confronted with complications beyond the legal employer/employee issues. *Hazel Kirke* was such a popular play that it was subject to rampant copying commonly referred to as piracy in the theatrical press – either the copying of the performance itself or copying of the manuscript text – which spawned sustainable, and lucrative, alternative markets for plays across the country. Piracy was a much larger, and longer-term, problem for the industry. Within two years of the 1856 amendment, newspaper reports started to voice dissatisfaction with the reforms in the face of the expanding theatrical piracy business.[15]

Between 1880 and 1897 the *Dramatic Mirror*, under the editorship of Harrison Fiske, set out on a crusade to make the public aware of the extent of play plagiarism, "naming and shaming" producers and actors involved in copying at every possible opportunity to do so. In most issues of the *Dramatic Mirror* during the 1880s and 1890s, there is a mention of alleged infringement. Harrison Fiske wrote in 1889: "THE MIRROR will continue its crusade until the pirates are all driven to cover or wiped out of existence by legislative enactment."[16] And the legislative revisions that victims pursued went beyond the usual account of profits or injunctive relief to include criminal penalties.[17]

11 Other incentives were based on the long-term profitability of the show. MacKaye, *Epoch: The Life of Steel MacKaye*, 369. *See also* Fisk, *Working Knowledge*, 154–158.

12 *See MacKaye* v. *Mallory*, 12 F. 328 (C.C. S.D.N.Y. 1882); Fisk, *Working Knowledge*, 158.

13 *See MacKaye* v. *Mallory*, 79 F. 1 (2d Cir 1897); *MacKaye* v. *Mallory*, 80 F. 256 (C.C.S.D.N.Y. 1897); *Mallory* v. *MacKaye*, 86 F. 122 (C.C.S.D.N.Y. 1898). *See also* "At Law About Hazel Kirke," *New York Sun*, March 24, 1896, transcribed in "Notes for Epoch," Box 48.50, MacKaye Family papers.

14 *See* Fisk, *Working Knowledge*, who writes at 157: "In the terms of the great debates of the 1880s about the relation of labor and capital, the Mallorys were extracting the entire surplus value of MacKaye's creative labor. The theatre press thus came down squarely on the side of labor … The court came down squarely on the side of capital."

15 *See, for example, Boston Saturday Evening Gazette*, June 19, 1858, 2 (the Act: "does not at all appear to have met the purpose for which it was intended.") *See also* generally, the ongoing problem of piracy and the attempts by Harrison Fiske to control theatre copyright infringement through the vehicle of *The Dramatic Mirror* (early 1880s to 1897). The *New York Dramatic Mirror* was founded in 1879 and ceased publication in 1922. It was originally titled the *New York Mirror*, renamed the *New York Dramatic Mirror* in 1889, and renamed again to become the *Dramatic Mirror* in 1917. For consistency purposes, I use two general titles for the publication which covers the entire period of publication (1879–1922): (1) In the body of the text I refer to the publication as the *Dramatic Mirror* and (2) In the footnotes I cite the publication as the *New York Dramatic Mirror*.

16 "Movements of the Pirates," *New York Dramatic Mirror*, April 13, 1889, 3. *See* Fannie Aymar Mathew's pleas to protect the dramatist against rampant piracy: "Dramatists' Rights," *New York Dramatic Mirror*, April 11, 1892, 5; "A Set-Back to the Pirates," *New York Dramatic Mirror*, July 1, 1887, 6.

17 The advocacy measures leading to the 1897 Act are examined by Zvi Rosen, "The Twilight of the Opera Pirates: A Prehistory of the Right of Public Performance for Musical Compositions," *Cardozo Arts & Entertainment Law Journal* 24 (2007): 1157.

*Hazel Kirke* was at the center of the conversation about theatrical piracy. The *Dramatic Mirror* reported how Chicago theatrical publisher Alexander Byers, with his "gang" of pirates, under the umbrella of the Chicago Manuscript Company, had in his possession unauthorized copies of *Hazel Kirke* that he was moving throughout the country to producing partners.[18] The expanding activities of Byers eventually led to the establishment of a "pirate play-bureau" in Chicago to deal with the highly organized group that operated in defiance of any potential legal rights of dramatists and their representatives.[19] The thriving market for copies of *Hazel Kirke* also triggered vigorous discussion in the theatre press about informal methods of dispute resolution,[20] and the need to introduce further federal copyright reform with stronger penalties to better protect American dramatists.[21] But despite the author rhetoric, a noticeable feature of the disputes reported in the *Dramatic Mirror* was that they often did not involve the original playwright. The party alleging infringement was usually a producer, and the alleged infringer was usually another producer, theatre manager, publisher, or actor.

According to the owners of *Hazel Kirke*, the resolution of disputes often demanded vigilante-like responses along with formal legal action. Buoyed by their "earnest and intelligent efforts to hunt the rascals down,"[22] the Mallorys – with help from Marc Klaw and the Frohman brothers Daniel, Charles, and Gustave, who would later form the nucleus of the all-powerful Theatrical Syndicate – "settled by payment" with Byers, and his accomplices,[23] in April

18 "A list of seventy seven copyrighted plays were found in the possession of this Chicago gang." *See* "Dramatic Thieves at Bay," *New York Dramatic Mirror*, March 11, 1882, 6; "Prosecuting Play Thieves," *New York Dramatic Mirror*, April 15, 1882, 8. Byers was described in 1909 as reminding one of "the cleverest and Shiftiest of the Standard Oil crowd." It was a reference Tom Lawson made of Henry E. Rogers: *see* "Chicago's Centre For The Disposal Of 'Lifted Stuff'," *Variety*, February 6, 1909, 6.

19 *See* "A Pirate-Play Bureau," *New York Dramatic Mirror*, July 6, 1889, 1.

20 *See* "Theatrical Litigation and the Remedy," *New York Dramatic Mirror*, January 15, 1881, 6, suggesting an industry arbitration process to resolve disputes and: "The law-courts begin by being absolutely ignorant of theatrical usage. The lawyers on both sides are generally quite as ignorant."

21 Many disputes commenced but settled before judgment. Indeed, the *Dramatic Mirror* opined in the early 1880s: "Who will be the Blaine to devise a Peace Congress for the settlement of all theatrical wars out of court and thus beat the lawyers?" *See New York Dramatic Mirror*, May 6, 1882, 8. *The Mirror* also suggested the establishment of a fund to litigate against piracy (a quote by manager George Harrison): "I wish some decisive action could be taken by the combination managers toward maintaining a fund to defray the expense of prosecuting men who allow a pay to be produced without guarantee that the right to do so is clearly in their possession. If this were done it would do much to remove the evil, and I shall be glad to put myself in communication with other travelling managers to attain this result." "On the Track of Pirates," *New York Dramatic Mirror*, October 1, 1887, 7 (citing theatre manager Seymour). However, *see also* "Drama at the Bar," *New York Dramatic Mirror*, October 13, 1888, 6 (where Fiske acknowledges "that the drama should have secured a lodgment in judicial minds," as a consequence of more engagement between the theatre industry and the courts).

22 *See* "Prosecuting the Play Thieves," *New York Dramatic Mirror*, April 15, 1882, 3; *see also* "Dramatic Thieves at Bay," *New York Dramatic Mirror*, March 11, 1882, 6; "The Examination of the Chicago Play Thieves," *New York Dramatic Mirror*, April 15, 1882, 3.

23 Mr. Laroque and Mr. Coby were Byers' accomplices and were also prosecuted: *see* "The Examination of the Chicago Play Thieves," *New York Dramatic Mirror*, April 15, 1882, 3.

1882.[24] The *Dramatic Mirror* published a declarative warning following the group's victory to all "managers, hall owners and hall agents throughout the United States."[25] Any attempt to trespass on the rights of the owners of *Hazel Kirke* "will be summarily dealt with in Civil and Criminal Courts, and offenders will be punished to the law's fullest extent."[26]

Eileen Curley suggests that although the 1856 Act, encouraging registration, "guarant [eed] playwrights the authority to control publication and performance of their texts," it also "aided and abetted play pirates."[27] As examined, the notion that the 1856 Act "guaranteed playwrights" authority in substance is questionable. But it is clearer that Alexander Byers knew how to harness a broader legal system that required copyright registration and play publication for federal protection, and required control over unpublished manuscripts at common law. The publisher's business sustained itself throughout a period in which the common law "play right" attached to unpublished manuscripts was evolving in the courts. Byers also weathered the federal legislative reforms of 1891, 1897, and 1909, aimed at, either directly or indirectly, circumventing his practices.[28] In the last two decades of the nineteenth century, Byers copied down performances in theatres and exploited the plays throughout the country outside the jurisdiction in which they were copied. Byers was probably aware that unpublished dramatic scripts were subject to protection under state common law copyright, but it was unclear whether state laws applied to activities outside the state. He sustained his business under a legal framework before 1909 where it was not yet definitively clear – although some intra-state cases were siding with the proprietor[29] – if it was illegal to copy a work down in one state and print and publish it in another. He also appears aware that many state jurisdictions did not require copyright transfers of unpublished scripts to be

24 *See* "Copyright Notice," *New York Dramatic Mirror*, April 1882, 12. "[A] unanimous Grand Jury at Chicago returned an indictment, and placed under heavy bail Alex. Byers and H. S. Corby for obtaining and selling stolen copies of Hazel Kirke."

25 *See* "Copyright Notice," *New York Dramatic Mirror*, April 1882, 12 (this was all capitalized in the original).

26 *See* "Copyright Notice," *New York Dramatic Mirror*, April 1882, 12. Within the year, there were numerous reports in the *Mirror* about the continuation of alleged illegal activities: *see* "An Illiterate Play-Thief," *New York Dramatic Mirror*, November 18, 1882, 7; "More Piracy," *New York Dramatic Mirror*, April 14, 1883, 10.

27 Eileen Curley, "A Shot over the Bow: William Gillette and Amateur Play Piracy," *Journal of American Drama and Theatre* 22, no. 3 (2010): 30.

28 There were specific ways that the three major enactments of 1891, 1897, and 1909 aimed to deal with play piracy as discussed in Chapter 1. The 1891 amendments of course provided protection to foreign works in the United States in a market that was flooded with foreign productions. The 1897 Act expanded protections to performance rights attached to musical compositions, but another critical dimension of the reforms was the addition of criminal penalties for copyright infringement – reforms that were driven by playwright advocates including Harrison Fiske and theatrical lawyer/judge Abram J. Dittenhoefer in the face of rampant piracy. Among the expansive 1909 amendments was the inclusion of the right to register unpublished works, thus hindering the ability of Byers to copy in one state and publish or perform in another. Byres survived throughout it all by adapting to different legislative interventions.

29 *See Palmer* v. *DeWitt*, 47 N.Y. 532 (1872).

in writing. And, as discussed, the parol transfer presumed that producers or publishers had acquired the author's copyright before publishing or performing the work, even with no suggestion that an assignment had occurred.

Byers also appeared to appreciate that a deficient registration system presented unique opportunities to establish a national business on the illusion of legitimacy. He could register titles, or derivations of original titles, where it was unclear whether the title was his to register. He assured notice of copyright was printed across many of the scripts he acquired, signaling to the theatrical economy that he owned the work. In jurisdictions far afield from the infringement, it was easier to presume Byers had lawful control over a work when the actual owner was unaware – and unable to police – that an infringement had occurred.

Byers was trading in the most lucrative American and foreign works across state boundaries. He, therefore, deprived American dramatists of potential royalties and opportunities in a market already flooded with the work of foreign authors. Byers had a business model that was evolving around the interests of mediating stakeholders and the gumption to take advantage of this environment to its "fullest extent." Byers was also an opportunist like French who moved in and out of the law when it best served his purposes. More importantly, he was a mediator with the resources and networks to control the movement of works between the author and the audience within the larger theatrical organizational structure.[30]

Despite the best intentions to bring the copyists to justice at the turn of the twentieth century, Byers continued to operate.[31] Table 3.1 below is a population of dramatic compositions – many of which are housed in the vast script collection of the Chicago Manuscript Company Archive[32] – that Byers allegedly pirated from the owners and authors of the works. The Table includes instances between 1882 and 1916 where the press identified a work that was: (1) attached to Alexander Byers and his Chicago Manuscript Company; and (2) the subject of a piracy complaint or piracy litigation.[33] That is, all the plays in the Table were housed and sold by the Chicago Manuscript

30 *See* Robert Spoo's work on contested understandings of piracy and trade courtesy. Spoo writes about literary property in nineteenth-century America being "a complex activity intimately bound up with legitimate publishing and the copyright law . . . Respectable houses and pirate firms were not always distinguishable." Robert Spoo, *Without Copyrights: Piracy, Publishing, and the Public Domain* (New York: Oxford University Press, 2013), 26, and *see* 26–28.

31 As soon as the *Hazel Kirke* dispute was resolved between Byers and Mallory in 1882, there were reports coming out of the west that the play was subject to piracy – illegal copies that were possibly coming from Byers' office: *see* "More Piracy," *New York Dramatic Mirror*, April 14, 1883, 10.

32 The extraordinary script collection of the Chicago Manuscript Company, purchased by Robert Sherman after Byers' death, includes scripts from the early 1880s, but is mostly concentrated after 1892: 1/3/MSS 175, Sherman Theatre Collection, Special Collections Research Center, Southern Illinois University Carbondale (86 Boxes) [hereafter Sherman Theatre Collection].

33 *See, for example*, the plays identified to have been stolen in: "Following up the Pirates," *New York Dramatic Mirror*, July 23, 1887, 2; "A Pirate Play Bureau," *New York Dramatic Mirror*, July 6, 1889, 1; "Beware of Play-Stealer Byers," *New York Dramatic Mirror*, February 13, 1892, 8; "Chicago's Centre for the Disposal of 'Lifted Stuff'," *Variety*, February 6, 1909, 6; "Play Piracy Must Stop," *New York Dramatic Mirror*, April 5, 1911, 13; "Byers Indicted," *New York Dramatic Mirror*, June 21, 1911, 14.

Company without (allegedly) the consent of the author or owner, and that author or owner either started proceedings or claimed rights in the work. The few plays highlighted in bold do not appear in the press reports. But the scripts of these works in the archive are highly suspicious (including, for example, multiple versions of scripts in handwritten and printed forms).

TABLE 3.1 *Dramatic compositions Alexander Byers allegedly pirated*[34]

| Play (Alternative Title) | Copyright Regis Yr/Name (1st regis)/published copies received by Copyright Office (0 c, 1 c, or 2 c) | Author (A) or Owner |
|---|---|---|
| After Dark | ("printed . . . for private use.")[35] | Dion Boucicault (A) |
| Alixe | 1873/Augustin Daly/ 0 c | Augustin Daly (A) |
| Across the Continent | 1870/Oliver Doud Byron/ 0 c | James McCloskey (A) |
| Alabama | No registration found | Unknown |
| Adam the Second | 1899/Will C. Matthews/ 0 c | Will M. Cressy |
| (Alias) Jimmy Valentine | 1909/Liebler & co., New York/ 1 c | Paul Armstrong (A) |
| Are You a Mason? | 1901/ Emanuel Lederer, Carl Herrmann (adapted)/ 2 c | Emanuel Lederer and Carl Herrmann (adpt) |
| Arrah-na-Pogue (Wicklow Wedding) | 1891/E. H. House/ 0 c (alleged piracy reported before registration) | E. H. House (A) |
| The Banker's Daughter (Lillian's Last Love) | 1878/B. Howard/ 2 c | B Howard (A) |

34 In the first column of Table 3.1 some plays have alternative names (the second name in brackets). In these instances, plays were registered or trading under either of the names – a strategy that may have been used to avoid detection of pirated works. The second column identifies the year that the work was first registered (either title and/or copies deposited – whatever is the most complete date), the name of person/organization under which it was registered, and where available how many published copies of the work were recorded as received by the Copyright Office (0c, 1c, 2c). There is however some uncertainty whether all compositions recorded as deposited were actually deposited. The third column identifies the name of the author (A) or owner of the work. Where there is "no registration" I could not find or determine the relevant registration record. The registration details were taken from: Library of Congress Copyright Office, *Dramatic Compositions Copyrighted in the United States: 1870–1916* (Washington, DC: Government Printing Office, 1918) Vol. 1 (A–N), Vol. 2 (M–Z). A note to be aware of when reading the data: In most instances, it was clear what registration record related to the alleged piracy complaint (for example, when there was only one registration in the record). In some instances, there were multiple works registered under the same title. In these situations, I attempted to match the physical script details in the archive (where a script was available) with the registration record, or I used the first (earliest) registration record. In some instances, in column 2, I have provided further descriptive details about the registration history, particularly where Alexander Byers was involved.

35 *See Daly* v. *Palmer*, 6 F. Cas. 1132, 1135 (1868): "The play of 'After Dark' has never been published by Boucicault, although printed by him for private use."

TABLE 3.1 *(continued)*

| Play (Alternative Title) | Copyright Regis Yr/Name (1st regis)/published copies received by Copyright Office (0 c, 1 c, or 2 c) | Author (A) or Owner |
|---|---|---|
| Baby Mine | 1910/M. Selwyn (alias M. Mayo)/ 1 c | M. M. Selwyn (A) |
| Bertha the Sewing Machine Girl | 1904–5/ A. H. Woods/ 0 c | Theodore Kremer (A) |
| Ultimo (Big Bonanza) | 1886/Augustin Daly/ 2 c | Augustine Daly (A) |
| Blue Jeans (Bluejeans) | 1888/Joe Arthur/ 0 c | J. Arthur (A) |
| Bunch of Keys (The Hotel) | 1883/C. Hoyt and W. Edouin/ 0 c | Charles Hoyt and Winnie Edouin (A) |
| The Builder of Bridges | 1909/Samuel French/ 2 c | Alfred Sutro (A) |
| Caprice | 1885/H. P. Taylor/ 2 c | Howard Taylor (A) |
| Captain Lettarblair | 1906/Bobbs Merrill Co./ 2 c (alleged piracy reported before registration) | Marguerite Merlington (A) |
| The Charity Ball | 1888/ D. Belasco and H. C. DeMille/ 0 c | D. Belasco and H. C. DeMille (A) |
| The Chorus Lady | 1906/ James Forbes/ 2 c | James Forbes (A) |
| The Climax | 1909/ Edward Locke/ 2 c | Edward Locke (A) |
| Colonel Sellers (Gilded Age) | 1874/Samuel L. Clemens/ 0 c | S. L. Clemens (A) |
| Confusion | 1883/John Stetson/ 1 c | Joseph Derrick (adapted by J. Stetson) |
| The County Fair | 1890/N. Burgess/ 2 c | Charles Bernard and Neil Burgess (A) |
| **Country Hero** | No registration found | Chas Perkins |
| The Country Boy | 1910/E. Selwyn (and others)/ 1 c | E. Selwyn (but script says Charles Perkins) |
| Dad's Girl (A Thief in the House) | 1912/Clara Hammond/ 1 c (alleged piracy reported before registration) | Clara Hammond (A) |
| The Danites "The Heart of the Sierras" | 1877/McKee Rankin/ 0 c | Joaquin Miller (A) |
| Davy Crockett | 1914/Alex Byers (a few versions registered going back to 1900 under other names)/ 2 c (alleged piracy reported in 1889) | Charles Hart writing for Byers |
| The Deacon's Daughter | 1886/A. C. Gunter/ 0 c | Archibald C. Gunter (A) |
| The Deep Purple | 1910/Liebler and Co/ 1 c | Paul Armstrong and Wilson Mizner (A) |
| Divorce (Fate) | 1873/Le Clercq (registered as Fate)/ 0 c | Bartley Campbell (A) |

TABLE 3.1 *(continued)*

| Play (Alternative Title) | Copyright Regis Yr/Name (1st regis)/published copies received by Copyright Office (0 c, 1 c, or 2 c) | Author (A) or Owner |
|---|---|---|
| Dew Drop (Sea Sands) | No registration found | Unknown |
| East Lynne | could be various – it is a 3-act play | Ms. Henry Woods |
| **The Elopement** | 1914/Alex Byers/ 2 c (multiple registrations of a play by this title in the 30+years before 1914) | Harold Hargerson for Byers (Edwin Emery crossed out)(A) |
| Esmerelda | 1882/Frances Hodgson Burnett/ 2 c | William Gillette and Frances Hodgson Burnett (A) |
| Bessie's Burglar (registered as Editha's Burglar) | 1884/Gus. Thomas and E. McP. Smith/ 0 c | G. Thomas and E. Mcp. Smith (A) |
| **Farmer and the Actress** | No registration found | Unknown |
| A Farmer's Daughter (Only a Farmer's Daughter) | 1914/Alex Byers (earlier registration in 1908 to E. Anderson)/ 1 c (alleged piracy reported in 1889) | Nelson Compston for Byers (another 1914 Byers' registration under Nelson Richards as author) |
| Forgiven | 1885/Frederic Bryton and Clay Greene/ 0 c | F. Bryton and C. Greene (A) |
| Fun in a Boarding School | 1882/Charles P. Brown/ 2 c | Charles P. Brown (A) |
| Forty Five Minutes From Broadway (The New Rochelle) | 1905/George M. Cohan/ 2 c | George M. Cohan (A) |
| A French Marriage | No registration found | Unknown (no author on the script) |
| The Fortune Hunter | 1909/Winchell Smith (alternatively under Byers' Library of tabloid plays in 1913)/ 2 c | Winchell Smith (A) (author is Nelson Compston on script) |
| The Georgia Minstrels | No registration found | no author on script |
| The Galley Slave | 1880/Bartley Campbell/ 0 c | Bartley Campbell (A) |
| Hazel Kirke[36] | 1880/J. Steele MacKaye/ 2 c | J. Steele MacKaye (A) |
| Hearts of Oak | 1879/James A. Herne/ 0 c | James A. Herne (with David Belasco) (A) |

36 Note here that the Mallory brothers were found to own this work as employers of MacKaye despite the registration (*see* commentary in the introduction of this chapter).

TABLE 3.1 *(continued)*

| Play (Alternative Title) | Copyright Regis Yr/Name (1st regis)/published copies received by Copyright Office (0 c, 1 c, or 2 c) | Author (A) or Owner |
|---|---|---|
| Held by the Enemy | 1898/William Gillette/ 2 c (alleged piracy reported before registration) | William Gillette (A) |
| The Henrietta | 1901/Bronson Howard/ 2 c (alleged piracy reported before registration) | Bronson Howard (A) |
| His Wife's Hero | No registration found | Unknown (no author on script) |
| How Hearts Broken (Queena) | 1883/James K. Tillotson/ 2 c | James K. Tillotson (A) |
| Huckleberry Finn | No registration found of dramatic work | Roy Lewis (on script) |
| **Hunting for Hooligan** | 1902/ C. E. Royal and A. Beeson/ 0 c (registered to Byers in 1917)/ 2 c) | James Strong (on script) but it is C. E. Royal and A. Beeson (A) |
| **The Imposter (Gentleman Dick/ Falsely Accused)** | note: Byers says he registered play in 1913 (as part of his Library of Tabloid Plays) | Nelson Compston (on script) |
| In Old Kentucky | 1897/Jacob Litt/ 2 c | Charles T. Dazey (A) |
| In the Place of the King | No registration found | Unknown |
| Ivy Leaf | 1884/William H. Power/ 0 c | Con. T. Murphy (A) |
| Josh Whitcomb | 1887/M. E. Osbon/ 0 c | M. E. Osbon (A) |
| Jim the Penman | 1898/L. J. Howard/ 0 c (alleged piracy reported before registration) | L. J. Howard (A) |
| Lion and the Mouse | 1906/Charles Klein/ 2 c | Charles Klein (A) |
| Little Sunbeam | No registration found | No mention |
| Little Lord Fauntleroy | 1889/Frances Hodgson Burnett/ 2 c | Victorien Sardou-(F H Burnett (adapted)) |
| The Littlest Girl (Her First Appearance) | 1898/Chas B. Davis/ 2 c | Robert Hillard (A) |
| Lord Chummley | No registration found | Unknown |
| The Lost Paradise | Various registrations 1897–99 | J. Ligon (A) (among other adapters and authors) |
| Lynwood | 1884/James K. Tillotson/ 2 c | James K. Tillotson (A) |
| The Masked Ball | 1914/Alex Byers/ 2 c (alleged piracy reported before registration in 1894) | W. C. Herman for Byers (A) |
| McKenna's Flirtation (Peril) | 1887/E. Selden/ 2 c | E. Selden (A) |

TABLE 3.1 *(continued)*

| Play (Alternative Title) | Copyright Regis Yr/Name (1st regis)/published copies received by Copyright Office (0 c, 1 c, or 2 c) | Author (A) or Owner |
|---|---|---|
| May Blossom | Various registrations 1883–85 and later (Martha Morton) | Martha Morton (A) |
| The Melting Pot | 1909/Macmillan Co. / 2 c | Israel Zangwill (A) |
| m'Liss | 1873/Henry A. Weaver/ 0 c | Harry B. Weaver (on script) registered Henry B. Weaver |
| Mixed Pickles | 1885/T. H. Sayre/ 2 c | T. H. Sayre (A) |
| **Monte Cristo** | 1906/Fredrick Conrad by E. Moore/ 2 c | Eugene Moore (A) |
| The [A] Mountain Pink | 1883/Edwyn A. Barron and Morgan Bates/ 0 c | Morgan Bates and Edwyn A. Barron (A) |
| Mr Barnes of New York | No registration found | A. C. Gunter (A) |
| Muldoon's Picnic (Irish Aristocracy) | 1914/Alex Byers/ 2 c (registered to others as early as 1881) (alleged piracy reported in 1889) | Langdale Williams for Byers (A) |
| My Partner | 1880/Bartley Campbell/ 0 c | Bartley Campbell (A) |
| My Geraldine | 1880/Bartley Campbell/ 0 c | Bartley Campbell (A) |
| Nobody's Claim | 1884/Edwin A. Locke/ 1 c | Edwin A. Locke |
| Night Off | 1886/Augustin Daly/ 2 c | Augustin Daly |
| Number 973 | No registration found | Robert Hilliard and Edwin Holland (in script record) |
| Our Boarding House | 1876/Leonard Grover/ 0 c | Leonard Grover (A) |
| Only a Farmer's Daughter | 1877/William E. Barnes/ 2 c | W. E. Barnes and later version by C. R. Gardiner (A) |
| One of the Bravest (Tim the Fireman) | 1883/E. E. Price/ 0 c | E. E. Price (A) |
| The Operator (The Flag Station) | 1891/S. D. Ferguson and Arthur Hornblow/ 0 c | S. D. Ferguson (and A. Hornblow) (A) |
| Passion's Slave | 1890/J. A. Stevens/ 0 c | John A. Stevens (A) |
| A Passing Fancy | 1914/Mark E. Swan/ 1 c (alleged piracy reported before registration) | M. E. Swan (A) |
| Peck's Bad Boy | 1914/Alex Byers/ 2 c. But multiple versions of this work registered to others back to 1883. The alleged piracy was reported in 1889 | W. C. Herman for Byers |
| Pat and the Genii | 1900/Thos. Nawn/ 2 c | Edmund Day and Thomas Nawn (A) |

TABLE 3.1 *(continued)*

| Play (Alternative Title) | Copyright Regis Yr/Name (1st regis)/published copies received by Copyright Office (0 c, 1 c, or 2 c) | Author (A) or Owner |
|---|---|---|
| Euchre (The Phoenix) | 1873/Tweetie Mongeon/ 0 c | T. Mongeon (A); F. J. Ziegler (under The Phoenix in 1916) |
| The Planter's Wife | 1880/James Tillitson/ 0 c | James K. Tillitson (A) |
| Prince Karl (The German courier) | 1886/Archibald C. Gunter/ 0 c | Archibald C. Gunter (A) |
| Queen's Evidence | 1878/J. H. Rowe (another registration by George Thompson, 1876)/ 0 c | J. H. Rowe (A) |
| Ranch 10 (Annie From Massachusetts) | 1882/Harry Meredith/ 0 c | Harry Meredith (A) |
| Rosedale (The Rifle Ball) | 1890/H. S. Taylor/ 0 c | John Lester Wallack (A) |
| Sam'l of Posen (The commercial drummer) | 1880/G. H. Jessop/ 2 c | G. H. Jessop (A) |
| Seven Sisters | No registration found | Unknown |
| Seven Days | 1909/Avery Hopwood/ 1 c | Mary Roberts Rinehart and Avery Hopwood (A) |
| Shenandoah | 1897/Bronson Howard/ 2 c; earlier version S. C. Mercer 1887/ 0 c. Alleged piracy reported in 1892, 1898, and 1900 | Bronson Howard (A) S. C. Mercer (A) |
| Springtime | 1909/Fredric Thompson / 1 c | Booth Tarkington and Harry Leon Wilson (A) |
| The Still Alarm | 1887/Joseph Arthur/ 2 c | Joseph Arthur (A) |
| The Stowaway | 1887/Hal S. Taylor/ 0 c | Hal S. Taylor (A) |
| Supper for Two | No registration found | Unknown |
| A Texas Steer | 1899/Charles Hoyt/ 2 c (alleged piracy reported before registration) | Charles Hoyt (A) |
| Ten Nights in a Bar Room | 1916/Alex Byers/ 2 c (title registered to others earlier in 1890, 1898, 1903.) Alleged piracy reported in 1907 | Nelson Compston (A) for Byers |
| A Tale of a Turkey | 1905/Edward R. Burton, Corney Brookes/0 c | Edward R. Burton and Corney Brookes (A) |
| A Touch of Nature | Multiple registrations under various names | H. P. Leonard (1905 version) (A) |

TABLE 3.1 *(continued)*

| Play (Alternative Title) | Copyright Regis Yr/Name (1st regis)/published copies received by Copyright Office (0 c, 1 c, or 2 c) | Author (A) or Owner |
|---|---|---|
| **Uncle Josh Perkins (Uncle Josh)** | 1891/T. S. Denison/ 2 c | Charles Townsend (A) |
| Uncle Tom's Cabin | 1912/Alex Byers/ 2 c; multiple earlier versions registered under different names. Alleged piracy reported in 1907 | Chas Morton adapted for Byers |
| Woman's Devotion (Vigilante) | 1904/Preston Gibson (also earlier 1889 version- John Barrington, Alfred Jones)/ 0 c (alleged piracy reported before registration) | Preston Gibson (A) |
| Waterloo | 1907/Samuel French/ 2 c | Arthur Conan Doyle (A) |
| Widow Bedott (A Hunt for a Husband) | 1879/D. R. Locke/ 0 c | D. R. Locke (A) |
| **Whirlpool** | 1911/Alexander Byers/ 2 c; Multiple registrations of this title to others before 1911 | W. C. Kaiser for Byers |
| Zigzag | 1888/ William Tillotson/ 2 c | William W. Tillotson (A) |
| Young Mrs Winthrop | 1882/ Marshall H. Mallory/ 2 c | Bronson Howard (A) |

The works in Table 3.1 provide possible insights into how Byers ran his business, interacted with the law, and used the copyright registration system.[37] Some authors in this Table worked for Byers, including identified "notorious" play copyists such as

[37] On the operations of the Chicago Manuscript Company *see*: "Pirated Plays and the Pirates," *New York Dramatic Mirror*, July 9, 1887, 2; "Following up the Pirates," *New York Dramatic Mirror*, July 23, 1887, 2; "A Pirate Play-Bureau," *New York Dramatic Mirror*, July 6, 1889, 1; "Pestiferous Pirates," *New York Dramatic Mirror*, July 13, 1889, 3; "Pirate Play Bureaus," *New York Dramatic Mirror*, May 24, 1890, 9; "Beware of Play-Stealer Byers," *New York Dramatic Mirror*, February 13, 1892, 8; "An Audacious Theft," *New York Dramatic Mirror*, July 2, 1892, 4; "A Pirate in Court," *New York Dramatic Mirror*, February 11, 1894, 11; "Dishonest and Audacious," *New York Dramatic Mirror*, March 16, 1895, 8; "A Foe to Pirates," *New York Dramatic Mirror*, June 15, 1895, 8; "Still at It," *New York Dramatic Mirror*, October 5, 1895. There is a degree of speculation in interpreting this material because it was sometimes difficult to establish that the work alleged to have been stolen by Byers was the relevant work in the registration record. For example, as previously noted, in column 2 of Table 3.1, I have tried to be as transparent as possible in outlining where there are multiple records registered under the same title. The fact that so much of Byers' material was alleged to be illegal also requires a degree of speculation in interpreting the material.

Nelson Compston.[38] Other plays, as identified in brackets, have multiple titles: a strategy to perhaps avoid detection from original authors or owners. Many works were commercial successes – *Uncle Tom's Cabin, Little Lord Fauntleroy, Hazel Kirke, Monte Cristo,* and *Big Bonanza* – suggesting that Byers was audacious enough to want to profit from the potentially more lucrative and well-known works.

Byers appears to interact selectively with the copyright registration system. He embraced the system when his interests were advanced and ignored it when these interests were hindered. The majority of alleged activities of piracy in the population were reported in the press before 1897 (the year when federal copyright law was revised to include criminal penalties for infringement).[39] Further, in many of these pre-1897 cases, an author or owner other than Byers registered the work. Therefore, Byers appears to exploit works in the pre-1897 period despite an author, owner, or another broker, registering the work. Indeed, throughout Byers' entire career, based on the population in Table 3.1, it appears that Byers had little fear acquiring and exploiting works registered under the name of the owner, author, or publisher/broker alleging infringement.[40]

But there is reason to pause before simply labelling Byers as a brazen copyist who acted in defiance of authors or owners of legally registered works. For example, there are works in the above Table where the record suggests published copies were not deposited with the Copyright Office to complete the record (see the second column with entries marked as "o c").[41] Thus, it is possible that these registrations were never perfected. There are also some examples in the Table

38 *See* "Some Notorious Play Pirates," *New York Dramatic Mirror*, August 27, 1887, 8. Compston is regularly identified in the *Mirror* as a stage manager. The *Mirror* had a regular column where they would name and shame companies and individuals.

39 This small population does not necessarily represent the full extent of Byers' alleged illegal activities, but is just a portion of those reported mostly in the *Dramatic Mirror*. The reduction in cases over time could suggest the legislation was a deterrent. But it must be noted that the editor of the *Mirror* Harrison Fiske seemed to mostly drop the issue after 1897 – when the copyright amendment was introduced that included criminal penalties – and focused his energy on the rise of the Theatrical Syndicate.

40 This strategy would sometimes backfire against the brazen Byers in the most public of ways. The *Dramatic Mirror* often posted names of plays – as well as the legal author and owner of the work – particularly where a play was possibly the subject of piracy. Edgar Selden, the author of *McKenna's Flirtation*, noticed in a list of "successful copyrighted plays" his work was included. Selden wrote in a comment to the *Mirror*: "in January, 1888, a man was discovered comfortably seated in an orchestra chair industriously engaged in taking down, in shorthand, the language, business of the play, etc., and who was promptly ejected from the theatre by the watchful usher, but unfortunately permitted to escape without arrest. Eventually his attempted theft must have met with success, and furthermore he was undoubtedly acting for and in league with this same Alex Byers." *See* "Pestiferous Pirates," *New York Dramatic Mirror*, July 13, 1889, 3.

41 These records were reconciled with the entries in: Library of Congress Copyright Office, *Dramatic Compositions Copyrighted in the United States: 1870–1916* (Washington, DC: Government Printing Office, 1918) Vol. 1 (A–N), Vol. 2 (M–Z). As previously discussed, the Office itself in the introduction to these volumes acknowledges that many of the records were not perfected. So even where a deposit is recorded the physical composition may not have been deposited.

where the alleged piracy occurs before the title is registered to the author or owner other than Byers.[42]

In the absence of federal copyright protection, authors and owners could still, of course, seek recourse at common law with respect to their unpublished manuscripts and associated performance rights. But as far as Byers may have been concerned, he was copying an unpublished work in one state and exploiting it – through printing, publication, or selling parts of the unpublished work – in another. Commentary from this period is preoccupied with the evils associated with rampant piracy and the compromises it meant for American authors. And by the 1880s, state courts appeared to be siding with proprietors of unpublished scripts on a more consistent basis.[43] But the law was still going through a period of transition. Byers reproduced unpublished scripts and moved them throughout the country where it was unclear whether the laws in one state applied to another.[44] Byers was as much a cunning speculator taking advantage of an ambiguous and evolving legal setting as he was a copyist exploiting the work of vulnerable dramatists.[45]

After 1908–1909 (following the major revisions to federal copyright law in 1909) there is some evidence in Table 3.1, based admittedly on a very small sample, that Byers was registering works that he was accused of copying and exploiting in the press.[46] In some instances, Byers waits for more than a decade to register the work after the owner/author submits an initial registration. For example, the play *Hunting for Hooligan* was registered at first under the names of the authors "Beeson and Royal" in 1902. In 1917, the Chicago Manuscript Company writes on the script "Copyright 1917 by Alexander Byers" and registers it under the name of Byers. A

42 *See, for example*, from Table 3.1: *Arrah-na-Pogue (Wicklow Wedding)*, *Captain Lettarblair*, *Dad's Girl (A Thief in the House)*, *Held by the Enemy*, *The Henrietta*, *Jim the Penman*, *The Masked Ball*, *A Passing Fancy*, *A Texas Steer*, *Woman's Devotion (Vigilante)*.

43 *See* developments in the memory doctrine by Derek Miller, *Copyright and the Value of Performance, 1770–1911* (Cambridge, UK: Cambridge University Press, 2018), Ch. 3 who shows how the doctrine was mostly rejected in the state courts by the early 1880s: *see, for example*, *Tompkins* v. *Halleck*, 133 Mass. 32 (1882) and *French* v. *Conelly*, 1 N.Y. Weekly Digest 196 (1875). There was a shift away from earlier common law cases where it was found that you could reproduce from memory (for example, a shift from earlier case of *Keene* v. *Kimball*, 82 Mass. 545 (1860).)

44 I am grateful to an anonymous reviewer for helping me with this point. Until 1909, the law was still evolving with respect to whether it was illegal for a stenographer to write down the dialogue of a play performed in one state and then print and sell copies of it in another state. The state common law in one state did not strictly apply to another. *See, however*, cases that clearly came down on the side of the proprietor to hold the first right to publish an unpublished manuscript at common law: *Palmer* v. *DeWitt*, 47 N.Y. 532 (1872) (as discussed in previous chapters).

45 The Mallory brothers, who ruthlessly exploited author Steele MacKaye in contractual negotiations, chased Byers to the end of the earth to protect *Hazel Kirke*. The private, abusive, contractual negotiations between the Mallory brothers and Steele MacKaye are difficult to distinguish from the very public, and supposedly illegal, activities of Byers operating in a rapidly developing legal environment.

46 In the population of Table 3.1 there are no examples of Byers attempting to register a work before 1909 that was alleged to have been pirated in press reports. This does not mean he did not attempt to register works he did not own, but in this small sample there are no examples.

"James Strong" is noted as authoring the script in the archive collection – another possible indication that Byers was seeking to distance the real authors from their work.[47] *Ten Nights in a Bar Room* was registered by Byers in 1916 with Nelson Compston acknowledged in the record as the author. There are multiple registrations of this title in 1890, 1898, 1903 to stakeholders other than Byers.

In some situations, Sarah Blackstone has argued that Byers registered unknown scripts under his own name,[48] or made slight changes to well-known works and registered them under his name or the name of his employees.[49] He also ran a separate entity which included abridged versions of popular compositions – registering these works as part of "Byers' Library of Tabloid Plays."[50] An interesting feature of the works registered by Byers – reported as pirated in the press – was that registration occurred after the alleged infringement.[51] Byers usually perfected the registration process by depositing two published copies ("2 c").[52] The depositing of two copies possibly enhanced the appearance of authenticity. But after 1909, this additional step of depositing two copies was not even necessary. Byers only needed to register the unpublished work. He could potentially take any script that he copied, make slight modifications, and then register it with the Copyright Office. The post-1909 framework in some cases might have assisted, not hindered, Byers. The Chicago Manuscript Company was already trading in the business of unpublished manuscripts, and now

47 *See* "Hunting for Hooligan," Box 31, Sherman Theatre Collection. At the bottom of the script it states: "Under the new copyright law the rights of production of a play are not secured by the purchase of a manuscript of it, are offences punishable by fine and if done willfully by imprisonment." Curiously, in the inside cover it states: "Copyrighted 1915." The registration record in the virtual catalogue is Card No. 32885 "D," published on Nov. 1, 1917, and two copies Nov. 30, 1917. "Hunting for Hooligan: A musical Comedy in Two Acts" by James Strong, copyright claimed by Alexander Byers. Entry No. D48442 (https://vcc.copyright.gov/browse).

48 *See* "The Elopement," Box 18, Sherman Theatre Collection.

49 *See, for example,* "East Lynne," Box 18, Sherman Theatre Collection; "Uncle Tom's Cabin" – multiple versions, Box 78, Sherman Theatre Collection; "Count of Monte Cristo," Box 13, Sherman Theatre Collection. As discussed in Sarah Blackstone, "Alexander Byers, Play Pirate Extraordinaire," *Theatre History Studies* 14 (June 1994): 107, 107–108. Noting that *East Lynne* and *The Elopement* have been used interchangeably for the same work in an earlier musical burlesque version of the play by James Barnes. *See* Internet Broadway Database: www.ibdb.com/broadway-show/east-lynne-438892. The later play version of *East Lynne* was the book adaptation of Mrs. Henry Wood (also written by Wood): www.ibdb.com/broadway-show/east-lynne-3246.

50 *See, for example,* "The Fortune Hunter," Box 23, Sherman Theatre Collection (is also filed in the registry under Byers' tabloid plays known alternatively as *Charlie's Aunt, The hustler, the bells*). *See* the list in Library of Congress Copyright Office, *Dramatic Compositions* Vol 1. A–N. p 269.

51 *See, for example, Davy Crockett* (Byers registers in 1914, alleged piracy reported in 1889); *Farmer's Daughter* (Byers registers in 1914, alleged piracy reported in 1889); *The Masked Ball* (Byers registers in 1914, alleged piracy reported in 1894); *Muldoon's Picnic* (*Irish Aristocracy*) (Byers registers in 1914, alleged piracy reported in 1889); *Peck's Bad Boy* (Byers registers in 1914, alleged piracy reported in 1889); *Ten Nights in a Bar Room* (Byers registers in 1916, alleged piracy reported in 1907); *Uncle Tom's Cabin* (Byers registers in 1912, alleged piracy reported in 1907).

52 *See, for example, Davy Crockett, The Elopement, Hunting for Hooligan, The Masked Ball, Muldoon's Picnic, Peck's Bad Boy, Ten Nights in a Bar Room, Uncle Tom's Cabin, Whirlpool.* But once again, even though the record states two copies were deposited, I did not verify whether they actually were deposited. The point is that Byers is creating the illusion of legitimacy.

they could do it under the auspices of the federal copyright registration system. And, as discussed, the Library of Congress was not scrutinizing the legitimacy of all registrations. The publisher also used the courts when he believed he was the victim of piracy, striking out over his pirated and registered plays. In many of these instances, it is unclear whether he was the legitimate owner of the work alleged to be stolen.[53]

Byers' use of the registration system can be read in several ways. For example, a more sympathetic reading of Byers' practices is that he was taking the opportunity to control a composition in which the registration may have lapsed, and the author/owner was not vigilant enough to renew the registration of the work. But this scenario is difficult to establish, particularly given that federal copyright protection periods were expanding after 1909.[54] Another possible reading, however, is that Byers used registration to create the illusion of perfected ownership. In this scenario, Byers never had any claim to ownership but could exploit a vulnerable copyright registration system where many scripts (published, or unpublished after 1909) were not submitted for registration, or the completeness, accuracy, or legitimacy of the registration was not scrutinized. Byers could, therefore, take any script and change the title, change the author (or even keep the same title), and be confident that his control over copyright in the work would not face interrogation in everyday practices with clients. He could wait for years to distance himself from the original registration to give the appearance that the registration was new and therefore legitimate. All the potential purchaser of the script views in the record is the name of Alexander Byers (if they even looked at the record at all.)[55]

53 Indeed, in some instances Byers was not possibly the owner of the work in which he was suing for piracy. One of the more interesting examples involved Byers' claim against George Clancy, a former employee of Byers who according to the *Dramatic Mirror*: "Clancy saw that Byers was making money rapidly in this dishonest business, and bethought him that if it was a good thing for one it ought to be a good thing for two." The court however was not able to determine whether the plays in question "belong to Byers" including *The Masked Ball, Esmerelda, The Danites, The Lost Paradise, Caprice, Held by the Enemy, The Old Homestead, Forgiven, and The Charity Ball* among "a score or more of other dramas." "A Pirate in Court: The Remarkable Case of Alexander Byers, Play Thief, of Chicago," *New York Dramatic Mirror*, February 11, 1894, 11. In other instances it appears that Byers may have been the victim of piracy – for example with respect to the plays *Rube and Mandy, Plain Molly, Why Lindy Ran Away, The Boss of Z Ranch*, and *Clouds and Sunshine* which were all registered under Alex Byers. *See* "The Suppression of Piracy," *Opera House Reporter*, February 4, 1916, 2; "Says he Stole a Play," *La Crosse Tribune*, June 24, 1915; "In Repertoire: Clouds and Sunshine," *Billboard*, June 15, 1918, 23.

54 It would require a thorough study of whether and when copyright protection periods ended for these works, whether they were renewed, and what were the lengths of copyright extensions, particularly after the major 1909 revisions. *See* Zvi Rosen's important ongoing work exploring the history of the registration system in deeper detail.

55 William Stout suggests that after 1909 Byers changed his business model to focus on tent managers as a "legitimate" playbroker. His "stable of writers included Myron Leffingwell, W. C. Herman, Nelson Compston, Clarence Black, and Langdale Williams." *See* William L. Slout, *Theatre in a Tent: The Development of a Provincial Entertainment* (Bowling Green, OH: Bowling Green University Popular Press, 1972), 77. Byers, however, was still the subject of ongoing litigation after 1909, a grand jury trial in 1911, and constant complaints about his activities in the press. Indeed, Byers may have acted as the broker for a limited number of legitimate works in order to disguise the extent of his overall operations.

The scripts in the Chicago Manuscript Company Collection provide further insights into how Byers successfully operated his business. He changed portions of the script, altered titles, reproduced scripts with new authors, stamped clear copyright notices on the title pages of scripts that gave the appearance of legitimate registration, or simply reproduced the script in full.[56] Many scripts in the collection that were the subject of piracy claims evolve in several different forms. Take *Seven Days*, written by Mary Roberts Rinehart and Avery Hopwood, and registered under the name of Hopwood in 1909.[57] The *Mirror* reported that Byers had stolen the work.[58] The first version (Figure 3.1) is handwritten – probably transcribed from attending the actual performance or copied from another manuscript.

The second version was usually typed up in Byers' back office rooms,[59] by a small team of stenographers as shown in Figure 3.2. Byers then transported the script across the country to his network of producing associates.

Many variations of this process appear throughout the collection. Sometimes a third version of the script exists in a more publishable or presentable form.[60] Suspicious annotations appear over copies of scripts throughout the collection including "George, Be careful, don't lose this. It will be impossible to replace it ... nothing left out,"[61] "ask mr byers if he wants copyright sheet,"[62] "cut the opening,"[63] "register the title of the script as regis as 'Editha's Burglar.'"[64] Cover notes query whether "you want to cut any out,"[65] and many script covers include a handwritten seal stating the version of the script was "original, don't sell."[66] The collection also includes handwritten notes that confirm the script in question is the

56 The 1870 amendment, Act of July 8, 1870, ch.230, § 86, 16 Stat. 198 provided that "authors may reserve the right to dramatize or to translate their own works." The Act provided an early form of a derivative right in federal legislation.

57 *See* "Seven Days," Box 66, Sherman Theatre Collection. Indeed, many of the scripts in the collection include a handwritten first version – the work of stenographers either transcribed in the theatre or copied from a script obtained by Byers.

58 *See* "Play Piracy Must Stop," *New York Dramatic Mirror*, April 5, 1911, 13.

59 *See* "To Kill Piracy," *New York Dramatic Mirror*, January 8, 1898, 15.

60 *See, for example*, "Seven Days," Box 66, Sherman Theatre collection; "Farmer's Daughter," Box 20, Sherman Theatre collection (Box not marked); "East Lynne," Box 18, Sherman Theatre collection; "Huckleberry Finn," Box 31, Sherman Theatre Collection; "Peck's Bad Boy," Box 56, Sherman Theatre Collection.

61 "Are You a Mason," Box 3, Sherman Theatre Collection. The "nothing left out" is stamped on a later page. This play was subject to a raid of Byers' office and subsequent litigation: *see* "Raid on Byers," *New York Dramatic Mirror*, May 31, 1902, 13.

62 Thus, suggesting Byers was using the requirement of notice to provide the appearance of copyright registration and ownership of a play that was alleged to have been stolen. *See* "Farmer's Daughter," Box 20, Sherman Theatre Collection.

63 "How Hearts Are Broken or Queena," Box 31, Sherman Theatre Collection.

64 Existing under the name of Bessie's Burglar or Editha's Burglar, Box 18, Sherman Theatre Collection.

65 "Why Lindy Ran Away," Box 84, Sherman Theatre Collection (noting this is a play which Byers claimed was the subject of piracy against him).

66 "Alias (Jimmy Valentine)," Box 1, Sherman Theatre Collection; "The Climax," Box 11, Sherman Theatre Collection; "Divorce (Fate)," Box 16, Sherman Theatre Collection; "The Fortune Hunter," Box 23, Sherman Theatre Collection; "The Galley Slave," Box 24, Sherman Theatre Collection (also

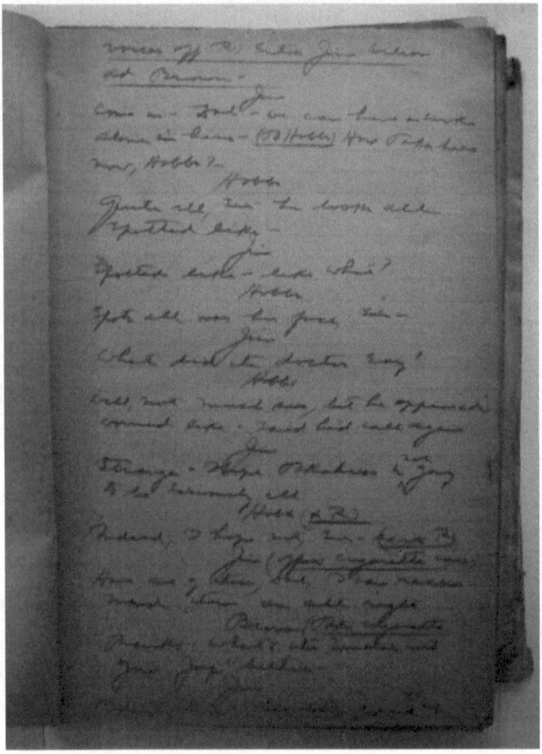

FIGURE 3.1 Handwritten version of *Seven Days*

exact copy of the one in the Copyright Office except for the title page.[67] Scripts contain significant deletions,[68] additions,[69] underlined text subject to further revision,[70] and include printed extracts of text copied and pasted from one version to another.[71]

Byers thus altered, added, and deleted material, revised titles, and changed characters in the plays. He manufactured manuscripts, attached copyright notices

says "cut version"); "Little Sunbeam," Box 39, Sherman Theatre Collection; "The Masked Ball," Box 44, Sherman Theatre Collection; "My Geraldine," Box 49, Sherman Theatre Collection.

67 *See* "Rube and Mandy," Box 64, Sherman Theatre Collection.

68 *See, for example*, "Huckleberry Finn," Box 31, Sherman Theatre Collection; "[An] Ivy Leaf," Box 33, Sherman Theatre Collection; "McKenna's Flirtation (Peril)," Box 45, Sherman Theatre Collection.

69 *See, for example*, "The Galley Slave," Box 24, Sherman Theatre Collection; "Ten Nights in a Bar Room," Box 73, Sherman Theatre Collection (the notes in finding aid also refer to "Sapho" and "St. Elmo" and "The Drunkard").

70 *See, for example*, "Bertha the Sewing Machine Girl," Box 5, Sherman Theatre Collection (and major cuts as well).

71 *See, for example*, "The Planter's Wife," Box 57, Sherman Theatre Collection; "The Masked Ball," Box 44, Sherman Theatre Collection.

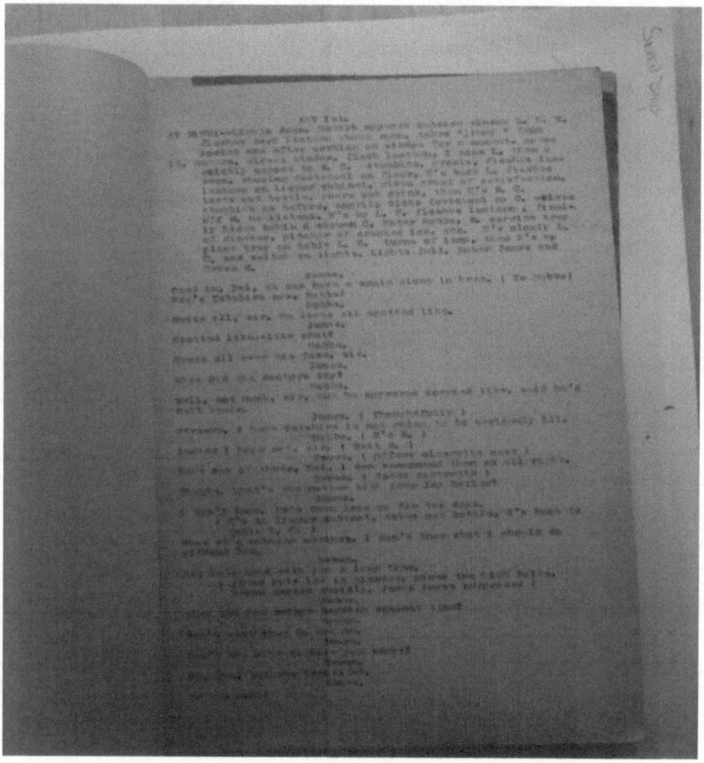

FIGURE 3.2 Typed version of *Seven Days*

to works, and published catalogues advertising his stock. Byers expanded his activities with help from new technologies. The Chicago Manuscript office space housed "the best plays now on the stage, together with three typewriters and two devices for mimeographing" for rapid reproduction.[72] Byers' office was described as "small and dingy" filled with "[s]everal stenographers … always at work, hammering out abstracted scripts and pilfered parts."[73]

For Byers, like Samuel French, control over theatrical material also involved efficient administrative processes that enabled the movement of creativity between authors and audiences.[74] The press provided detailed accounts of how Byers sold the physical text and licensed performance rights throughout the country. Byers published catalogues that included over 150 plays all in a manuscript form, and offered at "five dollars

72 *See* "To Kill Piracy," *New York Dramatic Mirror*, January 8, 1898, 15s.

73 *See* "Chicago's Centre for the Disposal of 'Lifted Stuff'," *Variety*, February 6, 1909, 6.

74 Eileen Curley also discusses Byers' business practices citing: "Says He Steals Plays," *Chicago Daily Tribune*, November 18, 1894, 1 (Eileen Curley, "A Shot over the Bow," 31–32).

apiece."[75] A script preview required a US$1 deposit (forfeited if not purchased).[76] A selection of the most popular plays from the decade before became available at a reduced rate – six for US$25 in one instance[77] – and side parts leased for performance, selling at US$5 to US$10 a piece.[78] Byers also harnessed modern transportation networks moving his product to the west along the train lines: "the express companies, knowing his trade, carried on business with him to the profit of both, and that many companies in Western one-night stands presented the stolen pieces."[79]

The business activities of Byers, in the second half of the nineteenth century, were a reminder that control over the production process required a range of skills and resources beyond the possession of intellectual property rights. Like French, Byers built a business based on unpublished works. In a circular to its patrons written in 1895, The Chicago Manuscript Company wrote that the "owner" of the few successful plays written in the United States[80]

> jealously guards his property, and by every means in his power endeavors to prevent others from obtaining a copy of it. For this reason successful plays are never printed until long after they have ceased to be sources of profit to their producers.

Byers claimed The Chicago Manuscript Company provided an alternative service that the owners had monopolized: "I am doing the public a favor by placing at their disposal works which would otherwise be restricted."[81] Byers candidly confessed that downtrodden authors, actors, and other publishers would sell him manuscripts to copy and exploit – "[t]here is always a leak somewhere, even in the best regulated shows."[82]

75 *See* "Following Up the Pirates," *New York Dramatic Mirror*, July 23, 1887, 2.

76 "Following Up the Pirates," *New York Dramatic Mirror*, July 23, 1887, 2. *See also* "Beware of Play-Stealer Byers," *New York Dramatic Mirror*, February 13, 1892, 8 where Byers' policy statement in his catalogue is revealed: "In order to avoid unnecessary correspondence, parties ordering plays will please conform to the following rules: Enclose $1 with order for each manuscript. Order will be filled and sent C.O.D. for the balance due, with privilege of examination: but will positively not send any manuscript entirely C.O.D. Correspondence solicited with parties having manuscripts not in this list."

77 *See* "To Kill Piracy," *New York Dramatic Mirror*, January 8, 1898, 15s.

78 "To Kill Piracy," *New York Dramatic Mirror*, January 8, 1898, 15s.

79 "To Kill Piracy," *New York Dramatic Mirror*, January 8, 1898, 15s.

80 *See* "Dishonest and Audacious," *New York Dramatic Mirror*, March 16, 1895, 8.

81 *See* "Chicago's Centre for the Disposal of 'Lifted Stuff'," *Variety*, February 6, 1909, 6. Of course a playwright's work was protected at common law when their work was in a manuscript unpublished form. On the common law play right *see* Jessica Litman, "The Invention of Common Law Play Right," *Berkeley Technology Law Journal* 25 (2010): 1381. Blackstone suggests that Robert Sherman continued Byers' practices after taking over the business. An examination of Sherman's play lists and correspondence shows that Sherman continued to provide copyrighted material that he did not own for lease. Sherman also seemed to distinguish the notion of leasing manuscripts (perceived as legal) and selling scripts (illegal). Even in some instances Byers was open to the idea of selling scripts where "there seems to be a quite a desire of the colleges to acquire copies of old plays, as well as new ones." *See* R. Sherman to G. Hughes, December 9, 1933, "Sherman Files," University of Washington School of Drama records, Accession # 70–002, Box 58, fol. 1. *See also* on Sherman's continuance of Byers' illegal activities: Blackstone, "Alexander Byers," 108–112.

82 "Chicago's Centre for the Disposal of 'Lifted Stuff'," *Variety*, February 6, 1909, 6.

Stakeholders who wanted to see Byers brought to what they thought was justice continued to torment the publisher throughout the life of The Chicago Manuscript Company. In 1898, a year after the revisions to federal copyright law providing for criminal penalties,[83] T. H. French triumphantly raided Byers' offices, which led to a remedy of 5 c. damages for five respective plaintiffs.[84] Byers was sued in Chicago for stealing *Are You a Mason* and slapped with a permanent injunction against using the work. When the plaintiffs were asked whether they wanted to pursue criminal proceedings they replied: "No; we have accomplished our purpose, and as I understand that Byers is ill, impoverished and practically in hiding, we do not care to proceed criminally against him."[85] Byers inevitably continued as he was the subject of several disputes in the following years and faced a grand jury for pirating numerous plays in 1911.[86] For his recalcitrance, Byers was fined US$500 and ordered to release a few hundred foreign works which formed a trivial part of his collection of thousands of plays.[87]

The system of control over production that Byers built in daily practices existed against the backdrop of a legal environment that suggested, by the end of the nineteenth century, American dramatists were the beneficiaries of an expanding legislative framework of copyright protections. The statutory copyright regime evolved from protecting just the mere published dramatic text to safeguarding performance of the dramatist's text, adaptations of the dramatic work, including translations of the work, and protecting the dramatist's work in foreign jurisdictions. The dramatist had various remedies, a new system of registration through the Library of Congress, and after 1897 access to criminal penalties could send an infringer to jail. The 1897 Act was supposed to be the crowning achievement of Harrison Fiske's twenty-year crusade to rid the industry of piracy in the name of advancing the interests of dramatic authors.[88]

83 *See* 29 Stat. 481 (1897).

84 *See* "Pays Only Five Cents Damages," *Boston Daily Globe*, December 14, 1900, 2.

85 *See* "Against Play Piracies," *New York Dramatic Mirror*, April 1, 1905, 15; *see also* "Against a Notorious Pirate," *New York Dramatic Mirror*, April 1, 1905, 12.

86 These plays included *Builder of Bridges; The Country Boy; Baby Mine; The Deep Purple; Alias Jimmy Valentine; The Melting Pot; In the Place of the King*: *see* "Byers Indicted," *New York Dramatic Mirror*, June 21, 1911, 14.

87 *See* "Flaw in Foreign Copyrights," *New York Dramatic Mirror*, April 23, 1913, 10.

88 29 Stat. 481 (1897). *See, for example*, a selection of the numerous articles in relation to the 1897 reforms including: "To Prevent Play Piracy," *New York Dramatic Mirror*, December 21, 1895, 13; "Play Piracy," *New York Dramatic Mirror*, June 29, 1895, 8; "For the Copyright Law Amendment," *New York Dramatic Mirror*, December 28, 1895, 23; "The Cummings Bill," *New York Dramatic Mirror*, January 18, 1896, 14; "Copyright Amendment," *New York Dramatic Mirror*, February 1, 1896, 11; "To Prevent Play Piracy," *New York Dramatic Mirror*, February 29, 1896, 10, 11; "The Copyright Bill," *New York Dramatic Mirror*, May 30, 1896, 12; "To Prevent Piracy," *New York Dramatic Mirror*, December 19, 1896, 3; "A Long-Needed Law," *New York Dramatic Mirror*, December 26, 1896, 15; "Piracy's Death," *New York Dramatic Mirror*, January 16, 1897, 11; "The Anti-Piracy Law," *New York Dramatic Mirror*, January 23, 1897, 11; "Views of the Copyright Law," *New York Dramatic Mirror*, February 6,

Byers continued to run his business throughout it all, however. He created a system for transferring theatrical material between authors and audiences that not only survived litigation in the early 1880s but endured until he died in 1922. Byers possessed the internal infrastructure to transform the creative labor of playwrights into material scripts and exploit this labor across the theatrical economy. His staff attended theatres and transformed the ephemeral performance into a material script. The workforce included an army of stenographers who could refine, alter, and reconstruct the original performance in ways suitable for potential exploitation. Byers also had a network of disgruntled theatrical practitioners willing to sell him closely guarded scripts, or parts of scripts. He had space to house printing technology and turn the intangible into the material. He also used evolving transportation technologies (the railroad system) to expand the reach of his enterprise to territories across the country.

Thus, Byers had the mediating expertise, which the playwright did not possess, essential for controlling the movement of creativity across the theatrical economy. He had the resources to reproduce the work on mass and exploit that material for profit. Byers was adept at using the law and capitalizing on evolving industry practices. He appears to manipulate the deficient registration process and was able to get the most out of an industry that traded in manuscripts. It was an environment that allowed the publisher to move his works across the country and outside the state jurisdiction in which they were copied. An obituary of Byers in 1922 describes him as simply "an authority on copyright law." Given his ability to navigate his way through the system for almost forty years, this assessment seems fair.[89]

1897, 15; "Dramatists and Managers Banquet," *New York Dramatic Mirror*, March 27, 1897, 10. Leading theatre lawyer Abram Dittenhoefer was consulted in 1894 by the Dramatists' Club with a view of amending copyright law to give better protection to dramatists against piracy: *see* "Copyright Law," *New York Dramatic Mirror*, April 7, 1894, 12; "Hope for a Just Law," *New York Dramatic Mirror*, February 22, 1896, 14; "To Prevent Play Piracy," *New York Dramatic Mirror*, February 29, 1896, 10–11 (major article on the Joint Committee of Dramatists and Managers meeting in Washington including comments of Bronson Howard at 10 who claimed the number of pirated plays had doubled between 1895 and 1896). On the issue of rampant piracy in the last decade of the nineteenth century still persisting across the country *see also* "As to Copyright of Titles," *New York Dramatic Mirror*, May 12, 1894, 12; "Theatrical Rights," *New York Dramatic Mirror*, May 12, 1894, 13, and an expansive article in the *Dramatic Mirror* in 1895: S. M. Gardenhire, "Play Privacy: With Some Suggestions as to the Difficulty of Practical Legislation to Prevent it," *New York Dramatic Mirror*, March 23, 1895, 4. (The articles were still claiming the protection for the performance – the "stage-right" – was inadequate.) On the Cummings Bill *see also* Rosen's "The Twilight of the Opera Pirates," 1157.

89 *See* "Obituary Alexander Byers," *Variety*, April 7, 1922, 8, 25.

# 4

# Brokering Theatre

American playbrokers – agents of playwrights – added another layer of mediation to the theatrical landscape in the second half of the nineteenth century and the first decades of the twentieth century. Recent theatre scholarship has highlighted the role that pioneering theatrical agents like Alice Kauser played in developing transatlantic business.[1] Playbrokers also shaped industry bargaining and contractual standards in the United States. The brokers, like the first mediating publishers, sought control over various processes and objects in the space between the author and audience. Such objects included printed and published dramatic scripts, rehearsal prompt scripts, advanced royalty notices, and accounting processes. Further, these brokers, like French and his associates, influenced the production process by forming personal relationships of trust with other mediating stakeholders in the industry.

Playbrokers presented both opportunities and new challenges for dramatists. The mediating brokers at the forefront of this industry, including Elisabeth Marbury and Kauser, implemented royalty systems on a wider scale and offered dramatists a gateway to expansive networks and broad audiences that would otherwise be unattainable. The determination of the earliest brokers to provide writers better access to the industry is unquestionable. The brokers, however, also built a system of reliance on their services which placed dramatists in an inevitable, often unintentional, position of compromise when they entered into the production process. The influential brokers shaping the industry were themselves beholden to mediating sources of influence in the form of the theatrical trusts – including the Theatrical Syndicate and the Shuberts – who were expanding rapidly in the first decades of the twentieth century. A system of reliance on brokerage services also complemented narratives of playwright business incompetence which in turn enhanced power disparities between mediators and dramatists. These stigmas implied that

[1] There has been excellent recent scholarship on cultural and transatlantic production and the brokers, particularly on Alice Kauser. *See, for example,* Marlis Schweitzer, *Transatlantic Broadway: The Infrastructural Politics of Global Performance* (Houndmills, Basingstoke, Hampshire, UK; New York, NY: Palgrave Macmillan, 2015); Nic Leonhardt, "Transatlantic Theatrical Traces: Oceanic Trade Routes and Globe-Trotting Amusement Explorers," *The Passing Show* 30 (2013/2014): 2.

playwrights were less able to negotiate the contractual terms of production and therefore should be removed from this process. Brokers held onto scripts for indefinite periods and continued to encourage the outright purchase of authors' rights for film adaptations. The agents often requested substantial reading fees from writers, refused to hold commissions in trust, and created verbal agreements with no written agency contract. The ambiguity surrounding contractual terms led to varying commission levels and unclear lines of responsibility for administrative expenses. The brokers, like the earliest publishers including Samuel French, built successful business structures in the United States on the back of European drama. Mediating playbrokers also possessed broad powers as arbiters of taste. As the broker is a central character determining taste, their influence goes beyond the economic to the aesthetic: the ability to reshape the work of the dramatist to shepherd it through the production process. Aesthetic compromise serves as a condition of entry into the industry.

And how did writers respond? The first societies – including Bronson Howard's Society of American Dramatists and Composers established in 1891, followed by the subordinate dramatist groups of the Authors' League of America (from 1912 to 1913) – were still very much in their infancy as far as having meaningful ability to negotiate with these new emerging mediating businesses. Dramatists, for the most part, were entering into agreements directly with other stakeholders in an environment where, as George Middleton suggests, contractual conditions were "too chaotic to be boxed into a formula."[2] The consequences of mediation cannot be understood through an economic lens alone. Power dynamics, and responses to that power, play out in the fluid personal interactions of the everyday. Mediating influence over the production process occurs in moments of incremental negotiation which on the face appear reasonable but over time represent sustained, and often unintentional, imbalances in power. Scrutinizing moments of place and time in ongoing negotiations provides the opportunity to consider the undeniable benefits, but limits, of the development of brokering services.

## I. THE EARLY AMERICAN PLAYBROKERS: ESTABLISHING GROUND RULES FOR ACCESS

### A. *The "Poor Businessman"*

Playwrights throughout most of the nineteenth century negotiated the contractual boundaries of their authority directly with producers.[3] Novel licensing systems developed by mediators like Samuel French paved the way for the publisher to act

[2] George Middleton, *These Things Are Mine: The Autobiography of a Journeyman Playwright* (New York: The Macmillan Company, 1947), 304–305.

[3] *See* Michael B. Leavitt, *Fifty Years in Theatrical Management* (New York: Broadway Pub. Co., 1912), 589.

as a broker for some of America's more successful dramatists in the latter part of the nineteenth century. French, for example, represented Bronson Howard.[4] But by the end of the nineteenth century, the field had expanded to the point that a new "class of middlemen," as M. B. Leavitt describes them, began to specialize in brokering negotiations between playwrights and producers.[5]

Commentators in the early twentieth century who wrote about the emergence of the theatrical playbroker often explain the need for the service because of the playwright's lack of business acumen. Leavitt, for example, suggests the playbroker relieved the dramatist of all business care to "responsible managers."[6] Although Arthur Krow acknowledges the business expertise of a playwright depends on individual temperament,[7] Henry Stewart suggests "[t]he average author is a poor business man, a timid, sensitive creature who shrinks from the ordeal of hawking his play around the managers' offices."[8] Lawyer Philip Wittenberg suggests "many authors" find business affairs "an unwelcome and undesirable intrusion. They [authors] either fail to understand, or are unwilling to understand."[9] By the early twentieth century, Archibald Selwyn was describing the playbroker as an "absolute necessity."[10]

A more generous reading of the emergence of the playbroker is that they were filling a needed information gap in the production process. A playwright does not necessarily have an understanding of the "pulse" of the market,[11] or lacks access to producers.[12] A broker can therefore establish processes for matching a play with a producer allowing the writer to focus on the business of writing plays. And of course, if the broker makes a successful deal with other stakeholders everybody benefits from that deal. But this process of reliance on brokerage services also situates playwrights in an inevitable position of compromise. Brokers were indeed acting on behalf of writers, but they were also establishing the ground rules for the terms of negotiation in the industry and how writers accessed the industry.

### B. C. R. Gardiner, "The Advisory Manager"

C. R. Gardiner was one of the first brokers to establish the ground rules for broker and author relationships, attracting considerable attention across the theatrical economy in the late 1870s and early 1880s. Gardiner played a critical role in not

4 *See* Henry T. Stewart, "The Playbrokers of New York," *Theatre Magazine* 5 (1905): 163.

5 Leavitt, *Fifty Years*, 589.

6 Leavitt, *Fifty Years*, 589.

7 Arthur E. Krows, *Play Production in America* (New York: H. Holt and Company, 1916), 1.

8 Stewart, "The Playbrokers," 163.

9 Philip Wittenberg, *The Protection and Marketing of Literary Property* (New York: J. Messner, inc. c. 1937), 177.

10 Stewart, "The Playbrokers," 165.

11 Krows, *Play Production in America*, 2.

12 *See* Alfred L. Bernheim, *The Business of the Theatre* (New York: Actors' Equity Association, 1932), 114.

only the development of the brokerage industry but also the centralization of the industry around booking agencies that would tour attractions across the country. Alfred Bernheim[13] and John Frick[14] suggest that Gardiner's *Managers' and Stars' Agency* was the first mediating business of its type to secure "exclusive control" over both theatres and attractions, and was a precursor to the Theatrical Syndicate organization.[15] The *Dramatic Mirror* described Gardiner's "great agency" as an "entirely new line of business."[16] Gardiner sent attractions out on the road along specified routes which meant the theatres would have to deal directly with the agent to access the best attractions.[17]

The focus of Gardiner's brokerage business was acting talent, but because he had considerable control over both theatres and attractions it was a natural extension of his operations to represent dramatists. With jurisdiction over both theatres and attractions – a narrative that would emerge again and again over the next forty years through different organizational structures – Gardiner was always in a strong position to define the terms of engagement with creators of theatrical material.[18] Gardiner's regular advertising campaigns in the *Dramatic Mirror* – published in 1880 (Figure 4.1) – provides an insight into the extent of his operations. The advertisement also shows how the broker established the terms of control over budding dramatists through standard contractual industry developments.

Gardiner's mediating activities extended to "advisory manager," "amusement broker," and "manager's agent," finally conceding that his agency is an all-encompassing "Information Bureau for those interested in Amusements" with transnational interests.[19] In terms of writers, Gardiner represented himself as a "Dramatic Agency on a large scale," and "an agent for several leading Dramatic Authors"; having "the right to produce their pieces."[20] Thus, Gardiner seeks to establish his credentials as a playbroker by claiming his association with leading authors, but he also uses the rhetoric of authorship to enhance his legitimacy. These leading authors grant Gardiner "the right" to produce their work.

13 *See* Bernheim, *The Business of the Theatre*, 114.

14 *See* John Frick, "A Changing Theatre: New York and Beyond," in *The Cambridge History of American Theatre. Volume 2, 1870–1945*, eds. Don B. Wilmeth, Christopher Bigsby (Cambridge, UK: Cambridge University Press, 1999), 204–205.

15 Sanger and Jordan, established by theatrical manager Frank W. Sanger in 1885, was one of the first brokers in the industry with connections across the globe, but Gardiner appeared to set up his agency business a decade earlier.

16 "Stock and Combinations," *New York Dramatic Mirror*, May 1, 1880, 6.

17 *See* Bernheim, *The Business of the Theatre*, 42. There were also earlier agents establishing combinations in the immediate years after the Civil War. Bernheim himself identifies circuits emerging in the 1870s and early 1880s all over the country. *See* Bernheim, *The Business of the Theatre*, 34–40.

18 *See* "Stars and Managers Agency," *New York Dramatic Mirror*, January 25, 1879, 6; "CR Gardiner and his Office," *New York Dramatic Mirror*, July 26, 1879, 5.

19 "C. R. Gardiner advertisement for Playwrights," *New York Dramatic Mirror*, November 13, 1880, 11.

20 "C. R. Gardiner advertisement," 11.

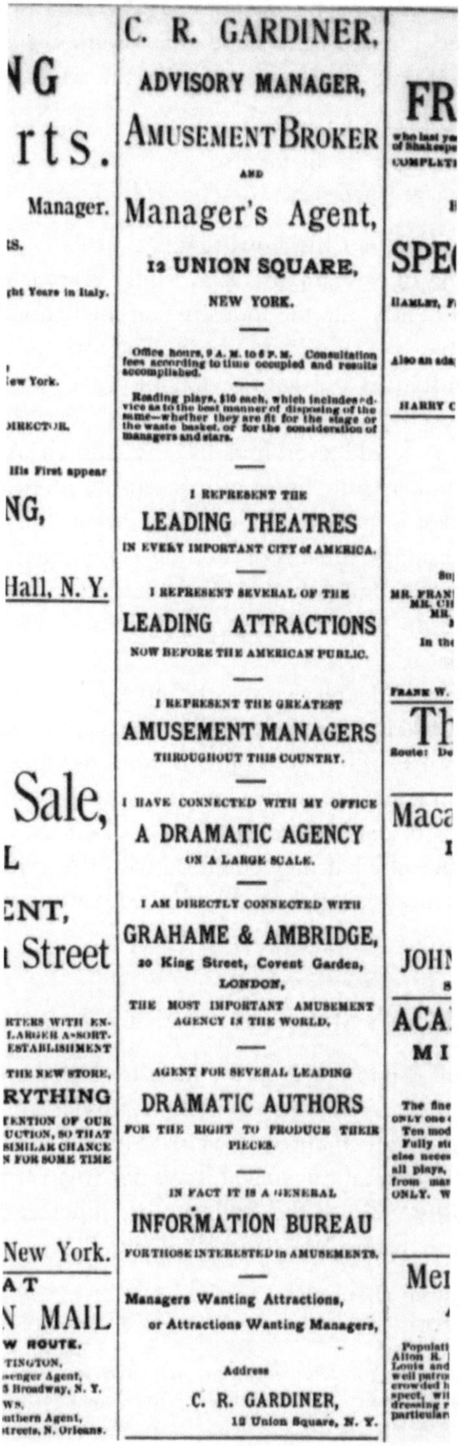

C. R. GARDINER,

ADVISORY MANAGER,

AMUSEMENT BROKER

AND

Manager's Agent,

12 UNION SQUARE,

NEW YORK.

Office hours, 9 A. M. to 6 P. M. Consultation fees according to time occupied and results accomplished.

Reading plays, $10 each, which includes advice as to the best manner of disposing of the same—whether they are fit for the stage or the waste basket, or for the consideration of managers and stars.

I REPRESENT THE

LEADING THEATRES

IN EVERY IMPORTANT CITY of AMERICA.

I REPRESENT SEVERAL OF THE

LEADING ATTRACTIONS

NOW BEFORE THE AMERICAN PUBLIC.

I REPRESENT THE GREATEST

AMUSEMENT MANAGERS

THROUGHOUT THIS COUNTRY.

I HAVE CONNECTED WITH MY OFFICE

A DRAMATIC AGENCY

ON A LARGE SCALE.

I AM DIRECTLY CONNECTED WITH

GRAHAME & AMBRIDGE,

20 King Street, Covent Garden, LONDON,

THE MOST IMPORTANT AMUSEMENT AGENCY IN THE WORLD.

AGENT FOR SEVERAL LEADING

DRAMATIC AUTHORS

FOR THE RIGHT TO PRODUCE THEIR PIECES.

IN FACT IT IS A GENERAL

INFORMATION BUREAU

FOR THOSE INTERESTED in AMUSEMENTS.

Managers Wanting Attractions,

or Attractions Wanting Managers,

Address

C. R. GARDINER,

12 Union Square, N. Y.

FIGURE 4.1 C. R. Gardiner advertisement, 1880

Although Gardiner uses the playwrights' legal relationship with the work to establish his own credentials, in the same advertisement he also reveals how he deals with dramatists in practice. Gardiner makes the rather benign statement:[21]

> Reading plays, $10 each, which includes advice as to the best manner of disposing of the same – whether they are fit for the stage or the waste basket, or for the consideration of managers and stars.

The condition represented an insidious practice in its earliest contractual form eventually outlawed by the Dramatists Guild fifty years later. Reading plays for a fee was a gateway for entry into the industry that mediating brokers controlled. It was also a gateway that was subject to abuse. The aspiring dramatist hands over US$10 with, in most instances, the delusional hope of access to "managers and stars." The broker enjoyed exclusive control over the script for a long time with a small chance that the script would ever find its way into the hands of a reputable manager.[22] Indeed, brokers sometimes purchased the more likely scripts outright for a flat fee. The broker would eventually license the work to theatrical producers, and license it into subsidiary streams of revenue – including adaptations and stock productions – for amounts much higher than what the playwright received for the initial sale. Therefore, in these instances, the dramatist never benefited from the future life of the work.

But what other option did a playwright with no experience have when the broker controls access to the stakeholders in the industry that could transform the work into a theatrical production? Further, what other options did American dramatists have but to compromise in a market of the late 1870s flooded by the work of foreign authors? There was a disconnection between a dramatist's initial control as an author and the realities of what they could do with this initial control when they negotiated with mediating stakeholders like C. R. Gardiner in the larger theatrical economy.

## II. MARBURY AND THE POWER TO NEGOTIATE

C. R. Gardiner's rapid rise to power in the industry ended only four years after his brokerage agency started operations. In 1882, Gardiner announced that he had entered into articles of agreement with Harry Smart and J. J. Spies who would "assume control" of the dramatic agency.[23] It was not Smart and Spies who expanded the brokerage industry toward the end of the nineteenth century, however. M. B. Leavitt's claim that a "class of middlemen" began to specialize in the

21 "C. R. Gardiner advertisement," 11.

22 *See* Bernheim, *The Business of the Theatre*, 113–114; *see also* "Play Brokers," *New York Dramatic Mirror*, July 22, 1914, 12.

23 "A New Firm of Agents," *New York Dramatic Mirror*, January 7, 1882, 10. Gardiner cited the reason for his retirement was that the agency "consume[d] all his time, and he is unable to give attention to any other business."

brokering business could not have been further from the truth. The innovators in the brokerage industry following Gardiner at the turn of the century were a group of extraordinary women including Elisabeth Marbury, Alice Kauser, and H. C. (Beatrice) DeMille.[24] Catherine Fisk suggests that renowned actor/manager Laura Keene also had a "play-brokering business" as early as the 1860s.[25]

A key to Elisabeth Marbury's ascendancy in the business was that she continued to perfect an organizational system developed by mediators including Gardiner and Samuel French.[26] The system involved controlling the contractual terms of how intellectual creation moved between the author and producer through exclusivity deals concerning performance rights. Marbury's sophisticated system for foreign authors shifted from an outright sale of rights to one that involved the licensing of rights (like the Samuel French model), a consistent royalty structure, and the payment of advances.[27] Marbury proposed the new system to the celebrated French playwright Victorien Sardou, who already had considerable success in the United States with plays including the Samuel French-controlled *Diplomacy*[28] and *Fedora*.[29] The risk of adopting a royalty licensing model, as proposed by Marbury, was that if the play failed, royalties – calculated on gross receipts – would likely be smaller than if there was an outright sale for American rights.[30]

Marbury, however, convinced Sardou that he would have acquired an "infinitely greater harvest" in previous American outings if he was paid a royalty rather than an outright sale.[31] Touring four companies across the major cities of the United States had the potential to reap extraordinary returns for all concerned. It was such a successful meeting that Sardou introduced Marbury to other leading French

24 Robert Grau, *The Business Man in the Amusement World; A Volume of Progress in the Field of the Theatre* (New York: Broadway Pub. Co., 1910), 203–205: writes in 1910 in what feels patronizing as a modern reader, of women's "adaptability to the conduct of theatrical business" (at 203 referring particularly to a dramatic agent Mrs. Fernandez in this instance).

25 Catherine Fisk, *Working Knowledge: Employee Innovation and the Rise of Corporate Intellectual Property, 1800–1930* (Chapel Hill: University of North Carolina Press, 2009), 145. Other successful brokerages of the period included Sanger and Jordan, Selwyn and Co, Bellows and Gregory, as well as Samuel French and Son. *See* Stewart, "The Playbrokers," 164.

26 Marbury first agreed to represent Frances Burnett to dramatize the novel *Little Lord Fauntleroy*, which eventually found its way to Broadway. This first production was successful, running from December 3, 1888, to May 11, 1889 (no details provided regarding number of performances). *See* Internet Broadway Database: www.ibdb.com/broadway-production/little-lord-fauntleroy-5718.

27 *See* Stewart, "The Playbrokers," 164. *See also* Elisabeth Marbury, *My Crystal Ball; Reminiscences* (New York: Boni and Liveright, 1924), 66–69.

28 Which he worked on with Samuel French and was the subject in the litigation *French* v. *Maguire*, 55 How. Pr. 471 (N.Y. Sup. Ct. 1878).

29 Sardou sold his rights in the United States in his previous productions, including the highly successful *Fedora*. In 1882 M. L. Mayer acting on part of Sardou "transferred and assigned all right title and interest ... for the United States" to Fanny Price for 20,000 francs. But the contract reveals that royalties were paid – 10 percent of gross for the first hundred performances and 5 percent thereafter. Contract: M. L. Mayer and F. Price, January 3, 1883, Box 23, American Play Company records, Billy Rose Theatre Division, The New York Public Library [hereafter American Play Company records].

30 Marbury, *My Crystal Ball*, 67.

31 Marbury, *My Crystal Ball*, 69.

authors and also received endorsement from the all-powerful Society of Authors.[32] With this support, Marbury's thirty-year reign as the preeminent playbroker in the United States began in earnest.

Marbury established a system that gave authors greater control over their plays by prioritizing licensing arrangements. But a closer examination of Marbury's expansive collection of agency agreements in the *American Play Company Collection*, reveals that playwright authority had its limits; especially as Marbury's influence expanded and her business morphed into the American Play Company directed by John Rumsey.[33] Marbury and her later associates who took over control of the agency[34] – like Gardiner and French before her – could make incremental adjustments to the terms of engagement in thousands of agreements for considerable personal benefit.

Marbury's agency agreements with playwrights included three standard terms that governed the relationship. The first clause usually provided for the appointment of Marbury/The American Play Company as an agent and also outlined, in general terms, the responsibilities of the agent. These responsibilities included identifying the specific play in question, the collection and receipt of all monies due, and making available to the author all accounting records for the production, if requested. The second clause usually provided the percentage commission rate a writer agreed to pay a broker for their services. And the third clause of the standard agency agreement usually provided details about the nature of the agency relationship. The commission was "a continued interest" paid by the author to the agent and was "not revocable" at "the pleasure" of the playwright. The clause is much like the "sole and exclusive" agency provision that Samuel French demanded of his clients, securing control over dramatic material for extended periods in markets that were managed by a small handful of mediators.[35]

Thus, these were some of the first standard agreements in the industry between playbrokers and playwrights. The agreement required responsibilities on the part of the agent to represent their client, and required the author to pay the agent an agreed-upon commission that was not revocable.[36] The generality of the agreements

32 So, a similar scenario to the exclusive relationship that Samuel French enjoyed with the British Society.

33 The American Play Company collection includes an expansive collection of agency agreements of Elisabeth Marbury. Marbury (who had previously partnered with Selwyn and Co) entered into an agreement with John Rumsey in 1914 to form a new mega brokerage agency. The new arrangement was in fact Marbury's relinquishing of control over daily business operations. She acted as a consultant to the American Play Company and Rumsey ran the brokerage. *See* "Play Brokers Combine," *New York Dramatic Mirror*, October 28, 1914, 9; "Play Brokers Combine," *Publishers Weekly*, 86 no. 18, October 31, 1914, 1378–1379.

34 And the vast majority of agreements in the American Play Company collection are forged under the leadership of John Rumsey.

35 *See* Chapter 2.

36 *See, for example*, Contract-The Conversion of Carrick: Evelyn Sutherland and Elisabeth Marbury, December 20, 1905, Box 16, American Play Company records; Contract-A Court Scandal:

provided parties enough flexibility to negotiate case-by-case. But this flexibility also presented opportunities for brokers to exercise considerable control over the process. Further, a lack of uniformity in any agreement with playwrights, as the Dramatists Guild would argue in the mid-1920s, harmed younger and less-experienced dramatists in particular. There are significant variances in the American Play Company agreement commission rates. For example, commissions for playbrokers at the turn of the century were as high as 10 percent of gross receipts across both foreign and domestic agreements.[37] But the Marbury agency agreements include many commission rates at varying levels. The most common alternative rate was 8 percent,[38] but there are examples in the collection of commissions as low as 5 percent[39] and one instance of 1 percent of gross receipts.[40] The agency amends the decrease or increase in the commission rate by hand,[41] and there are varying rates for adaptations and dramatizations.[42] There are also other agreements where Marbury and her

A. Boucicault/O. Shillingford and Elisabeth Marbury, February 3, 1899, Box 17, American Play Company records; Contract-Cupid's Camp: William Blatt and Elisabeth Marbury, July 3, 1909, Box 17, American Play Company records; Contract-Diplomacy: Square Bancroft and Elisabeth Marbury, March 5, 1902, Box 19, American Play Company records.

37 *See, for example,* Contract-The Acting Governor: Marie Owen and M. Selwyn, November 28, 1909, Box 9, American Play Company records; Contract-Le Affaires: Octave Mirbeau and Elisabeth Marbury, February 18, 1904, Box 9, American Play Company records; Contract-After All: Freeman Wills and Elisabeth Marbury, September 12, 1902, Box 9, American Play Company records; Contract-Cyranno: Gustave Roger/Edmond Rostand and Richard Mansfield, March 1898, Box 17, American Play Company records (up to 10 percent); Contract-Miss Ananias: Catherine Cushing and Elisabeth Marbury, June 14, 1910, Box 48, American Play Company records; Contract-Miss Cahart's Career: Eugene Walter and Selwyn and Co., January 22, 1909, Box 48, American Play Company records; Contract-The Modern Marriage: Harrison Rhodes and Elisabeth Marbury, August 20, 1910, Box 48, American Play Company records (10 percent + 1/10 interest).

38 *See, for example,* Contract-Dangerfield: Annie Russell and Elisabeth Marbury, January 17, 1899, Box 18, American Play Company records; Contract-The Gadfly: E. Voynich/Stuart Robson and Elisabeth Marbury, January 24, 1899, Box 26, American Play Company records; Contract-Cynthia: Herbert Davies and Elisabeth Marbury, February 14, 1902, Box 17, American Play Company records; Contract-Play to Be Titled (for Miss Amelia Bingham): H G Dam and Elisabeth Marbury, May 14, 1901, Box 18, American Play Company records; Contract-D'Arcy of the Guards: Louise Shipman and Elisabeth Marbury, May 23, 1901, Box 18, American Play Company records; Contract-Dorothy's Dilemma: Alfred Thompson and Elisabeth Marbury, August 24, 1891, Box 19, American Play Company records; Contract-Imagination: Sydney Rosenfled and Elisabeth Marbury, July 2, 1896, Box 33, American Play Company records; Contract-Play for Cohens and Harris: George Middleton and Elisabeth Marbury, June 9, 1906, Box 47, American Play Company records; Contract-Mr. Bar[nma]ster of Boston: John Cann and Elisabeth Marbury, April 19, 1894, Box 49, American Play Company records.

39 *See* Contract-Degenerates: Sydney Grundy and Elisabeth Marbury, October 2, 1899, Box 19, American Play Company records; Contract-Out in Illinoy: C. T. Dazey and Elisabeth Marbury, January 29, 1902, Box 54, American Play Company records (initially 5 percent).

40 *See* Contract-Miss Burdock's Lover: E. Stanton/D. Atherton and Elisabeth Marbury, October 1, 1891, Box 48, American Play Company records.

41 *See* Contract-House of a thousand Candles: Bob Marris Co. and Elisabeth Marbury, May 15, 1906, Box 32, American Play Company records.

42 *See, for example,* Contract-Deaco Bradbury: Edwin Dix and Marie Falls, June 18, 1902, Box 18, American Play Company records; Contract-various contracts: Paul Potter and Elisabeth Marbury, January 23, 1905, Box 53, American Play Company records; Contract-The Quality of Mercy: Edith

associates negotiated generous deals for themselves. The established playwright Rachel Crothers, for example, agreed to pay Marbury a "one-tenth interest in and to the said play," *A Man's World*, as well as a 10 percent commission.[43]

The broker also oversaw a contractual system that allowed for significant variations in author artistic control. A standard artistic control clause in contracts with dramatists, before the first Dramatists Guild Minimum Basic Agreement in 1926, provided the following:[44]

> It is mutually agreed and understood that no change in or additions to the text of the said play shall be made without the knowledge and consent of the parties of the first part [the author], but the parties of the first part shall make such change in the said play as may be mutually agreed upon.

The clause, therefore, required author consent but was also flexible enough to realize that changes may be necessary as the work transforms from the page to the stage. Ultimately, playwright consent was necessary, but there was some degree of anticipated negotiation between the parties before making the changes.

And these standards sometimes evolved into more objective tests, where the authors and managers agreed to: "make such reasonable, proper and necessary changes or modifications in the said play as may be mutually considered" during rehearsals or after the commencement of the production.[45] In other instances, parties could specifically negotiate changes during the rehearsal process.[46] Further, for adaptations, author consent was not always specifically required. For example, in some contracts, the author had to make "necessary changes" "agreed upon" between the parties.[47] Producers with significant power were in a stronger position to determine the boundaries of what was "agreed upon" between the parties. The emergence of, and variations in, the artistic control clause is examined further in the next chapter.

Furness and Elisabeth Marbury, April 5, 1910, Box 60, American Play Company records; Contract-Helmet of Harrare: Bertha Rumble and Elisabeth Marbury, May 14, 1901, Box 30, American Play Company records; Contract-Via Crucis: Lorimer Stoddard and Elisabeth Marbury, March 14, 1900, Box 74, American Play Company records.

43 *See* Contract-Man's World: Rachel Crothers and Elisabeth Marbury, September 20, 1910, Box 45, American Play Company records; *see also* Contract-The Modern Marriage: Harrison Rhodes and Elisabeth Marbury, August 20, 1910, Box 48, American Play Company records.

44 Contract-Commencement Days: Margaret Mayo/Virginia Frame and John Cort, August 28, 1908, Clause 8, Box 16, American Play Company records.

45 *See* Contract-High Life and Jail: The Shubert Theatrical Company/Archibald Selwyn and Louis Shipman/Ron Shields, January 5, 1910, Clause 9, Box 31, American Play Company records; *see also* Contract-Dolly Lane: A Stern and M Mayo and Selwyn and Co, December 29, 1910, Clause 10, Box 19, American Play Company records.

46 *See* Contract-The Sage of Milltown: Edgar Selwyn and Shubert Theatrical, August 6, 1908, Box 23, American Play Company records; *see also* Contract-The Miss Gower, Emma Brenner and Shubert Organization, December 19, 1908, Box 48, American Play Company records.

47 Contract-Divorcons: Margaret Mayo and William Brady, March 4, 1907, Clause 4, Box 19, American Play Company records.

Another variation in the artistic consent clause arises in the context of musical theatre collaborations. Sometimes agreements significantly favored the senior author of a co-authored piece. For example, T. W. Thatcher collaborated with Channing Pollock to write the book and libretto for the musical work *If Love Be Love*. The contract brokered by the agent provided that it was "expressly understood" that "any and all changes whatsoever" desired or required by Pollock in the book, were made "without any objection" on the part of Thatcher.[48] Thus, the consent clause was far from uniform in its application. Whether a manager could renegotiate the terms of artistic control with a playwright became an issue of considerable tension. Indeed, as examined in the next chapter, the Shuberts turned this clause into an ongoing battleground over the first half of the twentieth century. Most importantly, the playwrights themselves do not appear to be privy to most of these negotiations on artistic authority between the broker and the producer.

Another forum where brokers asserted influence over authors concerned the length of the relationship between agents and dramatists. Brokers sometimes locked authors, or particular works of authors, into long-term arrangements that left limited room for renegotiation as the relationship developed. An author with an exclusive agency deal could have their work sit on the shelf for years without the broker sending the play out to producers. The standard agreement between an agent and an author was one year.[49] There are examples in the collection involving the Selwyn Agency in particular,[50] which commit authors to five years,[51] and as much as twenty years for specific plays.[52]

Brokers also entered into contracts on behalf of dramatists to find a vehicle for a particular actor. Thus, in these instances, playwrights would have to tailor their work to satisfy the creative vision of the actor and producer.[53] Further, examples of outright payments for adaptations, negotiated by the broker, continued to exist

48 *See* Contract-If Love Be Love: W. Thatcher and Channing Pollock, December 1904, Clause 2, Box 33, American Play Company records.

49 This would be confirmed later by George Middleton and written into the Agency/Dramatists Agreement of 1928: *see* George Middleton, "The Dramatists' Guild Agency Agreement," *The Bulletin*, July–August 1928 in Dramatists Guild 1928, Box 25, George Middleton Papers, Manuscript Division, Library of Congress, Washington, DC [hereafter George Middleton Papers].

50 *See* relationship between Marbury and Selwyn: "Play Brokers Combine," *New York Dramatic Mirror*, October 28, 1914, 9. Rumsey and Marbury purchased the Selwyn Company acquiring capital stock of US$800,000.

51 *See* Contract-Mary Elston and a Frat: Philip Bartholomew and Selwyn Co., April 16, 1907, Box 46, American Play Company records; *see also* Contract-3 UK Plays, Marie Corelli and Elisabeth Marbury, March 26, 1909, Box 16, American Play Company records.

52 *See* Contract-D'Arcy of the Guards: Louise Shipman and Elisabeth Marbury, November 6, 1909, Box 18, American Play Company records; Contract-The Nabob's Daughter, Louis Shipman and Selwyn Co., November 6, 1909, Box 50, American Play Company records. (The long length of the agreement could be a consequence of it being a character role. But the length could also be a result of the role the actor may have played in developing the script.)

53 *See* Contract-No title as yet: Leo Ditchenstein and Elisabeth Marbury, April 1, 1903, Box 19, American Play Company records.

contrary to the Marbury/Sardou licensing model.[54] The agent also often burdened the author with administrative costs which included a fee for drafting contracts in addition to the commission for overall agency responsibilities.[55] There are examples in which the author's stock subsidiary rights are waived or purchased by the agent.[56] There are instances of arrangements in the American Play Company collection that appear to adopt the older "verbal agency" agreement as described by Alfred Bernheim.[57] In these agreements, the agent is a party to the production contract and therefore does not have a separate agency/playwright agreement. So the rights and responsibilities of the relationship between the agent and playwright are limited to the commission amount. But the contracts do not specify all other aspects of the relationship and thus the author is more exposed to agency exploitation.[58]

Elisabeth Marbury – and her later associates – was one of the first brokers in the United States to implement a comprehensive uniformed agency/playwright contractual framework that agents adopted across the industry in the first decades of the twentieth century. The system, however, highlighted that agency and playwright success did not neatly go hand in hand. The organizational framework created by agents left playwrights one place removed from the negotiating table but also dependent on broker services. There is no question it was an effective system with benefits for all, but the system also presented opportunities for considerable mediator incremental opportunism.

## III. ALICE KAUSER AND THE CONSOLIDATION OF THE BROKERAGE INDUSTRY

Alice Kauser was the natural heir apparent to Elisabeth Marbury in the American playbroker industry and Marbury viewed Kauser's ascendancy as a source of personal pride.[59] Kauser was born in Hungary in 1872. She immigrated to the United States with her family as a teenager and spoke several languages.[60] Marbury employed

54 Contract-Before and After: Selwyn Co. and Leo Ditrichstein, January 29, 1910, Box 12, American Play Company records.

55 *See, for example,* Contract-Evergreen: Constance Harrison and Elisabeth Marbury, February 16, 1893, Box 31, American Play Company records; Contract-Imagination, Sydney Rosenfeld and Elisabeth Marbury, July 2, 1896, Box 33, American Play Company records (US$25 for drafting contracts).

56 *See* Contract-Lover's Lane: Clyde Fitch and American Play Company, August 5, 1908, Box 43, American Play Company records; Contract-A Wild Irish Girl, George Broadhurst/George Hobart and American Play Company, January 13/16, 1911, Box 77, American Play Company records.

57 *See* Bernheim, *The Business of the Theatre*, 114.

58 *See, for example,* Contract-Dolly Lane: A Stern and M Mayo and Selwyn and Co., December 29, 1910, Box 19, American Play Company records (detail about the role of the agent); Contract-Mistress Penwick: Mrs Fenno and Co. and Elisabeth Marbury, May 21, 1900, Box 48, American Play Company records (generality of terms, but focused on agent benefits).

59 Marbury wrote in her biography of Kauser, "She is a brilliant woman and I have always rejoiced in the fact that I was instrumental in aiding her towards the founding of her subsequent career, now of many years' standing" (Marbury, *My Crystal Ball*, 136–137.)

60 *See generally* on Marbury's early life: Marbury, *My Crystal Ball*, 136.

Kauser as her assistant which presented a unique opportunity to learn the business. Marbury also believed that Kauser was a talented employee who acquired an extensive knowledge of contracting practices between playwrights and producers when employed at Marbury's agency.[61]

In January 1895, Kauser established her own "play bureau." Harrison Fiske's *Dramatic Mirror* announced that Kauser wanted to represent the interests of both foreign and American dramatists.[62] Kauser incorporated the standard contractual system of Marbury and focused on the foreign author market in the immediate years after the 1891 international copyright Chace amendments. The budding broker also expanded her interest in stock theatre companies across the country, cornering a monopoly on this market. The *Dramatic Mirror* describes how Kauser agreed with Marbury in 1898 to have the "sole authority to arrange with stock companies" the production of many of Marbury's well-known plays.[63]

By the first decade of the twentieth century, there was a mature mediating brokerage industry controlled by a handful of highly skillful stakeholders. Kauser was a beneficiary of mediation systems developed by Samuel French and Elisabeth Marbury that moved creation throughout the industry. In 1904, the *Dramatic Mirror* described Kauser's agency as "the largest play business in the world," with over 200,000 copies of stock on hand.[64] She also developed a reputation for advancing new innovative dramatic voices while meeting the financial realities of the industry. Kauser, in an interview conducted in 1911 at the height of her powers, explained her role as mainly involving the ability to match the dramatist with the appropriate manager and star. This process of matchmaking, for Kauser, involved finding the "balance" between "interesting managers in new ideas and new authors, and to pointing out to authors what the respective wants of stars and managers may be."[65] She was cautious not to advance assumptions that implied managers were overtly commercial at the expense of producing "the highest type of play." The broker suggested it was more important to find the appropriate collaboration between actor, manager, and dramatist to transform the work from a text into a production.[66]

Kauser thus viewed her role as one of facilitating a compromise between perfect artistic integrity and optimal commercial exploitation. But with considerable influence also came the opportunity to play a disproportionate role as an arbiter of taste. It

61 Marbury, *My Crystal Ball*, 136.

62 *See* "A New Play Bureau," *New York Dramatic Mirror*, January 26, 1895, 7; "Alice Kauser Returns," *New York Dramatic Mirror*, April 28, 1906, 15. Kauser would regularly update the *Mirror* on her extensive travels abroad to Europe and on her current projects: *see also* "A Talk with Alice Kauser," *New York Dramatic Mirror*, August 6, 1910, 6; "From the Agent's Point of View," *New York Dramatic Mirror*, August 23, 1911, 5; "Alice Kauser: A Chat with the Woman Who Presides Over the Largest Play Business in the World," *New York Dramatic Mirror*, December 31, 1904, 7.

63 *See* "Controls All Available Plays," *New York Dramatic Mirror*, November 19, 1898, 15.

64 *See* "Alice Kauser: A Chat with the Woman Who Presides Over the Largest Play Business in the World," *New York Dramatic Mirror*, December 31, 1904, 7.

65 "From the Agent's Point of View," 5.

66 "From the Agent's Point of View," 5.

is a form of market diversification, where the broker wants a reputation associated with the most reputable trade. Marbury's standard "agency responsibility" clause was also general enough for agents to exercise broad discretion over what writers and types of projects would have access to the industry.

The most direct way that Kauser played the role of gatekeeper was when a producer sought her advice on the type of play they should produce. Kauser acted as an exclusive agent for the Frohmans in the early years of the burgeoning Theatrical Syndicate business of the late nineteenth century.[67] Established producer Gustav Blau highlighted how a stream of scripts flowed between the agent and Syndicate until finding the right vehicle for production. In these exchanges, there is never direct correspondence between writer and producer. Blau wrote to Kauser that "all plays submitted to this office" had been "read promptly," but they had "not yet been fortunate in finding a manuscript suitable to our purposes."[68] Undeterred, Blau requested more scripts – "a good play, that is a significant and vital play," with the added postscript that he was "also looking for a vehicle for Miss Alice MacMahon, now under our management."[69] Playwright access to the industry is defined in this instance by interests other than that of the writer: a "vehicle" for a particular actor, or a "vital" play as determined by the broker.

Theatrical Syndicate member Marc Klaw also relied on Kauser's advice – reading, rejecting, and restating his wishes in an ongoing dialogue with the broker. But Klaw had limited direct correspondence with the playwright.[70] Kauser acted as an initial gatekeeper by determining what material to promote to producers – and what works to dismiss – from the expansive stable of emerging and established writers on her books. The Kauser collection includes many examples of playwright misery, where the broker had read and rejected the work.[71]

So Kauser provided the gateway for authors by determining whether they were the right fit for a particular producer or actor. As the conduit between a producer's needs and the dramatist's aspirations, Kauser also established her control over the production process as the physical repository for creative material in the industry. Kauser,

67 *See* "Alice Kauser: A Chat," 7 ("after they have run their allotted season" on Broadway).

68 Gustav Blau to Alice Kauser, October 24, 1927, Box B, Alice Kauser papers, circa 1895–1940, Houghton Library, Harvard University [hereafter Alice Kauser papers].

69 Gustav Blau to Alice Kauser, October 24, 1927, Box B, Alice Kauser papers. Similarly, Charles Hopkins rejected the play *The Radiant Release* stating that he wanted "a play that has real quality that would warrant publication and that will also act. Haven't you ONE like that? If so, I want to do it": *see* Charles Hopkins to Alice Kauser, December 23, 1922, Box HE–J, Alice Kauser papers. Along similar lines looking for something else, *see* Charlotte Wells to Alice Kauser, December 22, 1914, Box S, Alice Kauser papers; M. Phillips to Alice Kauser, January 27, 1928, Box P–R, Alice Kauser papers ("in need of a 'good play'").

70 *See* Alonzo Klaw to Alice Kauser, February 6, 1922, Box K, Alice Kauser papers (and others in the folder).

71 *See, for example,* Henry Chambers to Alice Kauser, no date, Box C, Alice Kauser papers; Children's Playhouse to Alice Kauser, no date, Box C, Alice Kauser papers; Stephen Gilman to Alice Kauser, November 22, 1934, Box P–R, Alice Kauser papers; Stephen Gilman to Alice Kauser, September 10, 1934, Box P–R, Alice Kauser papers.

like Samuel French, housed the physical copy needed to realize, or potentially realize, the production. The Kauser collection contains examples of both producers and playwrights requesting scripts, waiting for the scripts to be returned to a third party, or wanting to return scripts.[72] Control over the movement of creation in the industry and control over the physical object of creativity went hand in hand.

Kauser, like Marbury and her associates, also had significant influence over any alterations to the script despite no specific clause in agent/dramatist agreements about the right to make "artistic changes" to the manuscript. The presumption was that brokers would only suggest changes if they were in the author's best interests. But the less obvious examples of potential exploitation evident in the Marbury agreements are also noticeable in the Kauser brokerage deals. If a particular broker monopolized access to producers, writers were potentially more willing to compromise their artistic integrity to gain access to professional production. The Kauser collection includes extensive correspondence between Kauser and writers, both established and emerging, suggesting key changes to scripts.[73] The correspondence, however, rarely refers to whether the changes received the explicit consent of the playwright. The issue is not that the changes improved the work for ultimate production, but whether the suggestions to change the work occurred without the author's explicit desire to make the changes. Thus, the producer may be receiving a script that is precisely how the author desired it to be, or some reasonable compromised version worked out between the agent and writer. The producer might also be receiving a version that the writer has had to reluctantly accept because there are limited gateways to the production process.

Another complicating factor for Kauser was that several organizations who controlled touring circuits, theatre houses, and attractions across the country dominated the industry in the period of her ascendancy. The sheer size and influence of the large commercial businesses, including the Shuberts and Theatrical Syndicate as discussed in the next chapter, meant there were fewer opportunities to produce outside of the commercial system and outside of the terms on which these businesses wanted to negotiate.

Indeed, the Shubert Organization defied the authority of brokers constantly on different issues. The Shuberts challenged Kauser on whether they could hold onto authors' rights after they had expired,[74] they claimed the author had no interest in

[72] *See* Harrison Fiske to Alice Kauser, June 5, 1914, Box F, Alice Kauser papers; Charles Wagner to Alice Kauser, July 30, 1927, Box AM–AS, Alice Kauser papers; *see also* G. Bird, Shubert Theatrical Co. to Alice Kauser, June 2, 1914, Box S, Alice Kauser papers.

[73] *See, for example*, Kauser Office to Margaret Anglin, August 6, 1918, Box AM–AS, Alice Kauser papers; James Beury to Alice Kauser, January 22, 1925, Box B, Alice Kauser papers; "Dana" to Alice Kauser, June 6, 1920, Box D–E, Alice Kauser papers (marked "strictly private"); Alice Kauser to William DuBois, February 26, 1928, Box D–E, Alice Kauser papers; Alice Kauser to Howard Hull, October 27, 1925, Box D–E, Alice Kauser papers; Emile Hopgood to Alice Kauser, July 19, 1923, Box G–Ha, Alice Kauser papers; Arnold Kummer to Alice Kauser, March 24, 1924, Box K, Alice Kauser papers; Arthur Pinero to Alice Kauser, February 11, 1909, Box P–R, Alice Kauser papers; Anne Nichols to Alice Kauser, October 23, 1925, Box Ma–O, Alice Kauser papers.

[74] *See* Zoe Akins to Alice Kauser, February 18, 1929, Box AM–AS, Alice Kauser papers.

film rights,[75] they claimed foreign rights over Kauser's authors which they did not possess,[76] and accused Kauser of holding up productions for self-interested purposes.[77] The Shubert Organization threatened Kauser to not enter into alternative lease arrangements on behalf of her authors because they would directly compete with touring interests.[78] And, on occasions, they tried to undercut royalty rates.[79] They demanded that Kauser change her accounting practices to suit their practices better,[80] and accused the brokers of "hold[ing] up manuscripts in their Office after the production of the play," which caused great inconvenience and was an "unnecessary expense."[81]

It is quite a list of accusations. The Shubert Organization, in many of these negotiations, resisted attempts by playwrights to exercise greater artistic and economic authority over the work they created. As will be discussed in the next chapter, producer influence over writers was an ongoing process adapting to the unique circumstances of each production. And despite the exhaustive demands the Shuberts made of Kauser, the business relationship between the two groups continued. Kauser was in constant negotiation with the Shuberts about productions, new authors, and new opportunities.[82] The correspondence between Kauser and the Shuberts highlights that even the authority of the best brokers had its limits as the dramatists and brokers were often beholden to larger mediating organizational forces in the industry.

---

Mediating brokers built a system that relieved the playwright of business responsibilities so they could get on with the job of writing plays. The brokers presented opportunities for untried dramatists and introduced a licensing royalty system that complimented Samuel French's scheme. The presumption was that authors under these brokerage systems had greater control over their work and also better access to subsidiary streams of revenue. But a closer examination of the contractual systems established by Elisabeth Marbury and refined by brokers like Alice Kauser – two of the most reputable brokers of the period – shows that applying consistent standards was a constant challenge. This environment, in turn, leads to brokers having broad discretion over the negotiating process and persistent hidden moments of inequity.

75 *See* Shubert Theatrical to Zoe Akins, February 15, 1929, Box S, Alice Kauser papers (regarding the play Careers: note this is a letter, not a contract).

76 *See* John Biro to Alice Kauser, September 26, 1923, Box B, Alice Kauser papers (and enclosed letter – Biro calling J. J. Shubert "a thief").

77 *See* William Currie to Alice Kauser, September 7, 1917, Box C, Alice Kauser papers.

78 *See* G. Bird, Shubert Theatrical to Alice Kauser, November 30, 1914, Box L–Ma, Alice Kauser papers.

79 Shubert Theatrical to Alice Kauser (Zoe Akins), February 15, 1929, Box S, Alice Kauser papers.

80 G. Bird, Shubert Theatrical to Alice Kauser, June 2, 1914, Box S, Alice Kauser papers.

81 *See* J. W. Jacobs to Alice Kauser, August 4, 1917, Box S, Alice Kauser papers.

82 *See, for example*, W. Cuthers to Alice Kauser, July 2 (year unknown), Box C, Alice Kauser papers (Cuthers was directing for the Shuberts and asking Kauser for recommendations). *See more generally* Shubert Organization correspondence with Alice Kauser, Box S, Alice Kauser papers.

And if these inconsistencies occurred in the most reputable agencies, it is unsurprising that Alfred Bernheim claimed there was a "vast difference" in the quality of agents. Bernheim describes many agents as "lax and incompetent and do not serve their clients as they should."[83] The system provided opportunities for ordinary playwrights, but also embedded narratives about playwright business incompetence. The agency system handed expansive control to a group of influential brokers who determined which playwrights had access to the industry and the terms on which they entered.

And the dramatists did respond. As early as 1910, the *Dramatic Mirror* was reporting that the playbrokers and writers had "come to the parting of the ways."[84] Leading dramatists, in particular, were complaining that services provided by the brokers did not justify the handsome commissions they earned. A younger group presented an alternative system to the American Dramatists Club proposing the establishment of an in-house nonprofit agency service.[85] The proposal involved the brokers returning a percentage of their commission to the American Dramatists Club for causes including "clearing the theatrical seas of play pirates."[86]

The dramatists did not adopt any of the proposals, however. Throughout the second decade of the twentieth century, the brokers only grew in strength despite attempts by authors to establish standardized terms of engagement.[87] Accusations of broker exploitation were numerous. Critics claimed the brokers were "in reality agents for publishers and producers," particularly those brokers engaged in the exploitation of stage rights for the screen.[88]

83 *See* Bernheim, *The Business of the Theatre*, 114.

84 *See* "Playwrights and Playbrokers," *New York Dramatic Mirror*, March 5, 1910, 5.

85 "Playwrights and Playbrokers," 5.

86 "Playwrights and Playbrokers," 5.

87 The Authors' League developed agency contracts by 1919 (which appeared to apply across authors of all branches within the League before the Dramatists Guild formed as a group later in 1919). The standard agency agreement included clauses on greater transparency including presenting all offers to the author (clause 4) but also the author had an obligation to inform the agent of all potential agreements (clause 3). The agent also agreed to deliver "all such moneys" and accounts to the author within two days of collection and to deduct a ten percent commission (clause 5). This agent fee would be the only deduction, thus, further deductions would not include administrative expenses unless, importantly, "the Author requires or approves of special arrangements" which opened the opportunity for agent exploitation (clause 6). The standard agreement also provided that, on termination, the agent had no claim on commissions (clause 8), but importantly, the agreement does not provide guidance on the standard length of agreements. The length of agreements varied dramatically, and could tie up authors to agents for years. *See* "The League's Standard Agency Contract," *The Authors' League Bulletin* 7, no. 5 (August 1919): 15.

88 *See, for example*, L. J. V. Letter to the Editor, "As to Agents: An Open Letter," *The Authors' League Bulletin* (February 1920): 5. Implying here that the broker, acting for the publisher/producer, purchases the rights from the author at a reduced rate to benefit the producer of the adaptation. The author is paying two commissions in reality: one to the producers' representative and "one to mine" as he was made an offer through the third party producer (by way of the broker). All the time, however, the agent is claiming that they are an agent of authors, not producers.

Theatre and literary lawyer Philip Wittenberg, writing in 1937, reflected on the rise of the playbroker in the first decades of the twentieth century by providing playwrights a cautionary list of what they should demand in agency agreements.[89] The cautions reveal much about incremental agency opportunism over the previous fifty years. In particular, the issues that continued to compromise the writers included the length of playwright/agency agreements. Terms of stock and other subsidiary rights, varying commission levels, and responsibility for administrative expenses remained a source of contention. Holding onto scripts for indefinite periods, the outright purchase of authors' rights, requesting reading fees, not holding commissions in trust, and creating verbal agreements without written agency agreements continued to compromise dramatists.

In 1928, the Dramatists Guild decided to negotiate with the agents to "stabilize" conditions in the business.[90] Guild President George Middleton suggested the first Dramatists Guild's Agency Agreement provided, "a definite code of business ethics ... formulated between dramatists and agent by which each cannot help [but] profit."[91] The new agreement provisions included an arbitration mechanism, and clarification that the relationship was fiduciary in nature which meant royalties were payable by a fixed date and held in trust until payment.[92] As the relationship was personal, agency was not assignable, and the Guild under the agreement could inspect the agent's accounts "upon certain occasions." The agreement prevented any playwright from being committed to an agent for an indefinite period.[93] Thus, it took fifty years to establish the agency agreement between dramatists and brokers.

In the second half of the nineteenth century, the earliest playbrokers, publishers like Samuel French, and opportunists including Alexander Byers, were building an industry that relied on the movement of works through mediating organizations. The relationship between the dramatist and their initial intellectual property rights was inherently pragmatic in the context of the larger theatrical economy – a place to begin the process of production. And copyright law was evolving in ways that accommodated mediators. The transferral of copyright in the unpublished manuscript was often assumed to follow the outright assignment of the physical manuscript. The Copyright Registration record in this period includes the names of many mediators who had the resources to perfect registration or create the impression of perfected registration. The expansion of the idea of the "employer author" in the courts of the second half of the nineteenth century as examined by Catherine Fisk

89 *See* Wittenberg, *Protection and Marketing of Literary Property*, 179–188.

90 *See* Elmer Rice to Members of the Dramatists Guild, June 5, 1941, Dramatists Guild 1928, Box 25, George Middleton Papers. Rice had to send a letter to all members in 1941 reminding them that the 1928 agreement was still in effect as many members were "unaware of the existence of this agreement."

91 *See* George Middleton, "The Dramatists' Guild Agency Agreement," *The Bulletin*, July–August 1928 in Dramatists Guild 1928, Box 25, George Middleton Papers.

92 Also held in *Ziegfeld* case: *Caesar* v. *Ziegfeld*, 223 App. Div. 86, 226 N. Y. Supp. 510 (1st Dept 1928).

93 *See* Middleton, "The Dramatists' Guild Agency Agreement."

shifted power toward corporate mediators. And playwright responses, in a period where collective resistance was in its earliest stages, involved writers negotiating directly with mediators that asserted disproportionate power.

By the beginning of the twentieth century, all of these early mediating businesses were also beholden to a larger centralized industry structure as evident from Alice Kauser's relationship with the Shubert Organization. And these organizations, as we will now turn to, built empires through expansive theatrical real estate portfolios, by establishing booking systems across the country, and by controlling the movement of works in the space between authors and audiences.

# 5

# Negotiating Playwright Integrity

The story of the rise of the Theatrical Syndicate and the Shuberts as part of the larger mediating structures of the industry in the late-nineteenth and early-twentieth centuries has received extensive treatment in the theatre literature.[1] In the second half of the nineteenth century, the industry became increasingly centralized in the hands of a small group of businesses that coordinated venue bookings and attractions. The decentralized stock houses across the country developed into a star touring system, which then developed into a combination system.[2] Management of the physical theatre space and management of the attraction separated. As a touring system became a profitable model, individual theatres started to morph into local circuit groups. Theatrical organization centralized in the city centers, and the business of booking became essential to coordinate tours across the country.[3]

The Theatrical Syndicate formed in 1896 and was comprised of six men in three separate partnerships: Sam Nixon and Fred Zimmerman, Charles Frohman and Al Hayman, Marc Klaw and Abraham Erlanger. The Syndicate was a national booking agency which, through a process of vertical integration, eventually controlled theatre attractions, theatre venues, and circuit bookings across the country. It was a model that the Syndicate and the Shubert brothers continued to perfect in the first decades of the twentieth

1 I use the expressions commercial producer/manager, theatrical trusts, and impresarios interchangeably here in this chapter. I am, however more specifically referring to the Shuberts and the Theatrical Syndicate in nearly all instances, and their respective records held at the Shubert Archive. The press used these expressions interchangeably to advance different agendas (for example, drawing comparisons between the industrial trusts of the Gilded Age).

2 In the star touring system, a star performer would tour a group throughout the country, thus separating the attraction from the physical space. This system can be contrasted to the stock system where the stock company, in a town for example, provided the physical space and the attraction – actors and writers were employees of the stock house. As noted, the combination business usually toured the one production across the country along specific touring routes and regional circuits.

3 On the centralization process *see* Alfred Bernheim, *The Business of the Theatre* (New York: The Actors' Equity Association, 1932), 61.

century and has had a lasting influence on the theatrical property landscape to this day.[4]

A common criticism of the Theatrical Syndicate and Shuberts is that their aggressive commercialism conflicted with the artistic development of American drama.[5] The Syndicate's frankness about prioritizing box office receipts over other aspects of the production process, especially artistic sensitivities, may have informed negative public perceptions. It is also likely that the public's mistrust of the Syndicate resulted from an ambiguous broader public relations agenda. Charles Frohman was not shy in making comparisons between the Syndicate and other large commercial trusts of the period. At the same time, however, Frohman knew that such messages might draw the ire of many in the theatre community. Thus, on the one hand, the Syndicate promoted stability and professionalism by trying to associate itself with the practices of larger industries, while on the other, it tried to alleviate the monopolistic concerns of the theatre community. The following statement of Frohman embodies how the Syndicate hedged its public message:

> There is no doubt that the legitimate business management under which theatres are run today is the best that could possibly be devised. It is the business system which obtains with the large business and banking institutions, and is intended for the best interests of actors, playwrights, and employees. But the business of management is misunderstood, so far as the theatres in America are concerned. There is no "concentration" of managers. We managers have not formed an alliance. The public has been misinformed concerning "theatrical syndicates" and the condition of theatrical affairs.[6]

Older commentaries often interpret the activities of the Syndicate with suspicion, also drawing inevitable comparisons, in the most colorful of language, with the larger industrial trusts of the period. Commentary often highlights the apparent evils of monopolization, greed, and commercialism.[7] Harrison Fiske invested in a relentless

[4] Theatre owners who control the limited number of properties on Broadway have built these empires over the course of the twentieth century. *See* commentary in Epilogue.

[5] For commentary and, in particular, criticism of the Theatrical Syndicate *see* Steve Travis, "The Rise and Fall of the Theatrical Syndicate," *Educational Theatre Journal* 10, no. 1 (1958): 35; Burt L. Standish, "Dick Merriwell on the Boards; or, Fighting the Theatrical Syndicate," *Tip Top Weekly* 762, November 19, 1910, 1; Cecile Rukgaber, "The Theatrical Syndicate and Its Effects upon the American Theatre" (MA diss., University of Wyoming, 1955); Larry T. Menefee, "The Syndicate War in Little Rock," *Arkansas Historical Quarterly* 46 (1987): 27; Patricia Marks, "A Firestorm of Criticism: Metcalfe and the Theatrical Syndicate, 1904–1905," *American Periodicals* 8 (1998): 15; Norman Hapgood, "The Theatrical Syndicate," *The International Monthly* 1 (1900): 99; Walter P Eaton, "Rise and Fall of the Theatrical Syndicate," *American Magazine* 70 (1910): 832; David Belasco, "The Theatrical Syndicate: One Side," *Cosmopolitan* 38, no. 2 (December, 1904): 193; Editors, "The Great Theatrical Syndicate: How Six Dictators Control Our Amusements," *Leslie's Monthly Magazine* 59 (1905): 331; "A Theatrical Trust for the World," *Current Literature* XLIII (1907): 319.

[6] Charles Frohman, "New Phases of Theatre Management," *Harper's Weekly* 48 (1904): 2022.

[7] William Bryan during the 1900 Presidential campaign highlighted how: "The actors suffer from the Theatrical Trust": *see* "Mr Bryan was Right," *New York Dramatic Mirror*, October 6, 1900, 14. The *New York Dramatic Mirror* was very hostile toward the activities of the Theatrical Syndicate.

pursuit of the Syndicate in his *Dramatic Mirror* over multiple supplementary issues in the immediate year after the Syndicate's formation.[8] Thomas Dickinson described the Syndicate as "a bogey which is held up to the horror of the innocent."[9] William Winter, writing about the commercialization of theatre in the early twentieth century, observed:

> The major causes are the prevalence of materialism, infecting all branches of thought: and of commercialism, infecting all branches of action ... It has passed from the hands that ought to control it – the hands either of Actors who love and honor their art, or of men endowed with the temperament of the actor and acquainted with his art and its needs – and, almost entirely, it has fallen into the clutches of sordid, money-grubbing tradesmen, who have degraded it.[10]

The editorial in this article goes on at page 14: "From time to time the MIRROR has published the truth about the sinister operations of this combination that hinders freedom of enterprise and discourages the art side of the theater that has come to its knowledge and to the knowledge of newspapers whose articles on the subject have been republished in the MIRROR'S columns." *See also* Alfred Harding, "Chapter IV: America," in *Our Theater Today*, ed. Herschel L. Bricker (New York: Samuel French, 1936), 98–142, 114 (suggests trust formation was inevitable in light of the rapid development of industrialism after the Civil War – "The trusts were not creatures of the theatre, but they were happening all around it ... they were in the air, and the theatre could no more have hoped to escape their infection than a class in a school invaded by an epidemic of measles"). Ralph Gabriel similarly refers to the inevitability of trustification suggesting the "unprecedented possibilities for profit" offered by the theatre would attract enterprising managers: Ralph Gabriel, "Foreword," in Oral S. Coad and Edwin Mims, *The American Stage* (Vol. 14, New Haven, CT: Yale University Press, 1929), 5–6; *See also* Margaret Knapp, "Introductory Essay," in *Inventing Times Square: Commerce and Culture at the Crossroads of the World*, ed. William Taylor (New York: Russell Sage Foundation, 1991), 123, who writes: "just as the 'robber barons' had done with oil, steel, and railroads" there was a sense of inevitability that the Syndicate would do the same in the theatre industry by "cornering the theatrical market." Andrew Bennett Harris observes: "The Syndicate gained absolute control over both sides of the business, a monopoly. In his defense, one could say Erlanger and partners were only following a national trend, for this was the 'robber baron' period in American business, spawning the likes of Rockefeller, Gould, Harriman, Mellon, and Carnegie": Andrew B. Harris, *Broadway Theater* (London; New York: Routledge, 1994), 9. *See also* Andrew Davis, *America's Longest Run: A History of the Walnut Street Theatre* (University Park: The Pennsylvania State University Press, 2010), 182. Andrew Davis suggests in organizing its operations the Syndicate was: "[L]ike the other trusts of the day. The 1890s was the era of the robber barons, and the Syndicate sought to control theatrical bookings as John D. Rockefeller was doing with oil, and other industrialists were attempting in railroads, banking, and steel." Henry Zecher writes that "the Syndicate chiefs were guilty of the same corporate greed as the robber barons in industry," and Anthony Bianco refers to the Syndicate maturing into "a monopoly as noxious as Standard Oil or any of the other infamous industrial trusts of the robber baron era." *See* Henry Zecher, *William Gillette, America's Sherlock Holmes* (Bloomington, IN: Xlibris Corporation, 2011), 266 and Anthony Bianco, *Ghosts of 42nd Street: A History of America's Most Infamous Block* (New York: Harper Collins, 2004), 28.

8 *See New York Dramatic Mirror*, November 6/13, 1897 through to February 26, 1898, Supplement Crusade: Supplement Nos. 1–15. The Syndicate used the *Morning Telegraph* to make their case while also "vilifying" the Shuberts. The Shuberts in response were "not-so-silent partners" in *The New York Review* which ran from 1909 to 1931. *See* Maryann Chach, "Behind the Scenes of the New York Review," *The Passing Show* 12, no. 2 (1989): 2–14.

9 Thomas Dickinson, *The Case of the American Drama* (Boston and New York: Houghton Mifflin Company, 1915), 108.

10 *See* William Winter (cited in the *Saturday Evening Post*) in "American Stage in Danger, Says William Winter," *The Theatre* 7, no. 80 (October, 1907): 268. Note, in some other sources you see this reference

As the Theatrical Syndicate expanded across the country, the perception that commercialism and artistic compromise went hand in hand also took hold in the industry. Producer David Belasco, who at first resisted the Syndicate, but later softened his view, commented:

> The almost limitless resources at the beck and call of the trust have gradually enabled it to destroy competition in such a way that, with very few exceptions, the entire army of independent producers is now either bankrupt or in the employ of the syndicate. Men of artistic ability, of discriminating judgment, whose work was beneficial to the public at large, whose productions were an educational force, have been obliged to sink their individualities, either by submitting to the dictates of a business organization and practically becoming its servants, or by forsaking their profession and carrying themselves or their energies into other fields.[11]

Thus, the perception emerged that commercialism was a new and perverse phenomenon in the history of the American theatre.[12] Alternatively, if the producers gave artists too much control, there was a risk that the work would not be commercial enough to attract large audiences across the country under the prevailing organizational structure of the mediating booking system.

There is also an extensive theatre literature that investigates the war between the Shuberts and Syndicate for control over the industry in the first decades of the twentieth century.[13] And this literature often contemplates how the broader industry environment shaped the development of American drama and dramatists. In one of

ending with "degraded it into a bazaar" (*see* "Miseries of the Actor's Lot," *The Literary Digest* 37 (1908): 982.)

11 David Belasco, "The Theatrical Syndicate: One Side," *Cosmopolitan*, 38, no. 2 (1904): 195. On David Belasco's work as a director *see* Lise-Lone Marker, *David Belasco: Naturalism in the American Theatre* (Princeton: Princeton University Press, 1975).

12 The charge of commercialism, however, was not new. Some of the pioneering producers of the earlier nineteenth century accused of commercializing the industry before the formation of the Syndicate included Stephen Price, James Caldwell, James Wallack, and Augustin Daly: *see* Lloyd Morris, *Curtain Time; the Story of the American Theater* (New York: Random House, 1953); J. F. Daly, *The Life of Augustin Daly* (New York: The Macmillan Company, 1917); J. L. Smith, *Three Stock Companies: Wallack's, Daly's and Palmer's* (MA Thesis, University of Iowa, 1927); George C. Odell, *Annals of the New York Stage* 15 vols. (New York: Columbia University Press, 1927); M. B. Leavitt, *Fifty Years in Theatrical Management* (New York: Broadway Publishing Company, 1912). *See* Glenn Hughes, *A History of the American Theatre: 1700–1950* (New York: Samuel French, 1951), 228–259, for an overview of some of the leading producers in the second half of the nineteenth century.

13 Monroe Lippman, "The History of the Theatrical Syndicate: its Effect upon the Theatre in America" (PhD diss., University of Michigan, 1937); Cecile Rukgaber, "The Theatrical Syndicate and Its Effects Upon the American Theatre" (MA diss., University of Wyoming, 1955); Dorothy G. Baker, "Monopoly in the American Theatre: A Study of the Cultural Conflicts Culminating in the Syndicate and its Successors, the Shuberts" (PhD diss., New York University, 1962); Anthony Vickery, "The Logistics and Finances of Touring in North America, 1900–1916" (PhD diss., University of Victoria, 2001); Bernheim, *The Business of the Theatre*, 64–78. Marlis Schweitzer's more recent work calls on the need to examine the activities of the theatrical trust through a broader lens: Marlis Schweitzer, "Aggressive, Beleaguered, Commercial, Defiant: Marc Klaw and Abraham Erlanger," in *The Palgrave Handbook of Musical Theatre Producers*, eds.

the more measured studies, Monroe Lippman suggests the Syndicate did "nothing positive either to encourage or discourage good drama,"[14] but also claims that playwrights under the Syndicate system had more opportunities to develop their works over longer rehearsal periods. Lippman suggests that playwrights "profited commercially, because of an increase in royalty rates, and because of the greater receipts accruing from long-runs made possible by the booking reform."[15]

Cecile Rukgaber writes that the conditions of the American playwright "vastly improved after the decline of the Syndicate."[16] *The News of the World*, calling the Syndicate the "sordid and odious trust," wrote in desperation that, "[s]omething might be done, perhaps, in the dramatic line in the way of resistance if all the playwrights in the United States would combine their efforts and produce one really good play."[17] Dorothy Baker, in her expansive thesis on the Syndicate, concludes that the trust possessed the power to dictate the "capacities of playwrights as creators."[18] Some of the most robust criticism of the Syndicate was coming from influential quarters in the independent theatre movement. Augustin Daly, for example, wrote in frustration:[19]

> I do not believe that the best interests of dramatic art nor the highest aims of the theatre will be served if the spirit of competition is chilled, crippled or destroyed; and the first aim of all such combinations or syndicates must be to absorb opposition and to kill off rivals or rivalry.

An initial priority of the Syndicate and Shubert Organization was to produce commercially successful work over long tours.[20] Both the Syndicate and Shuberts suggested that "final vindication of a play came through the approval of the greatest number."[21] To use Lee Shubert's often quoted phrase, "the box office never lies."[22] Jack Poggi wrote that "[a] play produced under the combination system, if it was to be successful, had to satisfy not only a particular audience in the place where it was

Laura McDonald and William Everett (New York: Palgrave Macmillan, 2017), 60 (and some references therein on p. 60). Along these lines *see* Peter Davis, "The Syndicate/Shubert War" in *Inventing Times Square: Commerce and Culture at the Crossroads of the World*, ed. W. Taylor (New York: Russell Sage Foundation, 1991), 147.

14 Lippman, "The History of the Theatrical Syndicate," 198.
15 Lippman, "The History of the Theatrical Syndicate," 197.
16 Rukgaber, "The Theatrical Syndicate," 103.
17 As quoted by "The Usher," *New York Dramatic Mirror*, July 24, 1897, 13.
18 *See* Baker, "Monopoly in the American Theatre," 632. *See also* at 316–317: "If a playwright declined an unprofitable Trust offer for his play, expecting to seek production elsewhere, again the Trust query was, 'Where?' By the 'law' of 'survival of the fittest' the Syndicate was being made to seem the fittest."
19 Augustin Daly, "The Strong Blows Struck by the World," *New York World*, December 6, 1897, S5-l, c. 3 as reprinted in part in Norman Hapgood, *The Stage in America, 1897–1900* (New York: The Macmillan Company, 1901), 18.
20 Initially touring was the successful model, but touring rapidly declined in the early decades of the twentieth century.
21 Jack Poggi, *Theatre in America: The Impact of Economic Forces: 1870–1967* (Ithaca, NY: Cornell University Press, 1968), 255.
22 *See* Poggi, *Theatre in America*, 256.

first produced, but also many other audiences, scattered over the entire country."[23] The conditions created by the trusts consequently compromised the development of American drama as longer runs – often prioritizing the work of foreign authors – meant fewer opportunities for emerging dramatists to have their work performed.[24]

Therefore, a more general, but not universal, criticism in the theatre literature about the playwright, Syndicate, and Shubert relationship is that the managers promoted business before art to the overall detriment of the development of dramatists.[25] The claim is that the theatrical managers created a culture where the producer first considered the type of production that would sell, "thus making art the subservient to the business ends of the theatre."[26]

—

What this literature does not address is how the theatrical managers negotiated the terms of artistic control in ongoing transactions. Influence over contractual relationships was secured incrementally as part of a longer-term strategy to establish how works moved through the larger evolving mediating structures of the industry. And the theatrical managers did not always assert their will over the artistic shape of the work in the belligerent ways as often portrayed in the literature of the time. Control over the artistic direction of the work for the commercial producers happened through what appeared to be mostly reasonable transactions and compromises.

23 Poggi, *Theatre in America*, 254.

24 On the compromises in drama *see* Arthur Hopkins, *Reference Point: Reflections on Creative Ways in General with Special Reference to Creative Ways in the Theatre* (New York: Samuel French, 1948), 14–15; Morris, *Curtain Time*, 326; Dorothy and Joseph Samachson, *Let's Meet the Theatre* (New York: Abelard-Schuman, 1954), 42–47; *see, generally*, George Middleton, *These Things Are Mine: The Autobiography of a Journeyman Playwright* (New York: The Macmillan Company, 1947). However, others have highlighted the benefits of the Syndicate and Shuberts. Owen Davis suggested the competition between the Shubert and Syndicate organizations proved profitable for playwrights: "Thanks to the syndicate and to Lee Shubert . . . authors now began to eat as regularly as ordinary mortals, and the high-powered motor cars so common to playwrights today can trace their being to this source." *See* Owen Davis, *I'd Like to do it Again* (New York: Farrar and Rinehart, 1931), 71.

25 Rukgaber, "The Theatrical Syndicate," 116–117.

26 Rukgaber, "The Theatrical Syndicate," 117. This is probably the most general, but common, claim made against the Syndicate. *See* Leavitt, *Fifty Years in Theatrical Management*, Chap. XLI; David Belasco, "The Theatrical Syndicate: One Side," *Cosmopolitan* 38, no. 2 (1904): 193; Travis, "The Rise and Fall of the Theatrical Syndicate," 35–40; Standish, *Dick Merriwell on the Boards*. *See, generally*, Archie Binns, *Mrs. Fiske and the American Theatre* (New York: Crown Publishers, Inc., 1955); "Mrs Fiske's Address on Theatrical Trust," *New York Times*, November 13, 1901, 9; Walter P. Eaton, *At the New Theatre and Others. The American Stage: Its Problems and Performances, 1908–1910* (Boston, MA: Small, Maynard and Company, 1910). It is a curious claim, however, to imply that profitable drama is not "good" drama or financial priorities compromise the development of native drama. It also implies that all producers that went before the Syndicate were not motivated profit. Montrose J. Moses observes: "the play which does not draw is not acceptable to the people, and while the box office should not limit the art, at least the art should not hold the box office in contempt, since herein is worldly measure of its own excellence." *See* Montrose J. Moses, "The Disintegration of Theatre," *Forum* 45 (1911): 466.

The federal statutory basis for the development of the position that, as Daniel Gervais writes, "copyright could be infringed by making something other than exact, 'piratical' copies," can be traced to the 1870 Copyright Act.[27] In an early form of a derivative right, the 1870 Act provided that authors or proprietors had "the sole liberty of printing, reprinting, publishing, completing, copying, executing, finishing, and vending." In addition, with respect to dramatic compositions, authors had the right "of publicly performing or representing it, or causing it to be performed or represented by others." And further, "authors may reserve the right to dramatize or to translate their own works."[28] The major amendments under the 1909 Act extended the rights: "to dramatize it [the work] if it be a nondramatic work; to convert it into a novel or other nondramatic work if it be a drama."[29] The actual expression derivative right, however, was not introduced into legislation until the major overhaul of the 1976 Act.[30]

In the first decades of the twentieth century, the battle to control the artistic direction of the work evolved into something more than just the right to adapt or modify, however. The commercial producers and dramatists called on different justifications for controlling the artistic shape of the work. Commercial theatrical producers often justified their right to artistic control through a pragmatic lens. It was the producers who were in the position to realize the work on the stage – including control over the physical theatrical real property – and were undertaking this responsibility at considerable financial and reputational risk. The producers, therefore, believed they should have broad artistic control over the work as it transformed from a script to a performance. For the commercial producers, including the Shuberts and members of the Theatrical Syndicate, defining the pragmatic borders of artistic control required flexibility – an ongoing negotiation with both emerging and established dramatists on contractual paper and in the rehearsal room.

And playwrights eventually responded to these developments in more formal ways by developing industry-based uniform agreements and negotiating under the umbrella of increasingly formalized groups. In forming these groups, the dramatists began to use language that spoke to a personal relationship with their creation and preserving the integrity of their work – if modified without playwright consent, the honor or reputation of the author was at stake. So something resembling moral rights – used by the dramatists as a rhetorical tool to advance protections in industry contracts – entered the lexicon of early-twentieth-century theatrical

27 *See* Daniel Gervais, "The Derivative Right, or Why Copyright Protects Foxes Better Than Hedgehogs," *Vanderbilt Journal of Entertainment and Technology Law* 15 (2013): 792 citing Paul Goldstein, "Derivative Rights and Derivative Works in Copyright," *Journal of Copyright Society U.S.A.* 30 (1983): 209, 214.

28 *See* Act of July 8, 1870, ch. 230, 16 Stat. 198 § 86.

29 Act of Mar. 4, 1909, ch. 320, 35 Stat. 1075 § 1(b).

30 Copyright Act of 1976, § 106(2), 90 Stat. 2541, 2546 (codified as 17 U.S.C. § 106(2): which provides "to prepare derivative works based upon the copyrighted work."

practice on a larger scale.[31] The Guild today describes it as a right to "artistic integrity."[32]

This chapter speaks to a more recent body of scholarship that seeks to look beyond interpretations that, as Marlis Schweitzer observes referencing Vincent Landro, "has not been especially kind to Klaw & Erlanger or the Theatrical Syndicate." I move away from views which have "borrow[ed] the bombastic rhetoric of turn-of-the-century journalists to characterize the Syndicate as a 'rapacious monopoly under the dictatorship of a small group of vulgar and greedy hucksters whose only interest was money and whose power had a stranglehold over the American stage'."[33] Influence over the transformation of the work from page to stage was an overarching objective for the Syndicate and Shuberts. Indeed, Ken Bloom writes "during the worst of the Depression," more than 60 percent of Broadway productions were either produced by the Shuberts or staged in Shubert theatres.[34] Thus, the Shuberts had a strong sense of what they believed constituted successful, and profitable, theatre on the largest of scales. But the methods used to consolidate influence were far from crude or bombastic. The managers engaged in methodical ongoing negotiations, reinterpreting the language of artistic control production by production, author by author.

The centralization of the industry by the end of the nineteenth century, coupled with a previously chaotic contracting regime incapable of being "boxed into a formula,"[35] presented opportunities for impresarios to build a new theatrical contracting system. The system allowed commercial managers like the Syndicate and Shuberts to mediate the movement of works between playwrights and theatrical audiences and also into subsidiary streams of exploitation. The Shubert and Syndicate contractual engagements include examples of the earliest trading in motion-picture rights with the burgeoning film industry. And control over theatrical creation also stood on the foundations of an expansive real estate portfolio. The

31 For an interesting examination of the relationship between the rhetoric of moral rights and authorship *see* David Simon, "Analogies in IP: Moral Rights," *Yale Journal of Law & Technology* 21 (2019): 337.

32 The current Dramatists Guild's Bill of Rights provides the following "right": "Artistic Integrity-No one (e.g., producers, directors, actors, designers, dramaturgs) can make additions, deletions, alterations, and/or changes of any kind to your script–including the text, title, and stage directions – without your prior written consent. This is called 'script approval.' You should never permit this contractual requirement to be diluted by phrases such as 'such prior consent not be unduly or unreasonably withheld,' or by settling for 'consultation' rather than 'approval' of such changes, or by allowing a 'passive approval' mechanism (i.e., if you do not object to a request for script changes within a limited period, the changes are deemed 'approved')." Dramatists Guild of America, *Bill of Rights*, www.dramatistsguild.com/advocacy/bill-of-rights.

33 *See* Marlis Schweitzer, "Aggressive, Beleaguered, Commercial, Defiant: Marc Klaw and Abraham Erlanger," 60 citing Vincent Landro, "Media Mania: The Demonizing of the Theatrical Syndicate," *Journal of American Drama and Theatre* 13, no. 2 (2001): 23. *See also* Davis, "The Syndicate/Shubert War."

34 *See* Ken Bloom, *Broadway: Its History, People, and Places: An Encyclopedia* (2nd ed. New York: Routledge, 2004), 488.

35 Middleton, *These Things Are Mine*, 305.

eventual live performance, associated intangible rights, and material tools essential for production–including real property and contracts for administering production–placed the physical and ephemeral dimensions of creation in necessary conversation with each other.

## I. MEDIATING HUBS OF CONTRACTUAL CONTROL

By the first decade of the twentieth century, the Syndicate and Shubert organizations had developed a sophisticated contractual system to control the movement of creativity in the industry between different mediums. The Shubert Archive has an extensive collection of over one thousand contracts involving all aspects of the Shubert and Theatrical Syndicate's complicated business activities from 1900 to 1920. The collection includes contracts on the formation of subsidiary companies, contracts that deal with theatrical property holdings, and most importantly, for present purposes, hundreds of contracts with playwrights (both foreign and American), translators, adapters, and also many agreements relating to the sale and licensing of film rights. The collection covers a period when the industry went through significant growth, followed by a rapid decline in touring, around 1910. The decline in touring was followed by a period of renewed growth in New York theatre to the mid-1920s, fragmentation in audiences, and the emergence of the film industry which had an immediate influence on the organization of the theatre industry.[36]

The Shubert Archive collection, established in 1976, consolidates the business and archival records of the Shubert Organization. The Shubert Archive holdings concentrate on the first four decades of the twentieth century when the Shuberts controlled an expansive portfolio of theatrical properties and were also actively engaged in producing on Broadway.[37] Although there is no way to confirm that the contract collection in the Shubert Archive is complete, it is substantial in size and covers the entire period from 1904 to 1919. And, as examined below in Sections III and IV, the collection includes contracts between established and emerging writers. It is also possible that there is a small degree of bias in the population. Some of the Shubert agreements appear linked to the more experimental New Theatre project which may, or may not, have some influence on the degree of artistic liberty afforded writers. The New Theatre founded in New York, 1909, received funding from "[t]hirty wealthy men [who] contributed $35,000 each" to its development.[38] It was the exception for noncommercial companies to receive such significant funding where the goal was to produce more ambitious work under a repertory system. Lee

36 *See* Poggi, *Theatre in America*, 28–98. The ongoing empirical work of Derek Miller is continuously revising and updating earlier work of theatre scholars like Jack Poggi. *See, for example*, Derek Miller, "Broadway Real Estate and Economic Complexity in the Theater," *Visualizing Broadway*, www.visualizingbroadway.com/broadway/shuberts.html.

37 *See* Shubert Archive website: www.shubertarchive.org/index_flash.htm.

38 *See* Poggi, *Theatre in America*, 103.

Shubert served as the business manager for the new venture and the highly regarded Winthrop Ames acted as its director. The company folded after only two years of operation under the crippling weight of theatre maintenance and payroll expenses. No individual production ran for long enough to recoup costs.

The provenance of the Klaw and Erlanger/Syndicate contracts, also included in the Shubert Archive, is not as certain. The Shubert Archive found the Klaw and Erlanger records by chance in a theatre.[39] The Syndicate records cover the entire 1900–1920 period and include contracts with dramatists across all genres – musicals, revues, straight plays, adaptations, translations, and agreements with film studios.

The centralized organization of the industry around a handful of theatrical impresario operators provided an environment for the Shuberts and the Syndicate to create a web of advantageous contractual networks. The producers manipulated the many limbs of their operations – booking agencies, production of theatrical attractions, and larger-scale operations crossing over into new mediums such as film – to control the production process in the first decades of the twentieth century. Playwrights, with limited options because of the centralized structure of the industry, often transferred control of their work to producers in the form of an assignment or long-term license. Thus, the form of the transaction was a legally negotiated transfer between author and manager. The substance of the transferal, however, was that the producer acted as the exclusive central gateway between the author and theatrical audiences or the author and subsidiary mediums of exploitation. Figure 5.1 depicting Klaw and Erlanger's involvement in the book adaptation of *The Trail of the Lonesome Pine* is representative of how the theatrical managers occupied a central position of authority over the administration of the production process. The figure shows how the work evolves from a dramatization of the original book, to the first-class production on Broadway, theatrical tours in repertory seasons, one-night-stands across the United States, and beyond.[40] The figure also highlights the stream of subsidiary revenue related to the film rights of three film adaptations. Finally, there is the sale of the rights in the text to Samuel French (1936). In all instances, the theatrical producer has a significant interest in the subsidiary revenue streams without any claim to authorship in the original literary work or theatrical adaptation.

The broad appeal of the plot of *The Trail of the Lonesome Pine* and surprising commercial success of the novel captured the attention of Klaw and Erlanger. The Syndicate in 1908 was at the height of its powers but in competition with the Shuberts for supremacy over theatrical touring routes across America. For Marc Klaw, the rhetoric of the priorities was clear under the pressure of intense competition with the Shubert brothers: "The theatre is not primarily an educator for the public." Klaw continued: "It is out to satisfy

39 Thanks to Mark Swartz, Archive Director at the Shubert Archive, for discussions about the collection. The records were acquired later by the Shuberts.

40 On the *Trail of the Lonesome Pine see The Shubert Archive*, Contract Collection, Group III, no. 120; General Correspondence Collection, Series 10, Box 78, Folder 11; Script Collection, SB 120.

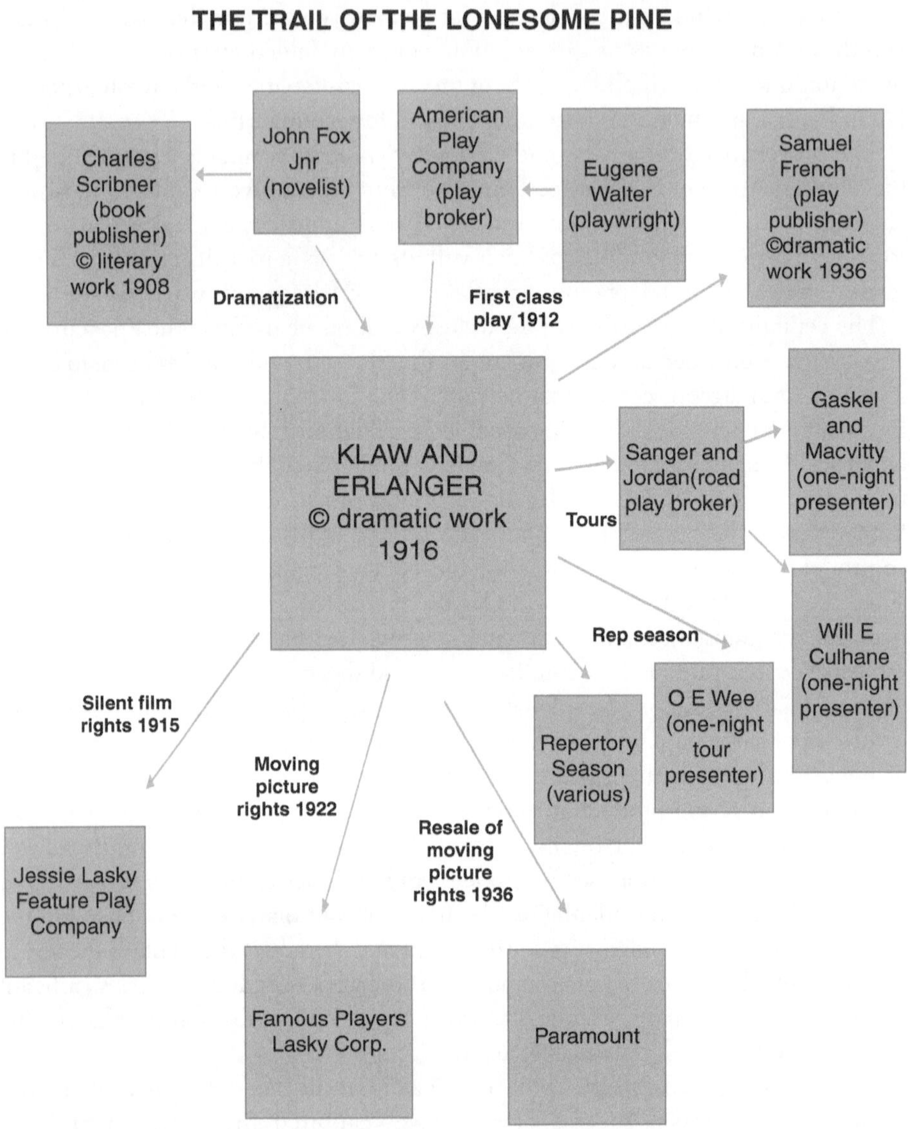


FIGURE 5.1 The Trail of the Lonesome Pine

the public demand ... What the public has the right to ask of the manager is that he shall give it good, clean, decent entertainment of a wholesome sort."[41] In 1912, Klaw and Erlanger secured the rights to dramatize John Fox's work and then contracted playwright Eugene Walter, through the playbroker American Play Company, to adapt the work for the stage, registering it under the name

[41] Marc Klaw, "The Theatrical Syndicate – the Other Side," *Cosmopolitan* 38 (1904): 200.

"Klaw and Erlanger" in August 1916.[42] The first theatrical adaptation of *The Trail of the Lonesome Pine* opened on Broadway at the New Amsterdam Theatre in January 1912, ran for a modest thirty-two performances, and received lukewarm reviews.[43]

Klaw and Erlanger, therefore, enhanced their control by first securing control over the intangible right. Through its resources and networks, the impresarios then exploited the work in several directions. Here, the playwright adapter of the book Eugene Walter – with no resources to create value in the intangible right – dissolves into the negotiating background as the work moves between mediums.[44]

Klaw and Erlanger negotiated directly with the literary author John Fox to have "authority to close for the picture rights of THE TRAIL OF THE LONESOME PINE, whether founded on the book or the play."[45] When entering into negotiations with the film companies, Klaw and Erlanger became the "sole and exclusive owners of all and every the [sic] motion picture rights."[46] Neither novelist John Fox nor playwright adapter Walter[47] seem to play a central role in the negotiation of the film rights for the first film production directed by Cecile B. DeMille in 1915,[48] and the later production in 1922.[49] Although the playbrokers for Walter were involved in the negotiation for film adaptation rights in 1922, the brokers wrote to Klaw and Erlanger that Eugene Walter had "sold all of his right, title and interest in this play to the

42 *See* "Copyright registration, Trail of the Lonesome Pine," August 25, 1916, Contract Collection, Group III, no. 120. *The Shubert Archive. See also* "The Trail of the Lonesome Pine," lc. Aug. 25, 1916; D: 44726; Klaw & Erlanger, New York. 55634 in *Dramatic Compositions Copyrighted in the United States: 1870–1916 (O–Z)*, ed. Library of Congress Copyright Office (Washington, DC: Government Printing Office, 1918): 2811.

43 The *New Yok Times*, for example, wrote that "The play, in short, is a sort of mixture of idyl and melodrama, with the idyllic quality, giving it a certain poetical charm and aloofness that is very nice, but serving at the same time to make the whole effect seem a little slow": "The Trail of the Lonesome Pine," *New York Times*, January 30, 1912, 7.

44 Thus, perpetuating a narrative of playwright complicity from the first half of the nineteenth century. On the role of the playwright as hired hand in the early nineteenth century *see* Howard Teichmann, *George S Kaufman: An Intimate Portrait* (New York: Athenaeum, 1972), 76.

45 *See* "Klaw and Erlanger to John Fox Jr," December 2, 1915, Contract Collection, Group III, no. 120, *The Shubert Archive* (where Eugene Walter would receive a percentage of advances and a percentage of 50 percent of the profits if the film made in excess of US$5,000 profit).

46 Agreement: M. Klaw and A. Erlanger with J. L. Lasky Futureplay Co. Inc, December 7, 1915, Contract Collection, Group III, no. 120, *The Shubert Archive.*

47 Agreement: M. Klaw and A. Erlanger with J. L. Lasky Futureplay Co. Inc, December 7, 1915, Contract Collection, Group III, no. 120, *The Shubert Archive.* Clause six provides that Klaw and Erlanger are the "sole owners of the moving picture rights in and to the said book and play and have full right and authority to grant to the party of the second part the sole right, license, liberty and privilege to make or cause to be made photographic reproductions and representations of the said novel and play."

48 There was in fact an earlier film in 1914 that was the subject of litigation on the basis of whether the agent was authorized to negotiate the motion picture rights. *See Charles Scribner's Sons, John Fox Jr, and Marc Klaw and Abraham Erlanger* v. *Broadway Picture Producing Company, and Ors,* "Complainant's Brief on Final Hearing," SDNY, 1914, Contract Collection, Group III, no. 120, *The Shubert Archive.*

49 Agreement: M. Klaw and A. Erlanger with Famous Players-Lasky Corporation, October 25, 1922, Contract Collection, Group III, no. 120, *The Shubert Archive.*

American Play Company on November 13, 1915."[50] Thus, Walter appears to play no role in the eventual direct negotiations with the film studios.

By 1935, when Marc Klaw granted and assigned all motion picture rights to Paramount Pictures for another film adaptation, it was clear that Eugene Walter and his estate had limited to no interest in the economic or artistic future of the work. Clause one of the "assignment" agreement read in part that Paramount was acquiring from Klaw and Erlanger:[51]

> All the motion picture rights, throughout the world, in and to and in connection with said play . . .; together with the sole and exclusive rights: to use, adapt, translate, subtract from, add to, and/or change said play and/or change the title thereof.

What did playwright Eugene Walter gain from all this? *The Trail of the Lonesome Pine* played on Broadway for a short run of thirty-two performances in 1912 and successfully toured across the country. In August 1915 Eugene Walter wrote to Erlanger:[52]

> [C]ompanies regularly organized to play THE TRAIL OF THE LONESOME PINE in one night stands should, in my opinion, pay a percentage royalty. They have always done so and there is no reason why they should not in the future. Otherwise, the author would not be receiving a fair share.

It is unclear whether Walter received the royalties for touring the theatrical production.[53] Walter assigned his interest in the motion picture rights to Klaw and Erlanger. As a result, he had a limited, if not negligible, stake in the profitable streams of revenue that came from the later film adaptations in 1922 and 1936 based on his adapted dramatization.

## II. THE NEW ELEPHANT IN THE ROOM: MOTION PICTURES

Eugene Walter's adapted version of *The Trail of the Lonesome Pine* suggests the theatrical trusts were intent on establishing the rules about how intellectual property moved between the theatre and other subsidiary mediums. Numerous film deals in

50 *See* "John Rumsey to Joseph Bickerton Jr," November 2, 1922, Contract Collection, Group III, no. 120, *The Shubert Archive*.

51 Agreement: M. Klaw with Paramount Productions Inc, August 22, 1935, Contract Collection, Group III, no. 120, *The Shubert Archive*. Clause one.

52 "Eugene Walter to A. L. Erlanger," August 7, 1915, Contract Collection, Group III, no. 120, *The Shubert Archive*.

53 All contracts for touring arrangements are between Klaw and Erlanger and the touring broker, and do not include the dramatist, Eugene Walter. *See, for example*, Agreement: M. Klaw and A. L. Erlanger with O. E. Wee Inc., March 23, 1917, Contract Collection, Group III, no. 120, *The Shubert Archive*; Agreement: Sanger and Jordan (agents for Klaw and Erlanger) with Will E. Culhane, July 10, 1915, Contract Collection, Group III, no. 120, *The Shubert Archive*. It is possible that the standard subsidiary touring royalty applied: 50 percent of the gross for the dramatist. This amount would have been paid through the American Play Company.

the Shubert contract collection between the theatre and film industries illuminate early twentieth-century practices. Motion picture rights became the new site of subsidiary contestation ripe for the theatrical producers to exploit. The theatre literature usually identifies several examples around 1925 of producers taking control over the sale of film rights.[54] The Shubert/Syndicate collection, however, includes much earlier examples, in the second decade of the twentieth century, of the trusts adopting inconsistent approaches to motion picture rights when dealing with playwrights.

Sometimes, the Shuberts, Klaw and Erlanger, and their affiliates, were reasonable when negotiating motion picture rights with dramatists. For example, the fairest contracts involved the playwright and producer agreeing with a film company directly for the sale or lease of film rights. In 1919, producer Winthrop Ames (an associate of the Shuberts) and playwright Mark Swan agreed to the sale of the motion picture rights in Swan's play *Her Own Money*.[55] The author was a party to the film rights negotiation, which granted the Famous Players' Lasky film studio the sole and exclusive right to the motion picture rights for the reasonable price of US$3,500. And the theatre producer and dramatist split the revenue from these rights 50/50 – the customary subsidiary split in the industry in other contexts such as stock rights.

This type of agreement was not consistently applied, however. What emerges throughout the collection are examples where the theatrical producers asserted considerable authority over the terms of motion picture rights. And although the 50/50 split on the sale of film rights seems reasonable, this custom developed despite theatre producers having no inherent right to film property.[56] In continental Europe, writers did not necessarily share film rights with theatre producers.[57] In some cases, these percentage splits were as high as 75/25 (theatrical producer/writer).[58]

54 *See, for example*, Bernheim, *The Business of the Theatre*, 85–92 (especially 90–91). These companies involved in contracts that were deemed oppressive toward dramatists include MGM and First National, but particular criticism was aimed toward the Fox Corporation and Famous Players' Lasky. *See also* John Tibbetts, *The American Theatrical Film* (Bowling Green, OH: Bowling Green State University Popular Press, c1985), 112–145; Robert McLaughlin, *Broadway and Hollywood: A History of Economic Interaction* (New York: Arno Press, 1974).

55 Marc Swan and Winthrop Ames with Famous Players Lasky, December 19, 1919, Contract Collection, Group II, no. 153A, *The Shubert Archive*.

56 *See* George Middleton, *The Dramatists Guild: What It Is and Does How It Happened and Why* (3rd ed. New York: Dramatists Guild, 1947), 16. Middleton notes that a possible reason why producers were able to negotiate a split on royalties for motion pictures was because the courts held that plays and pictures were competitive and therefore if a producer held rights in the dramatic work a dramatist would not be able exploit 100 percent of the motion picture rights at the same time. The compromise, therefore, was a split on motion picture rights between producer and author if the producer had an interest in the theatrical rights.

57 George Middleton, for example, writes that in France "no author shared these rights with the manager; he merely leased production rights for Paris and retained everything else." Middleton, *The Dramatists Guild: What It Is and Does*, 16.

58 *See, for example*, Shubert Theatrical Company with Lawrence Rising, June 15, 1914, Contract Collection, Group I, no. 90, *The Shubert Archive*. In this film adaptation of *The Cry for the Child*

There are examples in which an outright sale of film rights from playwright to theatre producer occurred for nominal amounts.[59] So there appears to be evidence of limited competitive bidding for film rights between studios. Rights were sold by theatre producers to film companies with minimal to no input from the original author. Studios made capital payments to theatre producers to fund the initial theatrical production in return for an exclusivity deal on the motion picture sale. In these instances, the producer often received an additional bonus payment from the film company for securing this advantage.[60] The theatre producer, therefore, received more than 50 percent of the film sale. In later years, this payment also sometimes included a "directing salary," which cut into author royalties.[61] In other circumstances, the theatre producer purchased the film rights from the playwright and then engaged another dramatist to rewrite the script as long as the second author received no income from subsidiary motion picture rights.[62]

clause five provides that should the Shuberts produce the play in either stock or as a moving picture the author will receive only "Twenty-five percent, (25%) of the amount received." In the film adaptation of *Round Up*, written by Edmund Day, Klaw and Erlanger were reluctant to give Day's wife, beneficiary of Day's estate, any more than 33 1/3 percent of motion picture rights in a work that was incredibly successful, refusing on multiple occasions over many years. In a letter from Day's lawyer to Klaw and Erlanger's lawyer in December 1915: "Klaw and Erlanger will not consent to give Mrs Day one-half of all moneys received by them from motion pictures of the 'Round Up'." "Mayer Goldman to David Gerber," December 15, 1915, Contract Collection, Group III, no. 99, *The Shubert Archive*. The original contract between Klaw and Erlanger and Day for the dramatic composition was signed in July 1906. It is unclear whether Klaw and Erlanger or Day ever agreed to the change.

59 *See, for example,* bill of sale between Shubert Theatrical Company and Charles Buck, for the *Battle Cry* moving picture rights, initially US$700 and then eventually negotiated for US$1000: August 15, 1917, Contract Collection, Group I, no. 303, *The Shubert Archive*; Shubert Theatrical Company with Eugene Walter, September 13, 1919, Contract Collection, Group II, no. 340F, *The Shubert Archive*. Walter would make an outright sale of film rights to the Shuberts for his play *The Heritage* for US$500.

60 *See, for example,* Agreement: Lee Shubert and F Ray Comstock Photoplay Inc with Fox Film Corporation, August 28, 1925, Contract Collection, Group II, no. 243, *The Shubert Archive*. In this agreement the Shuberts would agree to two separate payments as part of the sale of film rights for the motion picture adaptation of *The City* by Clyde Fitch: a full payment of US$25,000, made in a first payment on signing of US$10,000 and a second payment of US$15,000 in January of 1926. Interestingly, in correspondence between lawyers Ernst and Cane and the Shuberts more than ten years earlier, it was made clear regarding moving picture rights that they "have not been given to you [Shubert] either in whole or any part under the contract." Fitch passed away in 1909 and the Shuberts in the passing of time may have taken the opportunity to negotiate rights they never had in the absence of the author. *See* "Ernst and Cane to The Shubert Theatrical Co," January 17, 1914, Contract Collection, Group II, no. 243, *The Shubert Archive*; "Ernst and Cane to The Shubert Theatrical Co," June 16, 1910, Contract Collection, Group II, no. 243, *The Shubert Archive*. Under the original contract of 1909 they had to produce the work at least seventy-five times or the rights in the work would revert back to the author. They did not do this as John Rumsey of the American Play Company made clear in a letter in 1921: "John Rumsey to Frank Miller (General Manager National Play Company)," December 8, 1921, Contract Collection, Group II, no. 243, *The Shubert Archive*.

61 Middleton, *The Dramatists Guild: What It Is and Does*, 17.

62 *See, for example, Eyes of Youth* written by Charles Guernon (aka Carlton Glidden) who had a 50/50 split on motion picture rights with the Shuberts in a contract of April 4, 1917. However, on May 22, 1917, the Shuberts entered into an agreement with Max Marcin to "rewrite the play." Marcin received a 2.5 percent royalty but would "not receive anything from motion pictures." *See* "Unsigned memo to Lee Shubert," February 19, 1941, Contract Collection, Group II, no. 340M, *The Shubert Archive*.

The film-rights issues are often cited as the trigger that provoked the writers to establish the first uniform Minimum Basic Agreement of 1926. There was another issue, however, lurking within these agreements concerning motion picture rights that spoke to the emergence of the first derivative rights in the 1870 federal copyright revisions. During the negotiation of the 1926 Minimum Basic Agreement, dramatists believed that managers were specifically looking for works suitable for an eventual film sale. Although it is a difficult claim to prove from an artistic point of view, film adaptation appears to be a consideration for the Shuberts and Syndicate when they drafted contractual arrangements with dramatists.

For example, author Arthur Bennett agreed with Klaw and Erlanger to write an original play based on stories he had written in the *Evening Post* entitled *Sawdust and Sentiment.* Despite agreeing on a 50/50 split of motion picture rights,[63] the agreement also granted to the Syndicate the right to:[64]

> make or have made such changes, elaborations and additions as they [Klaw and Erlanger] deem necessary for such motion picture reproduction.

Suggesting a loss of "faith in the world in Bennett,"[65] Klaw and Erlanger demanded that Bennett work with a more "experienced" collaborator because "the changes [to the script] have not been satisfactorily made." Klaw and Erlanger felt that Bennett had not accepted collaboration "in the right spirit."[66] Bennett, like other less-experienced dramatists of the period, received an ultimatum: accept major changes to your script, with perhaps an eye on a motion picture adaptation in the future, or cancel the contract. *Sawdust and Sentiment*, a work of apparently some artistic merit, had a short theatrical run,[67] but the playwriting career of Arthur Bennett dissolved into the ether. In this case, mediators took control of the theatrical artistic process in the contractual negotiation so that the work was more palatable for subsidiary spaces of exploitation.

63 Agreement: Arthur Bennett with Klaw and Erlanger and George Tyler, October 1917, Contract Collection, Group III, no. 104, *The Shubert Archive*. Clause 8.

64 Agreement: Arthur Bennett with Klaw and Erlanger and George Tyler, October 1917, Contract Collection, Group III, no. 104, *The Shubert Archive*. Clause 8.

65 "Letter to Mortimer Fishel," November 10, 1917, Contract Collection, Group III, no. 104, *The Shubert Archive*.

66 "Letter to Arthur Bennett," February 23, 1918, Contract Collection, Group III, no. 104, *The Shubert Archive*.

67 Although probably not as a first class production on Broadway. The production was possibly limited to Baltimore, but could have been produced at other venues outside of New York. *See* advertisement in *Baltimore Sun*, February 9, 1919, 24: "Klaw and Erlanger and George C Tyler present–Sawdust and Sentiment by L. B. Yates." Bennett registered the work in 1917 under his name but identified the author under his publishing name L. B. Yates (registration 33013, D48615 on December 31, 1917). I could not find a record of the production, Arthur Bennett, or L. B. Yates on Internet Broadway Database.

## III. CONTRACTUAL ARTISTIC AUTHORITY

Determining whether the content of the work was commercially suitable for film adaptation was a subplot of a broader artistic issue that lived within the Shubert and Syndicate agreements. A striking feature of the producer contracts with playwrights in the Shubert Archive is the existence of a flexible clause about artistic control – the right to make alterations, additions, and omissions to the text. The managers embarked on a sustained effort in these contracts to alter the shape of these clauses and in turn the artistic direction of the work. Playwrights, in response, began to justify what appeared to be the right to adapt or modify their dramatic composition – provided for in the 1870 statutory revisions to copyright law[68] – by drawing on the rhetoric of a personal rights-type relationship with their work.[69]

Modifying the degree of artistic control in theatre contracts was an incremental process. Sometimes a playwright negotiated considerable control over the composition. There were also cases where the producer negotiated broad artistic control. In other instances, the parties settled on a compromised position. So the artistic control clause undergoes modification from contract to contract. But, as will be examined, the producers also appeared to assert control over the artistic direction of the work outside the glare of the contractual instrument – as the work transformed from the page to the rehearsal room.

Moments of artistic authority between dramatists and producers emerge in four ways in Shubert/Syndicate agreements. In this study, I examined 228 contracts. There are many contracts, about 18 percent of the population of 228, where the

68 *See* Act of July 8, 1870, ch. 230, 16 Stat. 198 § 86. It was an early form of the derivative right.

69 In the first decades of the twentieth century, an emerging view in the state courts was that the author did not retain a form of moral rights unless provided for in the contract. *See* Ilhyung Lee, "Toward an American Moral Rights in Copyright," *Washington and Lee Law Review* 58 (2001): 795, 813 citing from the period *De Bekker* v. *Frederick A. Stokes Co.*, 153 N.Y.S. 1066, 1068–69 (N.Y. App. Div. 1915), modified, 157 N.Y.S. 576 (N.Y. App. Div.), affd, 114 N.E. 1064 (N.Y. 1916); *Jones* v. *Am. Law Book Co.*, 109 N.Y.S. 706, 710 (N.Y. App. Div. 1908). It appears there is also case law from the period, that Lee identifies at note 99, suggesting the purchaser of literary property cannot do with it as they please in the absence of contractual moral rights language: *see Clemens* v. *Press Publ'g Co.*, 122 N.Y.S. 206 (N.Y. App. Term 1910) (Seabury J at 207–208). Commentators have claimed that by the mid-twentieth century, courts "applying state law, increasingly articulated a 'sui generis tort' of moral rights invasion," which subsequently stagnated in the second half of the twentieth century. *See* Patrick R. Goold, "The Lost Tort of Moral Rights Invasion," *Akron Law Review* 51, no.4 (2017): 1093. Another avenue where moral rights-type actions have been explored is in the context of the Lanham Act. *See also Gilliam* v. *American Broadcasting* 538 F.2d 14 (2d. Cir. 1976) which considered derivate rights doctrine could potentially protect the right of integrity. For an interesting examination of the intersection of race, copyright, moral rights, and performance *see* Brandon Johnson, "Whitewashing Expression: Using Copyright Law to Protect Racial Identity in Casting," *Northwestern University Law Review* 112, no. 5 (2018): 1137. The Copyright Act 17 U.S.C., § 106A provides attribution and integrity rights to authors in the limited context of the visual arts. Section 106A, 3(A) provides that the author of a work of visual art shall have the right "to prevent any intentional distortion, mutilation, or other modification of that work which would be prejudicial to his or her honor or reputation, and any intentional distortion, mutilation, or modification of that work is a violation of that right."

focus of the agreement is an assignment, subsidiary license, or sale of the motion picture rights. The following analysis does not include these agreements. The first group of contracts to consider between dramatists and theatrical producers are silent on the issue of artistic control ("silent contract"). This group makes up 16 percent of the total population. That is, there is no clause at all about changes to the text. These contracts resemble many agreements of the second half of the nineteenth century which would limit expression in the contract to the pecuniary terms such as advancement amounts and royalty percentages. The lack of a contractual term on artistic control suggests that any change to the dramatic composition was an ongoing verbal negotiation between writers and managers. More ominously for dramatists, the contractual silence was also a potential opportunity for managers to edit the work at will later in the rehearsal room.[70]

The second group of contracts, which makes up about 22 percent of the population, include artistic control clauses where the playwright has control over making additions or changes to the script ("pro-writer contract"). In these arrangements, explicit consent is needed to make changes, and the writer often has broad control over other aspects of the production process, such as casting. These contracts suggest there were times when members of the Syndicate and the Shubert groups were willing to afford authors a considerable degree of autonomy in the artistic decision-making process. For example, playwright Owen Davis agreed with the Shuberts in 1916 to produce *The Key to Room No. 10*. Under the agreement:[71]

> The managers agree that no alteration shall be made in the text without the consent in writing of the Author.

The Shuberts were also willing to provide less-established writers considerable artistic authority over their work. For example, in May 1909, the Shubert Organization agreed to produce Olive Porter's Broadway play *The Ringmaster*. The play explored the wheeling and dealing of early twentieth-century Wall Street finance and the "Ringmasters" of the New York financial world.[72] The Shubert script review department considered the play a work of some promise that "[e]vinces enthusiasm," but still required changes.[73] The contract with Porter provided that "no alterations or additions shall be made in the text of said play with the consent of the party of the second part [Porter]."[74] Here, there is a slight variation on the Owen

[70] This is what happened through the possible doctoring of scripts and eventual performance of the work itself. *See* further discussion below in Section V.

[71] Agreement: Owen Davis with Shubert Theatrical Company, June 7, 1916, Contract Collection, Group II, no. 317D, *The Shubert Archive*. Clause 6.

[72] On the plot of *The Ringmaster see* George Jean Nathan, "The Drama Comes into Season," *The Smart Set* 29, no. 1 (1909): 147; Channing Pollock, "Unmuzzling the Theatrical Season: The Ringmaster," *The Green Book Album* 2 (1909): 780.

[73] Review of *Ringmaster*, May 7, 1909, Play Criticism Collection: 1906–1909 Collection, "R," *The Shubert Archive*.

[74] Agreement: Shubert Theatrical Company with Olive Porter, May 11, 1909, Contract Collection, Group I, no. 233, *The Shubert Archive*. Clause 6.

Davis contract: no written consent required and a specific provision that no additions made without the author's consent.

In other circumstances, experienced writers secured extensive artistic control.[75] In the first decade of the twentieth century, just before the rapid expansion of the motion picture industry, narratives about wizards, witches, and mythical worlds were popular for stage adaptation. The Shubert brothers contracted with Frank Baum, author of the successful *Wizard of Oz* stories, to adapt three of his books for the stage, *The Marvellous Land of Oz*, *The Woggle Bug*, and *The Queen Sizi of Ix*.[76] The arrangement was a standard pro-writer agreement with Baum which granted royalties for the dramatization. The contract also stipulated that the Shuberts could not use "either directly or indirectly, characters known as the 'Tin Woodman' and the 'Scarecrow'."[77]

The third category of contract for artistic control seeks to secure the middle ground. In about 16 percent of the population, the producers and playwrights establish an objective standard for negotiation by incorporating a "reasonableness and necessary" benchmark ("balanced contract"). These contracts often involved prominent playbrokers such as Elisabeth Marbury or Alice Kauser negotiating the deal. In the early twentieth century, literary author Kate Douglas Wiggin wrote the classic and popular American children's novel *Rebecca of Sunnybrook Farm* which later developed into several books. Klaw and Erlanger felt the work was suitable for theatrical adaptation as well as film exploitation.

Kate Douglas Wiggin coauthored the theatrical adaptation with Charles Thompson. The agreement with Klaw and Erlanger for artistic control provided that:

> The said parties of the first part [the authors] agree to make such reasonable, proper and necessary changes or modifications in the said play as may be indicated by the

75 Another way in which authors attempted to control the script was to explicitly provide for the manuscript to be kept in manuscript form, thus, retaining all common law rights in the work. It was a strategy similar to that adopted by Samuel French. *See, for example*, Agreement: Edgar Alana Woolf and George Viereck with Shubert Theatrical Company, August 1908, Contract Collection, Group II, no. 158A, *The Shubert Archive* (clause 7); Agreement: Macpherson Turnbull with Shubert Theatrical Company, June 15, 1906, Contract Collection, Group II, no. 263, *The Shubert Archive* (clause 1). Further, a novelist would also sometimes negotiate artistic control in adaptation contracts in relation to issues of personal importance. For example, author Montague Glass entered into an agreement with the Shuberts to adapt his book *Potash and Perlmutter* for the stage. The contract provides that Glass shall have the right to "alter or veto any scenes or situations or lines that in the opinion of the said party . . ., may be in any way offensive to the Jewish race." Agreement: Montague Glass with Shubert Theatrical Company, July 8, 1911, Contract Collection, Group II, no. 393, *The Shubert Archive* (Clause 6).

76 *See* Agreement: Frank Baum with Shubert Theatrical Company, March 13, 1906, Contract Collection, Group II, no. 276A, *The Shubert Archive.*

77 Agreement: Frank Baum with Shubert Theatrical Company, March 13, 1906, Contract Collection, Group II, no. 276A, *The Shubert Archive.* Clause 1(e). On the theatrical works of the *Wizard of Oz see* Mark Swartz, *Oz Before the Rainbow: L. Frank Baum's The Wonderful Wizard of Oz on Stage and Screen to* 1939 (Baltimore, MD: Johns Hopkins University Press, 2000).

> said parties of the second part [producers]. The said parties of the second part agree not to make, or cause or permit to be made any changes or modifications or cuts in the said play, without the consent, in writing, of the said parties of the first part.[78]

Here, we see the evolution of the artistic control clause toward a recognition of the producer. Like the pro-writer contracts, the balanced agreements still often required written consent. But the author should not withhold changes when the suggested revisions were reasonable and necessary as indicated by the producers.

Who determined whether the changes were reasonable or necessary? The boundaries of reasonable and necessary, as will be examined, were refined by tinkering with the contractual language. The boundaries of what constituted reasonableness were also possibly renegotiated as the contractual relationship between author and manager evolved into an artistic one in the rehearsal room.

## IV. PRODUCER ARTISTIC AUTHORITY

The clearest indication that producers were intent on asserting artistic control over the work of authors arose when they would explicitly provide for this authority in agreements. Twenty-eight percent of contracts in the Shubert/Syndicate population examined include an artistic control provision that is "pro-producer" (fourth category). The common characteristic of all of these agreements regarding artistic control is that no express consent by the author is necessary to make any changes to the dramatic composition. Sometimes express consent was not required, but the manager simply agreed to avoid "affect[ing] substantially the structure of the said play."[79] The contractual language, however, is more assertive than that in the balanced clauses. For example, the Shubert Organization agreed to produce Lawrence Rising's *Apartment 12 K* in 1914 on the condition that they would not substantially alter the play. Rising, however, "will at the request of the said SHUBERT, make such necessary eliminations from the text of the play as the latter [Shubert] may require." And during the rehearsals, Rising will "make such changes, alterations, and interpolations at the request of the said Shubert as may be found necessary." There was no notice of written consent, or indeed any form of approval, except for the vague condition that no substantial alteration of the structure of the play occurs.[80]

The classic pro-producer clause, absent of any express author consent, is evident in a contract between the Shuberts and playwright Brandon Tynan to produce the play, *Vivian*, in 1909:[81]

78 Agreement: Kate Douglas Wiggin and Charlotte Thompson with Klaw and Erlanger, March 25, 1909, Contract Collection, Group III, no. 90, *The Shubert Archive.* Clause 7.

79 Agreement: Lawrence Rising with Shubert Theatrical, June 6, 1914, Contract Collection, Group I, no. 73, *The Shubert Archive.* Clause 1(c).

80 Agreement: Lawrence Rising with Shubert Theatrical, June 6, 1914, Contract Collection, Group I, no. 73, *The Shubert Archive.* Clause 1(c).

81 Agreement: Brandon Tynan with Shubert Theatrical Company, September 2, 1909, Contract Collection, Group II, no. 293C, *The Shubert Archive.* Clause 7.

> The party of the first part [author] agrees at all times to make such reasonable corrections and changes in the said book as may become necessary . . .
> and will make such excisions in the play as may become necessary during the performance thereof.

Klaw and Erlanger adopted a similar approach when seeking to avoid author consent. In a contract between Klaw and Erlanger and playwright Aaron Hoffman, the managers agreed to produce Hoffman's play *The Politicians* on these terms:[82]

> [A]ll changes that may appear to be necessary to the success of said play, be made in said play by the party of the first part [author] to the entire satisfaction of the parties of the second part [producers].

On other occasions, the producers used the language of reasonableness along with other provisions in the agreement to establish the framework of artistic authority over the dramatic composition. Klaw and Erlanger, coproducing with George Tyler, agreed with emerging dramatist Catherine Cushing to develop her play *The Belle* in 1917. Cushing agreed to "make such changes and modifications in said play as may be reasonably suggested by the parties of the first part [the producers]."[83] But the producers also required that to accept the manuscript for the first-class production, it had to be "satisfactory to them."[84] Thus, as was the case with so many contracts of the period, the lure of a first-class production came with conditions. Suggested changes had to be reasonable, but lurking behind the reasonableness of the changes was the veiled threat that if the overall manuscript was not satisfactory, the producer would not produce the play.

The Shuberts and Syndicate appear to adopt this approach throughout the collection. Despite the dramatist being the "sole owner and author" of the work, the dynamic established between manager and writer was such that in "delivering" the composition, the manager would dictate what was acceptable, and thus have influence over the artistic shape of the work. For example, in an agreement between author James Baldwin and the Shuberts to produce Baldwin's play *Twenty Two* the conditions provided:[85]

82 Agreement: Aaron Hoffman with Marc Klaw and Abraham Erlanger, August 21, 1909, Contract Collection, Group III, no. 113, *The Shubert Archive*. Clause 3.

83 Agreement: George Tyler and Klaw and Erlanger with Catherine Cushing, June 1, 1917, Contract Collection, Group III, no. 15, *The Shubert Archive*. Clause 9.

84 Agreement: George Tyler and Klaw and Erlanger with Catherine Cushing, June 1, 1917, Contract Collection, Group III, no. 15, *The Shubert Archive*. Clause 3.

85 Agreement: Shubert Theatrical Company with James Baldwin, June 21, 1909, Contract Collection, Group I, no. 253/8, *The Shubert Archive*. Clause 5. In the Shuberts initial review of the play it was concluded that *Twenty Two* was "an 'episode' of literary perfection." *See* Review of Twenty Two, June 8, 1909, Play Criticism Collection: 1906–1909 Collection, "T," *The Shubert Archive*.

> The party of the second part [author] agrees to make such additions and alterations or changes in the said play after its delivery and acceptance as may be deemed necessary in the judgment of the party of the first part [the Shuberts]

In a similar tone, the authors and owners of a play titled *Silk* signed an agreement with Klaw and Erlanger in 1913 to deliver a "full and complete manuscript" of their play to the managers on these terms:

> [T]he Licensors agree to make, to the best of their ability, the changes in the said play required by the Licensees.[86]

Inserting the language of reasonable or necessary modifications enabled producers to assert their authority over the artistic process without appearing to be unreasonable. Moreover, sometimes the producers even made an addendum to standard contracts to ensure that this language of reasonable or necessary changes enhanced their artistic control. In a 1915 contract between authors of the play *The Monster* and Shubert Theatrical, the contract provided "pro-writer" terms much like the Owen Davis contract above:[87]

> The manager agrees that no changes, interpolations, modifications, additions or eliminations of any kind in the said play or any part thereof shall be made without the consent in writing of the Authors.

The Shuberts made the following handwritten addendum to the contract:[88]

> [E]xcept such as may necessarily be made in the staging thereof

The Shuberts, therefore, were using the contract to articulate their need to assert artistic control over the composition as the creative process moved from the script to the more ephemeral space of staging the work. By adding the "exception," it is unclear whether in this transformation from the textual work to the performance of the work – the staging of the composition – actual formal consent is required.

The producers also tried to assert contractual artistic control over writers in other contexts. For example, producers often renegotiated casting control with dramatists.[89] And in some instances, writer artistic control was governed by how

86 Agreement: Irma Kraft and Frank Mandel with Marc Klaw and A. L. Erlanger, June 11, 1912, Contract Collection, Group III, no. 105, *The Shubert Archive.* Clause 4. Noting in this instance there had to be some prior discussion about the changes between the parties.

87 Agreement: Paul Dickey and Charles Goddard with Shubert Theatrical Company, April 1915, Contract Collection, Group II, no. 306B, *The Shubert Archive.* Clause V.

88 Agreement: Paul Dickey and Charles Goddard with Shubert Theatrical Company, April 1915, Contract Collection, Group I, no. 306B, *The Shubert Archive.* Clause V.

89 *See, for example,* Legrand Howard with F. Ray Comstock (on behalf of Shuberts), July 9, 1913, Contract Collection, Group II, no. 348A, *The Shubert Archive.* Howard's letter to Comstock initially provided that the cast of *Deborah* should "obtain[ . . .] my[author] approval of the said engagement and employment" (which is subsequently crossed out and initialed); Harry Smith with Marc Klaw and Abraham Erlanger, 1908, Contract Collection, Group III, no. 57, *The Shubert Archive,* Clause five, provides that Klaw and Erlanger will agree to produce the play *Little Nemo* "by a thoroughly

suitable the script was for a leading actor. J. Hartley Manners had an agreement with the Shuberts "to write an original play suitable for Miss Virginia Harned" based on a scenario "already accepted and approved of by [the Shuberts]."[90] In other situations, the Syndicate demanded that the author "furnish all the money necessary in making the production."[91] One area where the Shuberts were more insistent on maintaining artistic control was musicals – a lucrative and successful genre of the business and their area of theatrical specialization.[92] The Shuberts seemed determined to command control over the right to interpolate lyrics and musical compositions. In some cases, this right to interpolate was up to 50 percent of the original work. For the 1916 musical *The Cave Lady*, the Shubert artistic control clause provided:

> The party of the first part [Shuberts] shall be entitled at any and all times to interpolate musical numbers from time to time in said musical comedy, such interpolations however not to exceed 50% of the original score, and the parties of the second part agree to make any and all changes in the book, lyrics, and music as may in the judgment of the party of the first part be required.[93]

In another instance, Klaw and Erlanger applied the notion of reasonableness to the "popularity" of the musical work. In Harry Blossom's contract for a musical adaptation *Un Voyage Cook*, the managers agreed to make no changes to the work. But if any number "fail[ed] to meet with popular approval," and after a "reasonable

competent and adequate cast, and with a competent orchestra." Thus, there was broad discretion here for Klaw and Erlanger to cast production with no consent required from the author. *See also* Kellett Chambers with Joseph Brooks (on behalf of Shuberts), October 6, 1908, Contract Collection, Group III, no. 74, *The Shubert Archive*. The producers in this instance agreed to produce *My Permanent Husband* and were only required to give "reasonable deference" to the writer in casting and scenery decisions (Clause 6). *See also* Harry Smith with Shubert Theatrical Company, October 20, 1916, Contract Collection, Group II, no. 340D, *The Shubert Archive*. The author originally had a clause (2f) for his play *Ladies Change* that provided "The Shubert Theatrical Company agrees that the cast will be satisfactory to Harry James Smith," but this clause is crossed out (and initialed) and replaced by "It is understood that the cast and stage manager shall be mutually agreed upon." Finally, *see* Shubert Theatrical with Augustus Thomas, November 14, 1907, Contract Collection, Group II, no. 99B, *The Shubert Archive*. Clause 1, which provides that the author will write a play or drama containing a character "acceptable" to the Shuberts and also the actor John Mason Esq.

90 *See* J. Hartley Manners with Shubert Theatrical Company, March 21, 1906, Contract Collection, Group II, no. 127A, *The Shubert Archive* (unsigned).

91 *See, for example*, O. U. Bean with Marc Klaw and Abraham Erlanger, February 24, 1906, Contract Collection, Group III, no. 24, *The Shubert Archive*. Clause 4.

92 This included considerable artistic control over adaptations and translations of foreign language works. For example, the Shuberts negotiated a clause in the translation of the German work *Fortunate Fool*, "The Shubert Theatrical Company shall have the right to change the title if [sic] this work as well as to make other necessary changes of adaptation." Clause 4. Of course, there has to be a degree of flexibility with translation from one language to another, but the contract arguably allows for a degree of flexibility and potential to go beyond a mere translation into the new areas of artistic reconstruction. Verlag and Vortrieb with Shubert Theatrical, December 17, 1908, Contract Collection, Group I, no. 300B, *The Shubert Archive*. Clause 4.

93 Shubert Theatrical Company with Henry White, Charles Dickson, Harry Olsen, June 29, 1916, Contract Collection, Group I, no. 339A, *The Shubert Archive*. Clause 8.

opportunity" to replace the number, then "the Managers will have the right to interpolate any outside number in the place."[94]

When the manager owned the intellectual property and/or was an employer of the writer – for example, when they purchased the right to make a stage adaptation of a book – they would also specify artistic limits on the playwright who adapted the new work.[95] The esteemed writer, and noted playwright advocate, Channing Pollock agreed with Klaw and Erlanger and Joseph Brooks in 1909 to dramatize the book *The Inner Shrine* for the stage. After delivery, Pollock was to "make such changes and additions in the said manuscript or play as shall be suggested by the parties of the second part [the managers]."[96] In a 1912 agreement between playwright Henry Blossom and Lee Shubert (coproducing with A. H. Woods), the author agreed to adapt the book of the play *Aime de Femmes* for a musical. In clause eleven of the agreement the Shuberts simply crossed out the following pro-writer clause:[97]

> The managers agree that no changes, interpolations, additions or eliminations of any kind shall be made in the text of the said adaptation or version without the consent in writing of the Author.

Explicit playwright-centric artistic control clauses arise in only 22 percent of the population of contracts examined.[98] That is, playwrights were only able to negotiate a strong artistic control clause in about one in every four or five deals. And there is another noticeable feature of the "pro-author" contracts. Many of the writers who signed a pro-author contract had a track record of writing at least one successful production before signing their pro-author contract.[99]

94 Harry [Henry?] Blossom with Marc Klaw and Abraham Erlanger, September, 1911, Contract Collection, Group III, no. 63, *The Shubert Archive.* Clause VIII (unsigned).

95 Of course, as discussed, by 1909, the work-for-hire doctrine was enshrined in federal copyright doctrine and the employer had this greater control over the work.

96 Channing Pollock with Marc Klaw and Abraham Erlanger and Joseph Brooks, June 1909, Contract Collection, Group III, no. 44, *The Shubert Archive.* Clause 1.

97 Henry Blossom with Lee Shubert and A. H. Woods, November 1912, Contract Collection, Group II, no. 393A, *The Shubert Archive.* Clause XI. The Shuberts would cross out clauses in other instances to gain greater artistic control over the work. For example, the Shuberts contracted Harry Smith, author of a play *Ladies Change,* which originally provided clauses that required cast and director to be "satisfactory" to Smith. The cast clause was crossed out and replaced by the provision "It is understood that the cast and stage manager shall be mutually agreed upon" (clause 2f) and the director clause is simply crossed out 2(g). *See* Harry Smith with Shubert Theatrical, October 20, 1916, Contract Collection, Group II, no. 340D, *The Shubert Archive.* (Clause 2(f)(g)).

98 This is 22 percent of the entire population including the film contracts and about 26–27 percent of the contracts out of the four contract categories (silent, pro-writer, balanced, and pro-producer).

99 One hundred performances, anecdotally, is a crude financial break-even point for productions. Of these selected pro-author contracts, the authors involved had previous success in terms of breaking this 100-production minimum: *Milestones* (Arnold Bennett, Edward Knoblock: previous show had 184 productions); *The Thunderbolt* (Arthur Pinero: previous show had 127 productions); *Under Pressure* (Sydney Rosenfeld: previous show had 596 productions); *The Strange Woman* (William Hurlbut: previous show had 231 productions); *Moloch* (Beulah Marie: previous show had 216 productions); *Untitled Show* (Charles and Manuel Klein: previous show had 627 productions); *A Marriage of Reason* (Hartley Manners: previous show had 126 productions); *Her Own Money*

## V. REVISIONS IN THE REHEARSAL ROOM AND CODIFYING INTEGRITY

A contract may have specified a particular kind of artistic control, but changes to the script itself is another possible indication of how far a work diverted from the writer's original script as it moved from the page to the rehearsal room. Production scripts in the collection with balanced, pro-writer, pro-producer clauses, or where the contract is silent on artistic control, appear to undergo considerable revisions – particularly in musicals rather than straight plays. For example, Fanny Cannon and Georgia Earle, authors of the 1915 play *Mark of a Beast*, had their Shubert-produced script significantly altered. The dramatists' contract did not include an artistic authority clause.[100] The scripts of more established writers also underwent significant script editing. The Shubert Organization agreed to produce the J. Hartley Manners' musical comedy *The Girl and the Wizard* (workshopped as *The Magician*) in 1909.[101] The script in the archive includes major additions and omissions to the point where the revised work is far removed from the original composition other than the outline of the plot.[102]

Unsurprisingly, scripts attached to contracts with pro-producer artistic control clauses appear to be subject to many alterations, additions, and omissions. For example, there are significant omissions and additions to the script of *Apartment 12 K* by Lawrence Rising, produced by the Shuberts.[103] There are also examples of works that were significantly altered during the rehearsal process where the author had negotiated a pro-writer artistic control clause. *The Ringmaster* by Olive Porter, examined above, underwent many changes – page after page the work is doctored including new material and additions.[104]

Scripts attached to contracts with balanced clauses also provide an insight into how producers may have asserted authority over the dramatic composition. Thus, the boundaries of what constituted reasonable and necessary changes were possibly renegotiated in the rehearsal room. Kate Douglas Wiggin and Charlotte Thompson's dramatic adaptation of *Rebecca of Sunnybrook Farm* included a clause that required written consent by

(Mark Swan: previous show had 156 productions); *The Blue Mouse* (Clyde Fitch: previous show had 259 productions); *Marcelle* (Frank Pixley: previous show had 505 productions); *The Gay White Way* (Clarence Harvey, Sydney Rosenfeld (book and lyrics): previous show had 596 productions). The data was compiled from the Internet Broadway Database: www.ibdb.com/.

100 *See The Mark of the Beast*, 1915, Script Collection, 1713, *The Shubert Archive.*

101 *See The Magician (The Girl and the Wizard)*, 1909, Script Collection, 1801, *The Shubert Archive. The Girl and the Wizard* ran on Broadway from September 27, 1909 to January 1910 (music by Julian Edward, book by J. Hartley Manners and lyrics by Robert B. Smith, Edward Madden): *see* IBDB: www.ibdb.com/broadway-show/the-girl-and-the-wizard-3888. The script has the title typed *The Magician* which is crossed out and replaced in handwriting with "The Girl and the Wizard." Author is acknowledged as J. Hartley Manners.

102 *See The Magician*, 1909, Script Collection, 1801, *The Shubert Archive.* (Possibly script copy of actor Sam Bernard – written on the cover).

103 *See, for example*, Agreement: Lawrence Rising with Shubert Theatrical, June 6, 1914, Contract Collection, Group I, no. 73, *The Shubert Archive* (for *Apartment 12K*) and the script: *Apartment 12K*, 1914, Script Collection, 732, *The Shubert Archive; The Round Up*, 1907, Script Collection, SB 120, *The Shubert Archive.*

104 *The Ringmaster*, 1909, Script Collection, SB 2060, *The Shubert Archive.*

the authors to make any changes to the script. The authors were, however, also under an obligation to make "reasonable, proper and necessary changes or modifications" to the work when Klaw and Erlanger suggested such changes were necessary. Klaw and Erlanger had an ongoing interest in developing the play for motion picture adaptation.[105] The rehearsal script for the dramatic adaptation was subject to major omissions, additions, and alterations. Other scripts attached to contracts with balanced clauses deemed appropriate for motion picture adaptation also underwent major changes including Victor Herbert's musical *Trilby*, written in 1910.[106]

Caution, however, is needed in drawing definitive conclusions about the relationship between script changes and contractual artistic control. First, many of these scripts examined were prompt scripts and so the major changes to the script could simply be a product of the stage management process. Nor is there any way to confirm in all instances that writers disagreed with the changes in the scripts. Indeed, dramatists may have agreed to many of these alterations because they improved the work – a natural part of the process as the work moves from page to the stage – and also improved its commercial viability.[107]

There appears to be a correlation between scripts with major revisions and pro-producer artistic clauses, however. There are also examples where there are substantial changes to scripts when the contract is more balanced, the agreement is silent on artistic control, and where the clause in a contract favors playwright artistic control. Thus, although I have only been able to reconcile a few scripts with contracts,[108] a notable feature of these scripts is that major changes occur across all four types of

105 *Rebecca of Sunnybrook Farm*, 1909, Script Collection, SB 123, *The Shubert Archive*.

106 *Trilby*, 1910, Script Collection, SB 98, *The Shubert Archive*.

107 Authors including Bronson Howard had emphasized the importance of producing "satisfactory" drama that was "more acceptable" for a broader audience. *See* Poggi, *Theatre in America*, 258 (*see also* 257–260); Bronson Howard, *The Autobiography of a Play* (New York: Dramatic Museum of Columbia University, 1914), 26–27. And Howard held this view as well as being an advocate for writers.

108 In this note, I summarize records where I have been able to find a script that matches with a contract. I have identified whether the contract was either author-centric, producer-centric, balanced or silent on the issue of artistic control in each instance and whether the script had undergone changes. In some instances, there just was not enough information to determine whether there were changes and therefore to err on the side of the caution in these cases I have used the annotation "can't tell." *The Round Up*, 1906, Script Collection, SB 120, *The Shubert Archive* (significant changes/producer-centric); *The Trail of the Lonesome Pine*, 1915, Script Collection, SB 120, *The Shubert Archive* (minor changes/silent); *Trilby*, 1910, Script Collection, SB 98, *The Shubert Archive* (major changes/balanced control); *The Whip*, 1916, Script Collection, 2137(2), *The Shubert Archive* (major changes/producer-centric); *The Milestones*, 1912, Script Collection, 1232, *The Shubert Archive* (just blocking/author-centric); *Apartment 12K*, 1914, Script Collection, 732(1), *The Shubert Archive* (major changes/producer centric); *The Girl in Waiting*, 1906, Script Collection, 359, *The Shubert Archive* (no changes/author-centric); *The Secret Orchard*, 1905, Script Collection, 2004, *The Shubert Archive* (no changes/silent); *The Revellers*, 1909, Script Collection, 2057, *The Shubert Archive* (can't tell, no changes/producer-centric); *The Ringmaster*, 1909, Script Collection, 2060, *The Shubert Archive* (major changes/author-centric); *The Battle Cry*, 1914, Script Collection, 1530, *The Shubert Archive* (no changes/silent); *The Cave Lady*, 1916, Script Collection, 1688, *The Shubert Archive* (can't tell/producer-centric); *The Wolf*, 1908, Script Collection, 1810, *The Shubert Archive* (no changes/balanced); *The Land of the Free*, 1915, Script Collection, 1707, *The Shubert Archive* (no changes/silent); *The Mark*

contractual arrangements. Amendments to all the contract variations imply that – no matter what type of agreement – the producers wanted a degree of control over the shape of the work when it reached the rehearsal room.

This environment was obviously, and understandably, not a writer-driven process alone. Negotiations between dramatists and other collaborators were fluid.[109] Artistic control over script modification was continually evolving from contract to contract. Modifications in artistic control seem to have intensified as the relationship shifted from the contractual page to the rehearsal room. Indeed, perhaps the negotiating space was just too fluid for an alternative uniform industry code. Ongoing negotiations increased the possibility of opportunistic exploitation, but also allowed stakeholders to adapt to the unique circumstances of each relationship.

And the assertion that the managers did not consider advancing work of artistic quality – particularly if a work of artistic quality had the potential to translate into commercial success – deserves closer scrutiny. The producers were willing to reward writers of more ambitious works, on occasions, with considerable artistic control at both early and later stages of their careers. Producers relinquished control if there was something in it for them.[110] The Shuberts and Syndicate, based on this small

*of the Beast*, 1915, Script Collection, 1713, *The Shubert Archive* (changes/silent); *Just Like a Girl (The Love of Mike)*, 1915, Script Collection, 1386, *The Shubert Archive* (no changes/balanced); *Deborah*, 1913, Script Collection, SB 209, *The Shubert Archive* (no changes, can't tell/producer centric); *The Family*, 1910, Script Collection, SB 221, *The Shubert Archive* (no changes/author-centric); *The Piper of Burgundy*, 1904, Script Collection, 1292, *The Shubert Archive* (can't tell/producer-centric); *The Inner Man*, 1917, Script Collection, 1245, *The Shubert Archive* (can't tell/balanced); *The Marriage of Reason*, 1905, Script Collection, SB 122, *The Shubert Archive* (no changes/author-centric); *Rebecca of Sunnybrook Farm*, 1909, Script Collection, SB 123, *The Shubert Archive* (major changes/balanced); *The Golden Age*, 1919, Script Collection, SB 190, *The Shubert Archive* (can't tell/producer-centric); *The Woman Though Gavest Me*, 1914, Script Collection, 1983, *The Shubert Arche* (no changes/producer centric); *The Money Makers*, 1914, Script Collection, SB 207, *The Shubert Archive* (can't tell/producer-centric); *The Widow's Might*, 1908, Script Collection, 2082, *The Shubert Archive* (can't tell/producer-centric).

109 It must be noted this was a period where the theatrical director was still a relatively new collaborator in the creative process. The actor-manager often fulfilled a directorial role. Lew Fields had a long association with the Shuberts. In addition to his responsibilities as an actor, producer, and theatre manager, he also directed many Shubert productions. On Fields, *see* Armond Fields, *From the Bowery to Broadway: Lew Fields and the Roots of American Popular Theatre* (New York; Oxford: Oxford University Press, 1993).

110 And the "something in it for them" was that they would usually commit to someone who had previous success in terms of a longer running production. George Bernard Shaw has some of the strongest pro-playwright contracts in the Shubert/Syndicate collection. For example, Shaw's 1906 contract with Klaw and Erlanger for *Caesar and Cleopatra* includes strong artistic control and casting clauses. Further, the contract provides in clause four: "therewith pay to [Shaw] TEN PER CENTUM (10%) of gross receipts." This amount was a significant royalty rate for the period: M Klaw with George Bernard Shaw, July 1906, Contract Collection, Group III, no. 19, *The Shubert Archive*. But in the population there are also multiple examples of writers at the start of their career (less than ten productions) including *Milestones* (Arnold Bennett, Edward Knoblock), *The Strange Woman* (William Hurlbut), *Moloch* (Beulah Marie), *A Marriage of Reason* (Hartley Manners), *Seventeen* (Hugh Stanislaus Stange, Stannard Mears), *Her Own Money* (Mark Swan), *The Family* (Robert Davis), *Lady Teazle* (John Bangs, Roderic Penfield), *Kiddie (A Man's World)* (Rachel Crothers), *The Ringmaster* (Olive Porter). The first point to note is that three or four authors have been able to negotiate a robust artistic control contract on their first Broadway outing

population, appear to have been willing to give greater artistic control to writers who had written a previous work that ran for more than, or close to, 150 performances.

One, therefore, has to be careful in assuming that commercialism and artistic ambition were incompatible in the large commercial businesses of this period – a claim and criticism often made against the Syndicate and the Shuberts. Indeed, the dramaturgical notes of the Shuberts during the period between 1906 and 1909 suggest that the organization was looking for, and struggling to find, work of artistic quality to produce.[111] When they did find a work of some potential, the criticism was often thoughtful and reflective, and there was a keen interest in developing new work.[112] The theatrical impresarios wanted to control the work as it transformed from the page to stage, but their contractual practices suggest they were not overtly belligerent in achieving this goal. It was possible to influence the production process

(*The Family, The Ringmaster, Seventeen, Lady Teazle*). Mapping the history of these authors reveals different findings. For example, Olive Porter's script, author of *The Ringmaster,* appears to have undergone numerous revisions. In other instances, it appears that the managers were a good judge of future talent. Roderic Penfield, the coauthor of *Lady Teazle*, wrote the book and lyrics for the Shuberts' production of the *White Hen* in 1907 which ran for a respectable ninety-four performances. Hugh Stange, co-author of *Seventeen,* would write for Broadway for the next twenty years, although without a prominent hit production. It is notable, however, that in most instances where an emerging writer could negotiate a robust artistic control clause outside of the "first timers," the writer had at least one previous production that was not just successful, but a hit. Basing this on collection from Internet Broadway Database (IBDB) at www.ibdb.com.

111 The reviews, mostly written by George Broadhurst, were uncompromising in their criticism. *See, for example*: Review of Witches' Prophecy, Play Criticism Collection: 1906–1909 Collection, "W," *The Shubert Archive,* described simply as "Impossible"; criticism Review of General Grant, Play Criticism Collection: 1906–1909 Collection, "G," *The Shubert Archive,* reviewed as "Oh horror!" Many scripts, however, showed some potential and Broadhurst would keep them on "hold" – an insidious policy where the producers held onto scripts indefinitely so other producers could not get access to the script, but the works would often never be produced. *See, for example*, scripts placed on hold including Review of The Culprit, April 27, 1909, Play Criticism Collection: 1906–1909 Collection, "C," *The Shubert Archive*; Review of Tam Lin, May 7, 1909, Play Criticism Collection: 1906–1909 Collection, "L," *The Shubert Archive;* Review of Twenty Two, June 8, 1909, Play Criticism Collection: 1906–1909 Collection, "T," *The Shubert Archive* (concluding "might interest the New Theatre"); Review of Towers of Silence, May 1909, Play Criticism Collection: 1906–1909 Collection, "T," *The Shubert Archive;* Review of Vespers, April 1, 1909, Play Criticism Collection: 1906–1909 Collection, "V," *The Shubert Archive;* Review of The Brotherhood of Husbands, April 27, 1909, Play Criticism Collection: 1906–1909 Collection, "B," *The Shubert Archive.* Other scripts received extensive review: *see* Review of Hate and Love, Play Criticism Collection: 1906–1909 Collection, "H," *The Shubert Archive:* (reviewer Mathew Goldman wrote "Would advise close consideration of this manuscript"); Review of The End of Eustace Ede, September 1910, Play Criticism Collection: 1906–1909 Collection, "E," *The Shubert Archive:* ("recommended it for consideration" after detailed three-page review); Review of The Sensationalist, July 7, 1909, Play Criticism Collection: 1906–1909 Collection, "S," *The Shubert Archive* (despite the extensive review, Broadhurst concluded: "there is nothing in this piece to recommend it for consideration.") There are also examples of the Shuberts looking to support more adventurous work. For example, Broadhurst wrote of a comedy Unfaithful by Robert Bracco (adapted by Dirce St Cyr) that "The presentation of such a play would be something of an experiment, but I think it would be well worth the trial." Review of Unfaithful, no date, Play Criticism Collection: 1906–1909 Collection, "U–V," *The Shubert Archive.*

112 The Shuberts were involved in one of Broadway's first noncommercial companies to develop new work, the short-lived New Theatre.

through ongoing incrementalism that demanded reasonable compromises to secure longer-term control over the shape of the final realized production.

—

By the second decade of the twentieth century, the playwrights did not think this flexible contractual environment was working, however. There was a clear desire within the ranks of the playwrights to codify authority over the nonpecuniary artistic dimensions of the work they created. And the dramatists began to draw on the rhetoric of preserving the integrity of their work to justify protection.

The dramatists developed a flurry of industry codes between 1915 and 1920 which had limited to no influence on the producers. The dramatic subcommittee of the Authors' League – the forerunner to the Dramatists Guild – made an initial attempt to contract with managers under a standardized agreement in November 1915.[113] But this contract was only a guideline for stakeholders rather than a more formal uniform minimum basic agreement.[114]

Clause five of the 1915 contract provided that a manager agrees to announce the dramatist as a sole author. Further, the manager would make no changes "of any nature whatsoever" without having secured "the written consent to such changes of the AUTHOR."[115] The language was similar to the strongest pro-writer contracts in the Shubert and Syndicate collections and also embodied moral-rights rhetoric, punctuated with phrases like "integrity."[116] Clause eleven of the 1915 agreement provided that any rights will revert to the author when the manager violates the contract. Creation was not to be assigned away into the ether. Dramatists would assert control as the negotiation moved into lucrative new subsidiary forms of business, including film, through a licensing structure.

The slightly modified 1917 agreement was also critical in the evolution of a collective author-based artistic control framework. The 1917 agreement provided that the manager would "announce the name of the Author as the sole Author of said play"[117] on all printed material, programs, and related advertising material. The manager was also supposed to agree to "make no changes, alterations, or additions in

113 They published a dramatic contract in *The Authors' League Bulletin* "1915 Dramatic Contract," *The Authors' League Bulletin* (November 1915): 7–12. For a study of these industry agreements before the first basic agreement of 1926 *see also* Thomas Walsh, *Playwrights and Power: The Making of the Dramatists Guild* (Hanover, NH: Smith and Kraus, 2016), Ch 3. But also, still the most authoritative source, particularly on the 1920 Agreement, *see* Middleton, *These Things Are Mine*, 304–07.

114 This agreement was slightly modified in 1917 eliminating any mention of stock and motion picture rights, two of the most lucrative streams of income. *See* "1917 Dramatic Form Contract," *The Authors' League Bulletin* (August 1917): 3.

115 "1915 Dramatic Contract, Clause 5," *The Authors' League Bulletin* (November 1915): 8.

116 "1915 Dramatic Contract, Commentary," *The Authors' League Bulletin* (November 1915): 11 (annotations to Clause 5) – "members cannot be too emphatically urged to safeguard the identity and integrity of their compositions in every possible way."

117 "1917 Dramatic Contract Clause 3b," *The Authors' League Bulletin* (August 1917): 6.

or to the text of said play without the written approval of the Author," and to produce the work "only with a cast and stage director approved by the Author."[118]

As Thomas Walsh observes, the 1917 guide – like the 1915 agreement – was only that, and ultimately had a limited influence on contracting practices between dramatists and producers.[119] When the Dramatists Guild formed in 1919, in the wake of the Actors' Equity strike that pitted the producers against the actors, the writers sought to draft a new standard contract with the Producing Managers' Association (PMA).[120] Like its predecessors, the agreement was voluntary and

118 "1917 Dramatic Contract Clause 3d," *The Authors' League Bulletin* (August 1917): 6.

119 *See* Walsh, *Playwrights and Power*, 83–94. Walsh here seems to be referring to George Middleton, *These Things Are Mine*, 304–306.

120 *See* Middleton, *The Dramatists Guild: What It Is and Does*, 11; *see also* Walsh, *Playwrights and Power*, 92–95. Lee Shubert was the Vice President of the PMA. A copy of the revised 1920 contract has been difficult to locate and its terms are best pieced together through George Middleton's commentary (*These Things Are Mine* at 304–306) and the commentary from *The Authors' League Bulletin*, particularly in the years 1919–1920, which I document in this note. The negotiating process was protracted and the end result was an inconsequential organizational mess highlighting the early tensions with respect to the playwrights' status as independent contractors wanting to organize as a group. In June of 1919, Howard Kyle wrote to Editor-in-Chief Burges Johnson about a framework for establishing a "Standard Contract" although two agreements had been attempted before. The letter considers the development of a standard agreement in the context of "an alliance or coalition, indeed, of organized dramatic authors." Kyle sets out minimum royalty standards: "the manager assumes the responsibility of play production, binding himself to pay the author from 5% to 10% of all gross receipts of performances" and in addition "it is the practice" to pay the dramatist "a substantial sum of money designated as 'advanced royalties'." Kyle describes the author as a "creative proprietor who leases his product to a capitalist . . . on terms that *insure* him compensation for time and labor." Here, Kyle distinguishes the work of the author from that of the "employee" actor in their respective relationship to the manager which he concludes are "decidedly different." Kyle, who was consulted by the League on a way forward, suggests to the dramatists to first organize a subcommittee, consult with stakeholders – including managers and publishers – and then draft a standard contract. *See* Howard Kyle to Burges Johnson, "How to Establish a Standard Contract," *The Authors' League Bulletin* (June 1919): 12–13. By the next issue, the *Bulletin* editorial was warning dramatists to "STOP, LOOK, AND LISTEN!" – advocating for a cautious approach and to look out for exploitative deals with the motion picture industry. A primary concern, as outlined, identified how theatrical managers were being cut out of the negotiating process over stage rights (coordinated by theatrical managers). *See* "Of Interest to Playwrights," *The Authors' League Bulletin* 7, no. 4 (July 1919): 5–6. By the September 1919 issue, the *Bulletin* was reporting how Channing Pollock and Leroy Scott were leading the charge to formalize the Dramatists' Committee, "the biggest and most powerful body of playwrights ever banded together in America." The group finally came to a tentative (and unenforceable) agreement with the Producing Mangers' Association on September 6. The committee, which was the precursor to the Dramatists Guild chaired by Channing Pollock, formed three subcommittees on contracts for drama, musical plays, and motion pictures: *see* Channing Pollock, "The Dramatists Dawn Comes up Like Thunder," *The Authors' League Bulletin* 7, no. 6 (September 1919): 3–5. But the standard contract negotiations after this point stalled. In June 1920, Pollock provided an update on the glacial speed of drafting the standard contract, which Pollock attributed to lawyer delays, "the negligence of the Producing Managers' Association" and his own professional responsibilities as a playwright taking precedent. What is striking, however, is that no specific details about the contract to this point were provided. *See* Channing Pollock, "The Dramatic Contract," *The Authors' League Bulletin* (June 1920): 10–11. By November 1920, no copy of the new standard contract had appeared in the *Bulletin*, but the editors reported an agreement had finally been reached between the "Dramatists Guild of the Authors' League of America" and the PMA on the terms – "a most important event in the League's history." We see here one of the first uses of the term "a standard minimum contract," but still no specific details of the contract. *See* "Shop Talk," *The Authors' League Bulletin* 8, no. 8 (November, 1920):

unenforceable. It was treated with contempt by the PMA.[121] Lee Shubert's response to these fragile voluntary agreements was to state that "managers would treat with authors individually, and in no other way, and that the part of the good business man was to get the best and most he could."[122] Lee later claimed that

> The Producer is more important in the theatre than anyone else, including the author. I don't care how many plays a playwright writes, who could see them if there wasn't a producer? Who would know about a playwright unless a Producer invested his capital in it? That is why I say the Producer should *share* the copyright with the author.[123]

Unlike the methodical contracting strategy the Shuberts had established in everyday negotiations, Lee's language now turned more combative in the face of collective resistance. The Shuberts went as far as telling Channing Pollock and the dramatists in 1919 if they intended to organize as a group and refused to deal with the brothers on a contract-by-contract basis "they [the Shuberts] would write their own plays!"[124]

So protecting the integrity of the work was beginning to play a larger role in narratives of dramatist authority over theatrical creation in the first decades of the twentieth century. But the producers continued to resist as the playwrights tried to move toward a stronger standard agreement in the mid-1920s. And producer resistance focused on a new legal strategy outside the realm of copyright law altogether: testing whether the independent-contracting dramatists could organize as a group without falling foul of competition laws.

1–2. One of the only other statements on the new standard contract can be found in George Middleton's *These Thing are Mine*, 306. In the midst, and immediate aftermath, of the hostile dispute between Actors' Equity and the PMA, the dramatists again threatened to join the American Federation of Labor, which Middleton describes as "only a bluff," a negotiating tactic used throughout the twentieth century, which "sent such shivers down certain spines that creeping paralysis alone would then have prevented the new standard contract between the League and the M.P.A." *See also* "Dramatists Will Not Unionize," *New York Dramatic Mirror*, October 16, 1920, 680. But Middleton also provides further details about the significant limitations of the new agreement which had an extended gestation period (306–307): "In spite of some modern improvements, the agreement had two fatal defects: *its use was not mandatory, and its terms were not enforceable.* Neither individual managers nor authors were required to become members of their respective organizations, and nobody could be penalized for not using it – nothing except hisses could prevent its protective clauses from being red-inked. Some firms, in fact, soon made the contract a gory mess. Truth was, the Guild patted itself on the back to keep from admitting this. It still floated in the lofty realm or moral suasion, while managers and actors had already realistically dug in for self-leverage on the more solid ground of organized power."

121 *See* Middleton, *These Things Are Mine*, 305–306. Middleton refers to the producers here as the MPA (Managers' Protective Association) rather than the PMA.

122 *See* Walsh, *Playwrights and Power*, 83 (citing "The Dramatists Guild and the 'Equity Shop,'" *The Authors' League Bulletin* 5, no. 5 (August 1917): 3).

123 Jerry Stagg, *The Brothers Shubert* (New York: Random House, 1968), 249. Stagg writes that Lee made this statement "in arguments with the organizers of the Dramatists Guild."

124 *See* Channing Pollock, *Harvest of My Years* (New York: The Bobbs Merrill Company, 1949), 257. Pollock was, for a period, banned from Shubert playhouses despite working for the brothers for many years in a publicity role.

**PART II**

# The Organizational Response

In the second half of the nineteenth and early-twentieth centuries, theatrical stakeholders controlling the movement of theatrical works between authors and audiences included transnational and local opportunistic publishers and mediating brokerage agencies. Managers also emerged that booked tours across the country in regional circuits, controlled physical property spaces, and represented attractions. These stakeholders possessed the resources, administrative structures, and networks of influence to transform the intangible right into the final material production on stage. It was an industry that prioritized the preservation of manuscripts in an unpublished form and the trading in performance rights attached to these scripts. The evolving legal framework complemented the industry structure, providing ample space for parties to negotiate the terms of production. In case-by-case negotiations, mediating stakeholders shaped the terms of engagement through ongoing negotiations rather than acts of overt belligerence.

In 1919, playwrights happened upon a strategy of collective organization – in response to these mediating structures – known as the Dramatists Guild. The Dramatists Guild evolved out of a forty-year effort to organize the writers as a functional group.[1] In 1878, Steele MacKaye, before his disastrous contract with the Mallory brothers, remarked that "[t]he time has come for the organization and founding of a society of American dramatists somewhat on the plan of the well-known society in Paris."[2] MacKaye soon after joined forces with lyricist Clay Greene to establish the unremarkable American Dramatic Authors' Society. In 1891, Bronson Howard formed what George Middleton described as the "first effective group," eventually known as the Society of American Dramatists and Composers.[3] Under Howard's leadership, and Harrison Fiske's intense advocacy in the *Dramatic Mirror*, the group successfully lobbied Congress to amend federal copyright law in 1897 in the wake of expansive piracy. The new laws included criminal penalties for

[1] *See* George Middleton, *These Things Are Mine: The Autobiography of a Journeyman Playwright* (New York: The Macmillan Company, 1947), 304–309.

[2] Middleton, *These Things Are Mine*, 304 (Middleton citing MacKaye).

[3] Middleton, *These Things Are Mine*, 304.

copyright infringement.[4] By 1909, the group was rallying against the "clever, astute, experienced men ... in combination" to "acquire a power for drama and its authors."[5] In 1915 a small group of the Authors' League of America became the "dramatic subcommittee." This group drafted the first impotent agreements of 1915, 1917, and 1919/20 as discussed in the previous chapter.

But in 1919, the dramatists chose to reorganize again in the wake of the scenic artists establishing their own union in 1918 (United Scenic Artists) and the fierce Actors' Equity strike between the actors and the Producing Managers' Association in 1919. After a suggestion from Channing Pollock, the Authors' League allowed the dramatists to form an "autonomous committee," the birth of the Dramatists Guild. Owen Davis became the Guild's first President after the revision of a new constitution.[6] Flexing its independent-contracting muscles from the outset, the Guild condemned the union practices of the actors, declaring "no matter how great its power may become, the Guild will never desire the closed shop."[7]

Dramatists, therefore, responded to the prevailing organizational mediating structures in the industry by initially dealing directly with the mediators and then seeking to bargain as a collective. They first formed groups that resembled clubs or societies, but gradually moved toward an association structure, initially under the auspices of the Authors' League.

The introduction of the Dramatists Guild's Minimum Basic Agreement in 1926 represented a moment of consequence for how dramatists intended to organize their relationships with stakeholders in the theatrical economy. As noted, commentators often identify several unfair contractual deals between theatrical producers and the film industry as the specific trigger for the advocacy that led to the Basic Agreement of 1926.[8] The new Agreement went far beyond addressing the issue of film rights, however. Not only did the Agreement outline more transparent processes for the sale of film rights, but it also included provisions about artistic control, subsidiary rights, and minimum standards. George Middleton, author and architect of the Minimum

4 29 Stat. 481 (1897). *See* Zvi Rosen, "The Twilight of the Opera Pirates: A Prehistory of the Right of Public Performance for Musical Compositions," *Cardozo Arts & Entertainment Law Journal* 24 (2007): 1157.

5 *See* Thomas Walsh, *Playwrights and Power: The Making of the Dramatists Guild* (Hanover, NH: Smith and Kraus, 2016), 60–61 citing the "'Plan and Scope for Reorganization of the Dramatists Club,' Dramatists Club, 1909."

6 Middleton, *These Things Are Mine*, 306.

7 Middleton, *These Things Are Mine*, 307. *See, more generally*, George Middleton and Thomas Walsh have written treatments on the history of the Dramatists Guild, with coverage of the negotiations leading up to the adoption of the Minimum Basic Agreement on April 14. 1926. *See* Walsh, *Playwrights and Power*, Chs. 3–4; Middleton, *These Things Are Mine*, 298–327.

8 *See Shubert Theatre Corporation* v. *Arthur Richman, President of the Dramatists Guild*, May 6, 1927, New York Supreme Court, Record # 16847, Box 008047634, Hall of Records, New York Courts, "Memorandum of the Defendant in Opposition," at 1–2; Middleton, *These Things Are Mine*, 313–314; Arthur G. Hays, *City Lawyer* (New York: Simon and Schuster, 1942), 128–129; Walsh, *Playwrights and Power*, 97–99; Alfred L. Bernheim, *The Business of the Theatre* (New York: Actor's Equity Assoc., 1932), 89–91.

Basic Agreement, wrote in *These Things Are Mine*[9] about the difference between a prior industry of contractual chaos and the new regime which protected all authors, established or emerging, with a uniform arrangement.[10] Leading playwright lawyer Arthur Hays, who played a major role in drafting the Basic Agreement, stated in 1942 that "year after year" the Guild has grown and prospered. Hays concluded, "It [the Dramatists Guild] is perhaps more important to its members than a Bar Association to lawyers. No longer is the dramatist subject to chaotic conditions and the whimsy of producers and movie magnates."[11] Playwright Doug Wright, the winner of the Pulitzer Prize for Drama in 2004 for *I Am My Own Wife*, writes of the grueling negotiations before the signing of the Basic Agreement, where after five months "the writers emerge, victorious."[12] Arthur Train, a lawyer engaged in the volatile entertainment union movement of the early -twentieth century, described the Basic Agreement as "guaranteeing from Broadway only slightly less than the Barons exacted from King John at Runnymede."[13] The Agreement also continued to advance the narrative, sustained throughout the first half of the twentieth century, that any unauthorized alteration of the work was an assault on the playwright's integrity. Thus, language resembling moral rights, which did not exist in federal statutory copyright law, was used as a rhetorical tool to justify the author's personal connection to their creation and artistic control over that creation.[14]

Contemporary scholars and accounts have mostly praised the Basic Agreement for its enduring stability. Thomas Walsh writes of the evolution of copyright from "a printer/publisher-centered Act to an author/writer-centered Act."[15] Walsh suggests that the authority of the dramatist "is only gaining strength,"[16] and that "[t]he Dramatists Guild contract when used today is considered by many to be the

9 *See* Middleton, *These Things Are Mine*.

10 *See also* George Middleton, "The Dramatists Guild: What It Is and Does ... How It Happened and Why ...," Dramatists Guild Containers, George Middleton Papers, Manuscript Division, Library of Congress, Washington, D.C [hereafter George Middleton Papers].

11 *See* Hays, *City Lawyer*, 136–137.

12 *See* Doug Wright, "Playwrights and Copyright," *Columbia Journal of Law & the Arts* 38, no. 3 (2015): 302.

13 *See* Arthur Train, *My Day in Court* (New York: Charles Scribner's Sons, 1939), 313. *See also* William Klein II who writes in 1953 that "Suffice, that the Dramatists' Guild has now come of age." William Klein II, "Protective Societies for Authors and Creators," in *1953 Copyright Problems Analyzed*, ed. Theodore R. Kupferman (New York: Commerce Clearing House, 1953, Vol. 2), 62.

14 *See, for example*, George Middleton who throughout his various editions of "The Dramatists Guild What it is and does ... How it happened and Why ..." (1939, 1943, 1947, 1959, and 1966 – which circulated to all members) continued to retell this narrative of the relationship between artistic control and the author's integrity emanating from the first 1926 Agreement. In the 1959 edition, for example, Middleton writes one of the six "main objectives" on the 1926 Agreement was the "Preserved integrity of scripts. No changes without Author's consent." *See* George Middleton, *The Dramatists Guild What It Is and Does ... How It Happened and Why* (New York: The Dramatists Guild of the Authors' League of America, 1959 ed.), 11.

15 Walsh, *Playwrights and Power*, 16.

16 Walsh, *Playwrights and Power*, 16.

strongest writers' contract in America."[17] For Walsh, "American theatre as a dramatist-dominated, text-based theatre after the 1926 minimum basic agreement is difficult to challenge."[18] John Weidman, former President of the Dramatists Guild, claims that "as long as anyone can remember, the community of artists and businessmen who make theater have shared a common set of assumptions about how a play or a musical makes its way from the page to the stage."[19] Jessica Litman – although acknowledging the "controversy, and litigation" that followed the adoption of the Minimum Agreement – notes that during the evolution of the Basic Agreement over the twentieth century "the essential terms remained the same."[20] Litman continues: "Playwrights keep ownership of their copyrights and creative control of stage productions of their scripts. Producers pay playwrights a minimum percentage of box office receipts. Producers and playwrights share subsequent earnings and split the receipts from sales of film rights."[21]

A general uniformity of views in the literature, therefore, emphasizes a moment of transformation in 1926, followed by a slow-burning expansion in the dramatists' influence throughout the twentieth century under a relatively stable industry-created framework. Part II, however, examines the immediate resistance to the Basic Agreement and the Dramatists Guild's association status. And with immediate resistance follows the emergence of areas of law beyond copyright – beyond the intellectual property rights that stakeholders possess or aspire to possess – that become central in shaping relationships between theatrical stakeholders in the twentieth century.

In 1927, one year after the introduction of the Minimum Basic Agreement, Austin Strong drew the picture below (Figure II.1) of playwright George Middleton.[22] The illustration shows Middleton – tall, broad-shouldered, and imposing in stature – as "OUR ST GEORGE," "Fighting The Shubert DRAGON." It is a reference to the author going into battle with the impresarios over the dramatists' right to organize as an association and contract under a uniform Minimum Basic Agreement. For the Shuberts – who were used to arranging their affairs through flexible contract-by-contract arrangements – the new Basic Agreement represented a threat that could cripple any artistic and economic authority they had consolidated over the previous three decades. The brothers, however, as adaptable as ever, perhaps knew influence

17 Walsh, *Playwrights and Power*, 16.

18 Walsh, *Playwrights and Power*, 19.

19 John Weidman, "Protecting the American Playwright: The Seventh Annual Media and Society Lecture," *Brooklyn Law Review* 72 (2007): 640. The assumption of playwright authority over copyright, Weidman claims, has only come under threat from theatrical directors and Hollywood producers in the last two decades. The independent-contracting model deeply entrenched in the theatre and a producer-owned film model of copyright control come into direct conflict.

20 Jessica Litman, "The Invention of Common Law Play Right," *Berkeley Technology Law Journal* 25 (2010): 1421, 1420.

21 Litman, "Common Law Play Right," 1420–1421.

22 *See* Austin Strong, "Illustration of George Middleton: April 29, 1927," Austin Strong-Dramatist, Box 16, George Middleton Papers.

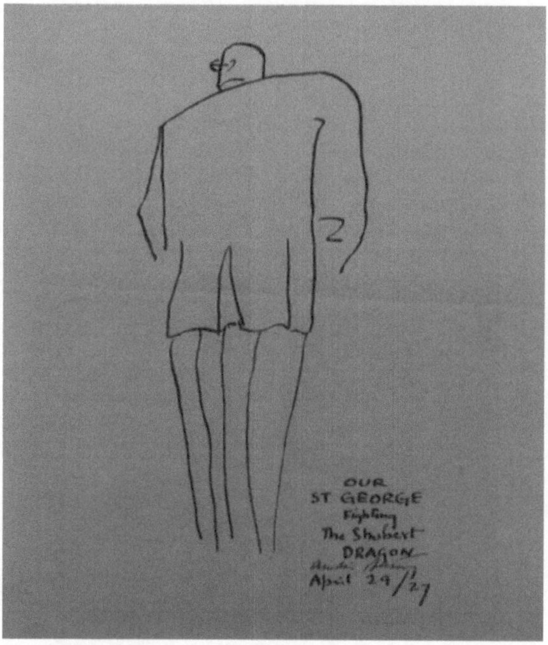


FIGURE II.1 Austin Strong's sketch of George Middleton

in the industry happened not only in the moment of reform but in response to reform. With crisis followed the opportunity to restructure responses around new organizational systems and new legal strategies.

The more illuminating feature of this picture is not the dominant image of Middleton – decisive, straight, and elongated lines, marching once more into the breach against those who would challenge playwright authority – but the note that Middleton scribbled on the back of the picture twenty-eight years later in 1955. Middleton writes, "In the reproduction of this in my autobiography, the word Shubert was omitted, for obvious reasons."[23] Thus, below in Figure II.2 is the reproduction in Middleton's book.[24]

The images reveal two understandings of authority that had become hallmarks of the ongoing negotiations in the American theatre by the mid-twentieth century. Resilient playwrights toiled and lobbied successfully for formal legal or industry-based reform, but lurking in the background was the constant fear of producer retribution. Authority was fragile.

[23] *See* Austin Strong, "Illustration of George Middleton: April 29, 1927," Austin Strong-Dramatist, Box 16, George Middleton Papers (handwritten note by George Middleton on the back of picture signed, GM June 1955).

[24] Middleton, *These Things Are Mine*, 323.

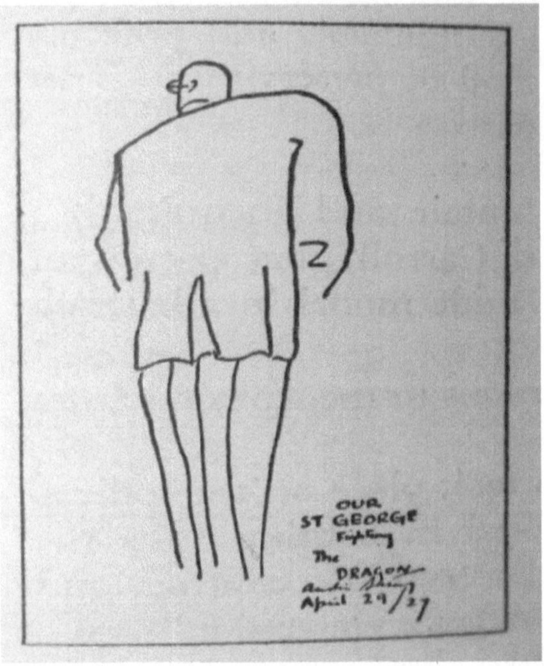


FIGURE II.2 Reproduction of Austin Strong's sketch of George Middleton in *These Things Are Mine*

The introduction of the Dramatists Guild's Minimum Basic Agreement in 1926 appeared to fill information gaps in dramatists' expertise – that had previously removed writers from the bargaining process – allowing them to negotiate better terms as a group. The Basic Agreement was the first uniform contract a majority of theatre producers and playwrights adhered to that established the legal architecture for production in the industry going forward. But as the Guild was an association, membership – and becoming a signatory to the Basic Agreement – was voluntary, not mandatory. Producers and writers still entered into private agreements with each other guided by the Guild's minimum standards.[25] And it was in this ambiguous space between private agreement and association that the managers saw an opportunity to undermine the writers through the lens of competition and labor law.

25 Dramatists Guild members and management signatories to the agreement have the approved contract certified by the Guild to assure "the revised contract doesn't have sub-standard terms that could negatively impact other DG members." *See* Dramatists Guild of America, "First Class and Broadway," www.dramatistsguild.com/broadway. So the Guild is removed from the initial negotiation only entering the process after an agreement has been made to assure, through certification, that minimum standards have been preserved. I am grateful for conversations with Ralph Sevush from the Dramatists Guild about this process.

# 6

# The Playwright Code

## I. THE FIRST AGREEMENT OF 1926

The major reforms to copyright law under the 1909 Act provided the appearance of an imposing author-centric legal landscape for American dramatists.[1] Among the protections, the 1909 Act separated the dramatic work into its own class,[2] dramatists had an exclusive right to "print, reprint, publish, copy, and vend" their copyrighted work,[3] and also the right to translate or convert it into a nondramatic work,[4] including novelization.[5] The 1909 Act also afforded reciprocal copyright for foreign authors[6] of the dramatic work.[7] Further, the 1909 Act provided copyright registration for unpublished plays.[8]

A *Report on Committee to the Association of Dramatists* written in 1925/26 also aimed to shape the writers' influence on a set of industry principles that complemented the extensive legislative protections.[9] These principles included artistic control over the title and content of the work, a more transparent and open competitive market for the bidding of motion picture rights, and greater control over subsidiary profits derived either directly or indirectly from the work of the playwright.[10] The Minimum Basic Agreement of April 1926 articulated the spirit of many of these

1 *See* Act of March 4, 1909, ch. 320, 35 Stat. 1075.

2 Under the class "Dramatic or dramatico-musical compositions." Act of March 4, 1909, ch. 320, 35 Stat. 1075 § 5(d).

3 Act of March 4, 1909, ch. 320, 35 Stat. 1075 § 1(a).

4 Act of March 4, 1909, ch. 320, 35 Stat. 1075 § 1(b).

5 *See* Act of March 4, 1909, ch. 320, 35 Stat. 1075 § 1(b).

6 Act of March 4, 1909, ch. 320, 35 Stat. 1075 § 8(b).

7 Authors could also dramatize a work *see* 35 Stat. 1075 (1909) § 1.

8 Act of March 4, 1909, ch. 320, 35 Stat. 1075 (1909) § 11. *See* Jessica Litman, "The Invention of Common Law Play Right," *Berkeley Technology Law Journal* 25 (2010): 1381, 1416–1417, 1383–1384. Still, even after these amendments many writers continued to not register their manuscripts, perhaps because of a fear that the work would be pirated. The author could still rely on the common law, or equity, for protection of their unpublished work against copying: Act of March 4, 1909, ch. 320, 35 Stat. 1075 § 2.

9 *See* "Report on Committee to the Association of Dramatists," Dramatists Guild Containers, George Middleton Papers, Manuscript Division, Library of Congress, Washington, DC [hereafter George Middleton Papers]. (The report is dated January 7, 1926.)

10 "Report on Committee to the Association of Dramatists," Dramatists Guild Containers, George Middleton Papers (Resolution IV).

revisions.[11] Negotiations for the new agreement, which is part of ongoing research, reveal the important role played by Joseph Bickerton, William Brady, Sam Harris, Lee Shubert, and Arthur Hammerstein for the producers. Arthur Richman, Owen Davis, Gene Buck, Otto Harbach, and George Middleton advocated on behalf of the dramatists. The committee respectfully debated the merits of each clause. Issues that consumed the group included the terms for film adaptation and small rights (such as radio rights), rights of foreign authors, and more generally the issue of whether the Dramatists Guild was creating an anticompetitive "closed shop."[12]

Indeed, whether the new agreement enforced a closed shop came up straight away in relation to the overarching first clause, "The Right to Contract."[13] William Brady, representing the managers – speaking to a much longer historical narrative about how mediators asserted expansive power over the production process – claimed that "[t]he author brings a script of a play which has no value until it is produced, and the manager puts his money and his experience against the author's script."[14] For Brady, limiting access to only those writers who were in good standing with the Guild – what was understood as the closed shop – "in any instance is un-American."[15]

The closed shop concept in the context of unions required conditions on both employer and employee: employers agreed to only hire members of the union and members of the union agreed to remain employed.[16] In contrast, American dramatists were a group of independent contractors forming together under the umbrella of a trade association, not a union. The language of open and closed-door policies was not new to the American theatre, however. The Shuberts had stressed an open-door policy with strategic success in the first decades of the twentieth century in their battle with the Theatrical Syndicate for supremacy over touring routes across the country. An open-door policy gave attractions and theatre managers the freedom to work outside the Shubert Organization without the threat of exclusion from Shubert-controlled theatres and attractions at a future date. In contrast, the Syndicate required attractions and venues to sign exclusivity deals: you perform in all our venues or none at

11 The Basic Agreement received wide publicity in the press. *See, for example*, "American Dramatists," *The Stage*, July 8, 1926, 14. By July of 1926 Lee Shubert was complaining about getting access to the American plays, as he was not a signatory to the agreement. Shubert, in turn, started to seek more content from Britain: *see* "American Dramatists: Their Basic Agreement," *The Stage*, July 15, 1926, 12.

12 *See* Joint meeting of Sub-Committee of the Producing Managers Association and the Dramatists Guild of the Authors' League of America Inc, held at Roosevelt Hotel, New York, with meeting starting on March 11, 1926 (at 4PM, after introductory session). At the time of writing, the minutes for the meeting are part of collection of the Dramatists Guild of America in the process of being recovered [hereafter PMA and DG Meeting]. My deepest gratitude to Ralph Sevush and Tina Fallon of the Dramatists Guild for access to this material.

13 PMA and DG Meeting, March 11, 1926, 5.

14 PMA and DG Meeting, March 11, 1926, 8.

15 PMA and DG Meeting, March 11, 1926, 8.

16 In the decades that followed, The Taft-Hartley Act of 1947, Pub.L. 80–101, 61 Stat. 136 prohibited a range of unfair labor practices including closed shops. *See* Chapters 7 and 8.

all.[17] In a market with two major competitors, the Shuberts could appeal to the importance and virtues of openness in their public relations agenda. In reality, however, one of the only other places that attractions and theatres could turn to was the Shuberts in a market dominated by two major stakeholders. Invoking an open-door policy was a shrewd form of promotion used to rapidly expand the Shubert business in its early years of operation.

During the committee meetings for the first Basic Agreement, the managers argued – using the emotive language of a closed shop – that the dramatists were potentially creating anticompetitive conditions. Thus, some of the most powerful producers in the country, which had built empires based on controlling theatrical markets over the previous three decades, were rallying against an imagined dramatist-created closed market before it had even been established.

The response from the dramatists was somewhat surprising. Instead of challenging the notion that they were establishing a closed shop some playwright representatives were receptive to an argument that it was necessary and important. George Middleton stated in the early stages of the meeting "that the principle of the closed shop is the one that is involved and I don't think we can see our way clear to make any concession on that question."[18] John Emerson followed Middleton's lead even more forcefully stating, "we [the dramatists] stand on this principle of the closed shop and that ... is the essential element on which this whole thing must be based."[19] The dramatists also agreed with the managers that any manager found to be in bad standing with cause after arbitration could be backlisted from working with Guild writers. As Brady noted, backlisted entailed "not living up to the basic agreement."[20]

In concluding initial discussions on the general principles of the first "Right to Contract" clause, John Emerson for the dramatists once again did nothing to specifically clarify that they were not creating a closed-shop framework. In this evasive response:

William Brady [for the managers]: We are going back with this: [to the full managers' committee] that you insist upon the closed shop and that you do not want to make any basic agreement unless you do get the closed shop.

John Emerson: You have got the exemption of the foreign author – the foreign language author.[21]

[17] Monroe Lippman describes how in the infant years of the Shubert Organization, 1900–1905, the brothers adopted an "open door" policy in direct opposition to the Syndicate. This policy, Lippman claims, was a significant factor in their rapid rise. *See* Monroe Lippman, "The History of the Theatrical Syndicate: its effect upon the theatre in America" (PhD diss., University of Michigan, 1937), 112.

[18] PMA and DG Meeting, March 11, 1926, 9.

[19] PMA and DG Meeting, March 11, 1926, 9.

[20] PMA and DG Meeting, March 11, 1926, 11.

[21] PMA and DG Meeting, March 11, 1926, 21. The broader conversation here was whether English writers or American citizens living in England should be members.

After further discussion about whether an adapter of a work, such as a foreign work, had to be a member of the Guild (where the dramatists felt they should), Brady pushed the point:

> They insist upon closed shop
> They agree to managers closed shop.[22]

Foreign authors writing in a foreign language did not need to be members. But adapters of foreign works into English required membership. It was clear that writers wanted to control who could access their work. Anyone could join, as Arthur Richman clarified, but if a manager wanted access to the best dramatists, one had to be in good standing with the Guild and the terms of this new agreement.

A week later, the group returned to the issue of the "Right to Contract" clause, focusing again on whether foreign authors were exempt from becoming Guild members when their work was produced in the United States. Arthur Richman, for the dramatists, continued to articulate the broader closed-shop agenda:

> Nobody wants to keep an Englishman's play from being produced. It is only certain conditions we are laying down.

| | |
|---|---|
| HARRIS [FOR THE MANAGERS]: | Does that same condition apply over in London? |
| EMERSON [FOR THE DRAMATISTS]: | No; because they have not been wise enough to get a closed shop; we are wiser than they are.[23] |

For Emerson, speaking specifically in this instance about membership of English authors, much was to be learned from the earlier punishing negotiations between Actors' Equity and the managers. If there was a split that allowed some writers to join, but not others, dissolution was inevitable:

> If we allow every person to say, "I am eccentric and different from the ordinary run; I claim my rights and will not join anything," – if we allow that principle to stand, our organization will not be worth a tinker's curse, exactly the same as the Actors' Equity organization was coming to the point of dissolution because a principle was allowed, and the only method of saving it was to institute what we call an "Equity Shop" – and I believe that this organization of dramatists will go through the same experience unless they insist right now on what the managers call the "closed shop" – for the sake of argument we call it "closed shop," but it is not a closed shop; they must go through the same heartaches and threats of dissolution of their organization as Equity went through.[24]

The statement speaks to the contested and confused understanding of what the new basic agreement was in practice. Did the dramatists simply want to accommodate

22 PMA and DG Meeting, March 11, 1926, 21.
23 PMA and DG Meeting, March 17, 506.
24 PMA and DG Meeting, March 17, 1926, 516–517.

the language of a closed shop the managers insisted on to achieve the larger objective of contract ratification? The Basic Agreement was negotiated in the shadow of the ferocious Actors' Equity proceedings a few years earlier, where the dramatists sided with the producers and argued against the perils of a closed market. At the same time, the dramatists were desperate to find a collective response, under a more stable uniform agreement, to the rapidly expanding powers of the film industry and other industry mediators. The dramatists wanted adequate reward and better protection as the work moved into new lucrative subsidiary mediums. Owen Davis, discussing the application of the new agreement to English authors, pleaded with the managers for greater security. For the dramatists, a closed shop was something "[w]e feel that we will have to get," and to preserve long-term interests "cannot live without it."[25]

The definitional details about the Guild's organizational structure emerge as unclear. The Guild was trying to find an immediate solution to the growing threats of new entertainment mediums while also attempting to maintain a consistent argument about how "open" or "closed" the new association and its agreement should be going forward. The dramatists at once wanted to give the impression of openness but insisted on a closed structure.

The committee could not immediately agree on the language for the "Right to Contract" provision. When the committee met later to clarify all the terms, William Brady, for the managers, emphasized that they reserved the right to also organize as a closed shop. Richman responded that the dramatists were satisfied with this arrangement, "so long as there is nothing that contravenes the law."[26] Whether the industry was operating under a closed shop would be the subject of litigation that followed in the twenty years after the first agreement and is still unresolved to this day. The dramatists have continually denied that they formed a closed shop. In response, the Shuberts, in particular, have argued this is exactly what the Guild created.[27]

The substance of the first "Right to Contract Clause" in the Basic Agreement of 1926 as adopted was an amalgam of the various manager and dramatist demands.

25 PMA and DG Meeting, March 17, 1926, 517. Even though Davis also states that he "hates it" – the idea of a closed shop.

26 PMA and DG Meeting, March 25, 1926, 596 (Arthur Richman).

27 *See* George Middleton, *These Things Are Mine: The Autobiography of a Journeyman Playwright* (New York: The Macmillan Company, 1947), 307; *see* "Memorandum of the Defendant in Opposition," at 4–5, *Shubert Theatre Corporation* v. *Arthur Richman, President of the Dramatists Guild,* May 6, 1927, New York Supreme Court; Complaint of: Select Theatres Corporation and Select Operating Corporation in *Select Theatres Corporation and Select Operating Corporation* v. *Elmer Rice*, Supreme Court of the State of New York, January 1941, General Correspondence Collection, Basic Agreement 1936–1941, Box 17, *The Shubert Archive.* Transcript: *Carl E. Ring* v. *Harold Spina et al*, December 15, 1948, 63–64. In the *Ring* v. *Spina* litigation, to be discussed in the next two chapters, Edward Greenbaum acting for the Dramatists Guild was assisted in his preparation for the case by George Middleton. In correspondence between the two, Middleton emphasized that a point often not made by the Guild was that if they were operating an absolute "closed shop" then theatre owners like the Shuberts, who had significant control over theatres, could be excluded from contracting with members, which was not the case. *See* G. Middleton to E. Greenbaum, November 11, 1948, Box 25, George Middleton Papers (and other correspondence between the two around this time).

The managers agreed to make no contract with any "playwright, author, writer, or composer" that was "not a member in good standing of the Guild." At the same time, writer members were prohibited from entering into agreements with managers not in good standing with the Guild. The exceptions – as debated during the committee meeting between the managers and dramatists – included foreign authors of a foreign language, translations of foreign-language works, and adaptations in relation to foreign works with certain conditions. Managers could not adapt more than one play a year from British authors who were not Guild members (to protect smaller producers).[28]

More broadly, all contracts between authors and managers under the 1926 Agreement were subject to minimum terms, "but nothing herein contained shall be construed to prevent the Author from obtaining better terms."[29] The agreement included author-friendly clauses about attribution,[30] alterations,[31] casting, and

28 *See* "Minimum Basic Agreement, 1926," § 1. Note that in its April 1926 edition, *The Authors' League Bulletin* (at 19–26) published the Basic Agreement approved by the Guild and Producing Managers after they had concluded their committee meetings of March and April. There is a version of first Basic Agreement from February 1926 in Middleton's Collection. Middleton handwrites on the cover, "This is the original M.B.A" approved by the Guild and Producing Managers. He also however writes "as [finally] agreed-after managers agreement April 14. 26" in Dramatists Guild Containers, George Middleton Papers. The revised April version that supplanted the earlier version is confirmed in the April *League Bulletin* at 19.

29 *See* "Minimum Basic Agreement, 1926," § 4.

30 "Minimum Basic Agreement, 1926," § 7.

31 "Minimum Basic Agreement, 1926," § 8. During the committee meetings in March of 1926 between the managers and playwrights, the participants debated the boundaries of Clause 8 (alterations) at length: *see* PMA and DG Meeting, March 11, 1926, 34–38; March 25, 1926, 598–607. Middleton refers to the protections of the writer here "bringing out what the custom of the theatre is" (at 35). The issue of what constituted reasonable changes was discussed in the context of written consent, additions belonging to the author (but also there being an agreement of mutual consent (602)), and making sure there are no delays in production. Owen Davis invokes the romantic author narrative as a justification for playwright control over alterations: "I must, after all, live or die, on the plays I write" (at 37). And later Davis speaks to the author not asking for anything more than "he has not had since the beginning of time" (604). The producers, like William Brady, speak to the need for greater manager control and some flexibility regarding the many writers that are not experienced like Davis "but the cranks who come in under the guise of authorship" (34). Lee Shubert, in the meeting of March 26, speaks directly to the contracting practices that he had developed over the previous twenty years: "Have we the privilege when we buy a play from you to say 'We agree to any changes that the managers want before you buy the play'"(604). A fascinating discussion ensues between Davis and Shubert (604–606) about what additional terms the manager and writer can agree to about making changes and would there be the potential for a manager custom to evolve where a right to make changes was the subject of abuse (manager will only produce work of writer if they agree to allow manager to make changes). A delicate balance is struck here, with Davis implying with oversight the right could be given "if you do not abuse it" (606). In terms of the provision itself, § 8 (Alterations in Play), the managers and producers settled on a compromise, which left default authority with the dramatists. The provision provided that "The Manager agrees to produce and present the play without any additions, omissions, or any alterations whatsoever except such as may be specifically authorized by the Author, or, if more than one, by all, provided, however that in regard to musical comedies, such consent shall not be unreasonably withheld. The Author shall make no changes, omissions or alterations in the manuscript of a play contracted for production without the consent of the Manager. Any change of any kind whatsoever in

rehearsals,[32] and an expense account to monitor these processes.[33] The Agreement also included minimum terms for the production and leasing of plays – a significant problem for authors under previous customary arrangements where managers and agents often held onto works for indefinite periods.[34]

The procedures for subsidiary rights received clarification, including stock rights, amateur rights, radio rights, foreign language rights and adaptations, as well as more general foreign and, in particular, British rights.[35] All of these conditions sought to ensure that the dramatist benefited from the movement of their work into subsidiary streams of exploitation. In addition, a more cost-effective arbitration mechanism aimed to resolve disputes between authors and managers.[36]

The Agreement gave voice to the most complicated, and potentially lucrative, subsidiary stream of revenue – motion picture rights.[37] The Basic Agreement provided "in no event" will the manager receive any more than 50 percent of all net profits derived from motion picture rights. And the sale of motion picture rights required an arbiter who had the "power to negotiate all sales and/or other disposition of motion picture rights of all plays produced or to be produced under any contract made under this agreement."[38]

In the immediate years after 1926, there were clear signs that the new agreement influenced theatre practice. By January 1927, over 150 managers signed the Basic Agreement, and author membership had grown from 185 to 690 members.[39] By the end of 1927, 293 managers signed the agreement, and author members had grown to 978.[40] Dramatists Guild membership over the next year grew to 1299,[41] and by the end of 1928 the Guild was receiving up to 25 calls a day from dramatists seeking advice about theatrical intellectual property.[42]

the manuscript, stage business or performance of the play at any time shall be the exclusive property of the Author; and any part omitted from the play shall belong to the Author." If the manager thought the writer was being unreasonable, they could complain to the Guild Council, but the Council "had no power to compel" the author to make changes. Further, exceptions existed with respect to revues where managers "may make alterations and additions therein as in the Manager's opinion may be necessary."

32 "Minimum Basic Agreement, 1926," § 9.
33 "Minimum Basic Agreement, 1926," § 10.
34 "Minimum Basic Agreement, 1926," § 11.
35 *See* "Minimum Basic Agreement, 1926," § 12.
36 *See* "Minimum Basic Agreement, 1926," § 21.
37 *See* "Minimum Basic Agreement, 1926," § 12 (H).
38 "Minimum Basic Agreement, 1926," § 12 (H).
39 *See* Arthur G. Hays, *City Lawyer* (New York: Simon and Schuster, 1942), 132; George Middleton, "'The Dramatist's Shop,' What It Is, Why It Is, and How It Came About," *The Bulletin*, January 1927, 11 in Dramatists Guild Containers, George Middleton Papers.
40 *See* Hays, *City Lawyer*, 132.
41 *See* George Middleton, "The Dramatists' Guild: What It Has Done and Plans to Do. The President's 1928 Report," *The Bulletin*, November 1928, 17 in Dramatists Guild Containers, George Middleton Papers.
42 George Middleton, "The Dramatists' Guild: What It Has Done and Plans to Do. The President's 1928 Report," *The Bulletin*, November 1928 in Dramatists Guild Containers, George Middleton Papers.

At the end of 1928, George Middleton, now president of the Dramatists Guild,[43] outlined the extraordinary achievements of his organization since adopting the Basic Agreement.[44] The Guild recovered, at a conservative estimate, more than US$75,000 in delinquent royalties for its members.[45] The members also saved a considerable amount of money on contract transaction costs – "of the 620 contracts registered at the Guild, the cost to the author need only have been twenty-five cents for the printing."[46] The Guild also began production "check-ups" on royalty payments which would have never occurred before the Basic Agreement. These investigations revealed miscalculated payments for stock performances – out of incompetence rather than dishonesty – by mediator agent brokers and theatrical producers. Arbitration also relieved the burdens of formal litigation.[47] In 1928, the Dramatists Guild reported sixty-five complaints of Minimum Basic Agreement abuses, compared to twenty-eight in 1927,[48] and twelve of these complaints went to arbitration.[49] The most common issues of complaint included nonpayment of royalties and the reversion of rights under contract.[50] Other cases involved breach of contract (including instances of managers trying to reduce, or not pay, royalties), plagiarism claims, and agency abuses.[51]

It was clear that by the end of 1928, under the guidance of the highly competent Secretary Luise Sillcox,[52] dramatists had become increasingly reliant on the Guild to solve a range of issues about theatrical intellectual property.[53] Lee Shubert claimed in an affidavit by April 1927 that 143 "legitimate plays" were produced on Broadway

43 Middleton had taken over the role from Arthur Richman.

44 *See* George Middleton, "The Dramatists' Guild: What It Has Done and Plans to Do. The President's 1928 Report," *The Bulletin*, November 1928 in Dramatists Guild Containers, George Middleton Papers.

45 *See* George Middleton, "The Dramatists' Guild: What It Has Done and Plans to Do. The President's 1928 Report," *The Bulletin*, November 1928, 16 in Dramatists Guild Containers, George Middleton Papers.

46 George Middleton, "The Dramatists' Guild: What It Has Done and Plans to Do. The President's 1928 Report," *The Bulletin*, November 1928, 16 in Dramatists Guild Containers, George Middleton Papers.

47 Hays, *City Lawyer*, 134.

48 George Middleton, "The Dramatists' Guild: What It Has Done and Plans to Do. The President's 1928 Report," *The Bulletin*, November 1928, 22 in Dramatists Guild Containers, George Middleton Papers.

49 *See* George Middleton, "The Dramatists' Guild: What It Has Done and Plans to Do. The President's 1928 Report," *The Bulletin*, November 1928, 22 in Dramatists Guild Containers, George Middleton Papers, re. breakdown: of sixty-five complaints, thirty-seven were settled, twenty-one were still pending at time, and seven were dropped because they were frivolous. Many of the settled claims were for nonroyalty payments and these claims resulted in the collection of over US$54,000.

50 George Middleton, "The Dramatists' Guild: What It Has Done and Plans to Do. The President's 1928 Report," *The Bulletin*, November 1928, 22 in Dramatists Guild Containers, George Middleton Papers.

51 George Middleton, "The Dramatists' Guild: What It Has Done and Plans to Do. The President's 1928 Report," *The Bulletin*, November 1928, 22 in Dramatists Guild Containers, George Middleton Papers.

52 *See* Hays, *City Lawyer*, 134.

53 Hays writes of Sillcox, "Without Luise Sillcox at the helm, this might have been a different story. The Russians make no mistake in designating their leader the 'Secretary of the Commissariat'." *See* Hays, *City Lawyer*, 134.

(with 109 written by American authors). Nonmembers wrote twenty-one of these plays and only two of these succeeded.[54]

But if history had taught the dramatists anything, it was that theatrical mediators were adept at reorganizing their practices and assimilating to evolving industry environments. Despite the initial success, the first Minimum Basic Agreement structure had a tension that the producers were eager to challenge. The dramatists were at once acting as a group to establish collective bargaining influence over the managers, but it was also critical for them to maintain their independent-contracting status. Indeed, the dramatists were so insistent on distinguishing the Guild from union operations, such as Actors Equity, they called themselves a "dramatists' shop"[55] rather than a closed shop. But, as noted, the dramatists, during the negotiation of the first Basic Agreement, also seemed receptive to the idea that they were creating something very much like a closed shop. They stressed the importance of good standing to protect the long-term interests of its membership. The lines between unionization and trade association, or openness and closure, were often contradictory in substance. For example, George Middleton continually emphasized the openness of the Basic Agreement by suggesting that any manager and author was free to sign.[56] A guiding principle of the Guild, however, was that managers who agreed to the Basic Agreement would not enter into contracts with playwrights who were "not a member of this Association."[57] It was open for all to join, but if you did not join, you were unable to work with most of the influential managers in the country. The

54 *See* "Deposition Answer of Lee Shubert," 3–4, *Shubert Theatre Corporation* v. *Arthur Richman, President of the Dramatists Guild*, May 10, 1927, New York Supreme Court, Record # 16847, Box 008047634, Hall of Records, New York Courts [hereafter New York Supreme Court]. These nonmember agreements are with managers who had also not signed. Lee suggests two works *Sex* and *The Virgin Man* were the only successes.

55 *See, for example*, George Middleton, "'The Dramatist's Shop,' What It Is, Why It Is, and How It Came About," *The Bulletin*, January 1927 in Dramatists Guild Containers, George Middleton Papers.

56 *See, for example*, Middleton, *These Things Are Mine*, 307; "A Menace of The Movie," *New York Times*, February 6, 1926, 14; "Dramatists Deny They Seek 'Closed Shop' in Contract," *The New York Herald*, March 24, 1926, 14. Although the language of closed shop was used regularly in the press: *see* "Dramatists Adopt Basic Contract Asking for Authors' Closed Shop," *Variety*, February 3, 1926, 21; "'Sales Czar' between Managers and Authors on Film Rights," *Variety*, March 24, 1926, 19; "Playwrights Win Closed Shop; Managers Threaten to Organize," *The Billboard*, March 27, 1926, 5; "Playwrights Start Closed Shop on Films; Expect Direct Dealing for Movie Rights," *New York Times*, February 5, 1926, 21; "Screen Yields to Closed Shop of Playwrights," *The New York Herald, New York Tribune*, February 6, 1926, 10; "Dramatists Reveal Closed Shop Terms," *New York Times*, February 6, 1926, 1; "Managers Line Up over Closed Shop," *New York Times*, March 9, 1926, 10; "Playwrights Are Granted 'Closed Shop,' *The New York Herald*, March 20, 1926, 1; "Managers Grant Dramatists' Closed Shop; W.A. Brady Hints at Producers' Guild," *New York Times*, March 20, 1926, 1; "Closed Shop," *Boston Daily Globe*, March 22, 1926, 14; "Playwrights Win First 'Closed Shop' Case," *New York Times*, November 5, 1926, 25.

57 *See* "Report of Committee to the Association of Dramatists," January 7, 1926, Principle IV (1) in Dramatists Guild Containers, George Middleton Papers.

writers, therefore, wanted it all. But the managers said this was not possible because of the Guild's organizational structure and problematic relationship with competition law.

## II. IMMEDIATE RESISTANCE AND ANTICOMPETITIVE TENSIONS

Arthur Garfield Hays was a New York lawyer who "made millions" as counsel for "Wall Street brokers and bankers, [and] best-seller authors."[58] Hays, however, also devoted his career to civil liberties causes, cofounding the American Civil Liberties Union and serving as its general counsel for the last two decades of his life.[59] Although Hays was at first "frankly ignorant of the strange tangled trade relationship,"[60] between dramatists and producers, he played a central role in authoring the final version of the first 1926 Minimum Basic Agreement. Hays's "crusading spirit," committed to the "correction of any unfair practices,"[61] coupled with an open and objective mind, made him an ideal mediator between dramatists and producers.

Despite Hays's experience, and best efforts to forge an agreement, it was a considerable challenge to secure the support of the managers before the relatively uncontentious final contract committee meetings held over March of 1926. A group of leading producers at first refused to sign the industry-wide contract.[62] When the producers resisted, rumors began to circulate that the dramatists would join the American Federation of Labor.[63] The dramatists had evoked the possibility of unionization during the negotiations of the ill-fated 1919/20 standard agreement. Middleton wrote that the mere "threat" of unionization "sent such shivers down certain [producer] spines that creeping paralysis alone would have then prevented the new standard contract."[64] The producers possibly viewed unionization as the

58 *See* "Arthur Garfield Hays Dies at 73: Counsel to Civil liberties Union," *New York Times*, December 15, 1954 in Box 9, George Middleton Papers.

59 *See* "The Arthur Garfield Hays Civil Liberties Memorial," NYU Law School in Box 9, George Middleton Papers.

60 George Middleton, "Draft: To the Editor of the NY Times," in Box 9, George Middleton Papers; *see also* Hays, *City Lawyer*, 130.

61 George Middleton, "Draft: To the Editor of the NY Times," in Box 9, George Middleton Papers.

62 *See, for example*, "Golden Suggests Managers Unionize," *New York Times*, February 7, 1926, 14; "Brady Asks Parley With Playwrights," *New York Times*, February 8, 1926, 6; "Union of Managers," *Billboard*, January 23, 1926, 7; "Managers Seek Changes in Playwrights' 'Union'," *The New York Herald*, February 10, 1926, 1; "Dramatists' Pact Is Denounced by Producers' Group," *The New York Herald*, February 13, 1926, 10; "Producers to Reject Dramatists' Demands," *The Washington Post*, February 13, 1926, 8; "Producers Insist Dramatists' Union Offer New Contract," *The New York Herald*, March 10, 1926, 18.

63 *See* Middleton, *These Things Are Mine*, 320; "Dramatists Draft Plan to Join A. F. of L. to Balk Film Corner," *The New York Herald*, December 6, 1925, 1; "Play Writers May Join Union to Combat Fox," *The Sun*, December 6, 1925, 1; "Leading Dramatists May Join A.F. of L. to Protect Rights," *The Washington Post*, December 6, 1925, 3.

64 *See* Middleton, *These Things Are Mine*, 306.

least preferred option because they had just witnessed the prolonged, and expensive, battles the industry had waged against the actors and stagehands.[65]

The threats of unionization, coupled with an astonishing groundswell of support among leading and emerging dramatists,[66] and constructive contract negotiations in March of 1926, eventually led to nearly all producers signing the 1926 Basic Agreement.[67] The Shuberts, however, refused to sign and attempted to establish their own contractual agreements with playwrights. In the second half of 1926, the Shuberts established what became known as a "dummy system" where a producer signatory to the Minimum Basic Agreement acted as a producing shopfront for the Shubert Organization.[68] For example, the producer Jacob Weiser and dramatist William Perlman, author of the play *My Country*, agreed to produce the play in New York. *My Country* opened as a "Shubert production," but was later changed to the billing, "Independent Players Inc."[69] Weiser's relationship with the Shuberts was unsure at best – he was employed by the organization "but had the right to produce on his own."[70] Indeed, the Shubert Organization owned 50 percent of the production, all bookkeeping went through the Shubert offices, Shubert staff helped produce *My Country*, and the author received royalties paid by Shubert checks.[71]

65 For a more recent examination of the Actors' strike *see* Sean P. Holmes, *Weavers of Dreams, Unite! Actors' Unionism in Early Twentieth-Century America* (Urbana, Springfield, Chicago: University of Illinois Press, 2013), 58–86. The dramatists sided with the managers during the actors strike, much to the consternation of the actors. *See* the damming attack on the dramatists and criticism of the concessions they made to the producers: John Emerson (President of Actors Equity), "An Inspiring Address" 28, no.1 *American Federationist* (Jan 1921): 234–235. *See also* "The Dramatists' Guild and the 'Equity Shop,'" *The Authors' League Bulletin* 8, no. 11 (February 1921): 3–5. The article includes the Guild's resolution opposing the Equity Shop of the Actors drawing the distinction between what they believed was a closed shop to their open policy. The dramatists' emphasized how they thought the closed shop system would restrict play content approvals, cast approvals, and limit opportunities for playwrights in an already difficult market because of the restricted options in terms of casting (*see* in particular conditions 3, 4, 5, 6).

66 Other key dramatists involved on the contract committee in the weeks leading up to the signing of the Minimum Basic Agreement included: Eugene O'Neill, John Emerson, Eugene Buck, Otto Harbach, George Kelly, Roi Cooper Megrue, Channing Pollock, J. Hartley Manners, Le Roy Clemens, George Kaufman, Rachel Crothers, Arthur Richman, and chairman George Middleton. *See* Middleton, *These Things Are Mine*, 323.

67 *See* "Producers Agree with Playwrights on Five-Year Peace," *New York Times*, March 28, 1926, 1; "Producers Bow to Playwrights on All Demands," *The New York Herald*, March 28, 1926, 1; "Managers Sign Tuesday," *New York Times*, April 25, 1926, 22; "Dramatists Guild Terms Ratified by Producers," *The New York Herald*, April 28, 1926, 14; "Producers' League Signs 5-Year Peace," *New York Times*, April 28, 1926, 29; "Peace Effected in Fight of Dramatists and Producers," *Variety*, March 31, 1926, 21; "Dramatists Lift Ban on Plays," *Billboard*, April 10, 1926, 9; "Final Contract Form Printed for Dramatists-Producers," *Variety*, April 21, 1926, 19. Although even in late March there was still tension between the mangers and writers: *see* "Brady Disputes Victory Claimed for Dramatists," *The New York Herald*, March 29, 1926, 13. The first Agreement was finalized by the end of April 1926.

68 *See* "'Dummy' for Shuberts Suspended by Authors' Guild," *Variety*, November 3, 1926, 44.

69 "Dummy for Shuberts Suspended by Authors' Guild," *Variety*, November 3, 1926, 44. *See also* "Dramatists Bar Weiser from Plays until March," *New York Herald Tribune*, November 5, 1926.

70 "Dummy for Shuberts Suspended by Authors' Guild," *Variety*, November 3, 1926.

71 "Dummy for Shuberts Suspended by Authors' Guild," *Variety*, November 3, 1926.

On this occasion, the dramatists aligned against any resistance to the standardized agreement. Weiser and Perlman received a suspension from the Dramatists Guild for four and three months respectively, with "no member of the [G]uild ... allowed to submit plays to [Weiser]" during his suspension.[72] Authors were now refusing offers from the Shuberts to write and adapt works for the organization.[73] The Shuberts, enraged by the circumstances, embarked on a new course of action.

## III. LAW AND THE REFRAMING OF AUTHORITY AROUND MONOPOLY

By April 1927, the Shuberts, now drained of access to content, and their dummy system exposed by the Dramatists Guild, decided to respond through the courts. Arthur Hays was once again called on to defend the Dramatists Guild. On April 29, 1927, the Shubert Theatre Corporation filed a complaint in the New York Supreme Court against Arthur Richman, then president of the Dramatists Guild.[74] The core of the complaint was that the dramatists had established an illegal monopoly under section 340 of the New York General Business Law known as the "Donnelly Act." The complaint, drafted by the Shuberts' loyal and long-serving attorney William Klein, provided the public with an extraordinary insight into the size of the Shubert operations. The Shubert Organization, at the time of filing the complaint, was valued at over US$15 million and operated "upwards of one hundred theatres throughout the United States of America and Canada."[75] They also held booking arrangements with "750 other theatres" across the United States.[76] The Shuberts claimed that the membership of the Dramatists Guild included "all the known and established authors, playwright, writers and composers in the United States of America and Canada,"[77] and through its membership it "controls and regulates substantially"[78]

72 "Dummy for Shuberts Suspended by Authors' Guild," *Variety*, November 3, 1926.

73 "Dummy for Shuberts Suspended by Authors' Guild," *Variety*, November 3, 1926.

74 *Shubert Theatre Corporation* v. *Arthur Richman, President of the Dramatists Guild*, April 29, 1927, New York Supreme Court, Record # 16847, Box 008047634, Hall of Records, New York Courts. The suit received wide attention in the press. "Shuberts in Court Against Dramatists," *Variety*, April 27, 1927, 43; "Shubert Firm Sues Dramatists' Guild," *Billboard*, April 30, 1927, 8; "Legitimate: Decision Reserved in Shuberts-Authors Suit," *Variety*, May 4, 1927, 42; "Decision Reserved in Fight Between Shuberts and Authors," *Billboard*, May 7, 1927, 6; "Shuberts Start War On Dramatists," *New York Times*, April 22, 1927, 9; "Shuberts Declare Guild Guilty of Play Boycott," *New York Herald Tribune*, April 23, 1927, 10; "Shuberts Seek Stay on Authors' Guild," *New York Times*, April 23, 1927, 15; "Shuberts Bring Suit to Break Dramatists Pact With Producers," *New York Herald Tribune*, April 30, 1927, 13; "Move to Enjoin Dramatists Guild," *New York Times*, April 30, 1927, 25.

75 *See* "Plaintiff's Complaint," 2, *Shubert Theatre Corporation* v. *Arthur Richman, President of the Dramatists Guild*, April 29, 1927, New York Supreme Court.

76 "Memorandum of Defendant in Opposition," 8, *Shubert Theatre Corporation* v. *Arthur Richman, President of the Dramatists Guild*, May 6, 1927, New York Supreme Court.

77 "Plaintiff's Complaint," 2–3, *Shubert Theatre Corporation* v. *Arthur Richman, President of the Dramatists Guild*, April 29, 1927, New York Supreme Court.

78 "Plaintiff's Complaint," 3, *Shubert Theatre Corporation* v. *Arthur Richman, President of the Dramatists Guild*, April 29, 1927, New York Supreme Court.

the supply of content in the industry. Further, they argued that the Guild "compelled, coerced or enlisted substantially all American producers and managers other than the plaintiff" into its "unlawful project," the Minimum Basic Agreement.[79] It was through this control and regulation that the Guild could "fix the terms and prices of and for such materials and services."[80] Such a conspiracy made it virtually impossible for any author to "sell or dispose" of their work and services except through the conditions as the Guild determined.[81] These conditions made it virtually impossible for the plaintiff to "purchase the dramatic and musical materials and services" of authors, except under the conditions "fixed by the Guild."[82]

The Shuberts had constructed an understanding of how creation moved between author and audience in a way that spoke to the language of monopoly rather than copyright. Theatrical copyright was being defined by the producers as an object of trade and commerce although the courts had found that theatre was not an activity of trade and commerce.[83] The author was "a factory" – an "independent manufacturer."[84] The "product of a playwright's mind" is a commodity supplying "raw materials," providing "services," and selling "products" to purchasers such as producers. The producers, the Shuberts argued, were deprived of purchasing these materials and services if they were not an organization found to be in "good standing" with the Guild.

The Shuberts, thus, complained that the "unlawful methods" of the Guild constituted a "monopoly and combination in restraint of trade." The Guild was also engaged in "an unlawful secondary boycott" of producers not in good standing with the Guild, but also other dramatists and composers.[85] It was indeed an audacious claim given the colossal size and scope of the Shubert business. But it was a claim built on an impresario-based understanding of how creation flowed through the industry. The movement of creativity involved the ongoing negotiation of "materials," with the contractual terms adapting to the unique circumstance of every transaction. The producer undertook the risks and costs involved in materializing the intangible right so it could be eventually realized on the stage. That is how the Shuberts had operated for the previous twenty years.

79 "Plaintiff's Complaint," 3, *Shubert Theatre Corporation* v. *Arthur Richman, President of the Dramatists Guild*, April 29, 1927, New York Supreme Court.

80 "Plaintiff's Complaint," 3, *Shubert Theatre Corporation* v. *Arthur Richman, President of the Dramatists Guild*, April 29, 1927, New York Supreme Court.

81 "Plaintiff's Complaint," 4, *Shubert Theatre Corporation* v. *Arthur Richman, President of the Dramatists Guild*, April 29, 1927, New York Supreme Court.

82 "Plaintiff's Complaint," 4–5, *Shubert Theatre Corporation* v. *Arthur Richman, President of the Dramatists Guild*, April 29, 1927, New York Supreme Court.

83 *See* the key decision of *People* v. *Klaw*, 55 Misc. 72 (1907); 106 N.Y. Supp. 341.

84 *See* "Memorandum of the Defendant in Opposition," 23, *Shubert Theatre Corporation* v. *Arthur Richman*, President of the Dramatists Guild, May 6, 1927, New York Supreme Court. Arthur Hays attributes these portrayals of the author to William Klein.

85 "Plaintiff's Complaint," 7, *Shubert Theatre Corporation* v. *Arthur Richman, President of the Dramatists Guild*, April 29, 1927, New York Supreme Court.

Lee Shubert reiterated these understandings of theatrical practice in a deposition submitted on the same day as the original complaint.[86] Lee claimed that the intimidating tactics of the Guild impeded "the plaintiff's right to deal with the said authors . . . and to have free access to their products."[87] Lee's deposition focused on the "practical monopoly" imposed on the industry.[88] Harry Smith, who had been engaged by the Shuberts as an adapter of many theatrical works, and party to several oppressive theatrical trust contracts,[89] was an example of an author deprived of business opportunities under the Minimum Basic Agreement. The Dramatists Guild wrote to Smith stating that as a member of the Guild he did not have the right to contract with a manager not in good standing with the Guild. In this case, Smith did not even own the work as he was an employee of the Shuberts. The Guild's response, however, was that the agreement was "not limited to plays written or owned by the author, and has to do with any contract concerning with any play."[90]

Other instances of "misconduct" that Lee documented in his deposition involved the adaptation of works controlled by the Shuberts. The Guild also urged author and adapter Martin Brown to not work on an adaptation of a Shubert production because it "would get him into difficulties with the defendant Guild."[91] Authors and adapters including Maurie Rubens,[92] and Laetitia Irwin,[93] received similar letters from the

86 "Deposition of Lee Shubert," *Shubert Theatre Corporation* v. *Arthur Richman, President of the Dramatists Guild*, April 20, 1927, New York Supreme Court. "Deposition of Lee Shubert," *Shubert Theatre Corporation* v. *Arthur Richman, President of the Dramatists Guild*, April 29, 1927, New York Supreme Court.

87 "Deposition of Lee Shubert," 2, *Shubert Theatre Corporation* v. *Arthur Richman, President of the Dramatists Guild*, April 29, 1927, New York Supreme Court.

88 "Deposition of Lee Shubert," 4, *Shubert Theatre Corporation* v. *Arthur Richman, President of the Dramatists Guild*, April 29, 1927, New York Supreme Court.

89 Especially with respect to artistic control. *See, for example*, Agreement: A. L. Erlanger and Harry Powers with Victor Herbert, Harry B. Smith, Robert B. Smith, October 1919, Contract Collection, Group III, no. 4, *The Shubert Archive*. Clause 5 (where managers could omit the names of authors on any advertising).

90 "Deposition of Lee Shubert," 6, *Shubert Theatre Corporation* v. *Arthur Richman, President of the Dramatists Guild*, April 29, 1927, New York Supreme Court (attached letter from Luise Sillcox to Harry Smith, February 16, 1927).

91 "Deposition of Lee Shubert," 7, *Shubert Theatre Corporation* v. *Arthur Richman, President of the Dramatists Guild*, April 29, 1927, New York Supreme Court.

92 Maurie Rubens was asked by the Shuberts to write music and lyrics for the musical titled *Green Fruit*. Shubert deposed "upon hearing of this, wrote a letter on February 1st, 1927" in which the Guild demanded to know why Rubens had written for the Shuberts "as they have not yet signed the Basic Agreement." *See* "Deposition of Lee Shubert," 9, *Shubert Theatre Corporation* v. *Arthur Richman, President of the Dramatists Guild*, April 29, 1927, New York Supreme Court. The included letter: "H. B. Tonge to M. Rubens," February 1, 1927. *See also* "L. Sillcox to M. Rubens," March 22, 1927.

93 "Deposition of Lee Shubert," 12, *Shubert Theatre Corporation* v. *Arthur Richman, President of the Dramatists Guild*, April 29, 1927, New York Supreme Court. Shubert also included in his deposition a general message sent out to manager signatories on March 3, 1927. The letter brought to the attention clause 18 of the MBA which provided: "It is agreed that no rights shall be assigned or sublet to *nor shall any manager contract* with any person, partnership or corporation which shall not be in good standing with the Guild, except with the consent of counsel of the Guild." The letter then went on to make it

Guild. Lee also insisted that Jacob Weiser, the "dummy producer" as discussed, acted as an independent producer.[94]

The Dramatists Guild and Arthur Hays, in the memorandum of opposition, responded to the complaint by outlining the history of the Guild, the writers' fight for legitimacy, and the legal justification for association.[95] The defendant's first response was that the Shubert Organization's grievances were much broader than their initial objections to the Minimum Basic Agreement. The defendant alleged that the only obstacle for the Shuberts, and the reason they did not sign the Agreement, was the provision about "small rights." This provision dealt with the collection of royalties for music played publicly in restaurants, for example. The Minimum Basic Agreement provided that these rights were the subject of future negotiation.[96]

The Guild framed their response around their legality as a "dramatists shop" rather than a "closed shop." The Guild was trying to reconcile their dual status as an association of authors that consisted of individual members with independent-authorship status. Hays (for Richman) wrote in his response:

> The "Dramatists Shop" is in no sense a "Closed Shop", since any one can enter. They are not dealing with a managers' organization but with individual managers. Since there can be no discrimination, they interfere with no one's business except by exercising the legal right of a group of men to deal collectively.[97]

Indeed, agreements about the specific issues of royalty rates, outright sales, and advances were subject to individual negotiation between managers and authors.[98] For Hays and the Guild, the Agreement standardized "the form of the contract" so

clear to the community that the Shuberts were not in good standing with the Guild: "The question has already been determined through an arbitration which was decided by Jules S Bache, as a result of which a manager was penalized for having had business dealings with the Shuberts." *See* "Dramatists Guild to Managers signatory to the Minimum Basic Agreement," March 3, 1927, in "Deposition of Lee Shubert" at 12–13, *Shubert Theatre Corporation* v. *Arthur Richman, President of the Dramatists Guild*, 29 April 1927, New York Supreme Court.

94 *See* "Deposition of Lee Shubert," 9, *Shubert Theatre Corporation* v. *Arthur Richman, President of the Dramatists Guild*, April 29, 1927, New York Supreme Court. *See also* deposition of Jacob Weiser: *Shubert Theatre Corporation* v. *Arthur Richman, President of the Dramatists Guild*, April 5, 1927, New York Supreme Court. Wesier wrote that "during the three-month suspension period, I was in fact deprived of the advantages of dealing with the numerous members of the defendant Guild." Arthur Richman, in response, deposed that in all of these instances the Guild acted properly. *See* "Deposition of Arthur Richman," 12–15, *Shubert Theatre Corporation* v. *Arthur Richman, President of the Dramatists Guild*, May 6, 1927, New York Supreme Court.

95 "Memorandum of the Defendant in Opposition," *Shubert Theatre Corporation* v. *Arthur Richman, President of the Dramatists Guild*, May 6, 1927, New York Supreme Court.

96 *See* "Minimum Basic Agreement, 1926," § 13. The provision provides: "The rights of the Manager are specifically limited to those granted herein. All other rights (excepting so-called 'small rights' in dramatico-musical compositions, which are the subject of present negotiation), and all rights which may hereafter come into existence, shall always be reserved to the Author."

97 *See* "Memorandum of the Defendant in Opposition," 4–5, *Shubert Theatre Corporation* v. *Arthur Richman, President of the Dramatists Guild*, May 6, 1927, New York Supreme Court.

98 *See* "Minimum Basic Agreement, 1926," § 5.

the author would "know where he stands."[99] It was an exercise in reducing costs through a standard contract and implementing arbitration procedures. The Guild also claimed many playwrights had not signed the Basic Agreement, and the Shuberts were free to sign an agreement with these writers on whatever terms they desired.[100]

Hays, in his response, also tried to walk the delicate line between the Guild's similarities with the unions while stressing the differences. For example, Hays responded that the "legal principles underlying the questions raised here"[101] mirrored those of the "struggle of labor unions."[102] At the same time, the work that the dramatist does "is not the same as that of the ordinary workingman,"[103] but:

> [T]he right to do his work and the right to join with his fellows in exacting terms for his service rests upon the same principle.[104]

Hays argued that numerous examples existed, in different industries, where workers associated as a group and had the right to organize,[105] rather than the right to unionize. Any manager had the right to sign the agreement, and any dramatist had the right to not work with a manager who refused to deal with the group.[106] Hays stated:

> It would be difficult to conceive of any reason why the principles laid down in labor union cases should not apply to any group of men, whether they directly sell the labor of their hands from day to day, or whether they sell or lease the result of the labor of their brains.[107]

99 "Memorandum of the Defendant in Opposition," 5, *Shubert Theatre Corporation* v. *Arthur Richman, President of the Dramatists Guild*, May 6, 1927, New York Supreme Court.

100 *See* "Deposition of George Middleton," *Shubert Theatre Corporation* v. *Arthur Richman, President of the Dramatists Guild*, May 6, 1927, New York Supreme Court.

101 "Memorandum of the Defendant in Opposition," 9, *Shubert Theatre Corporation* v. *Arthur Richman, President of the Dramatists Guild*, May 6, 1927, New York Supreme Court.

102 "Memorandum of the Defendant in Opposition," 9, *Shubert Theatre Corporation* v. *Arthur Richman, President of the Dramatists Guild*, May 6, 1927, New York Supreme Court.

103 "Memorandum of the Defendant in Opposition," 9, *Shubert Theatre Corporation* v. *Arthur Richman, President of the Dramatists Guild*, May 6, 1927, New York Supreme Court.

104 "Memorandum of the Defendant in Opposition," 9, *Shubert Theatre Corporation* v. *Arthur Richman, President of the Dramatists Guild*, May 6, 1927, New York Supreme Court.

105 Hays citing in "Memorandum of the Defendant in Opposition," for example, the needle trade industry at 18 (*Qunito* v. *Schlesinger*, 201 App. Div 487 [*Schlesinger* v. *Quinto* 201 App. Div. 487]; *Maisel* v. *Sigman*, 205 N.Y.S. 807); the trucking industry (citing at 18–19 *Reardon* v. *Caton*, 189 App. Div. 501); and *see also* (at 16) the woodwork industry (*Bossert* v. *Dhuy*, 221 N.Y. 342). Hays also discusses, in the earlier context of actors, how the Shuberts took a contrary position "where they were anxious to sustain the validity of the 'Equity' or Actors' Shop" (Hays cites at 12): *Producing Managers' Assn. Inc.* v. *John Emerson as President of Actors, Lee Shubert et al*, 209 App. Div 870.

106 *See* Hays, *City Lawyer*, 132.

107 "Memorandum of the Defendant in Opposition," 19–20, *Shubert Theatre Corporation* v. *Arthur Richman, President of the Dramatists Guild*, May 6, 1927, New York Supreme Court.

As for the specific response to the complaint – that playwrights were manuscript sellers, and therefore subject to section 340 of General Business Law – Hays sought to distinguish between the tangible production and the intangible right.[108] For the defendant Guild, the purchase of the play "would give nothing . . . which would be of any value" to the producer as it does not carry with it "the right to produce the play."[109] The playwright simply "grants right to the producer" which does not involve either articles or commodities,[110] and neither was the right a matter of trade, commerce, or manufacture.[111]

In reply, William Klein, for the plaintiff Shuberts, focused on an issue that would continue to haunt the Dramatists Guild throughout the twentieth century and beyond:

> The fundamental view in the defendant's contention lies in the attempt to portray the Dramatists Guild as a labor union of mere employees banded together in order to secure fair terms of employment from employers. It is, however, nothing of the sort. The dramatists (except in a few instances) are not employees. They write their plays for themselves.[112]

Here was the dilemma for the dramatists that the producers had provoked by starting the anticompetition claim in the first place. The playwrights wanted all the privileges of unionism but were unwilling to become employees. For the Shuberts, only two options were available. The Guild members could contract with producers as employees. As employees, the writers would relinquish control in the copyright of the work to their producer employers. Alternatively, if dramatists wanted to maintain control over the copyright that

[108] Section 340 "Contracts for Monopoly Illegal and Void" of the New York General Business Law as amended in 1921, commonly referred to as the "Donnelly Act": "Every contract, agreement, arrangement or combination whereby A monopoly in the manufacture, production or sale in this state of any article or product used in the conduct of trade, commerce or manufacture or of any article or commodity of common use is or may be created, established or maintained, or whereby Competition in this state in the supply or price of any article, product or commodity is or may be restrained or prevented, or whereby For the purpose of creating, establishing or maintaining a monopoly within this state of the manufacture, production or sale of any such article, product or commodity, the free pursuit in this state of any lawful business, trade or occupation is or may be restricted or prevented, is hereby declared to be against public policy, illegal and void."

[109] "Memorandum of the Defendant in Opposition," 22, 23, *Shubert Theatre Corporation* v. *Arthur Richman, President of the Dramatists Guild*, May 6, 1927, New York Supreme Court.

[110] "Memorandum of the Defendant in Opposition," 23, *Shubert Theatre Corporation* v. *Arthur Richman, President of the Dramatists Guild*, May 6, 1927, New York Supreme Court.

[111] "Memorandum of the Defendant in Opposition," 25, *Shubert Theatre Corporation* v. *Arthur Richman, President of the Dramatists Guild*, May 6, 1927, New York Supreme Court. *See* the key 1907 decision of *People* v. *Klaw*, 55 Misc. 72 (1907); 106 N.Y. Supp. 341 where the claim was that the Theatrical Syndicate member Marc Klaw was attempting to monopolize the play booking business. The indictment in this case was dismissed and the case stood for the general proposition that the theatre was not an activity of trade or commerce.

[112] *See* "Plaintiff's Replying Memorandum," 27, *Shubert Theatre Corporation* v. *Arthur Richman, President of the Dramatists Guild*, May 10, 1927, New York Supreme Court.

subsisted in their work as independent contractors, and desired to associate as a group, they were subject to competition laws.

The Shuberts dismissed the notion that most playwrights were not committed to an anticompetitive collective cause. Klein replied, supported by evidence provided by Lee Shubert,[113] that "[p]ractically all the playwrights in the United States and Canada who have any appreciable value are thus linked together."[114] And in a moment of devastating irony, the Shuberts perhaps revealed their true intentions for establishing an "open -door policy" in their fierce battle against the Theatrical Syndicate two decades earlier.[115] Klein, in his assessment of the Dramatists Guild's "open shop" status, wrote:

> Does it help the situation to argue, as the defendant does, that anyone may join the Dramatists Guild? The plain effect of that suggestion is really this: The Dramatists Guild invites outsiders to join so that its monopoly may be as complete as possible . . . it is good camouflage; it gives a misleading air of fairness to the whole illicit scheme.[116]

Arthur Hays, in the final reply brief of the defendant Guild, continued to push the claim that the position of the dramatists was analogous to that of the actor or the bricklayer – "the laboring man." In association "there is strength" through the "use of collective power."[117] Hays framed association in terms of the broader landscape of the period. He wrote:

> With the change in economic conditions and the social necessity for organization, the law has developed so that today workingmen may not form a union and provide for a union shop, but they may even go further than we have here and insist upon a closed shop. The same principles are applicable to those in other callings. The same social pressures are at work.[118]

Thus, Hays was still seeking to distinguish between closed shop/unionism and open shop/association. An open shop was less intrusive – how could you, therefore, deny open association while at the same time recognize closed unionism?

In the end, these were matters that the court did not have to resolve. The Shuberts abruptly sought a motion for discontinuance[119] and signed the Minimum Basic

113 *See* "Lee Shubert deposition in reply," *Shubert Theatre Corporation* v. *Arthur Richman, President of the Dramatists Guild*, May 10, 1927, New York Supreme Court.

114 "Plaintiff's Replying Memorandum," 31, *Shubert Theatre Corporation* v. *Arthur Richman, President of the Dramatists Guild*, May 10, 1927, New York Supreme Court.

115 *See* Monroe Lippman, "The History of the Theatrical Syndicate: its effect upon the theatre in America" (PhD diss., University of Michigan, 1937), 112.

116 "Plaintiff's Replying Memorandum," 31–32, *Shubert Theatre Corporation* v. *Arthur Richman, President of the Dramatists Guild*, May 10, 1927, New York Supreme Court.

117 "Defendant, Reply Brief," 12, 13, *Shubert Theatre Corporation* v. *Arthur Richman, President of the Dramatists Guild*, May 21, 1927, New York Supreme Court.

118 "Defendant, Reply Brief," 13, *Shubert Theatre Corporation* v. *Arthur Richman, President of the Dramatists Guild*, May 21, 1927, New York Supreme Court.

119 "Stipulation and Order of Discontinuance," Signed by both parties on July 8, 1927, *Shubert Theatre Corporation* v. *Arthur Richman, President of the Dramatists Guild*, Filed August 5, 1927, New York Supreme Court.

Agreement.[120] One line of argument suggests that the Shubert brothers changed their position because the dramatists once again threatened to join the American Federation of Labor.[121] Further, the cost of litigation was becoming too onerous for the Shuberts.[122] Arthur Hays, in his biography, implies that the presiding judge Aaron Levy was a man with "a social conscience," there was "more … involved in the case than a point of law," and that after the judge "conferred with the lawyers, … Shubert signed the minimum basic agreement."[123] Howard Teichmann suggests in his biography of playwright and journalist George Kaufman that Lee Shubert agreed to sign the Minimum Basic Agreement after a brief phone conversation with Kaufman. Lee apparently stated to the playwright, "I can't speak for my brother, but as far as I'm concerned, I'm not going to rock the boat."[124]

The turn in events given such fierce and persistent resistance highlights the vagaries of the life of the theatrical impresario. Negotiation was a fluid process. Indeed, both the Shuberts and the Dramatists Guild adapted their position throughout the negotiation of the 1926 Agreement and 1927 competition law dispute. William Klein II wrote:

> When the MBA was first formulated and presented to the Producers, the Shuberts took the position that they could produce plays without the Guild. The Guild countered that it was so strong the managers would have to sign.
>
> But when the suit was brought the Shuberts' attorney, William Klein (my uncle) argued that the theatrical business was controlled by the playwright. This, despite the fact that the Shuberts owned a multi-million dollar corporation, controlled 100 first-class theatres and booked exclusively in 750 others. On the other hand, the Guild now became modest. It argued that it was really unimportant; that many playwrights were not members; and that many producers had not signed the MBA.[125]

120 *See* "The Dramatic Stage: Shuberts Going Heavy for Dramatic Pieces," *Billboard*, July 30, 1927, 22; "Shubert Dispute with Dramatists Ends Peaceably," *New York Herald Tribune*, May 20, 1927, 14; "Shuberts at Peace with Dramatists," *New York Times*, May 20, 1927, 22; "Shuberts Settle with Dramatists' Guild," *Variety*, May 25, 1927, 41.

121 *See* Middleton, *These Things Are Mine*, 331; "Dramatists May Join A. F. of L.," *New York Herald Tribune*, May 6, 1927, 14; "Dramatists Move to Join the A.F. of L.," *New York Times*, May 6, 1927, 21; "Dramatists' Guild May Join A. F.-L. As Shubert Suit Result," *Variety*, May 11, 1927, 43; "Dramatists' Issues Labor Threat," *Billboard*, May 14, 1927, 6. In the aftermath of the dispute between the Shuberts and Guild, the screen writers were observing the developments in the theatre, contemplating whether to join the A.F.L.: *see* "Veteran Screen Writers May Seek Affiliation with A. F. L," *Variety*, June 29, 1927, 9.

122 Malcolm Goldstein, *George S Kaufman, His Life, His Theatre* (New York: Oxford University Press, 1979), 145.

123 Hays, *City Lawyer*, 133.

124 *See* Howard Teichmann, *George S Kaufman: An Intimate Portrait* (New York: Athenaeum, 1972), 78.

125 William Klein the author of this piece was the nephew of William Klein, lawyer for the Shuberts. *See* William Klein II, "Protective Societies for Authors and Creators," in 1953 *Copyright Problems Analyzed*, ed. Theodore R. Kupferman (New York: Commerce Clearing House, 1953, Vol. 2), 58.

The Shubert brothers perhaps knew too well that in apparent retreat lay the foundations for future litigation on the issue of whether the Guild's trade association structure was illegal under competition law. The introduction of the Minimum Basic Agreement represented the moment in which the industry organized itself around association in a more formal manner although these agreements were still voluntary. But the dramatists never explicitly explained how association and contractual independence could coexist other than appealing to broad notions of the right to associate as a group – a right analogous to unionism, but distinct from the "closed" nature of unionism.

—

In the immediate decade after the 1927 litigation, the Basic Agreement went through two further revisions in 1931 and 1936.[126] But at the same time, a diverse group of stakeholders emerged that shaped how works moved between the author and audience in new ways. And these stakeholders created unique challenges for the American playwright despite whatever protections they were assumed to have secured under copyright law and an evolving industry Basic Agreement framework. The dramatists' authority was inherently fragile and constantly disrupted in the face of larger industry organizational structures.

In May of 1927, *Billboard Magazine* reported the dramatists were confronting a wave of vexatious "plagiarism charges" requiring "Drastic Changes in the Law,"[127] that had become "so common as to be unreasonable."[128] Unknown authors were suing well-known dramatists who had written successful works. The Dramatists Guild believed these suits were orchestrated by "an organized group of get-rich-quick promoters."[129] League representatives suggested that in nine out of ten instances the defendant playwright ultimately absorbed the heavy trial costs of these mostly frivolous claims.[130]

Howard Barnes and playwright Channing Pollock wrote detailed articles, and made extraordinary claims, about the extent of the problem in 1929 and 1930. Channing Pollock suggested the "plagiarism suit business" was "the most thriving of our infant industries," estimating that by 1930 plagiarism claims consisted of "as many as 40 percent" of professional productions that ran for more than 200 performances.[131] Barnes and Pollock also noted the role that mediating lawyers played in encouraging dubious litigation. For suits costing the plaintiff "little or nothing,"[132]

126 *See* Walsh, *Playwrights and Power*, 139–142 on the evolution of these two iterations.

127 *See* "Author' League in Arms over Plagiarism Epidemic," *Billboard*, June 4, 1927, 9; *see also* "Dramatists' Guild to War on Fake Plagiarism Suits," *Billboard*, April 23, 1927, 6; "Dramatists Open Fight on Fake Plagiarism Suits," *New York Herald Tribune*, April 14, 1927, 21; "Dramatists to Fight Plagiarism Actions," *New York Times*, April 14, 1927, 24.

128 *See* "Authors' League in Arms over Plagiarism Epidemic," *Billboard*, June 4, 1927, 9.

129 "Authors' League in Arms over Plagiarism Epidemic," *Billboard*, June 4, 1927, 9.

130 "Authors' League in Arms over Plagiarism Epidemic," *Billboard*, June 4, 1927, 9.

131 Channing Pollock, "Shaking Down the Author," *New York Herald Tribune*, June 1, 1930, 3.

132 Channing Pollock, "Shaking Down the Author," *New York Herald Tribune*, June 1, 1930, 27.

lawyers encouraged litigation by offering their services on a contingency-fee-basis. The most startling claim, verifiable only by rumor, was that:

> a firm of solicitors ... keeps an agent in the Copyright Bureau to summarize unproduced plays. These are said to be card indexed, and when someone achieves success with a story more or less like one of them the unproduced author is invited to walk in and collect.[133]

Barnes wrote that for every "ten or twenty" infringement cases tried before a court, "[c]lose to 150 threatened plagiarism suits are each year negotiated behind a veil of secrecy."[134] And even if the case was frivolous, the playwright "must resign himself to spending considerable sums merely to protect his reputation for honesty." Further:

> If he fights with legal machinery the accusation that he is a thief, he must take part in one of the most complicated of present court procedures. If, as is generally the case, he is willing to sanction the action by paying off the plaintiff in a compromise, he is still a very heavy loser. On the other hand, the plaintiff usually stands to lose nothing if his suit fails, and to gain money and publicity if it wins.[135]

In nine out of ten instances it was easier for the defendant to settle, even in what were frivolous claims, as settling was about one-tenth of the cost of clearing one's name in the courts.[136] Thus, for the plaintiff, as Channing Pollock also suggested, the frivolous claim was "almost always, successful."[137]

Litigation was so appealing to the racketeers because it was often difficult to distinguish between instances of opportunism and a sincere belief that plagiarism had occurred.[138] Successful authors, including Eugene O'Neill and James Hagan, were the subject of plagiarism claims.[139] David Belasco, throughout his career, spent more than US$100,000 in defending infringement claims.[140] Channing Pollock estimated that by the end of the 1920s "all the earnings from his first fourteen plays

133 Channing Pollock, "Shaking Down the Author," *New York Herald Tribune*, June 1, 1930, 27.

134 *See* Howard Barnes, "The Plagiarism Racket: The Tribute Levied on Success in the Theatre," *Theatre Guild Magazine* (October 1929): 11.

135 Howard Barnes, "The Plagiarism Racket: The Tribute Levied on Success in the Theatre," *Theatre Guild Magazine* (October 1929): 11. Barnes claims that in the big complicated suits the cost for defense "may well be between" US$5,000 and US$7,500.

136 Barnes, "The Plagiarism Racket," 12.

137 *See* Channing Pollock, "Shaking Down the Author," *New York Herald Tribune*, June 1, 1930, 3.

138 Pollock describes from experience the five causes of actions that are brought in plagiarism suits. First, there are the cases of actual grievance; second, ignorance of the law and of literature; third, coincidence; fourth, common source; and finally, common fraud. Pollock concludes that "As indicated by the infrequency of verdicts for the plaintiff, 'actual grievance' is very rare." *See* Channing Pollock, "Shaking Down the Author," *New York Herald Tribune*, June 1, 1930, 27.

139 On the suits against O'Neill and Hagan, *see* Harry Weinberger Case Files Regarding Plagiarism. Yale Collection of American Literature, Beinecke Rare Book and Manuscript Library, Boxes 1 and 2. And *see also* further examples that Barnes provides in his second article "Plagiarism Suits," *Theatre Guild Magazine* (November 1929): 23–24, 51.

140 *See* Barnes, "The Plagiarism Racket," 12.

were eaten up in holding at bay the gangs of plagiarism criers."[141] In one instance, where an unsuccessful suit that cost him "in the neighborhood of $20,000," the real cost was the inability to work for two years and losses in potential income of about US $100,000.[142]

The dramatists outlined a reform plan that was "similar to the present Grand Jury system covering criminal actions."[143] The plan involved the plaintiff having to first present evidence of plagiarism to a judge who would then decide whether there was enough material to go to trial. When there was insufficient evidence, based on the judge's preliminary assessment, the plaintiff had to pay an upfront deposit to cover all potential court costs if they wanted to continue the suit. Progression on legislative reform stalled in part because the theatrical producers, and particularly the Shuberts, had concerns about copyright divisibility. The organization opposed the reforms "because of the fear that it would strengthen the hand of the dramatist and enable the dramatist to sell competing motion-picture rights while the play was still running."[144]

In the first decades of the twentieth century, local dramatists also started to find spaces for their writing through mediating vehicles outside of the larger commercial organizations. The New Theatre, the Little Theatre in Chicago, Eugene O'Neill's Provincetown Players, the Washington Square Players (which eventually became the Theatre Guild), The Civic Repertory, The Yiddish Theatre, The Neighborhood Playhouse, and The Group Theatre, to name just a few, all evolved with exciting

141 Barnes, "The Plagiarism Racket," 12.

142 "Channing Pollock to W. N. Seligeberg," June 24, 1931, Harry Weinberger Case Files Regarding Plagiarism. Yale Collection of American Literature, Beinecke Rare Book and Manuscript Library, Box 2, Fol. 22.

143 "Authors' League in Arms over Plagiarism Epidemic," *Billboard*, June 4, 1927, 9. Reform was proposed under a bill introduced initially by Albert Vestal: Vestal Bill, introduced initially in March of 1926 in the 69th Congress, H.R. 10434 (and several later reintroductions). Pollock and Weinberger attempted, unsuccessfully, to incorporate into the Vestal Bill a provision concerning the frivolous plagiarism claims: *See* "H. Weinberger to F. LaGuardia," January 5, 1931, Harry Weinberger Case Files Regarding Plagiarism, Box 2, Fol 20.

144 *See* A. L. Kaminstein with L. G. Margolis, A. Bogsch, "Study No. 11: Divisibility of Copyrights," *Committee on the Judiciary Subcommittee on Patents, Trademarks, and Copyrights* (86th Congress, 2nd Sess., June 1957), 32–33. The authors, writing about congressional hearings in 1928, provide a more detailed explanation for the Shuberts' resistance to the earlier Vestal proposals. The authors write: "The Shubert interests opposed the 'divisible portion' of the bill because of the fear that it would strengthen the hand of the dramatist and enable the dramatist to sell competing motion-picture rights while the play was still running. At the time, the Basic Dramatists Guild Agreement covered the arrangements between the dramatist and the producer, but the Shuberts feared that, if the bill passed, ways would be devised of circumventing or abrogating the agreement. The usual agreement provided that the producer dramatist and both shared equally in the sale of motion-picture rights." ... "The Shubert interests were still opposed, stating that if 'divisibility' became the law, it would 'kill the spoken drama.' After the hearings, Representative Vestal introduced a revised bill, H. R. 12549, which was reported out by the House Committee on Patents. The committee found that the whole pattern of disposing of copyrights had changed since 1909, and with it, methods of distributing and division of rights. In place of the old practice of merely selling a manuscript or a book, the author now sold separate rights, and the trade practices had made 'the act of 1909 impracticable and obsolete.'"

artistic ambitions in mind. The nonprofits, along with the motion picture industry,[145] were growing at an incredible rate – from about fifty toward the end of the First World War to 500 by 1925, and more than a thousand by 1929.[146] The goal of many of these companies was the development of American dramatists telling American stories. But the challenge for these organizations was how to balance financial sustainability while preserving artistic ambition.[147]

It was inevitable that the parallel expansion in nonprofits presenting new drama and the film industry would lead to new mediating enterprises emerging such as the Bureau of New Plays in 1935/36 – a nonprofit playwriting program created by the Theatre Guild's Theresa Helburn – funded by the seven major Hollywood film studios.[148] Control over works into the lucrative subsidiary medium of film became the focus of a bitter dispute between producers and dramatists during the 1930s.[149] The Bureau collapsed – despite Theresa Helburn's best intentions to create a laboratory for America's most promising young dramatists to produce work for the stage – because it was unclear whether its priority was to develop American playwriting or serve as an incubator for the motion picture industry.[150] At the intersection of artistic ambition and economic reality, a continuous renegotiation of control over the production process occurs through mediating stakeholders including nonprofits, theatrical impresarios, and the film studios. The Dramatists Guild itself was also left in conflicted positions. The Guild impeded specific opportunities for writers in order to advance broader goals of the association.[151] The interests and voices of

145 Jack Poggi writes, "When the movies came along, this is what probably happened: the 'first class' theatres lost part of their audience (at first mostly the patrons of the galleries) to the movies; the 'popular priced' theatres were wiped out altogether; the group that had rarely gone to either now found a home in the movie houses." Jack Poggi, *Theatre in America: The Impact of Economic Forces: 1870–1967* (Ithaca, NY: Cornell University Press), 266.

146 *See* Poggi, *Theatre in America*, 107.

147 *See* Poggi, *Theatre in America*, 276–286.

148 This work is subject to ongoing research of which much of the archival study has evolved out of Theresa Helburn's papers and the Theatre Guild's archive at Yale: Theresa Helburn Papers. Yale Collection of American Literature, Beinecke Rare Book and Manuscript Library; in Theatre Guild Archive. Yale Collection of American Literature, Beinecke Rare Book and Manuscript Library.

149 The seven studios involved in the funding of the Bureau of New Plays included Paramount, Columbia, Metro-Goldwyn-Mayer, Twentieth Century-Fox, Universal, Warner Brothers, and RKO. *See* Theresa Helburn, "Special for Associated Press," Theatre Guild Archive, Box 1450, Fol. 13700 (May 4, 1936).

150 And young writers who won the Bureau's play writing competitions, such as Robert Wetzel, were often caught in the crossfire between strong mediating interests such as the Dramatists Guild, film studios, playbrokers, and nonprofit executives: *see* Theatre Guild Archive, Boxes including 313, 1446, 1448, 1449, 1453, 1459, 1469.

151 *See, for example*, Robert Wetzel who had to make a choice between membership of the Dramatists Guild or accepting a position to have his play produced as winner of the Bureau of New plays writing competition. Luise Sillcox of the Dramatists Guild warned Wetzel that if he accepted the award, he "would undoubtedly incur a good deal of displeasure temporarily among ['some of' handwritten addition] the membership, while others might not care one way or the other." *See* "Memo on Conversation between Hope Newcombe and Robert Wetzel," Theatre Guild Archive, Box 1459, Fol. 13814 (March 9, 1937).

emerging writers dissolve into the background as larger mediators negotiate the terms of production between different entertainment mediums.

And as the nonprofits, organizations like the Bureau of New Plays, and film studios competed to secure the services of the best young writing talent in the industry, an alternative organizational model started operations on the eve of the introduction of the 1936 Minimum Basic Agreement. This new mediator was foreign to the American theatre industry: a government administrative program. In 1935, the Federal Government embarked on an expansive venture to find work for the unemployed in the wake of crippling depression. The initial appropriation of almost US$5 billion administered under a New Deal agency, The Works Progress Administration (WPA), included an ambitious relief program dedicated to the arts. In the first year of operations, this relief effort employed over 40,000 artists, or skilled workers in the arts, of which 90 percent came from the relief rolls.[152]

The Federal Theatre Project, under the leadership of the talented Hallie Flanagan, employed more than 12,700 people at its height.[153] Moreover, Flanagan, like Theresa Helburn, was determined to build on the art theatre movement of the 1920s and 1930s. Flanagan aimed to create an expansive national art theatre that Americans across the country would have access to for a nominal admission price.[154] Indeed, there was no admission fee for 65 percent of Federal Theatre productions.[155] From 1935 to 1939, Federal Theatre productions played to thirty million people, many of whom had never seen a live theatrical production.[156]

The Federal Theatre Project produced critically acclaimed drama from the canons of Eugene O'Neill and George Bernard Shaw, while also providing a platform for talents such as John Houseman, Orson Welles, and Arthur Miller. Notable triumphs for the Federal Theatre Project included the Negro Theatre Unit, often featuring all African American casts, technical staff, and playwrights.[157] The

152 *See* Lorraine Brown (interviewer), "Transcript of Interview with Irwin Rhodes," WPA Oral Histories Collection, Federal Theatre Project Collection (1935–1939) C0002, George Mason University (Box 8, Folder 27), 11. *See* Hallie Flanagan, *Arena: The Story of the Federal Theatre* (New York: Limelight Editions, 1969 ed.), 358.

153 *See* "National Service Bureau Pamphlet: Vital Statistics, 1935–1939," National Service Bureau Administrative Files, Hallie Flanagan Papers,*T-Mss 1964–002, Billy Rose Theatre Division, The New York Public Library for the Performing Arts (Series II, Box 8) [hereafter Hallie Flanagan Papers].

154 At the most, the Project charged US$1 admission. *See* Lorraine Brown (interviewer), "Transcript of Interview with Irwin Rhodes," WPA Oral Histories Collection, 15. William McDonald, however, states that "an exception made it possible for companies on tour by special permission from the national director to charge $1.50. One case is on record where, for a single performance, permission was granted to charge two dollars." *See* William F. McDonald, *Federal Relief Administration and the Arts* (Columbus: Ohio State University Press, 1969), 531.

155 Flanagan, *Arena: The Story of the Federal Theatre*, 434. This was the figure at the end, and at the beginning, and Project-created productions were 100 percent admission free.

156 *See* "National Service Bureau Pamphlet," Hallie Flanagan Papers (Series II, Box 8). (The pamphlet states "65% of them new to the theatre.")

157 In other ongoing research I examine the significant challenges writers faced in terms of royalty payments and the content itself when writing about African American themes: John Charles

Living Newspaper also shaped the legacy of the Federal Theatre Project. The Living Newspaper program created new plays on important social issues of the day including works on big business,[158] agricultural workers,[159] Mussolini's invasion of Ethiopia (which never opened),[160] affordable electric power,[161] and tenant slums.[162]

So Hallie Flanagan, like Theresa Helburn at the Bureau of New Plays, had ambitions that the Federal Theatre Project would foster a new generation of dramatic voices. The reality, however, was that dramatists connected to the Federal Theatre Project, like the Bureau of New Plays, had to navigate their way through a bureaucratic minefield that was constantly undermining their artistic control and access to payments. The agency was a government-subsidized theatre, and thus the rules of how intellectual creation moved between author and audience underwent constant redevelopment. Most importantly, the Project had to observe the strict formalities of the broader WPA agenda – relief for the unemployed – while also complying with an endless stream of paperwork to justify its relationship with the government. As the organizational structure of the program became increasingly centralized, the gateways for playwrights to enter the system narrowed. And despite the incredibly ambitious work being produced, much of the program had to meet generic standards at minimum cost.

And within the government structure of the Federal Theatre Project, authors faced substantial challenges to earn royalties and protect their work. For some authors, such as Eugene O'Neill and George Bernard Shaw, securing royalties involved constructing a minimum-payment framework that involved producing a cycle of their plays over an extended period.[163] Dramatists employed as part of the Project had to find ways to circumvent their position as employed hired hands of the government to have their work acknowledged.[164] The employee writers lacked authority because of stigmas surrounding their relief status: any playwright of repute

Brownell Papers Relating to Mississippi Rainbow. Yale Collection of American Literature, Beinecke Rare Book and Manuscript Library, Box 1.

158 *Injunction Granted* (1936).

159 *Triple-A Plowed Under* (1936).

160 *Ethiopia* (1936).

161 *Power* (1937).

162 *One-Third of a Nation* (1938).

163 Building on the idea of multiple productions of the one play, Flanagan proposed multiple productions of the O'Neill canon over a specified period in what was to become known as a production cycle. *See* Leslie White, "Eugene O'Neill and the Federal Theatre Project" (PhD diss., New York University, 1986), 66–106; *see* Lorraine Brown (interviewer), "Transcript of Interview with Irwin Rhodes," WPA Oral Histories Collection (Box 8, Folder 27), 26–27. This cycle idea was recommended by Irwin Rhodes from the Federal Theatre Project.

164 This is part of ongoing research. Another issue here was whether copyright subsisted in the work of government employees. Ben Russak, supervisor of the play department, proposed a similar model to the one adopted by Henrik Ibsen and the National Theatre of Norway. In this system, the authors repaid their work-for-hire obligation like it was an advance, and in return, claimed title over the work. *See* "Ben Russak to Paul Turner," Play Department Correspondence, 1938–1939 [2.1.79/FTP 000370], November 3, 1938, Federal Theatre Project Collection.

was supposed to work as an independent contractor either in the commercial theatre or as a contractor in the Project, not as a government employee. Yet at the same time, ordinary independent-contracting authors connected to the Federal Theatre Project needed to be doggedly persistent to receive opportunities and royalty payments under a laboring bureaucracy that often took months to process royalty payments.[165]

For the Federal Theatre Project, sustainability was the primary motivator because it complimented the Project's overarching welfare goals. If the Project was sustainable, workers requiring relief would remain employed. Control over the production process here is serving a different function unique to the American theatre – a public dimension to employ the unemployed. It did not exist to build incubators for emerging theatrical writing talent, or advance their rights as authors of copyrighted works, unless that development was in direct conversation with welfare priorities.

So, despite expanding protections under the Basic Agreement, dramatists had to negotiate their way through an increasingly complicated environment of mediating stakeholders. The mediators now included commercial producers, nonprofits, government agencies, "quick-rich promoters," lawyers, and other burgeoning groups including the film studios. These mediators also had a variety of agendas: economic, artistic, and welfare-based. The independent-contracting writers chose to respond to the broader mediating structures in the theatrical industry through a uniform voluntary basic agreement bound together as members of a trade association. And it was this unsettled tension between independent-contracting status and trade association that finally came to a head in the seven-year battle between novice producer Carl Ring and the authors of the musical about Abraham Lincoln, *Stovepipe Hat*.

165 *See, for example,* John Brownell's experience with his play *Mississippi Rainbow* as discussed in ongoing Federal Theatre research: John Charles Brownell Papers, Box 1.

# 7

# Carl E. Ring and the American Playwright Trade Association

The Shuberts were not only able to adapt but thrive between the early 1930s and early 1940s. Abe Erlanger passed away in 1930 and Marc Klaw in 1936. With their passing ended the last remnants of the Theatrical Syndicate established in 1896. The Shubert brothers acquired most of the remaining Syndicate properties.[1] In late 1931/1932, the Shubert Organization went into receivership. By 1933, under the banner of the Select Theatres Corporation, the group repurchased the more valuable Shubert assets for a meager US$400,000 with no other bidders.[2] By 1941, the Shuberts had an interest in approximately 75 percent of Broadway attractions, and 90 percent of the remainder were "compelled" to play at a Shubert theatre.[3] The biographer of the Shubert brothers Jerry Stagg described this period for the impresarios as "a monopoly, in the truest sense."[4]

Andrew Davis writes that the Shubert Organization's influence during the 1930s and 1940s also relied on controlling the theatres in major tryout cities including New Haven, Boston, and Philadelphia. Davis claims that over 90 percent of all future Broadway productions first trialed "out of town" which included one, or all, of these cities.[5] The tryout towns provided producers the opportunity to gauge audience reception and make changes to the work before coming back to New York. Thus, in an environment where the Shuberts controlled the tryout venues near New York, as well as many of the Broadway theatres, it was understandable that aspiring producers would take heed of any advice the brothers were willing to share, particularly about production alterations.

1 *See* Andrew Davis, *America's Longest Run: A History of the Walnut Street Theatre* (University Park: The Pennsylvania State University Press, 2010), 234.

2 Davis, *America's Longest Run*, 234; *see also* Anthony Vickery, "Did the Shuberts Save Broadway? The Corporate Producers," in *The Palgrave Handbook of Musical Theatre Producers*, ed. Laura MacDonald, William A. Everett (New York: Palgrave Macmillan, 2017), 78–79. Vickery writes the two new companies were Select Theatres (that held stock in the theatres) and Select Operating Corporation.

3 *See* Jerry Stagg, *The Brothers Shubert* (New York: Random House, 1968), 342.

4 *See* Stagg, *The Brothers Shubert*, 342.

5 Davis, *America's Longest Run*, 234–235.

Under the Minimum Basic Agreement, however, any changes to the work required the consent of the author. Artistic authority was expanding with each new iteration of the Basic Agreement. Article VII of the 1941 Basic Agreement provided that the manager present the work of the playwright "without any additions, omissions, or alterations whatsoever, except such as may be specifically authorized by the author."[6] The Agreement, however, had always placed an important caveat on this authority. If the manager believed the author was unreasonable in refusing a request to make changes, they were able to "complain to the Guild." An arbitration mechanism existed in the Agreement, but it was administered by the Guild that created a contractual framework to protect authors, not managers. Under the Agreement, the Guild did not have to compel the author to make changes, even when the author was unreasonable.

It is against this background that the next two chapters examine the brief and disastrous theatrical career of New Jersey lawyer Carl E. Ring – the plaintiff in one of the most important cases in American theatre history. The proceedings in *Ring* v. *Spina* ("*Ring*"), spanning the period between 1944 and 1951,[7] were about control over creativity in the industry but not so much about copyright law. The *Ring* proceedings involved an antitrust lawsuit against the Dramatists Guild that came to a legally ambiguous conclusion, and has kept the organization under a cloud of possible illegality for the last seventy years. Although the Shuberts were not parties to the proceedings, Carl Ring was a vehicle for a larger producer – and Shubert-driven – cause, involving the reconstruction of the legal conversation over theatrical creation through the rubric of antitrust, contract, and trade-association status.[8]

Around the same period, legislators and the courts were establishing the boundaries of what type of activity was exempt from antitrust.[9] The Clayton Act passed in 1914 provided that "[n]othing contained in the antitrust laws shall be construed to forbid the existence and operation of labor."[10] Critically, section 6 exempted the labor of a human being from being an article or act of commerce.[11] Under the

6 As taken from the 1941 Basic Agreement which was the subject of the dispute in the *Ring* v. *Spina* proceedings. 1941 Minimum Basic Agreement, Box 25, George Middleton Papers, Manuscript Division, Library of Congress, Washington, DC [hereafter George Middleton Papers].

7 *See Ring* v. *Spina et al.*, 148 F 2d. 647 (1945); *Ring* v. *Spina et al.*, 166 F 2d 546 (1948); *Spina et al.* v. *Ring*, 335 U.S. 813; 69 S. Ct. 30 (1948); *Ring* v. *Spina et al.*, 84 F Supp. 403 (1949); *Ring* v. *Authors' League of America Inc et al.*, 186 F 2d 637 (1951); *Ring* v. *Spina et al.*, 341 U.S. 935 (1951).

8 With the conversation starting in the year immediately following the first Basic Agreement of 1926: *Shubert Theatre Corporation* v. *Arthur Richman, President of the Dramatists Guild*, April 29, 1927, New York Supreme Court, Record # 16847, Box 008047634, Hall of Records, New York Courts.

9 *See* ongoing research of Catherine Fisk and Brent Salter on the historical relationship between labor and copyright law in the American theatre: "Assumptions and Fragilities of Labor Relations in the American Theatre," *Ohio State Law Journal* 83 (forthcoming 2022). For an illuminating study (as part of important ongoing work) on the relationship between the antitrust exemption and independent contractor *see* Sanjukta M. Paul, "The Enduring Ambiguities of Antitrust Liability for Worker Collective Action," *Loyola University Chicago Law Journal* 47, no. 3 (Spring 2016): 969.

10 Act of October 15, 1914, ch. 323, 38 Stat. 730 § 6.

11 Act of October 15, 1914, ch. 323, 38 Stat. 730 § 6.

statute, the key condition for exemption status was not that the member was an employee, but there was labor of a human.[12]

In 1932, Congress tried to clarify the purpose of the exemption in the Norris-LaGuardia Act.[13] A labor dispute under the Act included "any controversy" about employment without reference to the proximity of the relationship between employer and employee.[14] But the Act also provided in part that:

> No court of the United States shall have jurisdiction to issue a restraining order or temporary or permanent injunction upon the ground that any of the persons participating or interested in a labor dispute constitute or are engaged in an unlawful combination or conspiracy.[15]

Thus, an issue here was what constituted a labor dispute.[16] The Supreme Court was also wrestling with the boundaries of the exemption. In *United States* v. *Hutcheson*,[17]

12 I am indebted to ongoing conversations and joint research with Catherine Fisk on the union status of the Dramatists Guild.

13 Act of March 23, 1932, ch. 90, 47 Stat. 70.

14 Act of March 23, 1932, ch. 90, 47 Stat. 70 § 13(c). The actual text is "regardless of whether or not the disputants stand in the proximate relation of employer and employee."

15 Act of March 23, 1932, ch. 90, 47 Stat. 70 § 5. Sections 6 and 20 of the Clayton Act and sections 1, 4, 5, and 13 of the Norris-LaGuardia Act collectively exempt conduct in which "a bona fide labor organization acting in its own self-interest to further a labor objective, where the union has not combined with a non-labor group." *See* American Bar Association, *Antitrust Healthcare Handbook* (Chicago, IL: American Bar Association, Section of Antitrust Law, 3rd ed. 2004), 56 referring to *United States* v. *Hutcheson* 312 U.S. 219, 236 (1941). The two acts together make up what is referred to as the statutory labor exemption. *See* Kieran Corcoran, "When Does the Buzzer Sound?: The Nonstatutory Labor Exemption in Professional Sports," *Columbia Law Review* 194, no. 3 (Apr. 1994): 1048–1051. The other federal legislation relevant here is the National Labor Relations Act (NLRA "Wagner Act"), Act of July 5, 1935, ch. 372, 49 Stat. 449, as amended by the Labor Management Relations Act ("Taft-Hartley Act"), Act of June 23, 1947, ch. 120, 61 Stat. 136. Following the Wagner Act, cases emerged that found collective groups to fall between employee and independent contractor: *see N.L.R.B.* v. *Hearst Publications, Inc.*, 322 U.S. 111, 127 (1944). The Taft-Hartley Act of 1947, however, aimed to exclude independent contractors from its ambit. In the years that followed, the issue of whether one can bargain, or is bound to bargain, under the NLRA, has been relevant as to whether the collective group is immune from antitrust: (*see* Justice White, *United Mine Workers* v. *Pennington*, 381 U.S. 657, 665 (1965). In order to accommodate the conflicts and tensions between antitrust and labor law, courts have also developed the law around "nonstatutory labor exemptions." *See* Corcoran, "When Does the Buzzer Sound," 1051–1053. Important nonstatutory cases developed after the *Ring* proceedings including: *Local Union No. 189* v. *Jewel Tea Co.* 381 U.S. 676 (1965); *United Mine Workers* v. *Pennington* 381 U.S. 657 (1965).

16 In later years, the term "labor dispute" was interpreted as including "any controversy concerning terms or conditions of employment … regardless of whether or not the disputants stand in the proximate relation of employer and employee." *See Taylor* v. *Local 7, Int'l Union of Journeymen Horseshoers*, 353 F.2d 593, 595, 602 (4th Cir. 1965). As set out in Section 113 of the Norris-LaGuardia Act, 29 U.S.C.A. § 113 (c), defines terms and words used in 29 U.S.C.A. Chapter 6. Majority here finding at 607: "Fairly construed, the statutory definition is broad enough to cover the situation disclosed here – an effort by the farriers to compel the owners and trainers to use only union members, and to get $16 for shoeing each race horse." *See, however*, the dissenting opinion of Judge Sobeloff who writes at 608: "The term 'labor dispute' can in some circumstances encompass disputes between suppliers of labor and purchasers of labor, regardless of the label attached to their relationship."

17 312 U.S. 219 (1941).

the Court found that as long as the union was acting in "self-interest" and not combining "with non-labor groups" the union would be immune from antitrust. Justice Frankfurter held that "[t]he Norris-LaGuardia Act reasserted the original purpose of the Clayton Act by infusing into it the immunized trade union activities as redefined by the later Act."[18] The *Allen Bradley* decision of 1945[19] further clarified *Hutcheson*, by finding that unions were not exempt from antitrust when their activities combined with business interests.[20] A union was exempt from antitrust as long as it was pursuing proper objectives.

In *Hutcheson*, the Court identified nonlabor groups as an exception to those groups that would be immune from antitrust. But there was a critical question that the courts had never adequately resolved in the context of the theatre. Did the Dramatists Guild association, and its members, have the qualities of a labor group for antitrust exemption purposes? In a series of cases in the decade before the *Ring* proceedings, the courts were distinguishing the work of independent contractors that formed together as a group (mostly not exempt from antitrust),[21] and employees forming union-type groups (often immune from antitrust).[22] Indeed, leading antitrust treatises cite precedent from the immediate years before the *Ring* v. *Spina* litigation suggesting that "[t]he exemption, although uncertain in scope, does not apply unless the collaborators (on one side of the agreement) are employees and not entrepreneurs or independent contractors."[23] But, highlighting the uncertainty of the scope of the exemption, there were also examples of groups much like the Guild that argued successfully they were exempt.[24]

Carl Ring, the inexperienced first-time producer who ended up investing and losing almost US$150,000 in the production *Stovepipe Hat*, was unexpectedly confronted with the uncertain realities that lived at the crossroads of law and theatrical practice. He was confounded by an industry where playwrights demanded expansive control over the creative process. Ring believed dramatic changes to the script, staging, choreography, and orchestration were necessary to have any chance of recouping costs. Yet, the three authors – Walter Hannan, Edward Heyman, and especially Harold Spina – became increasingly hostile toward Ring's desperate requests for changes. For the producers, Ring was an ideal candidate to challenge

[18] 312 U.S. 219, 236 (1941). Justice Frankfurter here referring to § 20 at 236: "In this light, § 20 removes all such allowable conduct from the taint of being 'violations of any law of the United States', including the Sherman Law."

[19] *Allen Bradley Co.* v. *Local Union No. 3, International Brotherhood of Electrical Workers*, 325 US 797 (1945).

[20] 325 U.S. 797, 800 (1945).

[21] *See Columbia River Packers Association* v. *Hinton*, 315 U.S. 143, 145 (1942).

[22] *Drivers Union* v. *Lake Valley Co.*, 311 U.S. 91 (1940).

[23] *See, for example*, Phillip Areeda, Louis Kaplow, Aaron Edlin, *Antitrust Analysis: Problems, Text, and Cases* (New York: Wolters Kluwer Law & Business, 7th ed. 2013), 87 citing in particular *Columbia River Packers Assn.* v. *Hinton*, 315 U.S. 143 (1942) ("union of fishermen not within labor exemption because they were selling fish, not their services").

[24] *See, for example*, *United States* v. *American Federation of Musicians*, 318 U.S. 741 (1943).

the legality of how writers responded to theatrical mediators of influence, like the Shuberts.

The merging artistic and economic interests also framed the *Ring* antitrust dispute. Ring's grievances were financial – he was claiming treble damages for an alleged injury that led to his significant losses. The proceedings, however, were triggered by an artistic disagreement. Ring's desire to make significant changes to the work included changes to the title of the play. The artistic dispute consumes the 2000 pages of transcripts from the trial proceedings in the Southern District of New York. Ring started proceedings based on requests to make changes to *Stovepipe Hat* which the authors rejected. The novice producer challenged the arbitration process which would determine whether author resistance to making changes was unreasonable. Alternatively, the authors held the view that they had a right to resist making any changes without their consent – a right which they believed impeded the integrity of their work as independent contractors.[25] Thus, a critical dimension of the *Ring* proceedings was an exploration of encroachments on the author's integrity framed around the language of competition law.

## I. RESISTANCE TO NEW AGREEMENTS AND HARNESSING *HELLZAPOPPIN*

Stakeholders renegotiated the fourth iteration of the Minimum Basic Agreement in early 1941. In response, Shubert lawyers William Klein and Adolph Kaufman set about the task of resisting the expansion of the new agreement, clause by clause, and subsection by subsection.[26] The Shuberts were willing to challenge the Guild's Basic Agreement on some of the lesser-known clauses. For example, Kaufman suggested pushing back on the provision that only allowed American producers to stage one play a year written by a British author who resided in Britain.[27] Kaufman was also concerned that producers had no control over the leasing of rights outside of Britain and the United States. The leasing rights were left to the "sole discretion" of the author.[28] Kaufman wanted to challenge provisions that required producers to file a bond with the Guild to

25 During Carl Ring's cross examination, the point was raised by counsel for the Guild that this notion of integrity existed at common law: "it is the common law which maintains the integrity of the playwright, or any creative artist … Now Spina had these rights independently, totally independent of any Sherman antitrust business or any [Minimum Basic Agreement]": Transcript: *Carl E. Ring* v. *Harold Spina et al.*, United States District Court Southern District of New York, December 22, 1948, 922, National Archives at New York City [hereafter Transcript: *Carl E. Ring* v. *Harold Spina et al.*].

26 *See* A. Kaufman to W. Klein, June 14, 1940, General Correspondence Collection, Basic Agreement 1936–1941, Box 17, *The Shubert Archive*; *see also* A. Kaufman to W. Klein: Re Minimum Basic Agreement, January 2, 1941, General Correspondence Collection, Basic Agreement 1936–1941, Box 17, *The Shubert Archive*.

27 *See* A. Kaufman to W. Klein, June 14, 1940, General Correspondence Collection, Basic Agreement 1936–1941, Box 17, *The Shubert Archive*.

28 A. Kaufman to W. Klein, June 14, 1940, General Correspondence Collection, Basic Agreement 1936–1941, Box 17, *The Shubert Archive*.

remain in good standing,[29] and he believed that a producer deserved to have more influence over the flow of copyright into subsidiary fields including stock and film rights.[30] The Shubert lawyers also felt that producers had no stake in "any new performing rights [that] are discovered."[31]

For the Shuberts, the provision providing that the "manager cannot make any changes in the script without the author's consent" was a "troublesome clause."[32] They believed the arbitration process did not compel authors to make changes, even where producer requests were reasonable. And the brothers continued to resist the notion that playwrights should have discretion over casting and direction decisions. For the Shuberts, these decisions were "strictly a producer's function."[33]

Preempting the challenges ahead, the Shuberts, under the banner of the Select Theatres Corporation and Select Operating Corporation, started proceedings in the New York Supreme Court against Elmer Rice, President of the Dramatists Guild, in January 1941.[34] Select Theatres and Operating became the "successors" to the Shubert Theatre Corporation,[35] but were essentially holding companies formed after the liquidation of the Shubert Organization during the Depression.[36]

The central claim of the Shuberts was that the Guild and its Basic Agreement was a combination involved in the restraint of trade and conspiracy under New York Law.[37] The Shuberts resurrected the same "closed shop" arguments they made after

29 A. Kaufman to W. Klein, June 14, 1940, General Correspondence Collection, Basic Agreement 1936–1941, Box 17, *The Shubert Archive.*

30 *See* A. Kaufman to W. Klein, June 14, 1940, General Correspondence Collection, Basic Agreement 1936–1941, Box 17, *The Shubert Archive* once again asking for a 50/50 split on film.

31 A. Kaufman to W. Klein, June 14, 1940, General Correspondence Collection, Basic Agreement 1936–1941, Box 17, *The Shubert Archive.*

32 A. Kaufman to W. Klein, June 14, 1940, General Correspondence Collection, Basic Agreement 1936–1941, Box 17, *The Shubert Archive.*

33 A. Kaufman to W. Klein, June 14, 1940, General Correspondence Collection, Basic Agreement 1936–1941, Box 17, *The Shubert Archive.*

34 "Complaint of: Select Theatres Corporation and Select Operating Corporation" in *Select Theatres Corporation and Select Operating Corporation* v. *Elmer Rice*, Supreme Court of the State of New York, January 1941, General Correspondence Collection, Basic Agreement 1936–1941, Box 17, *The Shubert Archive.*

35 *See* "Complaint of: Select Theatres Corporation and Select Operating Corporation" in *Select Theatres Corporation and Select Operating Corporation* v. *Elmer Rice*, Supreme Court of the State of New York, January 1941, General Correspondence Collection, Basic Agreement 1936–1941, Box 17, *The Shubert Archive.*

36 As noted, the new Select Organization repurchased their own assets – including twenty-eight theatres, performance rights, and scripts – at a bargain-basement price with no other bidders. *See* Vickery, "Did the Shuberts Save Broadway?," 79–80.

37 New York General Business Law § 340. Contracts or agreements for monopoly or in restraint of trade illegal and void. Discussed at "Complaint of: Select Theatres Corporation and Select Operating Corporation" in *Select Theatres Corporation and Select Operating Corporation* v. *Elmer Rice*, Supreme Court of the State of New York, January 1941, General Correspondence Collection, Basic Agreement 1936–1941, Box 17, *The Shubert Archive.*

the introduction of the first Minimum Basic Agreement in 1926.[38] The key elements of the conspiracy claim included restrictions on relationships with foreign authors, narrow minimum conditions for royalty payments, and overbearing playwright artistic control which apparently caused:

> insufferable hardships upon the plaintiffs and other producers since as the play progresses throughout rehearsal and particularly to fit the particular talents and attributes of special performers, additions, omissions or alterations frequently become necessary.[39]

The new agreement of 1941, according to the plaintiffs, contained "substantially all of the same arduous, burdensome and oppressive terms as in the present agreement coupled with still more unreasonable and objectious provisions."[40] Dispelling assumptions that this was an exclusively Shubert-driven cause, producer William Brady commenced a similar claim against Elmer Rice.[41]

The 1927 proceedings had not adequately resolved whether the Minimum Basic Agreement was anticompetitive, and the Shuberts had a long memory. By January 1941, almost a month before the new Basic Agreement was to take effect,[42] the producers' complaint appeared to focus on Brady's claim against Elmer Rice.[43] The February 28 deadline for the new Agreement came and went, and on March 10 the producers began an industry-wide claim. The League of New York Theatres issued a summons against the Authors' League of America.[44] The complaint, drafted by Shubert lawyers Klein and Weinberger on March 10, sought a temporary injunction and costs under section 340 of the General Business Law of the State of New York for

38 *See* "Plaintiff's Complaint," *Shubert Theatre Corporation* v. *Arthur Richman, President of the Dramatists Guild*, April 29, 1927, New York Supreme Court, Record # 16847, Box 008047634, Hall of Records, New York Courts.

39 "Complaint of: Select Theatres Corporation and Select Operating Corporation" in *Select Theatres Corporation and Select Operating Corporation* v. *Elmer Rice*, Supreme Court of the State of New York, January 1941, General Correspondence Collection, Basic Agreement 1936–1941, Box 17, *The Shubert Archive* (page 7).

40 "Complaint of: Select Theatres Corporation and Select Operating Corporation" in *Select Theatres Corporation and Select Operating Corporation* v. *Elmer Rice*, Supreme Court of the State of New York, January 1941, General Correspondence Collection, Basic Agreement 1936–1941, Box 17, The Shubert Archive (pages 9–10).

41 "Complaint of: William A Brady" in *William A. Brady* v. *Elmer Rice*, Supreme Court of the State of New York, January 1941, General Correspondence Collection, Basic Agreement 1936–1941, Box 17, *The Shubert Archive*.

42 President of the Dramatists Guild, Elmer Rice, confirmed that the 1936 Agreement would end on February 28, 1941. Elmer Rice to Producing Managers, February 27, 1941, General Correspondence Collection, Basic Agreement 1936–1941, Box 17, *The Shubert Archive*.

43 *See* Milton Weinberger to W. Brady, January 22, 1941, General Correspondence Collection, Basic Agreement 1936–1941, Box 17, *The Shubert Archive*. At the bottom of the copy of the letter, comments are attributed to J. J. Shubert: "I hope Brady doesn't back out on what he apparently promised Klein."

44 "Complaint of: League of New York Theatres Inc" in *League of New York Theatres Inc* v. *Authors' League of America Inc*, Supreme Court of the State of New York, March 10, 1941, General Correspondence Collection, Basic Agreement 1936–1941, Box 17, *The Shubert Archive*.

a restraint of trade. Therefore, this was the same claim of fourteen years prior but now pitted the leading producer and dramatist associations against each other.[45]

The proceedings never went to trial. In June of 1941, the League of New York Theatres informed members it had reached a compromise deal with the dramatists.[46] Litigation compelled the dramatists to make considerable concessions. The new Basic Agreement would not apply to nonresident foreign language authors but would apply to the American writer who adapted the work.[47] In the revised agreement, the Guild needed to be more responsive to requests for reductions in royalties and requests to keep plays in production for longer periods. The dramatists also agreed to favorably modify producer participation in motion picture rights beyond the initial ten-year period,[48] and for a "more equitable arrangement" over producer access to subsidiary rights. It was a cordial compromise, although, by the end of June 1941, the Shuberts still refused to sign the new Basic Agreement. William Klein wrote to J. J. Shubert on June 25:

> In view of your determination not to recognize the Dramatists Guild under any circumstances, my advice in the matter is to go along pretty much as you have in the past and if need be revive Producing Associates Inc as your managerial company.[49]

In some respects, the willingness of the Shuberts to formally sign the new Basic Agreement was a moot issue in substance, however. In practice, the impresarios continued to assert artistic and economic autonomy when it suited their needs.[50] Julius Green, for example, implies that the Shuberts reshaped Agatha Christie's American production of *Ten Little Indians* – apparently "a rather different play from that seen in Britain."[51] When Christie's representative Edmund Cork requested a copy of the American production script, Adolph Kaufman told Lee Shubert to provide "the manuscript of the original play ... as it was written by Miss Christie,

45 The claim brought by the producers mirrored the draft versions of the Brady and Shubert claims.

46 *See* J. Reilly to Members of the League of New York Theatres Inc, June 10, 1941, General Correspondence Collection, Basic Agreement 1936–1941, Box 17, *The Shubert Archive*.

47 J. Reilly to Members of the League of New York Theatres Inc, June 10, 1941, General Correspondence Collection, Basic Agreement 1936–1941, Box 17, *The Shubert Archive*.

48 J. Reilly to Members of the League of New York Theatres Inc, June 10, 1941, General Correspondence Collection, Basic Agreement 1936–1941, Box 17, *The Shubert Archive*. Where before, these rights reverted back to the playwright.

49 Memo: W. Klein to J. J. Shubert, June 25, 1941, General Correspondence Collection, Basic Agreement 1936–1941, Box 17, *The Shubert Archive*.

50 They eventually signed in early January 1942 (Lee Shubert). The Shuberts wanted to sign under the Select Operating Corporation, but to be in good standing "persons in control" also had to be a signatory for the Corporation to be a signatory of the MBA. *See* A. Kaufman to W. Klein, January 7, 1942, General Correspondence Collection, Basic Agreement 1942–1955, Box 17, *The Shubert Archive*; W. Klein to Don Douglas, January 10, 1942, General Correspondence Collection, Basic Agreement 1942–1955, Box 17, *The Shubert Archive*.

51 *See* Julius Green, *Curtain Up: Agatha Christie, A Life in the Theatre* (New York: Harper Collins, 2015), 188. Note that the work did have an alternative, deeply offensive, title as produced on Broadway.

and not the playing version which is being produced."[52] Christie "would have been horrified to see her work advertised variously as a 'hilarious chiller thriller,' a 'hilarious mystery thriller' and a 'superlative comedy mystery'."[53] Christie was a signatory to the Minimum Basic Agreement,[54] and thus required consultation over any changes to the script, which appeared to be significant.

But the Shubert resistance to the Minimum Basic Agreement did not only come from a desire to exploit opportunities and maximize profits. Resistance sometimes involved acts of pragmatism to revive a production likely to fail without producer intervention. For example, Adolph Kaufman and Lee Shubert dutifully followed Minimum Basic Agreement protocols by asking Christie to make changes to her play *Towards Zero* – particularly the final act. Christie, however, was too busy to make changes.[55] To resuscitate the work, the Shuberts, as they had done on other occasions, took matters into their own hands and employed a writer Robert Harris to undertake the task of revising the script (apparently without Christie's consent). Harris's contract resembled that of an employee rather than an independent contractor. Harris relinquished all rights in the amended work to the Shuberts.[56] The production, however, appeared to be beyond redemption and the out-of-town production never found its feet. The Shuberts made further attempts to persuade Christie to make the necessary changes, but they never came.

In other instances, the Shuberts acted outside the confines of the Minimum Basic Agreement because they believed it created a better outcome for creators and producers.[57] For example, the Shuberts created flexible percentage-based service agreements for the musical revue *Hellzapoppin*, by "Ole" Olsen and "Chic" Johnson, which were revised as the production became increasingly popular.[58] The musical revue in two acts, an escapist comedy, ran at three Broadway theatres between 1938 and 1941 for a staggering 1404 performances.[59] Olsen and Johnson were

52 Green, *Curtain Up*, 188 citing note 60: "SA [Shubert Archive]: Memo from Adolph Kaufman to Lee Shubert: 21/7/44."

53 Green, *Curtain Up*, 188.

54 Green cites Edmund Cork writing to Christie: "We will pay your membership dues to the Dramatists Guild." Green, *Curtain Up*, 150.

55 Green, *Curtain Up*, 219–220.

56 Green, *Curtain Up*, 220.

57 During the *Ring* v. *Spina* trial, counsel identified several plays in which the Shuberts allegedly operated outside of the Guild system. Issue discussed at Transcript: *Carl E. Ring* v. *Harold Spina et al.*, December 21, 1948, 686–687. Edward Greenbaum acting for the Dramatists Guild refers to *Ten O'Clock Scholar, My Romance*, implying these plays were produced outside of the Guild system.

58 *See* supplemental agreement outlined in letter: Select Operating Corporation to Ole Olsen and Chic Johnson, July 25, 1939, Production Correspondence Collection, Hellzapoppin 1938–39, 3–254, *The Shubert Archive*. *See also* George Middleton, *The Dramatists Guild: What It Is and Does; How It Happened and Why* (New York: Authors' League of America, 1947), 4. Note also that revues were one of the remaining mediums where managers retained a degree of artistic control in the Basic Agreement until 1946 (*see* next chapter).

59 *Hellzapoppin* ran at the 46th Street Theatre (September 22, 1938–November 24, 1938); Winter Garden Theatre (November 26, 1938– November 23, 1941); and the Majestic Theatre (November 25,

vaudeville comedians. It was perhaps their dual role as performers and creators, coupled with the work being a revue rather than straight play or musical,[60] which provided the Shuberts an opportunity to create an independent arrangement outside the Minimum Basic Agreement framework. Olsen and Johnson were not initially members of the Dramatists Guild, although they would join for future projects. There are indicators, however, suggesting that Olsen and Johnson resembled authors. For example, posters and programs for *Hellzapoppin*, as reproduced in Figures 7.1 and 7.2, credited the duo as creators of the work.[61]

And *Hellzapoppin* was registered as an unpublished work with the Copyright Office in August 1938 under the names of Olsen and Johnson.[62] A private agreement between the Shuberts and the comedy duo of July 25, 1938, is careful to acknowledge the duo's rights as creators but avoids the specific language of authorship.[63] The Shubert Organization declared Olsen and Johnson as indemnified against any losses, as it was the Shuberts who were the producers of the work.[64] But the agreement also

1941–December 17, 1941): *see* The Broadway League, Internet Broadway Database: www.ibdb.com/broadway-production/hellzapoppin-12378.

60 Thus, under the 1936 Minimum Basic Agreement, the producer still had the right to make changes to revues without author consent.

61 *See* the Internet Broadway Database that credits Olsen and Johnson as producers and writers of the book: Produced by Olsen & Johnson; (Uncredited) produced by Messrs. Shubert (Lee and J. J.) Music by Sammy Fain and Charles Tobias; Lyrics by Sammy Fain and Charles Tobias; Book by Olsen & Johnson; Musical Director: Harold Stern; Assistant Musical Dir.: Edward A. Hunt; Vocal arrangements by Phil Ellis; Featuring songs by Don George, Teddy Hall, Annette Mills, Gonzalo Curiel, Paul Mann and Stephen Weiss; Featuring songs with lyrics by Oscar Hammerstein II. Production page at: www.ibdb.com/broadway-production/hellzapoppin-12378. Note Figures 7.1 and 7.2: The poster for Figure 7.1 (original poster: Artist: Frank Morgan, 1938) and Figure 7.2 is from the 1940 program of the Winter Garden production published by Playbill.

62 *See* letter, W. Hughes to W. Klein, March 17, 1939, Production Correspondence Collection, Hellzapoppin 1938–39, 3–254, *The Shubert Archive*–letter outlines the details of the registration of the unpublished script ("its authors" Olsen and Johnson, registered on August 1, 1938–entry D–unpublished–58266). (Record confirmed in the virtual card catalogue: https://vcc.copyright.gov/browse.) They also registered two-act versions in 1939 (D unpub 70930) and 1940 (D unpub 70929); *see also* letter, Library of Congress to W. Hughes, March 17, 1939, Production Correspondence Collection, Hellzapoppin 1938–39, 3–254, *The Shubert Archive* where letter identifies authors and that no assignment of this work has happened since registered. Interesting correspondence that follows where internal memo clearly states that Shuberts have no right or authority to copyright the script of Hellzapoppin: *See* W. Klein to A. Kaufman, March 18, 1939, Production Correspondence Collection, Hellzapoppin 1938–39, 3–254, *The Shubert Archive*. It is a right that appeared to be safeguarded carefully by Olsen and Johnson. *See also* W. Klein to G. H. Werner, March 17, 1939, Production Correspondence Collection, Hellzapoppin 1938–39, 3–254, *The Shubert Archive*. (Record also confirmed in the virtual card catalogue: https://vcc.copyright.gov/browse.) It looks like the Shuberts were interested in securing the rights to the work but the lawyers, Klein in particular, strongly advised against attempting to register the work and the potential for a breach of contract.

63 *See* Select Operating Corporation to Ole Olsen and Chic Johnson, July 25, 1938, Production Correspondence Collection, Hellzapoppin 1938–39, 3–254, *The Shubert Archive* (under William Morris Agency letterhead).

64 Select Operating Corporation to Ole Olsen and Chic Johnson, October 6, 1938, Production Correspondence Collection, Hellzapoppin 1938–39, 3–254, *The Shubert Archive*. This was clarified in a letter a few months later.

FIGURE 7.1 Poster for Winter Garden production of *Hellzapoppin*

provided that Olsen and Johnson would "supply" all material, and the material was "owned by you,"[65] including the title of the work. The duo was the "sole owners" of the material and that "we [Shuberts] shall have no rights whatsoever thereto."[66] A slight wrinkle in the agreement, which distinguished it from the Basic Agreement, was that the Shuberts could provide any additional material and cast as they saw fit. Further, any added material would be the "sole property" of the impresarios.[67]

65 Select Operating Corporation to Ole Olsen and Chic Johnson, July 25, 1938, Production Correspondence Collection, Hellzapoppin 1938–39, 3–254, *The Shubert Archive.*

66 Select Operating Corporation to Ole Olsen and Chic Johnson, July 25, 1938, Production Correspondence Collection, Hellzapoppin 1938–39, 3–254, *The Shubert Archive.*

67 Select Operating Corporation to Ole Olsen and Chic Johnson, July 25, 1938, Production Correspondence Collection, Hellzapoppin 1938–39, 3–254, *The Shubert Archive.*

WINTER GARDEN

1634-1646 BROADWAY REALTY CO., INC.

FIRE NOTICE: The exit, indicated by a red light and sign, nearest to the seat you occupy, is the shortest route to the street.
In the event of fire or other emergency please do not run—WALK TO THAT EXIT.
JOHN J. McELLIGOTT, Fire Chief and Commissioner

THE · PLAYBILL · PUBLISHED · BY · THE · NEW · YORK · THEATRE · PROGRAM · CORPORATION

BEGINNING MONDAY EVENING, MAY 6, 1940

It is urged for the comfort and safety of all, that theatre patrons refrain from lighting matches in this theatre.

MATINEES WEDNESDAY AND SATURDAY

OLSEN AND JOHNSON
present
THE NEW
HELLZAPOPPIN
The Screamlined Revue
Designed For Laughing
with
OLSEN AND JOHNSON
BARTO AND MANN CHARLES WITHERS THE RADIO ROGUES HAL SHERMAN
WALTER NILSSON THE CHARIOTEERS
BETTYMAE AND BEVERLY CRANE THEO HARDEEN
Cyrel Roodney and June Winters, Reed, Dean and Reed, Shirley Wayne, Bergh and Moore, Stephen Olsen, June Johnson, Billy Adams and 100 others.

Book by OLSEN and JOHNSON
Music and Lyrics by SAMMY FAIN and CHARLES TOBIAS
Production staged by EDWARD DURYEA DOWLING
Dances Arranged by GAE FOSTER
Costumes Designed by JOAN PERSONETTE

FIGURE 7.2 Playbill program for Winter Garden production of *Hellzapoppin*

As for compensation, Olsen and Johnson received a "percentage" based on the length of the run rather than a royalty as stipulated in the Basic Agreement: 2 percent of the gross on the first four weeks; 10 percent from the fifth week onwards; and 12.5 percent outside of New York.[68] The Shuberts also inserted an option that did not exist in the Minimum Basic Agreement. If Olsen and Johnson received twenty weeks of work during the 1938–1939 season, the Shuberts could engage their services for the next season.[69] Not one of

68 *See* Memo: A. Kaufman to L. Shubert, July 28, 1938, Production Correspondence Collection, Hellzapoppin 1938–39, 3–254, *The Shubert Archive*; A. Kaufman to L. Shubert, W. Klein, J. Waters, H. Kaufman, J. J. Shubert, August 1, 1938, Production Correspondence Collection, Hellzapoppin 1938–39, 3–254, *The Shubert Archive*.

69 *See* Memo: A. Kaufman to L. Shubert, July 28, 1938, Production Correspondence Collection, Hellzapoppin 1938–39, 3–254, *The Shubert Archive*.

the *Hellzapoppin* contracts, therefore, used the specific language of authorship, but the material was "owned" by Olsen and Johnson. And the Shubert Organization administered the duo under the category of actors. For example, a memo on "actors' contracts" of September 1938 lists the duo among the many performers in the compensation summary.[70]

The *Hellzapoppin* arrangement was precisely the kind of freedom the Shuberts wanted in their contractual relationships with creators built on not only their interests but also the pragmatic considerations of mounting a production. Creators had a degree of artistic control – especially successful creators – but the Shuberts needed some flexibility, and control, over artistic changes and compensation terms. The Dramatists Guild, however, viewed these contracts differently based on years of subordination. It was this kind of arrangement that the Dramatists Guild was trying to avoid. Flexibility encouraged exploitation.

It was clear that *Hellzapoppin* was a roaring success a few months into its Broadway run. The Shuberts rewarded Olsen and Johnson by entering into new agreements at the end of December 1938.[71] The new terms provided the creators with 12.5 percent of gross for weekly takings up to US$20,000 and 15 percent for gross amounts in excess.[72] The Shuberts continued to renegotiate in response to the success of the show, increasing the compensation rates at the end of 1940,[73] and again when they ended their successful run in 1941.[74] The above examples suggest that the Shuberts were obviously in the business of making money. But financial success did not necessarily come at the expense of exploiting creators. The impresarios believed that it was more likely creators and producers would reap the benefits of a successful production by negotiating agreements outside the Minimum Basic Agreement framework. A successful collaboration required flexibility over financial and artistic issues on a case-by-case basis.

The Shuberts, therefore, operated inside and outside the Dramatists Guild system, making incremental judgments in each production. In the process, they continued to challenge the validity of the Basic Agreement on various grounds including small rights (the public performance of music), film rights, subsidiary,

70 Memo: H. Kaufman, J. Waters, A Cohen, September 7, 1938, Production Correspondence Collection, Hellzapoppin 1938–39, 3–254, *The Shubert Archive*.

71 *See* A. Kaufman to L. Shubert, W. Klein, J. Waters, H. Kaufman, J. J. Shubert, John Shubert, December 27, 1938, Production Correspondence Collection, Hellzapoppin 1938–39, 3–254, *The Shubert Archive*; Select Operating Corporation to O. Olsen and C. Johnson, December 24, 1938, Production Correspondence Collection, Hellzapoppin 1938–39, 3–254, *The Shubert Archive*.

72 A. Kaufman to L. Shubert, W. Klein, J. Waters, H. Kaufman, J. J. Shubert, 27 December 1938, Production Correspondence Collection, Hellzapoppin 1938–39, 3–254, *The Shubert Archive*.

73 Memo A. Kaufman "Re Olsen and Johnson," December 23, 1940, Production Correspondence Collection, Hellzapoppin 1938–39, 3–254, *The Shubert Archive*.

74 *See* Memo A. Kaufman to L. Shubert, W. Klein, J. Waters, H. Kaufman, J. J. Shubert, March 24, 1941, Production Correspondence Collection, Hellzapoppin 1940–1941, 3–254, *The Shubert Archive*; "Rider Attached to and Forming part of the contract between Ole Olsen and Chic Johnson," February 11, 1941, Production Correspondence Collection, Hellzapoppin 1948–1949, 3–254, *The Shubert Archive*.

and foreign rights. For the Shuberts, the importance, and priority, of these issues would vary depending on what the dramatists were proposing with each new iteration of the Basic Agreement. But the issue that consistently frustrated the Shuberts was the right to make alterations, additions, and omissions to the work. The playwrights had invoked the language of something similar to personal rights for decades. For the dramatists, the integrity of the work was at stake. The Shuberts, however, believed the Guild carved the artistic control entitlement out of thin air with the introduction of the first Basic Agreement, and they were unwilling to let the issue slide.

## II. *RING* V. *SPINA*: THE PRELIMINARY PROCEEDINGS

Carl Ring had no experience in the theatre when he spoke to Josephine Nicosia at Wickersham Hospital, New York, in January 1944.[75] Ring admitted himself because he thought he had ulcers, which turned out not to be true. The excruciatingly painful events for Ring followed after his discharge from Wickersham. Nicosia was the wife of Ring's doctor and a relative of Harold Spina – one of the three authors of the musical *Stovepipe Hat*.[76] Ring may not have had experience in the theatre, but he was a successful entrepreneur. He graduated from the University of Maine with a degree in mechanical engineering and Harvard Law School in 1929.[77] Ring practiced as a patent attorney in New York after law school and also had a business in Massachusetts which manufactured sunglasses.[78] The entrepreneur eventually discontinued his legal practice and maintained an electrical engineering firm in New Jersey which provided services to the railroad industry.[79]

Nicosia perhaps saw in Ring someone with an entrepreneurial spirit and, even more importantly – for the survival of the fledgling theatrical production *Stovepipe Hat* – deep pockets. Nicosia invited Ring to a reading of *Stovepipe Hat*, he was captivated, and soon after was investing thousands of dollars into the venture. The press documented the brief history of the production with excited anticipation for an eventual Broadway transferal.[80] The musical about the career of Abraham Lincoln "through the eyes of his contemporaries,"[81] first produced by Irving Gaumont, was supposed to have out-of-town tryouts in New Haven beginning on May 18, followed

75 Transcript: *Carl E. Ring* v. *Harold Spina et al.*, December 15, 1948, 90.

76 Transcript: *Carl E. Ring* v. *Harold Spina et al.*, December 15, 1948, 90.

77 Transcript: *Carl E. Ring* v. *Harold Spina et al.*, December 15, 1948, 88.

78 Transcript: *Carl E. Ring* v. *Harold Spina et al.*, December 15, 1948, 89.

79 Transcript: *Carl E. Ring* v. *Harold Spina et al.*, December 15, 1948, 90.

80 *See, for example*, "New Musical Comedy Opens at Shubert," *New Haven Courier*, May 6, 1944; "'Stovepipe Hat': New Musical Show Due to Play Here," *New Haven Register*, May 7, 1944; "'Stovepipe Hat' Has Premiere at Shubert May 18," *Hartford Courier*, May 8, 1944 (Stovepipe Hat Collection, Library for the Performing Arts, Dorothy and Lewis B. Cullman Center, New York City) [hereafter Stovepipe Hat Collection].

81 Although Lincoln never appears in the play. *See* "Stovepipe Hat in Premiere," *The Christian Science Monitor* (no date), Stovepipe Hat Collection.

by Boston, and Philadelphia.[82] The intention was to return to Broadway by June 1944.[83] In the second week of April, the press was reporting that Carl Ring had joined the production as a coproducer with Gaumont.[84] The production started to turn sour over the next month. A week before opening in New Haven, the *New York Times* reported that "the newcomer in show business," Carl Ring, had become the sole sponsor of *Stovepipe Hat* after seeking temporary injunctive relief to restrain Gaumont from interfering with the show, and also after Ring had agreed to reimburse Gaumont about US$6,000.[85] Ring's investment in the production, by this stage, was US$55,000.[86]

The New Haven production received warm reviews. The press commended Robert Ross's staging for "crowding so many momentous moments into the space of two and a half hours."[87] The lead voices of the cast of over one hundred also received praise. The response to the book and lyrics was not as enthusiastic, however. Critics described the work of Walter Hannan, Edward Heyman, and Harold Spina as "typical" and "smacked somewhat of the treatment accorded allegorical presentations in radio work."[88] The production moved to the Shubert Theatre in Boston on May 22 where the reception was even more constrained. The press described some scenes as missing their mark,[89] with the use of fantasy in the work viewed as a "weakness." The production did not benefit from a "static" story that was "episodic and vague, told jerkily and without sharp focus,"[90] "badly confused,"[91] with "slow and ill-considered direction."[92]

In the next week, the *New York Times* reported that the production had "abruptly ended" in Boston.[93] Ring released a statement charging Spina with walking out of

82 Irving Gaumont entered into his initial agreement with the three authors Harold Spina, Walter Hannan, and Edward Heyman on February 7, 1944. "All royalties hereunder" were to be split between the three authors as follows: cl 2C.1.: Spina 63 percent; Hannan 23 percent; and Heyman 15 percent. Royalties were calculated on 6 percent of gross and 7 percent after recovery or for sale of film rights. *See* Edmond Pauker Papers, Yale Collection of American Literature, Beinecke Rare Book and Manuscript Library, Box 39, fol. 961.

83 *See* "Opening on May 18 for Stovepipe Hat," *New York Times*, March 28, 1944, Stovepipe Hat Collection.

84 *See, for example*, "Carl Ring Joins Gaumont," *Tribune McCord*, April 8, 1944; *Brooklyn Eagle*, April 10, 1944; *New York Times*, April 10, 1944, Stovepipe Hat Collection.

85 *See* "Mr Ring Sole Sponsor," *New York Times*, May 11, 1944, Stovepipe Hat Collection.

86 "Mr Ring Sole Sponsor," *New York Times*, May 11, 1944, Stovepipe Hat Collection.

87 *See* "Last Night's Play: Stovepipe Hat-A legend with Music," *New Haven Courier*, May 19, 1944, Stovepipe Hat Collection.

88 *See* "Last Night's Play: Stovepipe Hat-A legend with Music," *New Haven Courier*, May 19, 1944.

89 *See* "Stovepipe Hat in Premiere," *The Christian Science Monitor* (no date). *See* E. Hughes, "Review: Stovepipe Hat," *The Boston Herald*, May 24, 1944. Stovepipe Hat Collection.

90 *See* C. Durgin, "Review: Stovepipe Hat," *The Boston Daily Globe*, May 24, 1944, Stovepipe Hat Collection; Elliot Norton, " 'Stovepipe Hat: Play about Lincoln, Opens Here," *Boston Post*, May 24, 1944, Stovepipe Hat Collection.

91 E. Hughes, "Review: Stovepipe Hat," *The Boston Herald*, May 24, 1944, Stovepipe Hat Collection.

92 E. Hughes, "Review: Stovepipe Hat," *The Boston Herald*, May 24, 1944, Stovepipe Hat Collection. There were, however, other reviews suggesting it was well received: "'Stovepipe Hat' Pleases Large Shubert Audience," *Boston Traveller*, May 24, 1944, Stovepipe Hat Collection.

93 "'Stovepipe Hat' Closes In Boston: Musical Abruptly Ceases," *New York Times*, May 29, 1944, 19.

the show, while also identifying the need to complete the orchestrations and work on the book.[94] In response, the authors held that Ring had violated the Minimum Basic Agreement, "by altering scenes and by discharging players without their consent."[95] The authors threatened that all rights would revert to them if Ring refused to restore the play to its original form.[96] Included in the major changes to the work was the alteration of the name of the musical from *Stovepipe Hat* to *Johnny Drummer*.[97]

The authors sought arbitration under the Minimum Basic Agreement to which Ring was a reluctant signatory after taking over sole producing responsibilities from Gaumont.[98] In response, Ring wanted to test the legality of the arbitration process in the courts, and thus the legality of the Minimum Basic Agreement. The producer-initiated proceedings in the Southern District of New York, reported widely in the press,[99] sought injunctive relief against the authors for, among other things, restraint of arbitration. Ring also claimed treble damages under the Sherman Act.[100] Judge Caffey considered three questions which included whether the parties were engaged in interstate commerce and whether the Dramatists Guild trade association fell under an exemption to antitrust law. The Court also considered whether the arbitration process provided for in the Minimum Basic Agreement violated antitrust law.[101]

His Honor dismissed the interstate issue.[102] As for the exemption, Judge Caffey found that precedent had yet to find "the line of demarcation [between union and guild] with sufficient clarity to enable one with confidence to say that the defendant guild comes within the protection of Section 17."[103] And turning to the validity of the arbitration process, Judge Caffey concluded that not enough facts were furnished to

94 "'Stovepipe Hat' Closes In Boston: Musical Abruptly Ceases," *New York Times*, May 29, 1944, 19.

95 "'Stovepipe Hat' Closes In Boston: Musical Abruptly Ceases," *New York Times*, May 29, 1944, 19.

96 "'Stovepipe Hat' Closes In Boston: Musical Abruptly Ceases," *New York Times*, May 29, 1944, 19.

97 "Authors, Producers Row on 'Stovepipe,' Show Folds in Boston," *Variety*, May 31, 1944, 53.

98 Ring believed he was coerced into signing the Minimum Basic Agreement after taking over production from Gaumont. *See Ring* v. *Spina et al.*, 148 F 2d. 647, 649.

99 *See, for example*, "Producer asks in Stovepipe Hat," *Variety*, 21 June 1944, 48; "'Stovepipe' Hearing off until July 18," *Variety*, June 28, 1944, 53; "'Stovepipe Hat' Producer Sues 3 of Show's Authors: Ring Asks $424,300," *New York Herald Tribune*, June 17, 1944, 9A.

100 Transcript of Record at 102: *Carl Ring* v. *Harold Spina et al.*, United States Court of Appeal for the Second Circuit: Opinion of Judge Caffey, Denying Temporary Injunction, United States District Court, Southern District of New York, National Archives at New York City.

101 Transcript of Record at 103: *Carl Ring* v. *Harold Spina et al.*, United States Court of Appeal for the Second Circuit: Opinion of Judge Caffey, Denying Temporary Injunction, United States District Court, Southern District of New York, National Archives at New York City.

102 Transcript of Record at 103–104: *Carl Ring* v. *Harold Spina et al.*, United States Court of Appeal for the Second Circuit: Opinion of Judge Caffey, Denying Temporary Injunction, United States District Court, Southern District of New York, National Archives at New York City.

103 Transcript of Record at 104: *Carl Ring* v. *Harold Spina et al.*, United States Court of Appeal for the Second Circuit: Opinion of Judge Caffey, Denying Temporary Injunction, United States District Court, Southern District of New York, National Archives at New York City. *See* Act of Oct. 15, 1914, ch. 323, §6, 38 Stat. 731 as amended, 15 U.S.C. §17: "The labor of a human being is not a commodity or article of commerce. Nothing contained in the antitrust laws shall be construed to forbid the existence and operation of labor, agricultural, or horticultural organizations, instituted for the

determine "whether the minimum basic agreement as a whole, or its Article XV [regarding arbitration], constitutes a violation."[104] The Court denied the motion for a temporary injunction,[105] and on August 12, 1944, Judge Rifkind vacated the matter.[106]

Ring, representing himself, having now invested around US$120,000 in a failed production, immediately appealed the decision of the District Court to the Second Circuit on the denial of the interlocutory injunction. Judge Clark, writing on behalf of the Court,[107] found reason to reverse the decision of the District Court, and remanded the matter to the District Court for additional trial proceedings.[108] In the process, the Court expressed considerable doubt over the legality of the Minimum Basic Agreement that had operated in the industry for the previous twenty years.[109] First, the Court stated that it was "now well settled that a contract covering a large part of an industry will be void and illegal under the Sherman Act."[110] Identifying how the Basic Agreement prohibited different actions over subsidiary streams of revenue, the Court held that there was a prima facie case that the Agreement was a restraint of trade,[111] and a prima facie case of economic coercion.[112] The Agreement "indicate[d] an attempt to control the industry,"[113] and "a price-fixing combination is not saved by the high purpose for which it is conceived."[114]

As for the Guild's exemption status under section 17 of the Sherman Act,[115] the Court found that although the parties did not have to be in an employer/employee relationship, "the exception will not apply unless an employer-employee relationship is 'the matrix of the controversy'."[116] Given the temporal nature of the engagement between writer and producer, the lack of a wage, and lack of ongoing services or the

purposes of mutual help, and not having capital stock or conducted for profit, or to forbid or restrain individual members of such organizations from lawfully carrying out the legitimate objects thereof; nor shall such organizations, or the members thereof, be held or construed to be illegal combinations or conspiracies in restraint of trade, under the antitrust laws."

104 Transcript of Record at 104: *Carl Ring* v. *Harold Spina et al.*, United States Court of Appeal for the Second Circuit: Opinion of Judge Caffey, Denying Temporary Injunction, United States District Court, Southern District of New York, National Archives at New York City.

105 Transcript of Record at 106: *Carl Ring* v. *Harold Spina et al.*, United States Court of Appeal for the Second Circuit: Opinion of Judge Caffey, Denying Temporary Injunction, United States District Court, Southern District of New York, National Archives at New York City.

106 Transcript of Record at 108: *Carl Ring* v. *Harold Spina et al.*, United States Court of Appeal for the Second Circuit: Order of Judge Rifkind Vacating and Denying Temporary Injunction, United States District Court, Southern District of New York, National Archives at New York City.

107 Evans and Clark JJ.

108 *Ring* v. *Spina et al.*, 148 F 2d. 647, 654 (1945).

109 Since the introduction of the first Minimum Basic Agreement in 1926.

110 *Ring* v. *Spina et al.*, 148 F 2d. 647, 650.

111 *Ring* v. *Spina et al.*, 148 F 2d. 647, 650.

112 *Ring* v. *Spina et al.*, 148 F 2d. 647, 652.

113 *Ring* v. *Spina et al.*, 148 F 2d. 647, 650.

114 *Ring* v. *Spina et al.*, 148 F 2d. 647, 651.

115 As amended 15 U.S.C.§ 17.

116 *Ring* v. *Spina et al.*, 148 F 2d. 647, 651.

provision of working conditions, the Court held "the exception therefore inapplicable."[117] Finally, Judge Clark disagreed with the District Court on whether the claim should fail because the plaintiff sought both rescission and enforcement of the contract.[118]

The Second Circuit's 1945 decision would indeed cast some doubt over the legality of the Basic Agreement and encourage the producers to fight on over the next few years. Shubert lawyers Klein and Weinberger wrote to J. J. Shubert declaring with apparent glee that "I am sure you will read this [the judgment] with interest."[119] "Interest" translated into another opportunity to reject the Basic Agreement structure or at least make it as difficult as possible for the Guild to expand its authority in the ongoing negotiating process.

The judgment, however, which on the face appeared to be a clear victory for Ring, was in substance narrow, and shed no further legal light on whether the Minimum Basic Agreement was unlawful. Avoidance of the substantive antitrust issue would be a common theme throughout the seven years of the *Ring* litigation. The opinion was a preliminary ruling,[120] with "its main effect [being] to suspend arbitration proceedings pending adjudication of the validity of the contracts."[121] The judgment was therefore reversed and cause remanded for further proceedings.[122] The resolution of the substantive issue had to wait for the jury trial.

The press, for the most part, was careful in its reporting, stressing the preliminary nature of the proceedings. Journalists, however, still could not resist resorting to provocative article titles and attention-grabbing opening paragraphs which alluded to a restraint of trade.[123] In a *New York Herald Tribune* editorial titled "Unintelligible Distinction," the author found that similar actions brought against the musicians were "virtually laughed out of court." Was there in substance, the editorial argued, a distinction between "a guild of playwrights" and a "federation of musicians," where they both shared the same goal of group organization?[124] The playwrights, however, had never made this case as plaintiffs.

117 *Ring* v. *Spina et al.*, 148 F 2d. 647, 652.

118 *Ring* v. *Spina et al.*, 148 F 2d. 647, 653. The Court also disagreed with the lower Court on the interstate trade issue: *Ring* v. *Spina et al.*, 148 F 2d. 647, 650–51.

119 Memo: Klein and Weinberger to J. J. Shubert, March 22, 1945, Dramatists Guild Collection, Re Basic Agreement: 1942–1955, Box 17, *The Shubert Archive*.

120 *Ring* v. *Spina et al.*, 148 F 2d. 647, 654.

121 *Ring* v. *Spina et al.*, 148 F 2d. 647, 654.

122 *Ring* v. *Spina et al.*, 148 F 2d. 647, 654. Lawyer Sidney Fleisher wrote to George Middleton that the decision was "contrary to the modern trend of thought in monopoly suits" and was thus "confident of ultimate success." *See* S. Fleisher to G. Middleton, March 23, 1945, Box 25, George Middleton Papers.

123 *See, for example*, "Tough Appeals Court Decision May upset Dramatists Guild's Methods," *Variety*, March 21, 1945, 51; "Dramatists Guild contract held restraint of trade," *Billboard*, March 31, 1945, 1.

124 *See* "Unintelligible Distinction," *New York Herald Tribune*, March 22, 1945, 26. The musicians had been previously granted exemption status.

The producers began all of these proceedings.[125] The producers had an incentive to continue a narrative that suggested the organizational status of the Dramatists Guild was ambiguous. It was an extraordinary bargaining tool the producers could call on – as indeed they would in the future – with each new iteration of the Basic Agreement.

125 The editorial concluded that it was the responsibility of congress to consider the boundaries of what constituted a union for exemption purposes. This issue was not considered for another sixty years in the context of the theatre and the Basic Agreement. *See, generally, The Playwrights Licensing Antitrust Initiative Act: Safeguarding the Future of American Live Theatre: Hearing on S. 2349 Before the S. Judiciary Comm.*, 108th Cong. (2004). Representative Coble reintroduced the Bill in the 109th Congress. *See* H.R. 532, 109th Cong. (2005). As will be discussed in the Epilogue, it progressed no further.

# 8

# Trading On "Its Own Inherent Strength"

In the two years that followed the Second Circuit's decision to remand the matter for further proceedings in the District Court, the defendants moved to strike the case. Ring successfully appealed the motion to strike and requested a trial by jury. The appeal succeeded in the Second Circuit,[1] and the defendants had certiorari denied in the Supreme Court of the United States.[2]

The factual issues, therefore, for the first time, were now set to be examined in the Southern District of New York. In the interim between the Second Circuit's decision of 1945 and the trial proceedings at the end of 1948, the Dramatists Guild adopted a new Minimum Basic Agreement. As with all previous iterations, the producers resisted the Agreement in the months before and after the March 1, 1946, deadline. The *New York Times* reported that the managers "had taken exception" to forty-nine changes proposed by the dramatists. The stakeholders reached a preliminary agreement in March 1946, subject to review over the next six months.[3]

The specific proposals that the Shubert Organization opposed included an expansion in rights for foreign authors. The new Basic Agreement proposed that all contracts with foreign authors follow the Guild-form standard contract,[4] and comply with the minimum terms of the Basic Agreement.[5] The Guild also proposed stricter conditions for securing first-class rights after initial runs,[6] bond payments to

[1] *See Ring* v. *Spina et al.*, 166 F 2d 546 (1948).

[2] *Spina et al.* v. *Ring*, 335 U.S. 813; 69 S. Ct. 30 (1948). *See also* "Supreme Court Refuses to Act in Suit on Play," *Variety*, October 13, 1948, 49.

[3] *See* "Theatre Pact Extended," *New York Times*, June 20, 1946, 18. *See also* Richard Rodgers to Producing Managers Signatory to the Minimum Basic Agreement, February 15, 1946, Dramatists Guild Collection, Re Basic Agreement: 1942–1955, Box 17, *The Shubert Archive*.

[4] Internal Shubert Memorandum Re Dramatists Guild, June 4, 1946, Dramatists Guild Collection, Re. Basic Agreement: 1942–1955, Box 17, *The Shubert Archive*. (re. Art. 1, Sec. 5(b)).

[5] Internal Shubert Memorandum Re. Dramatists Guild, June 4, 1946, Dramatists Guild Collection, Re. Basic Agreement: 1942–1955, Box 17, *The Shubert Archive*. (re. Art. 1, Sec. 6(b)) (even when foreign author is not a member of the Guild).

[6] Internal Shubert Memorandum Re. Dramatists Guild, June 4, 1946, Dramatists Guild Collection, Re. Basic Agreement: 1942–1955, Box 17, *The Shubert Archive*. (re. Art. II, Sec. 8).

the Guild were now as high as US$10,000 for musicals,[7] and motion picture rights were triggered after only forty-five performances.[8] But the proposal which would have enraged the Shuberts more than any other concerned author artistic control. In a decades-long crusade, the dramatists had negotiated their way to require consent for any additions or omissions over straight plays, musicals, and now, in 1946, the final dagger was revues.[9] The writers also asked for approval over the choice of dance director, orchestra contractor, conductor, and music arranger.[10]

John Shubert signed the interim agreement in April 1946,[11] but J. J. continued to work behind the scenes with Adolph Kaufman and William Klein to reject the proposals of the authors over the summer of 1946. J. J. Shubert recommended that the artistic control provisions that gave the author the right to select creative teams be "positively out."[12] He also thought paying author expenses while in New York and providing better conditions for advances was "ridiculous."[13]

The new Basic Agreement eventually came into force in August 1946 but did not include either J. J. or Lee as signatories.[14] George Middleton described the 1946 Minimum Basic Agreement as "radically" different from its predecessors and most of the proposals as outlined above were adopted without amendment, including the

7 Internal Shubert Memorandum Re. Dramatists Guild, June 4, 1946, Dramatists Guild Collection, Re. Basic Agreement: 1942–1955, Box 17, *The Shubert Archive*. (point 8).

8 Internal Shubert Memorandum Re. Dramatists Guild, June 4, 1946, Dramatists Guild Collection, Re. Basic Agreement: 1942–1955, Box 17, *The Shubert Archive* (point 10).

9 Internal Shubert Memorandum Re. Dramatists Guild, June 4, 1946, Dramatists Guild Collection, Re Basic Agreement: 1942–1955, Box 17, *The Shubert Archive*. (re. Art. II, Sec. 3(b)). The Shuberts, over many years, attempted to limit the rights of adapters who were instrumental to their business. The Shuberts wanted greater control over whether they could reject the work of authors who adapted works. Further, if the work was accepted, it would be the sole property of the managers: *see* "Memorandum: Suggested Changes to Dramatists Guild Contract," no date, Dramatists Guild Collection, Re Basic Agreement: 1942–1955, Box 17, *The Shubert Archive*.

10 Internal Shubert Memorandum Re. Dramatists Guild, June 4, 1946, Dramatists Guild Collection, Re Basic Agreement: 1942–1955, Box 17, *The Shubert Archive*. (re. Art. II, Sec. 4(a)). By August of 1946 these matters still appeared to be open: "Memorandum of Principal 'Open' Matters Following Discussions with Dramatists Guild," August 8, 1946, Dramatists Guild Collection, Re Basic Agreement: 1942–1955, Box 17, *The Shubert Archive*. Note also George Middleton writing in 1947: "Today the composer has equal rights with the dramatist in the supervision of his material. Arranger and musical conductor must be approved by the composer. Dance director and director of musical shows, likewise by the authors." George Middleton, *The Dramatists Guild: What It Is and Does. How It Happened and Why* (New York: Dramatists Guild, 1947), 15.

11 Agreement signed by John Shubert (son of JJ) with Dramatists Guild, April 28, 1946, Dramatists Guild Collection, Re. Basic Agreement: 1942–1955, Box 17, *The Shubert Archive*.

12 Memorandum: J. J. Shubert to Klein and Weinberger, June 10, 1946, Dramatists Guild Collection, Re. Basic Agreement: 1942–1955, Box 17, *The Shubert Archive*.

13 Memorandum: J. J. Shubert to Klein and Weinberger, June 10, 1946, Dramatists Guild Collection, Re. Basic Agreement: 1942–1955, Box 17, *The Shubert Archive*.

14 *See* Klein and Weinberger to James Stabile (Dramatists Guild), August 21, 1946, Dramatists Guild Collection, Re. Basic Agreement: 1942–1955, Box 17, *The Shubert Archive* (executed by John Shubert). *See* Transcript: *Carl E. Ring* v. *Harold Spina et al.*, United States District Court Southern District of New York, December 21, 1948, 626, National Archives at New York City.

revue consent amendment.[15] The authors now appeared to have considerable artistic control over their work across different genres.

The brothers continued to adapt and produce on their own terms in defiance of the Agreement, however.[16] Indeed, on the eve of the *Ring* trial, J. J. proposed, and even established, an association called the International Guild of Theatrical Writers, Inc.; an alternative group that focused on foreign authors and existed outside the Minimum Basic Agreement framework. But Klein and his associates gave J. J. reason to pause before moving ahead with the new organization given the pending *Ring* trial. Gesturing to the significance of the proceedings to the broader industry, the lawyers wrote:

> There is no litigation pending by us now against the Dramatists Guild and the suit . . . brought by Carl E Ring, producer of "Stovepipe Hat" will not be tried until the Fall . . . The case against the Dramatists Guild, whenever it is brought, would, of course, be a great deal stronger if there were no other writers' organization in the field.
>
> . . . Under these circumstances we do not recommend that it commence to function until the legality of the Dramatists Guild contract is cleared up once and for all.[17]

## I. THE TRIAL

### A. *The Issues for the Jury*

In the trial proceedings of *Ring* v. *Spina*, counsel shepherded the jury through an expansive business history of the American theatre. The jury was left to decide "whether the Guild was a labor organization exempt from the antitrust laws under 15 U.S.C.A. § 17." And if there was not an exemption, the defendants were acting in violation of antitrust laws.[18] Ring was again seeking treble damages and injunctive relief against the arbitration process.

The producers believed they needed some level of control over the artistic direction of the work to respond to the immediate needs of the production process. These were the same battles that the Shuberts had been fighting with the writers for almost half a century. Alternatively, for the dramatists, it was once again the integrity of the work at

[15] *See* Middleton, *The Dramatists Guild: What It Is and Does*, 14.

[16] *See, for example*, Lee Shubert's 1951 negotiations with Agatha Christie's representatives over *The Hollow* and *The Suspects*. Lee, who would pass away in 1953, was still trying to cut a deal outside of the Minimum Basic Agreement framework. Julius Green, *Curtain Up: Agatha Christie, A Life in the Theatre* (New York: Harper Collins, 2015), 292–301.

[17] Memorandum: Klein and Weinberger to J. J. Shubert, May 13, 1947, International Guild of Theatrical Writers, Inc Collection, 1947–1952, *The Shubert Archive*. The press was framing the case in terms of its far-reaching implications for the industry: *See* "Suit by Carl Ring May Set Precedent," *Billboard*, December 25, 1948, 45; "Dramatists Guild Suit Can Affect All Other Unions," *Variety*, December 29, 1948, 2, 50.

[18] *Ring* v. *Spina et al.*, 84 F Supp. 403, 406 (1949). The jury was "left" to decide the exemption issue because the Second Circuit had previously decided that the Minimum Basic Agreement constituted an illegal agreement in restraint of interstate trade and commerce (*see Ring* v. *Spina et al.*, 148 F. 2d 647(1945)).

stake – the rhetoric of something that went beyond an economic relationship between the author and the work to a deeply personal one. It was a condition won through contractual negotiation over the previous twenty years and mythologized by the likes of George Middleton. But at the same time, the moral-rights rhetoric was a powerful way to advance the writers' economic interests. The artistic and economic motivations were entwined. Thus, counsel for both the plaintiff and defendants devoted considerable time to exploring the boundaries of consent to make changes through the lens of artistic pragmatism on one side and artistic integrity on the other.[19]

Counsel for the plaintiff Ring, Alfred Julien, also built much of his case on the imperfect dispute resolution procedures under the 1941 Minimum Basic Agreement.[20] It was the author who had to consent to changes. If the manager believed the author was unreasonable, a complaint to the Dramatists Guild was a possible option. The Guild, however, Julien argued, had no power to compel the author to make such changes. The jury would have to decide, explained counsel, whether the power to not compel the author to make changes was one element that damaged the plaintiff.[21]

The key antagonist in Julien's narrative was composer Harold Spina, credited as the coauthor of *Stovepipe Hat*. In the out-of-town runs of New Haven and Boston, the plaintiff characterized the production as one in desperate need of changes.[22] Spina, according to the plaintiff, was an author resistant to change,[23] enlivened by an iron-clad Basic Agreement that entitled him to complete control over all changes to the work.[24] Thus, the premature closing of the production in Boston, the prevented reopening, and injury of up US$140,000, was the result of "this combination,"[25] which was "called into operation by a single man"[26] acting with the "knowledge of and with the force of the Guild."[27]

In response, Philip Wittenberg, on behalf of the defendants Spina and Heyman,[28] tried to characterize the inexperienced Carl Ring as unwilling to

19 The defendants named on the transcript were the authors Harold Spina, Edward Heyman, Walter Hannan. The other defendants named were playbroker Edmond Pauker and the Dramatists Guild.
20 Transcript: *Carl E. Ring* v. *Harold Spina et al.*, December 15, 1948, 11–19.
21 *See* Transcript: *Carl E. Ring* v. *Harold Spina et al.*, December 30, 1948, 1901.
22 Transcript: *Carl E. Ring* v. *Harold Spina et al.*, December 15, 1948, 37.
23 Transcript: *Carl E. Ring* v. *Harold Spina et al.*, December 15, 1948, 38.
24 *See* Transcript: *Carl E. Ring* v. *Harold Spina et al.*, December 15, 1948, 38–40.
25 Transcript: *Carl E. Ring* v. *Harold Spina et al.*, December 15, 1948, 45.
26 Transcript: Carl E Ring v. Harold Spina et al, December 15, 1948, 45.
27 Transcript: *Carl E. Ring* v. *Harold Spina et al.*, December 15, 1948, 46.
28 As well as the authors' agent Edmond Pauker. Spina was the composer, Heyman and Hannan wrote the book. *See* Transcript: *Carl E. Ring* v. *Harold Spina et al.*, December 15, 1948, 49. The program for the Boston season attributed Book and Lyrics to Heyman, Hannan, and Spina. Harold Spina was attributed as the composer of the music. Carl Ring was attributed as the sole presenter at the top of the program. *See* Stovepipe Hat Program for Boston May 1944 Season, Shubert Theatre, Playbills and Programs from Boston Theaters, 1775–1988 (TCS 66). Harvard Theatre Collection, Houghton Library, Harvard University. The authors' agent had a copy of the script, archived at the New York Public Library, from what looks like the New Haven production (has the production dates for New Haven on cover). The front page credits Spina for the music, Hannan, Heyman and Willard Lampell for the book and

arbitrate, and "determined ruthlessly to kick everybody out of that play except himself."[29] Wittenberg highlighted what the defendants believed was an abuse of producer power, claiming that Ring stated: "You will do what I want or there will be no play."[30] Ring is characterized as a belligerent opportunist willing to break a contract with his producing partner Gaumont and willing to alter the cast and the work without author consultation.[31]

Edward Greenbaum, for the second defendant Dramatists Guild, structured his argument around the broader claim of the historical vulnerability of the playwright.[32] George Middleton assisted Greenbaum in his preparation for the case. Middleton emphasized to Greenbaum that if they were operating an absolute "closed shop" theatre owners like the Shuberts would be excluded from contracting with members (which was not the case).[33] The ambiguity surrounding whether the Guild's Basic Agreement created a closed shop – vigorously discussed but not resolved during the committee meeting between the managers and dramatists over the first Basic Agreement in March of 1926 – had come back to once again haunt the writers.

For Greenbaum, Carl Ring was the omnipotent producer consolidating power over three stages – what Greenbaum described as a "3-act show."[34] In act one, Gaumont is the producer of the fledgling *Stovepipe Hat* which had unsuccessfully sought to raise funds for an extended period. Ring enters the scene with a modest investment contribution of US$5,000. In act two, Ring begins to establish his authority over the production by investing more money and becoming a coproducer with Gaumont, eventually suing his partner to secure sole producing authority. Greenbaum then charts Ring's ultimate realization of authority in act three:

> He is the producer now. He is the big shot; he runs the show; he bosses everybody around. He gets into a fight with the authors, as his lawyer has told you, he gets into a fight with the other people in the show; he fires one after another; several lawsuits result from that; he changes this, that and the other, and he doesn't like the name of the show, either, Stovepipe Hat. He changes the name of the show without asking anybody about it.[35]

By the time the production reached Boston, Ring had therefore consolidated all his power over the production, as realized in the new program reproduced in Figure 8.1.[36] For Greenbaum, Ring was no more than "a gambler who has played

lyrics, and "original conception" by Spina. *See* Stovepipe Hat Typescript, Performing Arts Research Collections Theatre, RM 6950, New York Public Library for the Performing Arts, New York.

29 Transcript: *Carl E. Ring* v. *Harold Spina et al.*, December 15, 1948, 53.
30 Transcript: *Carl E. Ring* v. *Harold Spina et al.*, December 15, 1948, 55.
31 Transcript: *Carl E. Ring* v. *Harold Spina et al.*, December 15, 1948, 56.
32 *See* Transcript: *Carl E. Ring* v. *Harold Spina et al.*, December 15, 1948, 62–63.
33 *See* G. Middleton to E. Greenbaum, November 11, 1948, Box 25, George Middleton Papers.
34 Transcript: *Carl E. Ring* v. *Harold Spina et al.*, December 15, 1948, 65.
35 Transcript: *Carl E. Ring* v. *Harold Spina et al.*, December 15, 1948, 66.
36 *See* Stovepipe Hat Program for Boston May 1944 Season, Shubert Theatre, Playbills and Programs from Boston Theaters, 1775–1988 (TCS 66). Harvard Theatre Collection, Houghton Library, Harvard University.

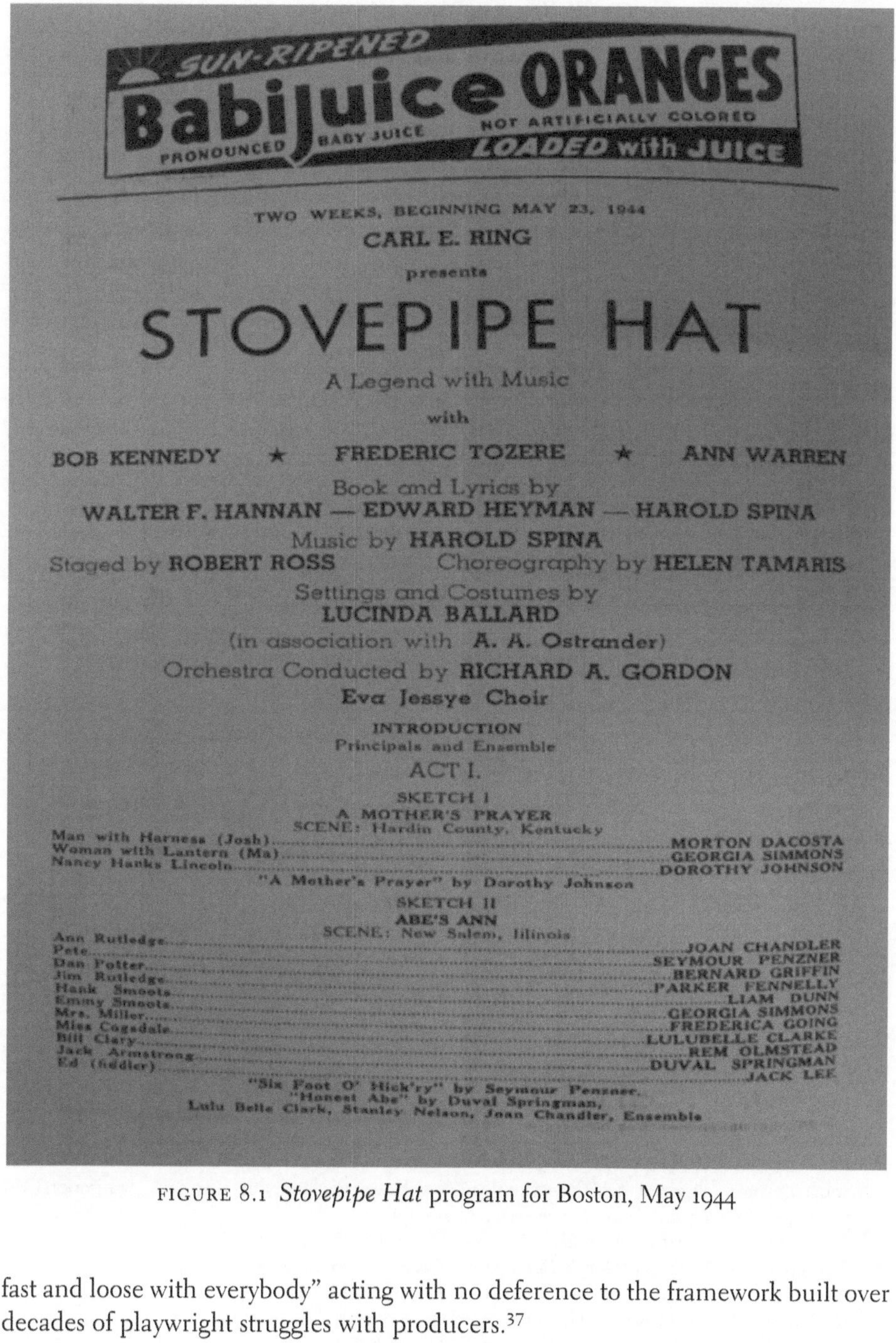
SUN-RIPENED
Babijuice ORANGES
PRONOUNCED BABY JUICE
NOT ARTIFICIALLY COLORED
LOADED with JUICE

TWO WEEKS, BEGINNING MAY 23, 1944
CARL E. RING
presents
STOVEPIPE HAT
A Legend with Music
with
BOB KENNEDY ★ FREDERIC TOZERE ★ ANN WARREN
Book and Lyrics by
WALTER F. HANNAN — EDWARD HEYMAN — HAROLD SPINA
Music by HAROLD SPINA
Staged by ROBERT ROSS Choreography by HELEN TAMARIS
Settings and Costumes by
LUCINDA BALLARD
(in association with A. A. Ostrander)
Orchestra Conducted by RICHARD A. GORDON
Eva Jessye Choir
INTRODUCTION
Principals and Ensemble
ACT I.
SKETCH I
A MOTHER'S PRAYER
SCENE: Hardin County, Kentucky
Man with Harness (Josh)... MORTON DACOSTA
Woman with Lantern (Ma)... GEORGIA SIMMONS
Nancy Hanks Lincoln... DOROTHY JOHNSON
"A Mother's Prayer" by Dorothy Johnson
SKETCH II
ABE'S ANN
SCENE: New Salem, Ilinois
Ann Rutledge... JOAN CHANDLER
Pete... SEYMOUR PENZNER
Dan Potter... BERNARD GRIFFIN
Jim Rutledge... PARKER FENNELLY
Hank Smoots... LIAM DUNN
Emmy Smoots... GEORGIA SIMMONS
Mrs. Miller... FREDERICA GOING
Miss Cogsdale... LULUBELLE CLARKE
Bill Clary... REM OLMSTEAD
Jack Armstrong... DUVAL SPRINGMAN
Ed (fiddler)... JACK LEE
"Six Foot O' Hick'ry" by Seymour Penzner,
"Honest Abe" by Duval Springman,
Lulu Belle Clark, Stanley Nelson, Joan Chandler, Ensemble

FIGURE 8.1 *Stovepipe Hat* program for Boston, May 1944

fast and loose with everybody" acting with no deference to the framework built over decades of playwright struggles with producers.[37]

[37] Transcript: *Carl E. Ring* v. *Harold Spina et al.*, December 15, 1948, 67.

## B. *The Testimony of Ring*

Carl Ring, one of the first witnesses to take the stand,[38] claimed that no disputes over the artistic direction of the work emerged until the second performance in New Haven.[39] The press clippings were encouraging.[40] Lee Shubert, who owned both New Haven and Boston theatres that staged the production, spoke with Ring on the second evening in New Haven and suggested that the work was promising, but needed changes. Shubert believed the show was too big – twice the size of *Oklahoma!* – and weighed down by slow scene changes, poor orchestration, and casting. The "amateurish" show would benefit from the experienced hands of "somebody like George Kaufman or George Abbott, a little more professional."[41]

Spina, Ring claimed, continued to insist that he would not make changes. Lee Shubert's involvement also infuriated the author. Ring testified that Spina defiantly stated, "Lee Shubert is not going to run my show."[42] Further, Ring claimed that with no artistic experience he was the mere agent of change; the director and other members of the creative staff made the actual changes.[43]

The tensions escalated when the production reached Boston for its two-week run. Ring was involved in a heated discussion with Spina at the end of the New Haven season leading Spina to once again assert his rights under the Basic Agreement. There was an update in the orchestrations and a script doctor, Richard Maloney, was engaged to make changes. Spina protested to Ring about the significant flaws in the revised production on the night before opening in Boston.[44] The show went on, and, in the next few days, the other authors Hannan and Heyman arrived in Boston. Spina and Heyman said they would write new songs, conceding the show was "deficient" in that respect.[45] Spina, however, was generally "disgusted" with the changes that were being proposed and implemented, many of which he believed did not receive his consent.[46]

After several performances in Boston, Ring felt Spina had finally, although reluctantly, agreed to allow revisions to the production. Everyone agreed if the changes did not improve the show, it would return to its original form in Philadelphia. The parties were unable to sustain a workable agreement, however. Spina left the show mid-season in Boston, never to return. The author hired counsel, Philip Wittenberg, to shut the Boston production down.[47] The production ended

38 Transcript: *Carl E. Ring* v. *Harold Spina et al.*, December 15, 1948, 88.

39 Transcript: *Carl E. Ring* v. *Harold Spina et al.*, December 16, 1948, 149.

40 Spina, however, observed that "these people in New Haven are kinder than Boston." Transcript: *Carl E. Ring* v. *Harold Spina et al.*, December 16, 1948, 178.

41 Transcript: *Carl E. Ring* v. *Harold Spina et al.*, December 16, 1948, 179.

42 Transcript: *Carl E. Ring* v. *Harold Spina et al.*, December 16, 1948, 181.

43 Transcript: *Carl E. Ring* v. *Harold Spina et al.*, December 16, 1948, 184.

44 *See* Transcript: *Carl E. Ring* v. *Harold Spina et al.*, December 16, 1948, 195, 197.

45 Transcript: *Carl E. Ring* v. *Harold Spina et al.*, December 16, 1948, 198.

46 Transcript: *Carl E. Ring* v. *Harold Spina et al.*, December 16, 1948, 199.

47 Transcript: *Carl E. Ring* v. *Harold Spina et al.*, December 16, 1948, 223–224.

prematurely in Boston and was unrevived until the proceedings in the federal courts of New York.[48]

Wittenberg, according to Ring, asserted the full weight of the authors' entitlements under the Basic Agreement: "You [Ring] are out under the Dramatists Guild contract, and that is all there is to it."[49] Wittenberg told Ring that he did not have a valid contract with Spina: "He [Wittenberg] says that they would consider an immediate arbitration to clean me out of the thing altogether, my rights, and I said I would like to talk about putting it on again, and my recollection is that he said nothing doing."[50]

The cross-examination of Ring focused on what changes he instigated between New Haven and Boston seasons, and his alleged antagonism toward the entire creative team.[51] The defense posited that under the Basic Agreement, to which Ring became a reluctant signatory, he was subject to its conditions.[52] And as a signatory to the Basic Agreement, the defense asked Ring whether he was subject to the artistic control Article Seven clause.[53] Indeed, Greenbaum continued to push Ring on whether his specific complaints were about undermining the authors' integrity. Ring first seemed ambivalent about the specific clause.[54] But when questioned further by Greenbaum on whether the provision was unfair, Ring conceded that "It [Article Seven] is unfair in that [it is an] agreement negotiated by somebody else and compelling me to sign."[55]

Ring was not willing to concede that the author had the sole authority to make changes. The producer testified that to "work the show into a final completed article,"[56] somebody had to make changes, and in this case, it should not have been Spina. In what appears to be a recollection of his conversation with Lee Shubert, Ring stated as for alterations:

48 Transcript: *Carl E. Ring* v. *Harold Spina et al.*, December 16, 1948, 227. The Boston season closed on May 27, 1944 – five days into what was supposed to be a two-week run.

49 Transcript: *Carl E. Ring* v. *Harold Spina et al.*, December 16, 1948, 224.

50 Transcript: *Carl E. Ring* v. *Harold Spina et al.*, December 16, 1948, 224.

51 Transcript: *Carl E. Ring* v. *Harold Spina et al.*, December 16, 1948, 231.

52 Further, the assignment from Gaumont to Ring was invalid because all rights vested in the author. Both the Guild and the authors, Greenbaum argued, needed to consent to the assignment. *See* Transcript: *Carl E. Ring* v. *Harold Spina et al.*, December 16, 1948, 268 (particularly the Guild not consenting).

53 Transcript: *Carl E. Ring* v. *Harold Spina et al.*, December 17, 1948, 311. This is Article VII of the 1941 MBA.

54 Transcript: *Carl E. Ring* v. *Harold Spina et al.*, December 17, 1948, 311–312.

55 Transcript: *Carl E. Ring* v. *Harold Spina et al.*, December 17, 1948, 319; although not conceding this is the reason why he made the claim (id. at 329). Greenbaum questioned Ring whether he knew the law with respect to these changes being made only with authors' consent, and Greenbaum refers to the Mark Twain case: *Clemens* v. *Press Pub Co.*, 122 NYS 206 (1910) [he cites as 67 Misc. 183]. A fascinating exchange ensues between Greenbaum and Ring, with regard to whether Ring believes this is a copyright issue or a contractual issue. *See* Transcript: *Carl E. Ring* v. *Harold Spina et al.*, December 17, 1948, 330 (referring to changes to script and the name of the play).

56 Transcript: *Carl E. Ring* v. *Harold Spina et al.*, December 17, 1948, 349.

> [I]t should have been someone else because Spina and Ross [the director] went as far as they could, and it was amateurish, and we needed professionals, and I mentioned names which had been suggested to me that we should get.[57]

According to Ring, investment in the production was a considerable risk that should have come with broad entitlements, including the right to make artistic choices. If the authors left the production, as Spina did in Boston, the producer "owner" of the work could make changes based on recommendations from experts,[58] including changes to the name of the play.[59] The process had to be flexible for the show to survive, and Ring claimed that Spina was opposing all changes.[60] Ring was speaking to a much broader issue. Although this may have been Ring's case and testimony, it was the Shubert Organization's fifty-year cause on trial.

### C. *The Testimony of Lee Shubert*

It is profoundly fitting that Lee Shubert, a central character in the history of American theatre law, was a principal witness for Ring in this moment of consequence for the industry.[61] Shubert first testified that *Stovepipe Hat*, after the second performance in New Haven, had a good chance of success if it underwent major changes.[62] The impresario, however, was careful not to specify whether managers should have the authority to make changes to the work. Thus, Shubert suggested under oath that creative experts were responsible for modifying *Stovepipe Hat*.[63]

These initial conciliatory overtones soon faced scrutiny under examination, however. Shubert testified that he was no longer a signatory to the Basic Agreement, and now was only "interested in plays that other people produced."[64] John Shubert, son of J. J., was a signatory to the 1946 Agreement. For Lee Shubert, previous incarnations of the Minimum Basic Agreement were "different" to the 1946 version in that they afforded "more privileges" to managers.[65] The key issue that

57 Transcript: *Carl E. Ring* v. *Harold Spina et al.*, December 17, 1948, 349.

58 Transcript: *Carl E. Ring* v. *Harold Spina et al.*, December 17, 1948, 404 (suggesting there were recommendations for changes from as many as fifteen to twenty people).

59 Transcript: *Carl E. Ring* v. *Harold Spina et al.*, December 17, 1948, 353.

60 *See* Transcript: *Carl E. Ring* v. *Harold Spina et al.*, December 17, 1948, 421; Transcript: *Carl E. Ring* v. *Harold Spina et al.*, December 17, 1948, 438; Transcript: *Carl E. Ring* v. *Harold Spina et al.*, December 17, 1948, 441.

61 *See* Transcript: *Carl E. Ring* v. *Harold Spina et al.*, December 17, 1948, 407–408. (Shubert telling Ring in New Haven that the cast was too big and show too heavy.) It was unsurprising that Shubert was given media attention during the trial: "Lee Shubert Testifies for Ring in 'Stovepipe' Suit Re Guild 'Monopoly'," *Variety*, December 22, 1948, 49.

62 *See* Transcript: *Carl E. Ring* v. *Harold Spina et al.*, December 21, 1948, 609; Transcript: *Carl E. Ring* v. *Harold Spina et al.*, December 21, 1948, 620; Transcript: *Carl E. Ring* v. *Harold Spina et al.*, December 21, 1948, 623.

63 Transcript: *Carl E. Ring* v. *Harold Spina et al.*, December 21, 1948, 620–621.

64 Transcript: *Carl E. Ring* v. *Harold Spina et al.*, December 21, 1948, 626.

65 Transcript: *Carl E. Ring* v. *Harold Spina et al.*, December 21, 1948, 629; Transcript: *Carl E. Ring* v. *Harold Spina et al.*, 21 December 1948, 631.

counsel sought to explore with Lee Shubert was whether he had entered into contracts with authors that conflicted with the Minimum Basic Agreement.[66] For Shubert, the central issue was not about specific economic formulations including royalty rates and structures, but more generally, "how we are to proceed with our contract without any interference."[67] In terms of artistic control, Judge Rifkind asked Shubert whether, under the 1941 Agreement, he entered into contracts with authors that did not provide author consent. Shubert responded: "Well, before this new contract, the old contract, we had more liberty . . . We would arrange that [changes] with the author by himself."[68] When pressed further by Wittenberg on whether the Shuberts made contracts with authors to make changes without author consent:[69]

A: Well, we used to get the author's approval whenever we wanted it.

Q: In other words, they generally consented?

A: They generally consented because we stood for something in the theatre.

Q: You mean they respected your judgment?

A: Yes.

Of course, up until the 1946 Agreement, all signatories to the Basic Agreement had to acquire the author's consent to make changes except in the limited context of revues, which were also off the table after the 1946 Agreement. When counsel pressed further on this issue, Shubert responded with a hint of ambivalence. Shubert also contradicted himself, perhaps trying to evade the question:[70]

Q: But the contract still required their consent?

A: No changes could be made without their approval. I believe they did require consent.

Q: You never made a production contract which made a different provision with respect to that?

A: Well, I would always have it understood.

Q: With the author?

A: Yes. . . .

Q: In writing?

A: Never had it in writing?

Q: Always verbal?

66 Transcript: *Carl E. Ring* v. *Harold Spina et al.*, December 21, 1948, 629.
67 Transcript: *Carl E. Ring* v. *Harold Spina et al.*, December 21, 1948, 632.
68 Transcript: *Carl E. Ring* v. *Harold Spina et al.*, December 21, 1948, 634.
69 Transcript: *Carl E. Ring* v. *Harold Spina et al.*, December 21, 1948, 635.
70 Transcript: *Carl E. Ring* v. *Harold Spina et al.*, December 21, 1948, 635–636.

A: Verbal

Q: That you could make changes?

A: That is right.

The Shubert Archive records, as examined previously, reveal that before 1926 the Shuberts made hundreds of agreements with a written consent clause. On many occasions, these artistic control clauses favored the producer, on some occasions they favored the playwright, and in other instances, the artistic control clause balanced the interests of managers and writers. The response may perhaps be a further indicator of how the Shubert Organization regularly negotiated the terms to make changes beyond the contractual space and in the rehearsal room.

In cross-examination, Greenbaum asked Shubert whether he had "any objection to the paragraph or clause in the [Minimum Basic Agreement] in regard to the author's right concerning changes in script," to which Shubert responded, "I had objections to it, yes."[71] Julien, for the plaintiff, objected when Shubert explained the grounds for his resistance to the clause. The Court sustained the objection because a response called "for too much mental cognition."[72] Shubert's position on the issue, however, would once again emerge in cross-examination by Greenbaum:[73]

Q: Did you have any experience where you wanted to change the script and the author would not permit it?

A: Yes.

Q: What happened in those cases . . . ?

A: We had arguments about it, discussions about it . . . – some of them did what we wanted and some did not.

For the Shuberts, negotiating artistic control also extended to changing the name of plays.[74] The testimony of Lee Shubert then went to the more significant issue of whether the Guild restricted production. Shubert testified that although the Guild thinks they protect writers, "They keep plays from being produced."[75] He continued: "They have inserted in their last contract such conditions that made me stop producing and a lot of other people who produce."[76]

In concluding his cross-examination, Greenbaum, counsel for the Dramatists Guild, turned to the Shubert production *Hellzapoppin*. The production was, as

71 Transcript: *Carl E. Ring* v. *Harold Spina et al.*, December 21, 1948, 679.

72 Transcript: *Carl E. Ring* v. *Harold Spina et al.*, December 21, 1948, 679-A: Greenbaum claimed it was valid as it was "the basis of this lawsuit."

73 Transcript: *Carl E. Ring* v. *Harold Spina et al.*, December 21, 1948, 680–681.

74 Transcript: *Carl E. Ring* v. *Harold Spina et al.*, December 21, 1948, 681. Shubert stating "there were so many of them." There is some confusion here whether they always asked for author consent. Shubert appears to contradict himself.

75 Transcript: *Carl E. Ring* v. *Harold Spina et al.*, December 21, 1948, 685.

76 Transcript: *Carl E. Ring* v. *Harold Spina et al.*, December 21, 1948, 685.

discussed, one of the Shubert Organization's greatest successes. The Shubert Archive shows that as early as 1938 copyright in the unpublished manuscript of *Hellzapoppin* was registered under the names of Olsen and Johnson. And William Klein wrote to the Shuberts recommending that the brothers should not claim an interest in the rights as Olsen and Johnson were the "owners" of *Hellzapoppin*. Despite this history, Shubert, under oath, continued to deny there was any authorship in the work. Shubert believed it was a vaudeville act "augmented" by Olsen and Johnson: "They were in vaudeville; they had what they call a unit, and I took it over and made a musical play out of it. That did not require authors or composers."[77] Shubert explained that they paid them "a salary and a percentage."[78] He sought to clarify his answer:[79]

Q: ... [H]ow [were] Olsen and Johnson ... paid?

A: They were paid a percentage of the gross receipts.

Q: And were they paid anything for their services as actors?

A: Well, that was their payment as actors.

Q: Didn't they get a salary as actors?

A: That was the salary as actors.

Q: And the whole thing was a percentage?

A: A percentage.

Q: That is, on a royalty basis?

A: Well, it is not royalty. It is a percentage. You call it any way you wish.

Q: You had no author to pay you say?

A: No.

An exchange ensues between Greenbaum and Shubert over the work having no author, and Greenbaum sarcastically remarks that authorship "just burst[s] out" of thin air.[80] Although conceding Olsen and Johnson owned the act, Shubert denounced the notion that anybody wrote the show. Thus, nobody received a royalty.[81] A revue-type production like *Hellzapoppin* was the kind of work more likely to be improvised and fall under the revue consent exception of the 1941 Basic

77 Transcript: *Carl E. Ring* v. *Harold Spina et al.*, December 21, 1948, 703.

78 Transcript: *Carl E. Ring* v. *Harold Spina et al.*, December 21, 1948, 703.

79 Transcript: *Carl E. Ring* v. *Harold Spina et al.*, December 21, 1948, 704.

80 *See* Transcript: *Carl E. Ring* v. *Harold Spina et al.*, December 21, 1948, 706. Lyrics and book for the work certainly existed and a copy is in the Shubert Archive: Production Correspondence Collection, Hellzapoppin, *The Shubert Archive* (copy on file).

81 *See* Transcript: *Carl E. Ring* v. *Harold Spina et al.*, December 21, 1948, 705. Including the Shuberts, who claimed to have enlarged the show into a musical.

Agreement. The Shuberts, however, had no title in this work and sought to establish there was no author in the creation of *Hellzapoppin*.

Why would Lee Shubert go to such exhaustive lengths to dispute any claim to authorship? Lee Shubert, as always, adapted and found ways around institutional frameworks. Perhaps he knew it was harder to escape having to comply with the charter of the Dramatists Guild if *Hellzapoppin* was considered a work of authorship. Shubert perhaps knew to define his relationship with Olsen and Johnson as an employee/employer-type agreement so the duo would not think of themselves as authors.

Lee's testimony reveals the lengths that the Shuberts would go to escape a system that he believed compromised his ability to produce theatre. The Shuberts, under their own agreements, could suggest and implement changes to the script and pay percentages rather than royalties on their own terms. It would, however, be unfair to characterize the arrangement between the Shuberts and Olsen and Johnson as one of pure exploitation, which counsel for the defense was trying to establish. The Shubert Organization rewarded the duo handsomely and renegotiated, for everyone's benefit, as the work grew in success. It is a reminder that authority was fluid and renegotiated continually – a fact lost in the quest to often neatly identify binary tensions between consent and nonconsent, unionism and association, or author contractors and employees.

## D. A "*Right to Freedom from Illegal Restraint*"

Most of the remaining witnesses were artists for the defense who spoke to the boundaries of consent and the need to protect the integrity of the work. Harold Spina, the first defendant in the proceedings, testified that Ring told him his "services were no longer required" in Boston, and that "he was going to have the play put on the way he wanted to and that I should not come along."[82] Spina testified that there were many cuts made without his notification,[83] and he only learned about the change in the title at the end of the Boston run.[84] Edward Heyman also testified that Ring approached him about changing the title, which he objected to given the association of the play with Abraham Lincoln.[85] Heyman testified that Ring said, overall, the show needed "lightening up."[86] The suggestions were in

[82] Transcript: *Carl E. Ring* v. *Harold Spina et al.*, December 28, 1948, 1374.

[83] Transcript: *Carl E. Ring* v. *Harold Spina et al.*, December 28, 1948, 1379. Although, during cross examination, Spina replied to the Court that he did consent to some changes in Boston: Transcript: *Carl E. Ring* v. *Harold Spina et al.*, December 29, 1948, 1452–1453. Edward Heyman testified that Ring asked Spina and Heyman to sign a consent form allowing Ring to make any changes in Boston "without interference of any kind": Transcript: *Carl E. Ring* v. *Harold Spina et al.*, December 21, 1948, 713.

[84] Transcript: *Carl E. Ring* v. *Harold Spina et al.*, United States District Court Southern District of New York, December 28, 1948, 1384, National Archives at New York City.

[85] Transcript: *Carl E. Ring* v. *Harold Spina et al.*, December 21, 1948, 715.

[86] Transcript: *Carl E. Ring* v. *Harold Spina et al.*, December 21, 1948, 720.

direct tension with the creators' vision to stage a sincere work of drama.[87] Director Robert Ross and choreographer Helen Tamaris Nagrin both testified to the major changes between New Haven and Boston. Ross, in particular, claimed that script doctor Richard Maloney was involved in many of these changes, apparently with no author consultation.[88]

Acclaimed dramatist Marc Connelly was called as an expert witness for the defense and spoke to the conditions of the playwright before 1926 – "almost devoid of recourse to any authority that would help him secure his rights and obtain royalties when they should be paid."[89] As for changes, Connelly, marshaling moral rights rhetoric, testified that although producers "promise[d]" to "preserve the integrity" of dramatists' scripts, the manager was "given carte blanche to make changes in the script over the playwright's protest."[90] Defendant counsel Greenbaum wanted to admit into evidence that during the negotiations of the first Minimum Basic Agreement, Lee Shubert was the only producer who voiced strong opposition to the artistic control clause.[91] But Connelly also conceded that applying the Minimum Basic Agreement artistic control clause was far from an exact science, with each side just as likely to be a "temperamental" party when an impasse occurred.[92]

Witnesses on both sides had therefore explored the pivotal artistic control clause in exhaustive detail between December and January 1948–1949. Wittenberg's summation to the jury, as counsel for the authors, pointed to the moment in the production at the Shubert Theatre in New Haven where the play was no longer a coproduction between Ring and Gaumont, but Ring's alone. With this newfound authority, Ring saw the opportunity to change the script, change the choreography, the orchestration, and the direction.[93] By the time the production reached Boston, it was an irredeemable mess and the creatives, including Maloney the dramaturg, had abandoned ship.[94] The inexperienced Ring was the sole reason why it was an

87 Transcript: *Carl E. Ring* v. *Harold Spina et al.*, December 21, 1948, 721.

88 *See* Transcript: *Carl E. Ring* v. *Harold Spina et al.*, December 29, 1948, 1550–1554 (Re. Tamiris); Transcript: *Carl E. Ring* v. *Harold Spina et al.*, December 29, 1948, 1568, 1579–1580, 1582 (Re. Ross). Although Julien in summation claimed Spina consented generally to Maloney's participation in the process: Transcript: *Carl E. Ring* v. *Harold Spina et al.*, December 30, 1948, 1910.

89 Transcript: *Carl E. Ring* v. *Harold Spina et al.*, December 27, 1948, 1182. *See also* testimony of Owen Davis who speaks to the pre-1926 conditions and the "bullying tactics" of producers: Transcript: *Carl E. Ring* v. *Harold Spina et al.*, January 11, 1949, 2142.

90 Transcript: *Carl E. Ring* v. *Harold Spina et al.*, December 27, 1948, 1189.

91 *See* Transcript: *Carl E. Ring* v. *Harold Spina et al.*, December 27, 1948, 1196. Indeed, Greenbaum during Connelly's testimony wanted to show that Shubert was an interested witness thus tainting his evidence as an expert: "he has been fighting this bitterly since 1926." *See* Transcript: *Carl E. Ring* v. *Harold Spina et al.*, December 27, 1948, 1199.

92 Transcript: *Carl E. Ring* v. *Harold Spina et al.*, United States District Court Southern District of New York, December 27, 1948, 1211–1212, National Archives at New York City.

93 Transcript: *Carl E. Ring* v. *Harold Spina et al.*, December 30, 1948, 1812.

94 Transcript: *Carl E. Ring* v. *Harold Spina et al.*, December 30, 1948, 1827.

unsuccessful show, and now he was trying to reconstruct authority in the theatre through the legal prism of antitrust to recover his catastrophic losses.

Greenbaum, for the Dramatists Guild, framed his summation around the significant power that producers, and Hollywood, had yielded over playwrights for years. The Minimum Basic Agreement, claimed Greenbaum, had finally addressed these abuses in 1926. Counsel also emphasized the many changes Ring orchestrated, "by the time all these changes were made it is doubtful that the defendants wrote any part of the book that was produced."[95] Ring also changed the name of the play – a "final act of arrogance and desecration."[96] Greenbaum spoke to the irony of Lee Shubert claiming that the dramatists had a monopoly given that the Shubert Organization "owns and controls half the theatres in New York" and "several hundred" throughout the country.[97] As for *Hellzapoppin*, Greenbaum summarized:

> You heard his [Lee Shubert's] testimony on Hellzapoppin. The author is nobody. The play was however written by Olsen and Johnson, they were the authors . . . How would you like to be a playwright trying your first or second or third play out and dealing with Mr Shubert? How would you like to deal with Mr Ring? The two extremes. It just well illustrates the purpose and the legitimate purpose of having a Dramatists Guild or a union and having a Minimum Basic Agreement.[98]

In response, Ring's counsel argued the defendants had based their case on assassinating the plaintiff's character.[99] Julien emphasized that in its twenty-six-year history, the Guild had never called itself a labor union "until they come into this case and it suits them to do it."[100] In reality, Julien argued, the Minimum Basic Agreement was a "32-page straitjacket" for the industry.[101] When the production reached New Haven it needed major changes, as recommended by Lee Shubert, a producer with extensive experience.[102] Julien claimed that Ring never wrote a single word of the script,[103] but was entitled, given his involvement in the production, to give his opinion: "Why isn't his business judgment of some value."[104]

In conclusion, Julien explained to the jury the importance of the connection between the consenting to change issue – which had "been built up to such tremendous proportions"[105] – and the larger antitrust case:

95 Transcript: *Carl E. Ring* v. *Harold Spina et al.*, December 30, 1948, 1841.
96 Transcript: *Carl E. Ring* v. *Harold Spina et al.*, December 30, 1948, 1870.
97 Transcript: *Carl E. Ring* v. *Harold Spina et al.*, December 30, 1948, 1836.
98 Transcript: *Carl E. Ring* v. *Harold Spina et al.*, December 30, 1948, 1836–1837.
99 Transcript: *Carl E. Ring* v. *Harold Spina et al.*, December 30, 1948, 1875.
100 Transcript: *Carl E. Ring* v. *Harold Spina et al.*, December 30, 1948, 1931. So, the Guild here is making the claim their association is akin to union status as a defendant, not a plaintiff. They have never made a claim that they are a union as a plaintiff.
101 Transcript: *Carl E. Ring* v. *Harold Spina et al.*, December 30, 1948, 1891.
102 Transcript: *Carl E. Ring* v. *Harold Spina et al.*, December 30, 1948, 1894.
103 Transcript: *Carl E. Ring* v. *Harold Spina et al.*, December 30, 1948, 1897.
104 Transcript: *Carl E. Ring* v. *Harold Spina et al.*, December 30, 1948, 1898.
105 Transcript: *Carl E. Ring* v. *Harold Spina et al.*, December 30, 1948, 1901.

> Now, the issue in this case again is not will Ring make the changes or should Spina make the changes? That is not the issue. And you are not going to be called upon to decide that question. You are going to be called upon to decide whether damage resulted to Ring because the [Minimum Basic Agreement] says, "If you make changes and the author protests you can't compel him not to protest, you can't compel him to make those changes." ... You are going to be asked to decide whether that is one of the elements of damage, one of the elements that damaged Ring in his business property.[106]

Judge Rifkind charged the jury to decide whether the Guild was a labor organization exempted from antitrust law under section 17 of 15 U.S.C.A. The jury found that the Guild was not a labor organization, not exempt under antitrust law, and that the defendants had violated antitrust law.[107] Having found that the defendants violated antitrust law, the jury then had to decide whether the violation caused injury to the plaintiff. To this question, the jury decided Ring had not suffered injury from either the Dramatists Guild, Spina, or Heyman.[108] The Court thus dismissed the complaint on the issue of treble damages,[109] which left whether to grant injunctive relief in equity.[110]

The specific, narrow, issue for Judge Rifkind to decide was whether to grant Ring an injunction enjoining arbitration as provided for in the Minimum Basic Agreement.[111] The grounds appeared on the face to be limited. The production contracts were illegal, and Ring had no contractual rights in *Stovepipe Hat*.[112] But his Honor held that despite the absence of contractual rights, it did "not follow that the plaintiff is entitled to no relief."[113] Judge Rifkind held that Ring's equitable relief existed in "his right to freedom from illegal restraint," which is protectable by enjoining the defendants from conspiring to interfere "with [the] plaintiff's acquisition of any and all rights in plays, including 'Stovepipe Hat'."[114] Thus, Ring was

106 Transcript: *Carl E. Ring* v. *Harold Spina et al.*, December 30, 1948, 1900–1901.

107 Transcript: *Carl E. Ring* v. *Harold Spina et al.*, January 4, 1949, 2050–2051. This was a result that the defendants perhaps always contemplated as possible despite their belief in their legal position given the whims of jury panels. Alexander Lindey representing the Guild with Greenbaum wrote to George Middleton: "I have practiced law too long and have been fooled too often by juries to venture a prediction as to the outcome." A. Lindey to G. Middleton, December 18, 1948, Box 25, George Middleton Papers.

108 Transcript: *Carl E. Ring* v. *Harold Spina et al.*, January 4, 1949, 1998; Transcript: *Carl E. Ring* v. *Harold Spina et al.*, January 4, 1949, 2050–2051.

109 Obviously, the jury did not have to consider the third question of the amount of damages because they answered no to the question of whether the plaintiff had suffered injury at the hands of the defendants. Transcript: *Carl E. Ring* v. *Harold Spina et al.*, January 4, 1949, 2013.

110 *Ring* v. *Spina et al.*, 84 F Supp. 403.

111 *Ring* v. *Spina et al.*, 84 F Supp. 403, 406. Counsel for the Guild also notes that another issue to decide was whether "the Guild be enjoined from enforcing the Minimum Basic Agreement." *See* A. Lindey to G. Middleton, January 12, 1949, Box 25, George Middleton Papers.

112 *Ring* v. *Spina et al.*, 84 F Supp. 403, 406.

113 *Ring* v. *Spina et al.*, 84 F Supp. 403, 407.

114 *Ring* v. *Spina et al.*, 84 F Supp. 403, 407.

unable to receive terms "less favorable than those offered any other producer,"[115] or could not be compelled to sign the Minimum Basic Agreement if entering into agreements with Guild members. So Rifkind enjoined the arbitration.[116]

## II. LEARNED HAND'S RESOLUTION OF NOTHING: "SO FAR AS THEY ARE NECESSARY"

Three days after Judge Rifkind made his ruling in the District Court, Executive Director of the Dramatists Guild Mills Ten Eyck sent George Middleton, founding father of the Guild and architect of the original Minimum Basic Agreement, a copy of the decision.[117] Ten Eyck attached an anxious handwritten note to the decision signing off with the valediction, "Hastily":

> As you will see it's about as bad as it could be for us. The Council has been called to meet on Tuesday to decide what we do next.[118]

At the end of the summer of 1949, after the Guild had time to digest the Rifkind District Court decision and discuss the next steps forward, Guild Secretary Herbert Kubly circulated a sober letter to members.[119] The Guild suggested three possible "long-range" responses which included appealing the decision, negotiating a new Basic Agreement with the producers, or advocating for an exemption to the Clayton Act "afforded . . . to other workers." This final option was a strategy the Guild also pursued, unsuccessfully, more than fifty years later in 2004 but never litigated in the courts.[120]

In the interim, the Guild prepared three separate agreements for straight plays, musicals, and revues, but also delivered the following ominous warning to its members:

> The Guild cannot require the use of these contracts nor require you to secure any minimum terms. However, the terms and conditions of the recommended production contracts represent established practice and what we consider fair, workable and generally acceptable arrangements for play production.[121]

115 *Ring* v. *Spina et al.*, 84 F Supp. 403, 407.
116 *Ring* v. *Spina et al.*, 84 F Supp. 403, 407.
117 *See* letter and decision of *Ring* v. *Spina et al.*, 84 F Supp. 403: M. Tenn Eyck to G. Middleton, May 20, 1949, Box 25, George Middleton Papers.
118 Letter and decision of *Ring* v. *Spina et al.*, 84 F Supp. 403: M. Tenn Eyck to G. Middleton, May 20, 1949, Box 25, George Middleton Papers. Some members of the press painted the result in similar ruinous terms. *Billboard* declared the Basic Agreement as "illegal" and that the Antitrust laws were invoked: "Minimum Basic Agreement Illegal, Court Rules Vs Scripters," *Billboard*, May 28, 1949, 46.
119 Dramatists Guild letter to Members, August 17, 1949, Box 25, George Middleton Papers.
120 *See generally, The Playwrights Licensing Antitrust Initiative Act: Safeguarding the Future of American Live Theatre: Hearing on S. 2349 Before the S. Judiciary Comm.*, 108th Cong. (2004).
121 Dramatists Guild letter to Members, August 17, 1949, Box 25, George Middleton Papers.

Kubly concluded that although the decision was "a bitter disappointment," and the Guild would not prescribe the use of the Minimum Basic Agreement, it was just another chapter in the long struggle of the Association.[122]

In the year that followed, the Guild lived under a cloud of uncertainty, and correspondence from the Association suggested that producers were beginning to reassert greater authority over contractual arrangements with authors. Luise Sillcox of the Guild exchanged anxious letters with George Middleton.[123] Contractual variations, "bad for the authors," started to emerge, particularly over royalty arrangements.[124] Sillcox, who had been on the frontline of Dramatists Guild causes for years, conceded that the current environment was "frightening me badly," and felt that for now, "we are going to be unable to protect our members in this regard."[125]

The Dramatists Guild decided to focus its attention on the appeal process to the Second Circuit as it believed, understandably, that Judge Rifkind's decision was "neither conclusive nor final."[126] The Guild appointed Arthur Garfield Hays for the appeal.[127] Hays, therefore, had come full circle, intimately involved in the formation years of the Guild, and its earliest antitrust disputes with the Shuberts.[128] Both Carl Ring and the Authors' League of America eventually brought the appeal to the Second Circuit, highlighting the inconclusive and universally unsatisfying nature of the proceedings to date. Ring, now in a substantial financial hole, appealed the damages component dismissed at the District Court level. The Authors' League made a cross-appeal against the injunction.[129]

Chief Judge Learned Hand assigned himself the task of writing the judgment in the appeal and cross-appeal. Hand and the two other circuit judges, Thomas Swan and Harrie Chase, circulated three enlightening memorandums before the decision. The memorandums suggest the injunction issue did not favor one party over the other, but there was an antitrust violation. Learned Hand, in his first internal memo to Swan and Chase on December 14, 1950, felt the injunction had become a moot issue and should be reversed, but not on the merits.[130] Hand's reasoning was

122 Dramatists Guild letter to Members, August 17, 1949, Box 25, George Middleton Papers.

123 *See* L. Sillcox to G. Middleton, March 1, 1950, Box 25, George Middleton Papers.

124 L. Sillcox to G. Middleton, March 1, 1950, Box 25, George Middleton Papers.

125 L. Sillcox to G. Middleton, March 1, 1950, Box 25, George Middleton Papers.

126 Dramatists Guild letter to Members, August 17, 1949, Box 25, George Middleton Papers; *see also* reporting suggesting this lack of clarity: "DG not to make changes Pending Clarification on 'Monopoly'," *Variety*, January 12, 1949, 57 and 61.

127 L. Sillcox to G. Middleton, October 20, 1949, Box 25, George Middleton Papers.

128 Hays was counsel in the 1927 dispute with Shuberts that was discontinued before trial. *See Shubert Theatre Corporation* v. *Arthur Richman, President of the Dramatists Guild*, April 29, 1927, New York Supreme Court, Record # 16847, Box 008047634, Hall of Records, New York Courts.

129 *Ring* v. *Authors' League of America Inc et al.*, 186 F 2d 637 (1951).

130 Internal Memo, *Carl Ring* v. *Harold Spina*: L. Hand to H. Chase and T. Swan, December 14, 1950, Box 213, fol. 13, Learned Hand Papers, Historical and Special Collections, Harvard Law School Library [hereafter Learned Hand Papers].

pragmatic, suggesting "[t]he only troublesome issue" was whether Ring could recover the deposit of US$1,500 from Gaumont. The Chief Judge wrote that Ring was not a professional producer and it was unlikely that he would ever produce again. In addition, Hand believed, if Ring wanted to use the work in the films, "he would not be dealing with the Guild."[131] Learned Hand then appears to turn to equitable considerations stating that although the discontinuance of a tort matter did not "put an end to an injunction; . . . the doctrine is not absolute."[132] His Honor suggested the judgment would probably upend the Guild: "[t]he balance between the conflicting interests seems to me to be strongly against continuing an injunction."[133] The Chief Judge voted to modify as above and affirm the Guild's appeal. Hand, however, appeared to be open to a different interpretation. He suggested that the injunction question was no different from the one considered by Judge Clark in the earlier Second Circuit proceedings where the Court reversed a decision to vacate the plaintiff's temporary injunction.[134] Indeed, as discussed, Judge Clark writing for the Court, held that Ring had established a prima facie case.[135] Further, in that case, the Court did not feel compelled to make a final ruling on the issue of whether there was a violation of antitrust.

Judge Chase responded the next day, frustrated by what he felt was a "somewhat emotional brief" submitted by counsel for Ring.[136] Judge Chase wrote that although Judge Clark lacked access to the full facts, "there seems to be nothing which changes the result he reached as to the illegality of the M.B.A."[137] Chase concluded that there was "enough interstate commerce" for the Sherman Act to apply and an exception did not exist under the Clayton Act as it would for a union: "These authors sell their produce to buyers and not their services to employers."[138] Despite raising these issues, Judge Chase also voted to affirm.[139]

[131] Internal Memo, *Carl Ring* v. *Harold Spina*: L. Hand to H. Chase and T. Swan, December 14, 1950, Box 213, fol. 13, Learned Hand Papers. This is not correct if he had an interest under the Minimum Basic Agreement. Hand here might be suggesting as the Minimum Basic Agreement was illegal he could negotiate with film companies in whatever way he liked.

[132] Internal Memo, *Carl Ring* v. *Harold Spina*: L. Hand to H. Chase and T. Swan, December 14, 1950, Box 213, fol. 13, Learned Hand Papers.

[133] Internal Memo, *Carl Ring* v. *Harold Spina*: L. Hand to H. Chase and T. Swan, December 14, 1950, Box 213, fol. 13, Learned Hand Papers.

[134] *Ring* v. *Spina et al.*, 148 F 2d 647 (1945).

[135] Of course, the case was remanded for further trial by jury, as examined above.

[136] Internal Memo, *Carl Ring* v. *Harold Spina*: H. Chase to L. Hand and T. Swan, December 15, 1950, Box 213, fol. 13, Learned Hand Papers.

[137] Internal Memo, *Carl Ring* v. *Harold Spina*: H. Chase to L. Hand and T. Swan, December 15, 1950, Box 213, fol. 13, Learned Hand Papers. Chase also agreed with the lower court in that all Ring "had was a right to produce the play as the court correctly held."

[138] Internal Memo, *Carl Ring* v. *Harold Spina*: H. Chase to L. Hand and T. Swan, December 15, 1950, Box 213, fol. 13, Learned Hand Papers.

[139] Internal Memo, *Carl Ring* v. *Harold Spina*: H. Chase to L. Hand and T. Swan, December 15, 1950, Box 213, fol. 13, Learned Hand Papers.

Judge Swan wrote to his fellow judges that he also felt that Ring's brief was "almost useless."[140] As for the Guild's appeal, Swan believed that "[Judge] Clark's opinions conclude us."[141] Swan wrote that royalty payments for the author remain the same after the sale, although "rewriting continues after the play is sold to a producer."[142] Therefore, a dramatist, Swan wrote, was in a similar position to a "manufacturer of stoves who incorporates a service policy at no extra price in the contract of sale."[143] So the writer is a service provider, not exempt from antitrust. Swan, with not much conviction, also concluded that the Guild's appeal should be affirmed "[w]ith some doubt."[144]

So the internal memos suggest there was significant doubt over the legality of the Guild and Basic Agreement framework. In its written opinion,[145] the Court first dealt with the damages issue and whether the plaintiff had sustained an injury.[146] The Court affirmed the position of the lower court. Ring, therefore, received nothing from the proceedings.[147] The District Court held before that Ring had no right or title in *Stovepipe Hat*.[148] The Court held that whatever interest obtained by Ring through contract "was unlawful because it was part of the unlawful conspiracy."[149] Ring's repudiation of parts of the contract left him with no interest in the play.[150]

Chief Judge Hand, therefore, up to this stage in the decision, agreed with the District Court. The issue on which the Second Circuit diverged from the lower court was whether Ring should have the opportunity "to bid for the right to 'produce'" the work in the future on the same terms as other producers.[151] It was here that the Chief Judge tread with caution around the core matter of concern for everyone in the industry that had confused since the first Basic Agreement of 1926. The Court reasoned that if it provided the plaintiff producer an opportunity to bid for the right to produce, it would have to decide "the 'Agreement' in fact was

[140] Internal Memo, *Carl Ring* v. *Harold Spina*: T. Swan to H. Chase and L. Hand, December 17, 1950, Box 213, fol. 13, Learned Hand Papers.

[141] Internal Memo, *Carl Ring* v. *Harold Spina*: T. Swan to H. Chase and L. Hand, December 17, 1950, Box 213, fol. 13, Learned Hand Papers.

[142] Internal Memo, *Carl Ring* v. *Harold Spina*: T. Swan to H. Chase and L. Hand, December 17, 1950, Box 213, fol. 13, Learned Hand Papers.

[143] Internal Memo, *Carl Ring* v. *Harold Spina*: T. Swan to H. Chase and L. Hand, December 17, 1950, Box 213, fol. 13, Learned Hand Papers.

[144] Internal Memo, *Carl Ring* v. *Harold Spina*: T. Swan to H. Chase and L. Hand, December 17, 1950, Box 213, fol. 13, Learned Hand Papers.

[145] *Ring* v. *Authors' League of America Inc et al.*, 186 F 2d 637.

[146] The memos did consider this issue, and were critical of the plaintiff's brief. As noted, the only issue of some contention was whether Ring was able to recover Gaumont's US$1,500 deposit, which was the balance of the assignment of rights in the play which relieved Gaumont of any obligations going forward with the production.

[147] *Ring* v. *Authors' League of America Inc et al.*, 186 F 2d 637, 641.

[148] *Ring* v. *Authors' League of America Inc et al.*, 186 F 2d 637, 641.

[149] *Ring* v. *Authors' League of America Inc et al.*, 186 F 2d 637, 641.

[150] *Ring* v. *Authors' League of America Inc et al.*, 186 F 2d 637, 642.

[151] *Ring* v. *Authors' League of America Inc et al.*, 186 F 2d 637, 642. If the authors decided to stage the play again, they could not offer Ring less favorable terms than those offered to any other producer.

a conspiracy forbidden by the Anti-Trust Acts."[152] The Second Circuit could make a final ruling because the District Court had now conducted a "definitive hearing" on the facts. The Court, however, held that despite the opportunity it had to make final rulings, it was "equally true" that it "need do so only so far as they are necessary to a disposition of the suit."[153] Chief Judge Learned Hand added:

> We hold that once it is decided that the plaintiff has no rights in the play, he has no standing to invoke a declaration that he is entitled to an opportunity to bid for a second "production" contract, or an injunction which will secure such a right. He has no existing interest to protect beyond that of any possible newcomer in the field, and that is not enough to support either a declaration or injunction.[154]

The Court stated there was no particular difference between the position of Ring and any other "future newcomer" that wanted to produce the work except that the inexperienced Ring had lost almost US$150,000 from his first failed venture into show business.[155] The Court held, with respect to being a victim of an unlawful conspiracy, the standards for injunctive relief were high when considered in the context of future conduct, and even higher when brought by an individual. And when the matter pertains to the public interest, "there must be some tangible probability that the wrong will be repeated to justify an injunction."[156] As for individuals, "he must then prove that there is a 'dangerous probability' of a repetition of the wrong to him individually, and the plaintiff at bar did not prove anything more than the most tenebrous probability."[157]

Ring's background and unlikely future as a producer appeared to influence the Court, as Chief Judge Hand outlined in his internal memorandum. Ring was a lawyer – not, "by profession," a "producer" of plays – and the work had not been staged in the seven years since its initial demise. The Court stated, given Ring's unfortunate experience, there was no reason to suppose he would produce again.[158] Alternatively, the Authors' League, "vigorously protests its innocence and beneficence; it is conscious of no wrongdoing, and asserts that its existence is essential to the protection of authors and composers."[159] Chief Judge Hand resolved that, of

152 *Ring* v. *Authors' League of America Inc et al.*, 186 F 2d 637, 642. Here again, referring back to Clark J's decision on behalf of the Court in 148 F 2d. 647.

153 *Ring* v. *Authors' League of America Inc et al.*, 186 F 2d 637, 642.

154 *Ring* v. *Authors' League of America Inc et al.*, 186 F 2d 637, 642.

155 *Ring* v. *Authors' League of America Inc et al.*, 186 F 2d 637, 642. Ring had repudiated the Agreement and was left without any interest.

156 *Ring* v. *Authors' League of America Inc et al.*, 186 F 2d 637, 643 citing cases at note 6 of the judgment: *United States* v. *United States Steel Corp.*, 251 U.S. 417, 445, 40 S. Ct. 293, 64 L. Ed. 343; *Hecht Co.* v. *Bowles*, 321 U.S. 321, 329, 64 S. Ct. 587, 88 L. Ed. 754; *Walling* v. *Helmerich & Payne*, 323 U.S. 37, 43, 65 S. Ct. 11, 89 L. Ed. 29; *Walling* v. *Youngerman-Reynolds Hardwood Co.*, 325 U.S. 419, 421, 65 S. Ct. 1242, 89 L. Ed. 1705; *Securities and Exchange Commission* v. *Torr*, 2 Cir., 87 F.2d 446; *McComb* v. *Goldblatt Bros.*, 7 Cir., 166 F.2d 387; *Walling* v. *T. Buettner & Co.*, 7 Cir., 133 F.2d 306.

157 *Ring* v. *Authors' League of America Inc et al.*, 186 F 2d 637, 643.

158 *Ring* v. *Authors' League of America Inc et al.*, 186 F 2d 637, 643.

159 *Ring* v. *Authors' League of America Inc et al.*, 186 F 2d 637, 643.

course, such conclusions about the League would "not protect it" if it was a combination in restraint of trade, "but they are relevant in deciding whether we should decide issues in which the plaintiff has only the most shadowy interest."[160]

The Court, therefore, lifted the injunction. But there was no resolution on the lingering, much larger, issue. Learned Hand felt it necessary in his final remarks to emphasize that all legal questions were to be left "open" over any future revival. The Court's position was the same as when the Second Circuit first granted the temporary injunction:[161] It was unnecessary to address the antitrust issue.[162]

It was clear that Ring had lost but unclear whether the dramatists had won. The Court lifted the injunction against the defendants on the arbitration issue, and Ring never received a cent. The jury, however, in the District Court answered in the affirmative regarding whether the defendants had violated antitrust law. The jury's verdict was the only direct pronouncement on the antitrust issue in any of the proceedings – trial or appellate level – apart from preliminary or prima facie decisions and the illuminating internal memorandums between Learned Hand and his fellow judges. All of these statements (whether preliminary or in internal memorandums) appeared to suggest there was considerable doubt whether the Guild and its Basic Agreement had not violated antitrust law.

The trade press was keen to report the decision as a victory for the dramatists,[163] but the Dramatists Guild was more cautious in its assessment. *Authors League News* reproduced Chief Judge Hand's decision on the front page of its January 1951 edition with the accompanying measured title: "Ring Decision Favorable."[164] The editors, in their brief commentary on the case, highlighted Learned Hand's parting comments that held, in essence, the issue of whether the Minimum Basic Agreement violated antitrust law "was specifically left unanswered by this court."[165] The League and Guild concluded that they were essentially left in the same position as they were before Ring began his proceedings in 1944. The dramatists did, however, feel that the decision to lift the injunction "dispels the stigma of illegality cast upon the Minimum Basic Agreement."[166] The decision also opened the door to renegotiate the Basic Agreement. But the managers' ever-present bargaining tool – the possibility to challenge the legality of the dramatists' guild association status – had survived.

—

Ring sought certiorari in April 1951.[167] *Variety* reported that Ring claimed the Minimum Basic Agreement had crippled the success of the production and

160 *Ring* v. *Authors' League of America Inc et al.*, 186 F 2d 637, 643.

161 This was the decision of Judge Clark on behalf of the Court: *Ring* v. *Spina et al.*, 148 F 2d 647.

162 *Ring* v. *Authors' League of America Inc et al.*, 186 F 2d 637, 643.

163 *See, for example*, "Court Rules in Favor of Drama Guild," *Billboard*, January 20, 1951, 36.

164 "Ring Decision Favorable," *Authors League News*, Vol. II (2) January 1951, 1.

165 "Ring Decision Favorable," *Authors League News*, Vol. II (2) January 1951, 1.

166 "Ring Decision Favorable," *Authors League News*, Vol. II (2) January 1951, 1.

167 "Carl Ring Takes 7-yr-old Case vs. Dramatists Guild 'Monopoly' to High Court," *Variety*, April 11, 1951, 58.

prevented the novice producer from changing the work.[168] The Supreme Court denied certiorari,[169] as the Guild expected,[170] and the matter appeared closed.[171] In late 1951, Harold Spina's agent Edmond Pauker sought to resurrect a new *Stovepipe Hat* production.[172] Spina expressed interest, but reluctance, in a revival. In the previous three years he had turned to write, "strictly commercial popular songs" to pull himself "up by the bootstraps, out of the dregs of chaos caused by the STOVE-PIPE HAT fiasco" and to relieve the "financial indebtedness" from the whole affair.[173] Spina did, however, go back to the script, writing to his agent in early 1952 about the "many-many, changes," he had made.[174]

Carl Ring was an accomplished man successful in business as a lawyer and engineer. He competed in the 1928 Olympics as a high hurdler and unsuccessfully ran for the United States Senate in 1952, a year after the finalization of his dispute with the dramatists.[175] He was perhaps motivated to reform the law in the wake of his traumatic experiences. Despite these impressive achievements, Ring's notoriety was attached to his dispute with the Guild. Ring's obituary in the *New York Times* remarks that "he drew national attention with a Federal suit against the Dramatists Guild of the Authors League of America" when the courts "did not award damages" for Sherman Act violations. The obituary continues, "[h]e sought to make changes in the play, but the authors refused, citing a contract provision that any changes required the author's approval."[176] It is a reminder of what narratives survive, and what continues to resonate – an amalgam of organizational, economic, and, just as importantly, artistic forces.

George Middleton wrote in response to whether the Guild had ever affiliated with any labor union by stating that the organization "has always relied on its own

168 "Carl Ring Takes 7-yr-old Case vs. Dramatists Guild 'Monopoly' to High Court," *Variety*, April 11, 1951, 58.

169 *Ring* v. *Spina et al.*, 341 U.S. 935 (1951).

170 Luise Sillcox informed George Middleton that Ring had lodged an appeal to the Supreme Court, but "[c]onfidently I doubt that they will grant the writ." L. Sillcox to G. Middleton, January 18, 1951, Box 25, George Middleton Papers.

171 This was certainly the view of the industry press, perhaps as exhausted as the parties themselves given the matter had now run for seven years. *See* "Supreme Court Refuses to Accept Ring Appeal; Case Now Seen Closed," *Variety*, May 23, 1951, 57.

172 *See* "Edmond Pauker to Harold Spina," November 15, 1951, Edmond Pauker Papers, T-Mss 1960–001, Box 75, fol. 7, Billy Rose Theatre Division, The New York Public Library.

173 "Harold Spina to Edmond Pauker," November 25, 1951, Edmond Pauker Papers, T-Mss 1960–001, Box 75, fol. 7, Billy Rose Theatre Division, The New York Public Library.

174 "Harold Spina to Edmond Pauker," February 28, 1952, Edmond Pauker Papers, T-Mss 1960–001, Box 75, fol. 7, Billy Rose Theatre Division, The New York Public Library. In 1953, the National Republican Committee was also interested in mounting a tribute production to celebrate Lincoln which "might take the form of an outdoor spectacle, condensed version, Washington and road showings or even possibly a Broadway production." *See* "Edmond Pauker to Harold Spina," August 12, 1953, Edmond Pauker Papers, Yale Collection of American Literature, Beinecke Rare Book and Manuscript Library, Box 39, fol. 962.

175 "Carl E. Ring, 89, Dies; Lawyer and Engineer," *New York Times*, June 14, 1991, D19.

176 "Carl E. Ring, 89, Dies; Lawyer and Engineer," *New York Times*, June 14, 1991, D19.

inherent strength."[177] The Dramatists Guild is an extraordinary success story. The Association is now more than a hundred years old. But there is also something inherently fragile about this history. The dramatists are constantly negotiating the circulation of material throughout the theatrical economy with various influential mediating stakeholders holding wide-ranging agendas. The dramatists join together as an association – "its own inherent strength" – where there is ambiguity about whether they have equivalent protections to employees of a union or whether they are shielded from antitrust exemptions. Writers come together as an association but ultimately still enter into individual agreements with producers as independent contractors. Within the broader organizational structure of the industry, the dramatic author's original intellectual property rights play a fundamentally practical role – the place to begin to transform the work from the page to the final realization of the production. And the stakeholders that control the space between original words and final production is the subject of constant renegotiation.

In the years following the Ring *v.* Spina litigation, courts continued to explore the exemption issue in other entertainment contexts. In *H. A. Artists & Assoc., Inc.* v. *Actors' Equity Association* the Supreme Court in a note, citing previous decisions,[178] stated that "a party seeking refuge in the statutory exemption must be a bona fide labor organization, and not an independent contractor or entrepreneur."[179] In the same case, however, an exemption applied to independent contracting agents of actors because commissions needed to be regulated to protect the union actors' minimum payment.[180] The Supreme Court has also found that the standard for whether orchestra leaders were a "labor group" party to a "labor dispute" was: "presence of a job or wage competition or some other economic relationship affecting legitimate union interests between the union members and the independent contractors."[181] In response to the dramatists after 1926, theatrical producers – and particularly the Shuberts – told an alternative story outside of intellectual property about control over creation in the space

177 *See* Draft Pamphlet of George Middleton, "Court Actions and Other Trials," no date, Box 25, George Middleton Papers.

178 Citing *Meat Drivers* v. *United States*, 371 U.S. 94; *Columbia River Packers Assn.* v. *Hinton*, 315 U.S. 143.

179 *H. A. Artists & Assoc., Inc.* v. *Actors' Equity Ass'n*, 451 U.S. 704, 717 (1981) (note 20) citing *Meat Drivers* v. *United States*, 371 U.S. 94; *Columbia River Packers Assn.* v. *Hinton*, 315 U.S. 143.

180 *See H. A. Artists & Assoc., Inc.* v. *Actors' Equity Ass'n*, 451 U.S. 704, 720–721 (1981). Justice Stewart delivering the opinion of the Court held in "[t]he peculiar structure of the legitimate theater industry" the "theatrical agents must, therefore, be considered a 'labor group,' and their controversy with Equity is plainly a 'labor dispute' as defined in the Norris-LaGuardia Act." Further, the agents "perform a function-the representation of union members in the sale of their labor-that in most nonentertainment industries is performed exclusively by unions."

181 *See American Federation of Musicians* v. *Carroll*, 391 U.S. 99, 105–106 (1968) where the Court held the correct criterion was applied by the District Court (this is the quotation from the District Court cited by the Supreme Court). In this instance it was band leaders who competed with union-member musicians for a share of club fees.

between authors and audiences. This was not a story about what intellectual property rights stakeholders held or aspired to hold in works of authorship. It was about how stakeholders organized their labor relationships in response to mediating structures and whether these labor relationships were anticompetitive. These narratives have endured. As a consequence, the authority that dramatic authors are often assumed to have over the work they create remains tenuous and unclear.

# Epilogue

The first renegotiated Basic Agreement after *Ring* in 1955 – consisting of multiple contracts – provided a preview of the issues that would occupy the industry over the next fifty years.[1] George Middleton suggests by the mid-1950s commercial productions had become reliant on external "angel" funders who were not receiving timely or adequate returns on their substantial upfront investments. Production costs in 1955, according to Middleton, "were 500 percent higher than on similar plays produced between 1935–1942."[2] Thus, higher production costs meant it took longer for backers to recoup which was a disincentive to invest. In 1955, the playwrights made their first of many compromises over royalty structures as Middleton explained:

> It was ... a realistic decision, which the Guild's Council itself made when it authorized its Negotiators to meet head on the Producer-Backer problem. The art of the possible thus pointed to the need of *modifying* royalty terms and conditions of acquiring interest in subsidiary rights, so that, until the play became a success, the Backers' investment against loss should be improved and some chance be given them to recoup. It was the philosophy which directed and prompted the 1955 contracts.[3]

1 The 1955 revisions included the following agreements: 1. A Producer/Manager Contract (between the Guild and Producer); 2. A Minimum Basic Production Contract (between Producer and Author of Dramatic Productions): 3. Minimum Basic Production Contract (between Producer and Book Author/ Lyricist/Composer of a musical); and schedules for additional terms and sale /lease of motion picture rights. *See* George Middleton, *The Dramatists Guild: What It Is and Does ... How It Happened and Why* (New York: Dramatists Guild, 5th ed, 1966), 16.

2 Middleton, *The Dramatists Guild: What It Is and Does ... How It Happened and Why* (1966), 16. Note also in 1955 the Supreme Court handed down its antitrust ruling on the issue of whether to break up the control the Shuberts had over houses across the country. Producers had to book their shows exclusively in Shubert houses contrary to the expansive rhetorical "open door policy" of the organization in the first decades of the twentieth century during their battle with the Syndicate. *See United States* v. *Shubert* 348 U.S. 222 (1955). As a result of the litigation, Select Theatres stopped its booking services, and the Shuberts had to sell off about twelve theatres in six cities. The UBO (the booking office) also ceased operations.

3 Middleton, *The Dramatists Guild: What it is and Does ... How it Happened and Why* (1966), 16.

Playwrights carried a considerable burden because of the broader industry forces of rising costs. As an alternative to the standard minimum royalty structure, the 1955 Agreement included terms that guaranteed authors upfront payments rather than royalties. In return, investors and producers received a greater interest in subsidiary streams of revenue. In the decade that followed, further concessionary options aimed to minimize the impact of crippling costs. For example, one option was to reduce author royalties by half for a certain number of weeks or until the production recouped its initial investment. In return, playwrights were supposed to receive higher advances or renegotiated terms on subsidiary rights.[4]

Developments in the commercial theatre on Broadway must also be read along with expansions in the nonprofit industry. The emergence of the League of Residential Theatres (LORT) in the second half of the twentieth century accompanied new dramatic voices in extraordinary regional spaces across the country. These theatres over the last fifty years, however, have undertaken considerable financial risks by investing in new unproven works. LORT and other regional-based theatres have placed new demands on authors for a stake in the later life of the work to, in some way, offset these risks.

A deeper archival study of the last fifty years is beyond the scope of this book. Important ongoing work is being conducted by other scholars. For example, Derek Miller's pathbreaking empirical research makes a significant contribution to our understanding of the American theatre economy advancing the earlier work of Jack Poggi and Alfred Bernheim.[5] But industry developments after the *Ring* litigation follow familiar entrenched patterns in the longer history of the American theatre. Mediators adapt practices to influence how works move between authors and audiences. Production is shaped by control over physical spaces (theatre ownership),

4 Middleton describes how advances were maintained, and even increased, but in order to keep costs down in the 1955 Agreement, "the Author might accept a maximum of $750 a week Minimum Standard Royalty for plays, $1500 for musicals, during the first four out-of-town weeks prior to the New York opening." And after opening, authors might forgo a percentage of royalties to be recouped in subsidiary streams. *See* Middleton, *The Dramatists Guild: What It Is and Does . . . How It Happened and Why* (1966), 17.

5 *See, for example*, Derek Miller, "Broadway Real Estate and Economic Complexity in the Theater," www.visualizingbroadway.com/broadway/shuberts.html (ASTR 2016 Working Session, November 4, 2016); Derek Miller, "Average Broadway," *Theatre Journal* 68, no. 4 (December 2016): 529. Marlis Schweitzer's examination of the early American impresarios and transatlantic networks set the scene for developments over the last one hundred years as examined in this book. *See, for example*, Marlis Schweitzer, *Transatlantic Broadway: The Infrastructural Politics of Global Performance* (Houndmills, Basingstoke, Hampshire UK; New York: Palgrave Macmillan, 2015); Christin Essin and Marlis Schweitzer, "Communities of Production: A Materialist Reading with an Offstage View," in *A Cultural History of Theatre in the Modern Age*, ed. Kim Solga (London; New York: Bloomsbury, 2017). *See also* George Pate, *Enter the Undead Author: Intellectual Property, the Ideology of Authorship, and Performance Practices since the 1960s* (Vancouver ; Madison: Fairleigh Dickinson University Press; Lanham, Maryland: The Rowman & Littlefield Publishing Group, Inc., 2019); Philip Auslander, *Liveness: Performance in a Mediatized Culture* (London; New York: Routledge, 2008); Anthea Kraut, *Choreographing Copyright: Race, Gender, and Intellectual Property Rights in American Dance* (New York: Oxford University Press, 2016).

and the control of administrative processes (how royalty and subsidiary-right systems are constructed through accounting practices). Mediators also continue to organize legal strategies around areas of law outside of copyright, including competition law. In response, the dramatists in 2004, almost half a century after *Ring*, proposed legislation "to resolve a sixty-year-old, but intractable, problem."[6] Over the last few years, the Dramatists Guild has continued to argue that renegotiation of the Approved Production Contract with producers is thwarted by "what they [the Producers League] claim are anti-trust issues."[7]

## I. APPEASING ANGELS FROM ABOVE

The 1976 United States Copyright Act presented an opportunity for all theatrical stakeholders to reshape their relationship with intellectual property law. Before 1976, the industry built models heavily reliant on the circulation of unpublished manuscripts and the intangible common law rights attached to unpublished manuscripts. After 1909, playscripts received protection under the federal statute if they were published and registered or alternatively registered as an unpublished work. Many were not. Theatrical litigants continued to move in and out of the federal and state common law system to advance their claims. For the most part, however, the industry avoided expensive and drawn-out litigation preferring to create internal rules through the various iterations of the Minimum Basic Agreement and relational contracting. Furthermore, state and federal courts continued to adopt the parol transfer that presumed that mediators had acquired the author's copyright before publishing or performing the work, even with no evidence to support the acquisition.[8]

The outsized effects of these rules contrast with the 1976 Copyright Act which in form discarded them. After 1976, copyright protection became automatic for authors who reduced their work to "fixed in any tangible medium of expression."[9] The Act extended the term of protection to "the life of the author and fifty years after the author's death,"[10] and expanded the scope of protection. For example, the author

6 *The Playwrights Licensing Antitrust Initiative Act: Safeguarding the Future of American Live Theater: Hearing on S. 2349 Before the Subcomm. on the Judiciary*, 108th Cong. (2004) ("Dramatists Guild Submission," 37).

7 *See* Ken Davenport: in conversation with Ralph Sevush, *The Producer's Perspective* (Podcast, Episode 35, August 2015) available at www.theproducersperspective.com/my_weblog/2015/08/podcast-episode-35-transcript-ralph-sevush.html.

8 I am grateful to an anonymous reviewer who initially highlighted to me the continued impact of the parol transfer after the 1909 Act.

9 *See* Copyright Act of 1976, Pub. L. No. 94–553, § 102, 90 Stat. 2541, 2544–45. Registration is a requirement in certain circumstances, however. For example, 17 U.S.C. §§ 411–12 required "Registration as prerequisite to infringement suit" and "Registration as prerequisite to certain remedies for infringement."

10 *See* Copyright Act of 1976, § 302(a). And, of course, was followed by much further extensions in the years to come.

could now license or assign any part of the exclusive right that they owned.[11] This was in form a playwright's framework despite the absence of the word playwright or dramatist from the 1976 Act or any previous iteration. Dramatists were assumed to be authors of dramatic works as they reduced their work to a tangible medium of expression.[12]

But the industry after 1976 also became preoccupied with placating the interests of mediating external investors by developing royalty pools and new models for the distribution of subsidiary revenues. Thus, the concerns that led to the 1955 Basic Agreement intensified in the late 1970s and early 1980s. The result was a collision between antitrust and larger organizational issues over who was entitled to a stake in the life and afterlife of original productions. And these developments did not only occur in the commercial sector. For example, the success of the Public Theatre's original production of *A Chorus Line* transformed relationships between authors and producers when the nonprofit wanted to transfer the work to the commercial theatre. Producer for the Public Joseph Papp and lawyer John Breglio designed a model in which the nonprofit secured options for the commercial transfer, a stake in future royalties, as well as subsidiary rights in third-party productions.[13] Major nonprofits soon followed suit including the Manhattan Theatre Club, Playwrights Horizons, Second Stage, and Roundabout in New York as well as the Goodman, La Jolla, and the Old Globe in other regional centers.[14]

The royalty issues only intensified after an article appeared on the front page of the *New York Times* in November 1981 claiming the industry was unsustainable if it continued to operate in its current form.[15] The smash-hit film adaptation *Woman of the Year* starring Lauren Bacall was grossing up to US$300,000 a week at the box office by its thirty-fifth week of production. The investors had hardly seen a cent returned on their original investment, however. By the early 1980s, concerns in the industry over rising costs leading to an inability to pay investors only deepened. Artists who received royalties, including playwrights, were at the center of the tensions.

11 *See* Copyright Act of 1976, § 201(d). Regarding the divisibility of copyright into subsidiary streams of revenue and the exclusivity arrangements that have been controlled by mediating publishers, *see* Shane Valenzi, "A Rollicking Band of Pirates: Licensing the Exclusive Right of Public Performance in the Theatre Industry," *Vanderbilt Journal of Entertainment and Technology Law* 14, no. 3 (2012): 778.

12 But after 1976 important scholarship emerged arguing how nonwriter collaborators could begin to frame arguments: *see, for example*, Jessica Litman, "Copyright in the Stage Direction of a Broadway Musical," *Art & the Law* 7, no. 4 (1982–1983): 309; and investigating the intellectual property language that stakeholders might want to include in standard agreements: Alan Littman and Jane C. Ginsburg, "The Rights of Stage Directors and Choreographers" (Mar. 30, 1984) cited in Margit Livingston, "Inspiration or Imitation: Copyright Protection for Stage Directions," *Boston College Law Review* 50, no. 2 (March 2009): 4451 (note 187).

13 *See* John Breglio, *I Wanna Be A Producer: How to Make a Killing on Broadway ... Or Get Killed* (Milwaukee, WI: Applause Theatre and Cinema Books, 2016), 135–137.

14 Breglio, *I Wanna Be A Producer: How to Make a Killing on Broadway*, 136.

15 *See* Sandra Salmans, "Why Investors in Broadway Hits Are Often Losers: Why Investors in Broadway Hits Are Often Losers," *New York Times*, November 22, 1981, D1. *See also* Breglio, *I Wanna Be A Producer: How to Make a Killing on Broadway*, 82–84.

Royalty percentages for plays and musicals enshrined in the first Basic Agreement, and applied for decades, were calculated on gross profits.[16] Royalties, however, were a highly variable expense based on box office takings. And by the early 1980s, there were multiple other parties beyond playwrights who had a negotiated royalty stake in the life of the production including designers, directors, star actors, and producers.[17] In contrast, investors had always received payment out of profits. Thus, the larger the royalty expense the smaller the profit, and the longer it would take to just repay investors let alone return them a profit on their original investment.

In the last months of 1981, *Woman of the Year* was suffocating under the weight of its expenses. Bacall was receiving 10 percent of the gross and other significant ongoing payments were applied to the underlying rights holder MGM and the Palace Theatre. Outside of these stakeholders, 20 percent of the gross went to combined creative interests which included the writers. Lead producer Lawrence Kasha predicted that investors would probably receive a return on their investment after approximately two years (a long run for a Broadway production).[18] Investors, the critical source of capitalization on Broadway, had little incentive to invest. The production finally reorganized its model to control costs, paying royalties out of a capped percentage pool taken from operating profits rather than gross (at a ratio of 2:1–2 for combined royalty holders to 1 for investors).[19] Thus, the royalty pool based on operating profits was born (although earlier variations of the model had been in operation for shows in similar dire circumstances).[20]

In response to the emergence of the pools, President of the Dramatists Guild Peter Stone declared that "[g]ross" for the playwright "is our birthright. You don't touch that."[21] But invariably the industry encroaches on the playwright as a way to reduce costs in the first weeks of production. Mediators that could transform words on a page into the final material performance began the systematic process of reshaping the production processes through shrewd accounting processes.

A royalty pool posed new challenges for all stakeholders. Each new production continually reconstructed the pool: royalty percentages and stakeholders changed

16 *See* net gross as defined in 1985 "Approved Production Contract for Plays of 1985" §4.03 less administrative expenses that come to approximately 10 percent of the "gross" amount (§4.03 subsections i–viii).

17 So, for example, in *The Woman of the Year* Lauren Bacall received 10 percent, MGM who owned the underlying rights took 2 percent, the three authors: book writer, lyricist and composer received 9 percent, the director 3 percent, choreographer 1.5 percent, costume designer, 0.25 percent, and the producers received 4 percent. The Nederlanders, who owned the Palace Theatre, received both operating costs (rentals) and a "share of ticket sales that averaged 6% of gross." *See* Salmans, "Why Investors in Broadway Hits Are Often Losers."

18 Salmans, "Why Investors in Broadway Hits Are Often Losers."

19 For example, operating profits are $x per week and 20 percent of profits are dedicated to paying royalties. Collaborators receive two lots and investors get one. The lots in the industry are known as "points" based on what percentage of the gross creators are entitled to.

20 *See* Salmans, "Why Investors in Broadway Hits Are Often Losers."

21 Salmans, "Why Investors in Broadway Hits Are Often Losers."

from one production to another. Thus, producers wanted to negotiate agreements on a case-by-case basis and inevitably the playwrights resisted. The producers, therefore, returned to what was becoming an incredibly useful way to encourage a more flexible negotiating framework: threaten the Guild that it operated as an illegal monopoly.

## II. THE INEVITABLE ANTITRUST RESPONSE

The 1982 antitrust litigation involving plaintiff Richard Barr – independent producer, and president of the New York League of Theatres – against the Dramatists Guild, and three of its member officers, became a forum for all parties to articulate their ongoing frustrations unresolved after *Ring*. Royalty pools, tensions over minimum standards, encroachments on royalties, investor interests, and the fact that the Basic Agreement had not been renegotiated for almost twenty years, were some of the issues in which all parties were seeking clarity. Negotiations for a new Basic Agreement had stagnated and thus the producers turned to the law. The arguments were familiar, however. The plaintiff claimed that the Guild had conspired to fix minimum prices and other terms under the standard agreement. This time the dramatists counterclaimed, arguing that the producers had also been involved in a conspiracy against authors contravening federal antitrust law.[22]

Barr framed the initial complaint around "the nature of trade and commerce" in the industry – how the producers created value in the production. For Barr, the author's work was "an integral and indispensable part of the presentation." On completion of the rehearsal, however, the work took on a new life in which the producer becomes central to the transformation process. The assemblage, rehearsing, and arranging process are all facilitated through the administration of the theatrical producer at considerable risk and cost: "a dramatic play generally costs $500,000 or more to produce and a musical generally $1,000,000 to produce."[23] Producers thus have the resources and networks to transform intellectual creation into a material production but they do so at considerable risk.

The claims for relief covered various grievances producers had with writers since the first Agreement of 1926. For example, the complaint highlighted restrictions on the ability to modify work, the coercion of authors to conform to minimum Guild standards, and the restrictions on access to subsidiary rights. Barr's complaint

[22] *See* "Complaint," *Richard Barr* v. *The Dramatists Guild Inc., Peter Stone, Ruth Goetz and Sheldon Harnick*, July 27, 1982, Records of District Courts of the United States, Record Group 21, National Archives and Records Administration: Northeast Region (New York City), Civil Case file 82 cv 4876, US District Court for the Southern District of New York; "Answer to Initial Complaint," *Richard Barr* v. *The Dramatists Guild Inc., Peter Stone, Ruth Goetz and Sheldon Harnick*, September 16, 1982, Records of District Courts of the United States, Record Group 21, National Archives and Records Administration: Northeast Region (New York City), Civil Case file 82 cv 4876, US District Court for the Southern District of New York.

[23] "Complaint," 5.

claimed that the Guild restrained interstate commerce, fixed minimum prices, and lessened competition.[24] Barr also sought a declaration that the alleged conspiracy to fix minimum prices violated Section 1 of the Sherman Act. He sought injunctive relief for the use of the minimum contract, and an enjoinment against the Guild to not interfere with direct negotiations between producers and playwrights.

The dramatists' response, counterclaim, and third-party response, identified the "economic realities" of vertical integration in the industry – how the monopoly theatre owners were also often engaged, or had an interest in, the production itself. The Guild believed theatre owners conspired "to fix, stabilize and/or maintain at artificially low and non-competitive levels the compensation received by playwrights" and "enforce[d] unfavorable terms and conditions in the contracts that are offered to playwrights by [producers]."[25] The Shuberts and Nederlanders, the defendants claimed, controlled 70 percent of first-class theatres, dominated the League, and ultimately the terms on which playwrights worked in the industry.[26]

The producers, following familiar previous strategies, highlighted what they viewed as inherent contradictions in the dramatists' position. In their response, as counterclaim defendants to the dramatists' antitrust claim, Barr argued that it is

> factually untenable and legally impermissible for defendants simultaneously to (a) defend the past and continued use of their Minimum Basic Production Contract, the "MBPC", as lawful, reasonable and necessary, and (b) argue that the same MBPC was coercively imposed on dramatists to their detriment and monetary injury.[27]

Part of the strategy of the dramatists, led by counsel Floyd Abrams, was to reframe the antitrust conversation into a potentially new area of inquiry. Abrams sought to admit documents that went to the issue of how the producers renegotiated in the shadow of formal frameworks. Abrams argued:

> We want to know what they have in their files which relates to what we are supposedly doing, what we supposedly said to our members, what they have said to us, what we have said to them, what we are restraining. We want to deal with the economics of the industry.[28]

24 "Complaint," 5–9.

25 *See* "Defendant's amended answer, counter claim and third party complaint," April 28, 1983, Records of District Courts of the United States, Record Group 21, National Archives and Records Administration: Northeast Region (New York City), Civil Case file 82 cv 4876, US District Court for the Southern District of New York, [45a,b].

26 *See* "Defendant's amended answer, counter claim and third party complaint," [37].

27 *Cited in Richard Barr, Plaintiff,* v. *The Dramatists Guild, Inc., Peter Stone, Ruth Goetz and Sheldon Harnick, Defendants and Third-Party Plaintiffs,* v. *The League Of New York Theatres and Producers, Inc., The Shubert Foundation, Inc., The Shubert Organization, Inc., Gerald Schoenfeld, Bernard B. Jacobs, Nederlander Organization, Inc., and James M. Nederlander, Third-Party Defendants,* 573 F. Supp. 555, 558 (1983).

28 *See* "Hearing Transcript before Judge Werker," September 13, 1983, Records of District Courts of the United States, Record Group 21, National Archives and Records Administration: Northeast Region

And an issue related to the "economics of the industry" rarely, if ever, discussed in legal discourse was the practice of cutting.[29] As explained by Abrams, "cuts" was the process of informally renegotiating terms between the author and a producer when a play had started its run and was proving unsuccessful or the run was starting to slow down. Abrams stated, "it is common place, and we want to show you this at trial, for different arrangements to be made and negotiated between the authors of the plays and the producers of them."[30]

Preliminary proceedings before trial suggested the defendant dramatists' counterclaim would receive careful consideration. Judge Werker in the Southern District of New York denied the motion by the plaintiffs to dismiss or stay the counterclaim.[31] The Court found that the Guild had standing to seek an injunction under the Clayton Act as Guild members could sue in their own right.[32] The door was open, fleetingly, for the dramatists to get clarification in a case first advanced by the producers.

## III. A NEW BASIC AGREEMENT

The Barr proceedings came to a grinding halt when the parties settled in the form of a newly negotiated industry contract known as the Approved Production Contract (APC).[33] The expansive and convoluted agreement that followed the Barr antitrust litigation provided no clear resolution on the Dramatists Guild's monopoly status, however. The APC was also an agreement for the entire industry negotiated by a handful of stakeholders. John Breglio writes:

> An open town meeting of sorts was held for the industry in a Broadway theatre when the APC was first unveiled in 1985. Most who attended the meeting were annoyed, if not downright angry, that so few people had been involved in or consulted about the negotiations. The APC was being presented as a fait accompli with no opportunity to object or recommend changes. The community was told that, since the new contract arose out of a very contentious lawsuit, participation by outside parties

(New York City), Civil Case file 82 cv 4876, US District Court for the Southern District of New York, 3.

29 "Hearing Transcript before Judge Werker," 3.

30 "Hearing Transcript before Judge Werker," 3.

31 573 F. Supp. 555, 563.

32 573 F. Supp. 555, 562–563. The court applied Hunt v. Washington State Apple Advertising Commission, 432 U.S. 333, 342–343, 97 S. Ct. 2434, 2441, 53 L. Ed. 2d 383 (1977), that allowed an association to have standing to seek injunctive relief. The Court found the counterclaim also properly alleged antitrust injury.

33 Even on settlement, or close to settlement, the parties' negotiations were intense with over fifty meetings after the 1983 preliminary findings. And they were also acrimonious. *See, for example*, Abram's opposition to a motion to dismiss in early April of 1983. Abrams did not want to settle until the new APC was formally adopted. "Affidavit of Floyd Abrams," April 5, 1985, Records of District Courts of the United States, Record Group 21, National Archives and Records Administration: Northeast Region (New York City), Civil Case file 82 cv 4876, US District Court for the Southern District of New York.

> would have been neither appropriate nor productive. In other words, the so-called Approved Production Contract hadn't been approved at all, except by a handful of lawyers not particularly conversant with the day-to-day negotiations in the theater, a few producers, and one writer – Peter Stone.[34]

After the parties approved their contract, *Variety* declared the "sweeping overhaul" of the Basic Agreement, last negotiated in 1961, was "recasting the authors' deal" and would result in a "lower weekly royalty in return for upfront coin."[35] At the heart of the new contract, emerging out of the investor *Woman of the Year* tensions and Barr litigation, was a restructure in the way playwright royalties were calculated. Playwrights' received "a sharp reduction" in gross box office receipts in return for higher advances and options.[36] Norman Kean, chair of the production committee for the League of New York Theatres, stated that the new Agreement "creates a climate which will serve as a significant first step toward stabilizing the weekly operating costs of production and thus increase the investors' opportunity of recouping and earning profit more quickly."[37] More specifically, the new Agreement replaced the rate of up to 10 percent for authors of plays and 6 percent for the combined authors of musicals on net gross.[38] Authors of plays now received 5 percent before recoupment and 10 percent after. And for musicals, these rates were 4.5 percent pre-recoupment for the three authors and 6 percent post-payoff.[39] If the show was an "early hit," and the work was still in its recoupment stage, writers would not benefit from the early success but investors recouped their money in less time.[40]

The APC also provided a new way to calculate weekly royalties. Royalties to this point were calculated on Gross Weekly Book Office Receipts (GWBOR) which were gross receipts less minor administrative adjustments of about 10 percent to get to the net gross figure.[41] Royalties were now calculated on an adjusted figure "by

34 Breglio, *I Wanna Be A Producer: How to Make a Killing on Broadway*, 115.

35 Richard Hummler, "B'Way Recasting Authors' Deal: Lower Weekly Royalty in Return for Upfront Coin," *Variety*, February 27, 1985, 56.

36 Hummler, "B'Way Recasting Authors' Deal," 56.

37 Hummler, "B'Way Recasting Authors' Deal," 56.

38 Between the 1936 iteration of the Basic Agreement and the Approved Production Contract of 1985, the standard royalty rate gradations of 5 percent, 7.5 percent, and 10 percent depending on the box office takings did not change in substance. *See* Joel Bassin, "The Minimum Basic Agreement of the Dramatists Guild: A History of Inadequate Protection," *The Journal of Arts Management Law and Society* 25, no. 2 (1995): 167. And the rates since 1935 increased based on gross box office takings: 5 percent on the first US$5,000, 7.5 percent on the next US$2,500 and 10 percent on everything thereafter and, as noted, a flat 6 percent split between all authors of a musical. *See also* Middleton, *The Dramatists Guild: What It Is and Does ... How It Happened and Why*, 17. The name of the Basic Agreement was changed to the Approved Production Contract in 1985.

39 *See* "Approved Production Contract for Play," 1985, §505(a)(b). *See* "Approved Production Contract for Musical Plays," 1985, §506(a)(b). Note of course, the writers were supposed to surrender royalties for upfront advances.

40 *See* Bassin, "The Minimum Basic Agreement of the Dramatists Guild," 167.

41 Gross Weekly Box Office Receipts (GWBOR) defined in 1985 "Approved Production Contract for Plays of 1985" §4.03 as "the Royalties for such Performance Week shall be computed upon all sums

subtracting the 'weekly breakeven' from total box-office receipts."[42] Thus, a significant shift had occurred. The calculation of royalties went from essentially a gross amount of box office receipts to a percentage of weekly operating profits. The tradeoff was supposed to be that writers would hopefully receive a higher rate in the future after recoupment. But even if the show had an extended run, production royalties at the higher rate were still calculated on weekly operating profits rather than gross receipts.[43]

And as Joel Bassin observes, the gross weekly amount available for royalties received a further cut under the APC as a losing week was defined as not exceeding 110 percent of GWBOR.[44] The breakeven point to start calculating royalties was 10 percent above the actual breakeven point. In such instances when the production did not meet the breakeven threshold, the writer received a guaranteed US$1,000. The writer of a play, therefore, went from a rate of up to 10 percent on net gross to a new system where before recoupment they received 5 percent of weekly operating profits. Even where the production made back an amount up to 10 percent above the real breakeven point, writers only received a guaranteed US$1,000. In many respects, this was a producer-driven agreement aimed at paying back investors as quickly as possible. The new system was a significant encroachment on the playwright's royalty – a primary source of income for writers.

Thus, the industry shifted to a model based on weekly operating profits. And the new APC did not even begin to directly consider the other evolving industry practice of royalty pools. The total "royalty" that came out of the weekly operating profit was shared among a pool of multiple participants, including the producers. No minimum standards were established in terms of who received what percentage of the total pool of royalties.[45]

## IV. ENHANCING THE CLAIMS OF NONPROFITS

The success of *A Chorus Line*, first produced Off-Broadway at Joseph Papp's Public Theatre, added another wrinkle in the developing royalty story in the immediate years following the 1976 Act. The production not only raised critical issues over what stake an originating producer was entitled to in the future, but also highlighted where original plays and new dramatic voices were being fostered and produced in

received by Producer from all ticket sales to the Play, allocable to performances given in such week, less the following deductions." And the gross less the deductions is what royalties are calculated on, known more commonly as the "net gross" figure. These deductions include state and federal taxes, ticket commissions, subscription fees, and fees that go toward the Dramatists Guild Fund, inter alia.

42 *See* Bassin, "The Minimum Basic Agreement of the Dramatists Guild," 168. *See also*, "Approved Production Contract for Play," 1985, §501; "Approved Production Contract for Musical Plays," 1985, §501.

43 *See, for example*, "Approved Production Contract for Play," 1985, §505.

44 "Approved Production Contract for Play," 1985, §505. *See also* Bassin, "The Minimum Basic Agreement of the Dramatists Guild," 168.

45 *See* Breglio, *I Wanna Be a Producer: How to Make a Killing on Broadway*, 87.

the United States. The League of Residential Theatres (LORT) – a coalition of regional theatres from across the country including New York – had been developing important work since its formation in 1966.[46] The regional theatres had become "the major source of productions, income, and creative focus for playwrights who belong to the Guild" while Broadway, in contrast, shifted its focus to housing transfers.[47]

As the success of the regional theatres grew, so did opportunities to transfer works to Broadway and its lucrative streams of revenue. But with success followed new complications. The regional theatres had to balance their tax-exempt status as a nonprofit with the future commercial production of the work.[48] The regional theatres also had to negotiate their stake in the future subsidiary exploitation of the work. A primary ambition for the nonprofits was to develop new dramatists. Encroaching on the future royalties of writers they developed undermined that role. But access to new revenue sources through Broadway transfers, touring, or film adaptation was an opportunity to create sustainable nonprofit theatres into the future. The nonprofit dilemma of the early decades of the twentieth century reemerges – expand and potentially have to make artistic compromises or maintain nonprofit status and risk destruction. For the regional theatres, balancing all of these interests demanded a model of negotiation with dramatists case-by-case. Thus, the regional theatres channeled the instincts of the Shuberts from decades earlier. Greater contractual flexibility allowed for more control over how works moved from the original author to the regional stage and then into subsidiary streams of exploitation. Flexibility for the LORTs was also important because case-by-case contracting was a way to circumvent the cumbersome APC.[49]

In contrast, the Dramatists Guild set about the task of ratifying a uniform agreement with LORT. The proposed agreement faced immediate resistance.[50] Indeed, many playwrights who had built long-term relationships with particular theatres were reluctant to enter into a uniform agreement.[51] The regional theatres, like their commercial managing colleagues, also suggested a uniform agreement would be an antitrust violation.[52]

By late 1992, the protracted negotiations over a uniform agreement ended. The Guild abandoned pursuing the uniform agreement because, among other reasons,

46 The New York theatres who use LORT agreements include the influential Lincoln Center Theater, Roundabout Theatre Company, Manhattan Theatre Club, and Theatre for a New Audience.

47 *See* Richard Hummler, "Major playwrights threaten no show at nonprofits," *Variety*, October 15, 1990, 96.

48 *See* Breglio, *I Wanna Be a Producer: How to Make a Killing on Broadway*, 132–135.

49 Hummler, "Major playwrights threaten no show at nonprofits," 96.

50 One of the arguments for a uniform agreement was that the Dramatists Guild needed new sources of funding and the nonprofits provided an avenue to derive revenue from a percentage of royalties in the wake of rich play production developing off Broadway. *See* Thomas Walsh, *Playwrights and Power: The Making of the Dramatists Guild* (Hanover, NH: Smith and Kraus, 2016), 201.

51 *See* Walsh, *Playwrights and Power*, 202–203.

52 Hummler, "Major playwrights threaten no show at nonprofits," 96.

many Guild members felt there was no need to change the flexible contracting process already in place.[53] The LORTs had become an influential gateway for playwright access to the industry and they could now continue to deal with writers on a case-by-case basis.[54]

But greater flexibility also opened the opportunity for new avenues of, often unintentional, exploitation. In the years that followed, regional theatre negotiating power became particularly noticeable in the context of royalties and subsidiary rights. By February 1993, the *New York Times* was reporting on a case involving Chicago's celebrated Steppenwolf Theatre that also highlighted the new favored place of the theatrical investor in the nonprofit context.[55] In a contract that the Guild thought was "quite literally the worst [it] has ever seen," the first-time author of *The Song of Jacob Zulu*, Tug Yourgrau, agreed to forgo all royalties for a flat fee until the production recouped its investment. Under Guild conditions, if the popular show sold to near capacity, the author could have received up to US$20,000 a week. Steppenwolf negotiated a flat fee of US$3,750 a week until recoupment.[56] For the nonprofit producer, it was an issue of viability and controlling costs. Steppenwolf raised funds for the production independently and the quicker they repaid investors the quicker they could also reward creators. The producers hoped to recoup in eight weeks.

Yourgrau was locked into a contract with Steppenwolf and had no guarantee that the work would make money after recoupment. The playwright was also in an agreement that breached the Dramatists Guild's minimum standards. Yourgaru fulfilled his contract with Steppenwolf, but at the same time the Dramatists Guild also reluctantly suspended his membership because his contract had breached the minimum standards of the APC. Reflecting on the event, Yourgrau stated: "I feel like a guy whose wife is giving birth at the same time there's a sickness in the family . . . I really regret having to choose between a Broadway production and sticking in the guild."[57] *The Song of Jacob*

53 *See* Walsh, *Playwrights and Power*, 204–205. Walsh outlines how a supporter of the uniform agreement Executive Director David Levine was replaced by Andrew Farber in early 1993. The Guild also changed its position, agreeing to negotiate with each individual LORT company.

54 Over time, contracts beyond the reach of the APC have become the subject of the certification process. For example, the Dramatists Guild writes: "In 2005, to accommodate the ever-changing landscape of Broadway, the full membership of the Guild voted to amend its bylaws and expand the range of productions which would be subject to assessment. Now, in addition to certified contracts, members are assessed on ALL their first-class productions in New York City, whether or not a production is produced pursuant to an APC. This includes any Tony Award-eligible production, whether or not it's designated 'first-class' pursuant to the contracts of the various unions involved with the production." *See* Dramatists Guild of America, "First Class and Broadway," www.dramatistsguild.com/broadway.

55 Bruce Weber, "On Stage, and Off," *New York Times*, February 19, 1993, C2. *See also* Bassin, "The Minimum Basic Agreement of the Dramatists Guild."

56 *See* Weber, "On Stage, and Off," C2. After recoupment he was to receive 16.7 percent of the weekly operating profit.

57 *See* Weber, "On Stage, and Off," C2. For another example of the choices between production on terms outside of the Guild and having to forgo Guild membership see my ongoing work with the Bureau of New Plays and Robert Wetzel: Brent Salter, "The Ordinary Authors of the Bureau Of New

*Zulu* was eventually nominated for six Tony Awards and ran for fifty-three performances on Broadway between March and May 1993 (approximately eight weeks).[58]

In the decade that followed, instances of significant encroachments and variances in LORT contracts surfaced, particularly over subsidiary rights. Craig Lucas removed his play *Prayer for My Enemy* from Roundabout Theatre because the company was taking as much as 40 percent of author royalties from subsidiary rights.[59] In more recent years, however, the regionals have been responsive to the playwright concerns, taking specific actions to revise subsidiary-right policies.[60]

Nonprofits continued to tinker with administrative processes in other ways to advance their stake in the later life of the work. For example, enhancement deals over transfers to the commercial theatre added another layer of potential compromises for the American dramatist. Enhancement deals involve commercial producers financing nonprofit productions to cover portions of budgets, special costs, or agreed upon amounts. In return, the commercial producer will secure a stake in the eventual transfer of the work and the subsidiary life of the work.[61] The enhancement deals in the 1980s originated from two distinct sources. The nonprofits sought enhancement money for potential commercial transfer. Alternatively, commercial producers sought out new writers and nonprofit companies where they could first test the work off-Broadway with the hope of eventually making a transfer. The obvious benefit of an enhancement is that it provides previously unavailable funding for authors and nonprofit companies. But as Todd London, and coauthors, note, the enhancement deals also lock parties into options early in the process. Thus, it is more difficult for playwrights to renegotiate the deal if the work is a success. And as enhancement deals proliferate, the creative focus potentially shifts from one where the work is given the space to develop, to one where the work must develop for commercial transfer. London and his coauthors observe the circumstances can lead to greater "pressure on playwrights to come to the theatres bearing money of their own."[62]

Plays: Copyright and Reallocating Authority in the American Theatre (1936–1949)," *Cardozo Arts & Entertainment Law Journal* 39 no. 1 (2021).

58 *See* "The Song of Jacob Zulu," Internet Broadway Database: www.ibdb.com/broadway-production/the-song-of-jacob-zulu-4708. The production ran at the Plymouth Theatre from March 17, 1993 to May 9, 1993 for nine previews and fifty-three performances. No information is provided regarding royalties or subsidiary money that the author made from the production.

59 *See* Patrick Healy, "Policy Change to Benefit Playwrights," *New York Times*, March 24, 2010.

60 Following the lead of Lincoln Center Theatre which made the decision in the 1980s to make no claim to subsidiary rights. The turnaround by many of the large nonprofits seems to have followed in the wake of Todd London's Report: Todd London, Ben Pesner, and Zannie Giraud Voss, *Outrageous Fortune: The Life and Times of the New American Play* (New York: Theatre Development Fund, 2009). *See* for some of the reforms theatres have made in recent years: Healy, "Policy Change to Benefit Playwrights."

61 *See* Breglio, *I Wanna Be a Producer: How to Make a Killing on Broadway*, 137–138; London et al., *Outrageous Fortune*, 160–167.

62 London et al., *Outrageous Fortune*, 165.

## V. ENCROACHMENT ON THE SACRED GROSS

So in the decades after the introduction of the 1976 Act, theatrical producers in both the nonprofit and commercial sectors – and investors demanding a faster return on their initial outlay – gradually reconstructed practices in the hope of greater stability and profits. The royalty system shifted from one based on gross receipts to royalty pools calculated on weekly operating profits. The creation of new original American drama centers on the regions and consequently these new incubators start to understandably seek a stake in the future of the work.

Broadway between the late 1980s and early 2000s appears to go through a significant transformation. Mega musicals staged by highly successful modern producers,[63] and productions adapted by Hollywood studios as part of a larger urban development project, reconstructed the physical midtown space.[64] The theatre literature has devoted considerable attention to these developments.[65] Former President of the Dramatists Guild John Weidman identified a new type of producer following in the footsteps of musicals like *Cats* and the *Phantom of the Opera*. For Weidman, "when that new breed arrived, predictably, it came from Hollywood"[66] and these producers sought to transform the business:

> What the most aggressive of the movie studios brought with them was a desire to do business, not according to the theater model which put the playwright in first position, but according to the Hollywood model, in which the producing studio owned the author's copyright and writers could be hired and fired at will.[67]

A concern was that, as discussed elsewhere,[68] the lure of astronomical studio money would transform playwrights into employees of multinationals, foregoing all intellectual property rights in the process. The studios and theatre industry appear to have

63 *See, for example*, the blockbuster musicals including *Phantom of the Opera* (still playing on Broadway) and *Cats* as well as the extraordinarily successful long-running productions including *Les Miserables*, *Miss Saigon*.

64 *See* Brent Salter and Kathy Bowrey, "Dramatic Copyright and the Disneyfication of Theatre Space," in *Law and Creativity in the Age of the Entertainment Franchise*, eds. Kathy Bowrey and Michael Handler (Cambridge UK: Cambridge University Press, 2014), 123.

65 *See, for example*, Steve Nelson, "Broadway and the Beast: Disney Comes to Time Square," *The Drama Review* 39, no. 2 (1995): 71; John Bell, "Disney's New Time Square: The New American Community Theatre," *The Drama Review* 42, no. 1 (1998): 26; Mark Sussman, "New York's Facelift," *The Drama Review* 42, no. 1(1998): 34; Elizabeth Wollman, "The Economic Development of the 'New' Times Square and Its Impact on the Broadway Musical," *American Music* 20, no. 4 (2002): 445; Mauyra Wickstrom, "Commodities, Mimesis, and The Lion King: Retail Theatre for the 1990s," *Theatre Journal* 51, no. 3 (1999): 285; Susan Bennett, "Theatre/Tourism," *Theatre Journal* 57, no. 3 (2005): 407; Frank Roost, "Synergy City: How Times Square and Celebration Are Integrated into Disney's Marketing Cycle," in *Rethinking Disney: Private Control, Public Dimensions*, eds. Mike Budd and Max Kirsch (Middletown, CT: Wesleyan University Press, 2005), 261.

66 John Weidman, "Protecting the American Playwright: The Seventh Annual Media and Society Lecture," *Brooklyn Law Review* 72 (2007): 644.

67 Weidman, "Protecting the American Playwright," 644.

68 *See* Salter and Bowrey, "Dramatic Copyright and the Disneyfication of Theatre Space," 123–139.

come to an agreement of sorts, balancing dramatist and studio interests.[69] Despite the appearance of a major transformation, these stories are far from new, however. Agreements are fragile and in constant threat of collapse or renegotiation.[70] New entertainment mediums enter the theatrical space. Theatrical impresarios since the early 1900s built empires on the back of the control of theatrical properties. In turn, control over the physical space translates into control of the negotiation process as the work transforms from the words of a playwright on a page to a realized production. Control over physical properties translates into significant power over who has access to these theatres or whether the theatre owner wants to coproduce or produce themselves. There are forty-one theatres on Broadway, thirty-one of which were built between 1910 and 1930, five between 1930 and 1990, and five since 1990.[71] Thirty-one of these theatres are controlled by three organizations: the Nederlander Organization (nine), Jujamcyn Theatres (five), and the Shubert Organization (seventeen).[72]

The concentration of ownership means a focus on a particular theatre experience including how the broader public space is used, which conceivably appeals to a more homogenized audience: "it is areas of law largely disinterested in questions of creativity – urban planning policy, tourism strategies and local employment rules – that set the conditions for the profitability of this kind of theatre, rather than copyright."[73] This environment has the potential to lead to more generic work, another significant rise in production costs, the need for higher investment, greater

69 *See* Carol Kaplan who suggests the studios have come to a compromise position adhering for the most part to the customs of the theatre. This is particularly challenging in circumstances where the studio owns the underlying work. In a 2005 agreement between *Shrek* producers Dreamworks and the creatives, which was based on a similar earlier agreement forged by Disney for their production of the *Little Mermaid*, the creatives were allowed to "copyright their material" even though that work was based on a Dreamworks movie. This was a substantial win for the writer on first appearance. However, in exchange, Dreamworks bargained to keep a larger piece of the financial pie by participation in the show's royalty streams at the end of the standard agreement period. *See generally*, Carol Kaplan, "Once More unto the Breach, Dear Friends: Broadway Dramatists, Hollywood Producers, and the Challenge of Conflicting Copyright Norms," *Vanderbilt Journal of Entertainment and Technology Law* 16, no. 2 (2014): 297; Jessica Brater, Jessica Del Vecchio, Andrew Friedman, et al., "'Let Our Freak Flags Fly': Shrek the Musical and the Branding of Diversity," *Theatre Journal* 62, no. 2 (May 2010): 151; *see also* Kimon Keramidas, *The Play's the Thing: Intellectual Property and the Political Economy of Contemporary American Theatrical Production* (PhD diss., City University of New York, 2008).

70 *See* Kaplan, drawing on some of the corporatization of theatre themes as noted in the literatures above and potential dangers: "[I]n the long term, a pervasive shift away from customary business terms and the legal structure that undergirds them could result in the irreversible loss of Broadway's cultural identity in New York City and nationally." Kaplan, "Once More unto the Breach," 351.

71 *See* Patrick Healy, "In Broadway Lights: No Vacancy," *New York Times*, April 28, 2010.

72 Healy, "In Broadway Lights: No Vacancy." Disney Theatrical owns the New Amsterdam Theatre which housed the *Lion King* for years and *Aladdin* since 2014. Other owner operators include the large LORT's like Roundabout (American Airlines Theatre and the Stephen Sondheim Theatre), the Lincoln Center Theatre (Vivian Beaumont) and the Manhattan Theatre Club (Samuel J Friedman Theatre).

73 *See* Salter and Bowrey, "Dramatic Copyright and the Disneyfication of Theatre Space," 130.

pressures to recoup capitalization on larger amounts because the risk is far higher, and ultimately greater pressure to restructure the way that creators, including playwrights, are paid. And these developments are the continuation of a history where one of the first places to look when cutting costs is creative royalties. When investor tensions over the *Woman of the Year* surfaced, production costs for musicals were between two and three million dollars. Today, these costs can be anywhere between six and ten million dollars and beyond.[74] In April 2018, The *New York Times* was reporting *Harry Potter and The Cursed Child* was the most expensive nonmusical ever produced on Broadway for US$65 million of which US$35 million was initial investor capitalization.[75]

Out of these pressures over the last few decades emerges amortization, the next encroachment in the royalty narrative. In effect, amortization represents a fixed amount, calculated on the show's production costs, to come out of the weekly operating profits before determining what is available to the royalty pool.[76] The amortization amount, therefore, reduces the total weekly pool of funds from weekly operating profits available to creators. In return, like previous models, customs develop around higher upfront playwright advances and, for example, a greater percentage of the royalty pool after recoupment.[77] But this once again represents an incremental playwright compromise. If a production is an initial hit, writers will not have a chance to recoup larger returns on box office takings during this initial period.

Thus, the writer's position shifts from a percentage of the gross, to a royalty pool taken from weekly operating profits, and is then reduced further by a fixed amortized

74 Breglio, *I Wanna Be a Producer: How to Make a Killing on Broadway*, 95.

75 Michael Paulson, "Another Harry Potter Landmark: At $68 Million, the Most Expensive Broadway Nonmusical Play Ever," *New York Times*, April 14, 2108. This includes US$35 million in capitalization. Breglio writes *Spider-Man: Turn Off the Dark* produced in 2010 cost US$75 million. Breglio, *I Wanna Be a Producer: How to Make a Killing on Broadway*, 95.

76 Breglio, *I Wanna Be a Producer: How to Make a Killing on Broadway*, 96. Breglio writes there are "several factors" that govern the calculation of the fixed amortization amount, but uses the example of "some contracts call for an amount equal to 2 percent of the capitalization with a cap of $200,000." The basic example Breglio uses for calculating the impact of amortization is as follows: net gross takings of US$900,000 and weekly operating costs of US$750,000 leaves US$150,000 operating profits. If the fixed amortization amount is US$100,000 this leaves US$50,000 to be divided between the investors and royalty holders. As Breglio notes at 96, investors are receiving two separate payments: the US$100,000 amortization amount plus "a portion (60%) of the $50,000 weekly operating profits that's shared with the royalty holders."

77 Breglio, *I Wanna Be a Producer: How to Make a Killing on Broadway*, 97. Other terms that can be renegotiated in favor of writers in light of amortization include reductions in amortization when the show surpasses a certain capacity, higher weekly guaranteed royalty rates, reduction in producer share of subsidiary rights, and actual share in the net profits of production. As Breglio notes at 97, all of these factors can lead to "lengthy and sometimes very contentious negotiations" including deferring amortization amounts until later in the production when budgets are clearer. But these further negotiations over amortization on concessions also calls into question the relative bargaining power of parties – for example, whether established writers are in a much better position to negotiate amortization concessions than emerging writers.

amount.[78] The promise is that the writer will be rewarded for their upfront concession in a far from certain recoupment period sometime in the imagined future. Of course, producers and investors will understandably argue that these reforms were necessary for the industry to be sustainable in the face of rising costs.

Theatre owners leave the royalty pool early on, they own and control the few spaces at the center of power in the American theatre, and determine who has access to the kingdom. The stakeholders with the resources and abilities to transform written words and intangible rights into productions, reinforce longer narratives about mediating influence:

> The laws of supply and demand put the theatre owners at the very top of the food chain. They are beneficiaries of rents paid on the gross, 100 percent recovery of their expenses, restoration fees, and fees for credit card charges and other ticketing services. Suffice it to say, at heart, they are owners of the most valuable and limited resources necessary to produce a play. Season after season, producers vie for the best theaters, or any theater, for their plays. So long as there are a finite number of theaters on Broadway and a plentiful supply of plays and investors sitting in the wings, theater owners will continue to issue rental contracts that dictate nonnegotiable terms for a Broadway house.[79]

Recent research, however, provides a deeper historical and empirical understanding of theatre ownership on Broadway which suggests the notion of nonnegotiable is not always clear. For example, Derek Miller examines the inconclusive historical relationship between gross box office and theatre management decisions such as invoking "stop clauses" (ending a run when a production's gross falls below a certain level as specified in a contract).[80] The inconclusiveness of results highlights the need to conduct more research on how theatre owners assert their power – including how they influence intellectual property structures – in a market characterized by limited supply.[81] It will

78 John Breglio presents a striking summary of the chain of accounting reforms since the early 1980s (not considering the unknown future success or failure of the work.) Breglio assumes, as examples, the weekly net gross of a commercial musical is US$800,000 (scenario 1), weekly operating profits are US$150,000 (scenario 2), and weekly operating profits with a fixed amortization amount of US$100,000 is US$50,000 (scenario 3). Based on respective royalty rates, and not considering future success or upfront variable negotiated positions, the weekly royalties are as follows: Scenario 1: US$12,000 (prior to early 1980s period); Scenario 2: US$7,500 (post *Woman of the Year* and 1985 APC amendments); Scenario 3: US$3,000 (the era of increased use of amortization, the early 2000s). For details *see* Breglio, *I Wanna Be a Producer: How to Make a Killing on Broadway*, 97–98.

79 Breglio, *I Wanna Be a Producer: How to Make a Killing on Broadway*, 99. It is important to note, however, organizations like the Shubert Foundation make an extraordinary contribution to the broader development of the American theatre as "the nation's largest funder dedicated to unrestricted funding of not-for-profit theatres and dance companies": *see* The Shubert Foundation Inc., www.shubertfoundation.org/ (thanks to Derek Miller for this point).

80 *See* Miller, "Broadway Real Estate."

81 *See* Michael Paulson, "Theaters Fight over 'Harry Potter' and 'Evan Hansen' in San Francisco," *New York Times*, September 28, 2018. Paulson reports on the dispute between the Nederlanders and Carole Shorenstein Hays over exclusive rights to tours of *Dear Evan Hansen* and *Harry Potter and the Cursed Child* in San Francisco. Hays asked the producers to stage concurrent productions and the

also be important to continue to scrutinize assumptions about access and, for example, the extent of creative homogenization. One has to be careful about generalizations in this space. To give an example, Miller shows – in making the larger argument against the notion that Broadway has become an increasingly difficult place to produce new plays – that Broadway has always been "an inhospitable environment" to create new works. But Miller also suggests the number of nonmusical plays since the rise of "Disneyfication" on Broadway in the early 1990s has remained steady.[82] Small, as it has always been, but steady.

## VI. BUYING INTO THE SHUBERT ANTITRUST NARRATIVE

By the middle of the 2000s, the dramatists had become increasingly frustrated on several fronts. The APC was in operation for twenty years with no substantive amendments. Royalty pools were central to the way that the industry organized commercial royalties but the rules for how they operated were not addressed in the APC. The APC was the compromise that came out of the *Barr* litigation. Over time, however, the producers and investors tinkered with its boundaries to best create models for controlling the movement of theatrical creation in the industry. And the shadow that loomed over all these developments – the negotiating tool which the producer could call upon as they had for the previous eighty years – was the threat of antitrust litigation.

In 2004/2005, the playwrights finally decided to respond by attempting to amend federal antitrust law rather than seeking clarity through the courts. Copyright law was not at the center of how the industry thought about authority structures over creation. The Shuberts had established an eighty-year alternative narrative around the issue of whether the playwrights could organize as a group and be exempt from antitrust law. The playwrights wanted their association status finally resolved. The *Playwrights Licensing Antitrust Initiative Bill*,[83] proposed a narrow statutory exception, "designed to solely address the legal status of the playwrights with regard to

Nederlanders argued that Hays's productions would cause "'irreparable harm' in breach of an agreement between the families restricting competition." Exclusivity agreements potentially restrict writers from multiple royalty streams where a limited number of organizations have extensive control over venues across the country. This story is of course familiar to the history of the American theatre.

82 *See* Derek Miller, "Response to Terry Teachout's 'Trying to Get on Broadway? Don't Write a Play *Wall Street Journal*, Sightings, April 9, 2015,'" *Visualizing Broadway* http://visualizingbroadway.com/broadway/teachout_response.html. *See also* Elizabeth Wollman, "Five Myths About Broadway," *The Washington Post*, July 10, 2020.

83 *See generally*, *The Playwrights Licensing Antitrust Initiative Act: Safeguarding the Future of American Live Theater: Hearing on S. 2349 Before the Subcomm. on the Judiciary*, 108th Cong. (2004), April 28, 2004. Representative Coble reintroduced the bill in the 109th Congress. *See* H.R. 532, 109th Cong (2005). It progressed no further. The long title of the Bill was: "To modify the application of the antitrust laws to permit collective development and implementation of a standard contract form for playwrights for the licensing of their plays."

labor and antitrust law."[84] Other commentators have written about the Bill, its potential benefits, and its eventual failure to progress to the floor of either house.[85]

The producers succeeded because nothing happened. The ambiguity surrounding whether the dramatists could negotiate as a group continued. Ambiguity meant the producers retained the eighty-year bargaining mechanism that they could invoke whenever playwrights wanted to expand their protections during internal negotiations. Gerald Schoenfeld, Chair of the Shubert Organization and Chair of the League of American Theatres and Producers, focused his Senate Hearing testimony on arguments his organization had pursued over the previous century. Channeling Lee Shubert from the *Ring* proceedings, Schoenfeld stated that "[o]bviously" the Dramatists Guild believed it was subject to antitrust law "[o]therwise, it would not be seeking an exemption from its provisions."[86] Schoenfeld's focus, however, was on what he believed was a disjuncture between how the theatre operated and the inflexible minimal, and anticompetitive, conditions the dramatists imposed on the industry. The specific tension, for Schoenfeld, was that the Guild had unilateral negotiating control, assuring the author received a certain percentage of weekly net profits through an approval process, "regardless of what the dramatist might otherwise receive as a Royalty Pool participant."[87] Thus, Schoenfeld believed that a uniform agreement did not necessarily reflect the value of the author in each circumstance, placed pressure on negotiations with other royalty participants, and pressures on overall costs. Schoenfeld remarked, "all dramatists are not equally talented."[88]

84 Section 2 of the Bill provided in part: "the antitrust laws shall not apply to any joint discussion, consideration, review, action, or agreement for the express purpose of, and limited to, the development of a standard form contract containing minimum terms of artistic protection and levels of compensation for playwrights."

85 *See* Ashley Kelly, "Bargaining Power on Broadway: Why Congress Should Pass the Playwrights Licensing Antitrust Initiative Act in the Era of Hollywood on Broadway," *Journal of Law and Policy* 16, no. 2 (2008): 877 (as the title suggests, Kelly argues that the growing pressures and presence of Hollywood studios adapting works for the stage necessitates the urgency to adopt the federal antitrust exemption for playwrights). *See also* Alison Zamora, "The Playwright Licensing Antitrust Initiative Act: Empowering the Starving Artist through the Convergence of Copyright, Labor, and Antitrust Policies," *DePaul-LCA Journal of Art and Entertainment Law* 16, no. 2 (Spring 2006): 395 (advocating for the introduction of the new amendment, but also focusing the strategy on a states-based approach, and making comparisons between playwrights and doctor independent-contractors); Bassin, "The Minimum Basic Agreement of the Dramatists Guild," 157 (preempting the antitrust legislative initiative mapping the inadequacies of protections and the fragility of the dramatists' status in the twentieth century).

86 *The Playwrights Licensing Antitrust Initiative Act: Safeguarding the Future of American Live Theater: Hearing on S. 2349 Before the Subcomm. on the Judiciary*, 108th Cong. (2004) ("Gerald Schoenfeld Statement," Chairman of The League of American Theaters and Producers, 9).

87 "Gerald Schoenfeld Statement," 10.

88 "Gerald Schoenfeld Statement," 11, attempted to show how dramatists' agreements varied in practice: "significant provisions of a dramatist's agreement are set forth in the offering documents. They demonstrate no uniform provisions manifesting the existence of a conspiracy on the part of producers."

Several Guild members testified in support of the Bill, including Arthur Miller and Stephen Sondheim, latching onto the moral-rights rhetoric that had also deeply informed the playwrights' position since the first decades of the twentieth century – the need to protect the integrity of the work. Indeed, in a fascinating observation, Sondheim went as far as to make a distinction between his "intellectual property rights" on the one hand and economic issues on the other. Sondheim testified:

> This is not just an economic issue, however. It is one of intellectual property rights. I, like my colleagues here, have often had to fight for these rights. For example, one show I wrote called "Merrily We Roll Along" is a piece that goes backwards in time. It starts with the end of the story and scene by scene proceeds back to the beginning.
>
> One producer tried to reverse the order of the play because he believed it would be easier for the audience to understand. Needless to say, it did not improve matters, but even if it had, it was not the show we had written or intended to be presented. Because I was a recognized name in the theater and had a certain amount of what is known as clout, I was able to protect the piece and stop the production, thus preserving the integrity of my intellectual property. Not every playwright is so lucky.[89]

So the Shuberts continued to invoke the potential monopoly issues from which the dramatists should not be exempt. And the authors continued to invoke the personal relationship they had with their work as embodied in their independent-contracting status. But perhaps it was the Dramatists Guild's submission that best encapsulated a much longer history. The Guild wrote in their submission that the amendment was "surgically designed to correct a singular anomaly in the case law relating to playwrights in the American theater."[90] For the previous sixty years since *Ring*, the Guild wrote, the dramatists "have operated under the constant threat of the application of the Sherman Act" and there was "no clear resolution of the basic legal questions."[91] The issue was exacerbated by the inconsistency of recent decisions in the entertainment industry,[92] highlighting the complexity of "the century old effort by our legal system to reconcile and accommodate two facially inconsistent national policies: labor and anti-trust."[93] The playwrights, however, viewed their position as exceptional:

89 *The Playwrights Licensing Antitrust Initiative Act: Safeguarding the Future of American Live Theater: Hearing on S. 2349 Before the Subcomm. on the Judiciary*, 108th Cong. (2004) ("Stephen Sondheim Statement"), 17.

90 *The Playwrights Licensing Antitrust Initiative Act: Safeguarding the Future of American Live Theater: Hearing on S. 2349 Before the Subcomm. on the Judiciary*, 108th Cong. (2004) ("Dramatists Guild Submission"), 36.

91 "Dramatists Guild Submission" citing the *Ring* v. *Spina* line of cases, 148 F2d 647 (2d Cir., 1945); 84 F. Supp 403 (SDNY 1949); 186 F2d 637 (2d Cir. 1951).

92 *Bernstein* v. *Universal Pictures, Inc.*, 517 F.2d 976 (2d Cir. 1975) (finding television and movie composers independent contractors, not employees); *Julien* v. *Society of Stage Directors and Choreographers, Inc.*, 1975 WL 957 (S.D.N.Y. Oct. 14, 1975) (finding that stage directors were employees, not independent contractors).

93 "Dramatists Guild Submission," 37.

> This accommodation/reconciliation is a challenge in the abstract; it is a daunting challenge in the unique environment of the Broadway Theater – itself part of a unique industry, the entertainment industry. The effort to categorize dramatists as common law employees or independent contractors in the classic analytic mode is a far different exercise than that involving fishing boat captains [See, *Columbia River*[94]]. The Broadway Theater is not the New York City electric supply industry [See, *Allen-Bradley*[95]]. Death of a Salesman is not a widget.[96]

Thus, the playwrights were seeking "to resolve a sixty year old, but intractable, problem in a single, but nationally important, venue – the American theater."[97] It was, however, a much deeper problem for the dramatists tracing back to the nineteenth century. The long-term response of playwrights to mediating power – to define themselves as independent contractors who combined under the umbrella of a trade association – had created freedoms to negotiate but also considerable complications. The Shuberts had created this alternative anticompetition narrative in the immediate years following the first Basic Agreement of 1926 and now the dramatists were seeking to resolve the issue through the lens of a special exemption to antitrust law. The Bill never passed and the ambiguity remains. J. J. and Lee Shubert could not have written the script any better themselves.

## VII. NEW GATEWAYS AND KNOWN MEDIATORS

Industry contractual relationships after 1976 had, therefore, followed a familiar path to that of the decades before: Playwrights negotiate an internal agreement as independent contractors and members of an association while mediators of influence seek to reconstruct the industry relationship invoking the threat of antitrust law. Amendments allowing for the greater divestment of copyright also presented opportunities for mediators of influence to shape how creation flowed into profitable subsidiary streams of exploitation. Before 1976, all rights that subsisted in a work could be sold in a bundle or licensed separately. After 1976, authors in form had greater flexibility with the option to sell or license all subsisting rights as a bundle or separately.[98] In the last three decades, new markets for the copyright owner have rapidly evolved in stock and amateur rights – high schools and local theatre groups, for example.[99] Thus, nonprofits and commercial producers found rewarding markets in the later life of the work in schools and community halls across the country that could be mined for decades after the original production.

94 *Columbia River Packers Assn.* v. *Hinton*, 315 US 143 (1942) (note added).
95 *Allen Bradley Co.* v. *Local Union No. 3, International Brotherhood of Electrical Workers*, 325 US 797 (1945)(note added).
96 "Dramatists Guild Submission," 37.
97 *See* "Dramatists Guild Submission," 37. Submission goes on to suggest that "It is not intended to, nor does it, attempt to resolve – or even address – larger issues of antitrust or labor law."
98 *See* 17 U.S.C. (of 1976) § 201.
99 *See generally*, Robert Hofler, "Life After Death on Broadway," *Variety*, November 20, 2009, 1,42.

The new more flexible transferal arrangements also presented extraordinary opportunities for mediators who patrolled the gateways to subsidiary mediums of exploitation. For example, theatrical publishers play a critical role in negotiating the afterlife of the work, including the stock and amateur rights. Shane Valenzi describes, in 2012, the networks of authority that grant access to these subsidiary audiences:

> To manage the immense effort it would take for authors to negotiate licenses with each company, authors lease the stock and amateur production rights to licensing houses that specialize in those transactions. Presently, six licensing houses control close to 100 percent of the market for theatrical works. Dramatists Play Service and Samuel French license nearly every "straight play" (drama without music) ever produced on or Off-Broadway available for license. Both also dabble in musical theatre: Dramatists Play Service owns the stock performance rights to several recognizable musical theatre works, and Samuel French licenses a small number of low-overhead, highly popular musicals like *Grease* and *Chicago*.[100]

Samuel French – the company built on the back of the unpublished works of foreign authors – maintains its influence over the production process in the twenty-first century through stock and amateur markets. French, and a handful of other publishers, control the small gateway to theatrical markets and establish many of the rules of entry.

Building exclusive-rights networks in geographical regions is another way that the mediators control the circulation of material.[101] Indeed, exclusivity deals based on geographical location often highlight how mediators shape subsidiary markets through contractual customs developed over decades. In February 2019, mediators including Broadway producer Scott Rudin, Dramatic Publishing Company, and the estate of Harper Lee, were engaged in a dispute that played out on the front page of the *New York Times* over competing dramatic adaptations of Harper Lee's *To Kill a Mockingbird*.[102] Rudin's version of the work written by Aaron Sorkin was successful on Broadway. And with success inevitably followed an intention to tour into subsidiary markets throughout the United States. Rudin sent letters to at least eight nonprofits across the country demanding that they cancel an alternative widely used adaptation of the work written by Christopher Sergel and published by Dramatic Publishing Company (DPC).[103] The basis for the complaint was a fifty-year-old contract which included an entrenched boilerplate provision prohibiting

100 Valenzi, "A Rollicking Band of Pirates," 779–780.

101 Valenzi, "A Rollicking Band of Pirates," 782.

102 *See* Michael Paulson and Alexandra Alter, "Legal Threats From Broadway's 'Mockingbird' Sink Productions around the Country," *New York Times*, February 28, 2019.

103 Including the "Dayton Playhouse in Dayton, Ohio, the Grand Theater in Salt Lake City and the Curtain Call Theater in Braintree, Mass": *see* Alexandra Alter and Michael Paulson, "'Mockingbird' Play Publisher Demands $500,000 from Harper Lee Estate," *New York Times*, March 8, 2019.

productions within a specified distance of a major city while a first-class production is running and/or touring:

> The letters invoked a 1969 contract between Lee and Dramatic [DPC] that blocks "Mockingbird" productions within 25 miles of cities that had a population of 150,000 or more in 1960 (the last census year before the agreement was signed) while a "first-class dramatic play" based on the novel is playing in New York or on tour.[104]

Rudin, in immediate response to the barrage of criticism he received for shutting down community productions often deep into their rehearsal process, defiantly stated: "We hate to ask anybody to cancel any production of a play anywhere, but the productions in question as licensed by DPC infringe on rights licensed to us by Harper Lee directly."[105]

As the criticism continued to swell, Rudin retreated, offering "an olive branch to the affected theaters, letting them put on a version of the play."[106] But Rudin also turned his scorn toward DPC. He suggested that Christopher Sergel III (the grandson of author Christopher Sergel and head of DPC), "erred in issuing licenses to present the play to theaters that should not have received them,"[107] based on the long-held traditions of the geographical boilerplate stipulation. Sergel, in response, commenced arbitration proceedings "to protect the ability of local theaters to stage his grandfather's adaptation and to award damages ... He accused the estate of the 'Mockingbird' author, Harper Lee, acting in concert with Mr. Rudin." Sergel sought damages "of at least $500,000."[108]

The solution for some, like Valenzi, seems clear. Playwrights, through the Guild, should negotiate more flexible arrangements with licensing houses over performance rights. For example, the licensing house, such as Samuel French or DPC, secures the exclusive right to the work itself but does not have an exclusive right to the performance of that work. Such an arrangement "would allow [licensing houses] to issue multiple performance licenses to a given geographic area rather than being pressured to limit a performance license to a single, powerful theatre."[109]

But will there be an incentive for mediators to modify practices going forward? Networks that facilitate the transformation of rights into material performances in the publishing space are becoming increasingly narrow. Valenzi, writing in 2012, highlights the hierarchical structure in the musical theatre publishing industry:

104 Paulson and Alter, "Legal Threats from Broadway's 'Mockingbird'."
105 Paulson and Alter, "Legal Threats from Broadway's 'Mockingbird'."
106 Michael Paulson and Alexandra Alter, "'Mockingbird' Producer Reconsiders, Letting Local Plays Go Forward," *New York Times*, March 1, 2019.
107 Paulson and Alter, "'Mockingbird' Producer Reconsiders."
108 Alter and Paulson, "'Mockingbird' Play Publisher Demands $500,000."
109 Valenzi, "A Rollicking Band of Pirates," 793–794. Note that this article was written in 2012. The Dramatists Guild is constantly engaged in facilitating the negotiation of agreements between its members and mediating stakeholders in specific circumstances. Many thanks to Ralph Sevush for ongoing conversations.

> Tams-Witmark continues to license the Cole Porter and George Gershwin musicals; Rodgers & Hammerstein Theatricals licenses the works of its namesake duo along with the works of Lerner and Loewe (*My Fair Lady* and *Camelot*, among others) and Andrew Lloyd Webber (*Phantom of the Opera, Evita, Cats*, and many more); and Music Theatre International remains the titan of the market, licensing the works of most every successful musical theatre author not mentioned above, including the Broadway musicals of the Disney Corporation.[110]

By December of 2018, music publishing giant Concord had acquired Tams-Witmark, the Rodgers and Hammerstein Organization, a joint venture with The Musical Company, and finally Samuel French (the company's first "foray into the nonmusical play business").[111] In an extraordinary consolidation of mediating control over theatrical titles in a short period, Concord not only publishes and licenses its theatrical scripts but also releases cast albums and invests in theatrical productions.[112]

The longer-term benefits of consolidating authority in the hands of a few mediating stakeholders are of course yet to be seen. But can writers say no to opportunities controlled by consolidated mediating businesses when the gateways to industry access are so few? President of Samuel French Nate Collins suggests the merger presents considerable benefits for creators including better access to technological innovation and producers. Collins gestures toward the other pragmatic justifications for the merger:

> The reason that this completely makes sense is given the competitive outlook of the industry, especially with Concord having acquired some of the major players – I just knew that competition was going to be a lot more fierce, and we were going to run into some headwinds.[113]

—

And these "headwinds" include how the industry continues to organize its relationships with the digital economy. In recent years, tech mediators including Amazon's Audible, Broadway HD, and Fathom Events provide audiences alternative ways to view live theatre through digital platforms and the comfort of their homes: "reshaping the experience, evolving it past the quaint notion of patrons filing into an arena, turning off their phones and sitting quietly in the dark."[114] Audible claims that it is "disrupting

[110] Valenzi, "A Rollicking Band of Pirates," 780.

[111] *See* Michael Paulson, "Concord Music Acquires Samuel French in Big Push Into Theater Business," *New York Times*, December 17, 2018.

[112] Michael Paulson writes of Concord's investment in *Jagged Little Pill*, a musical based on the works of Alanis Morissette which at the time of writing had just transferred to Broadway: Paulson, "Concord Music Acquires Samuel French."

[113] Paulson, "Concord Music Acquires Samuel French."

[114] *See* Mark Kennedy (AP) "Technology is remaking how we see the ancient art of theater," *Chicago Daily Herald*, October 23, 2019: www.dailyherald.com/article/20191023/entlife/310239934/. Livestreaming or simulcasting is not a new development; it has been adopted by companies for years. In August 2020 it was announced that Digital Theatre+, "the digital education service focusing

the theatre space"[115] between authors and audiences presenting opportunities for emerging writers to have their work produced on the stage and eventually adapted for an audiobook.[116] Recent world events shift these digital developments from the periphery to the center of conversations about the future of live performance. In a new world seeking to comprehend the longer-term ramifications of a pandemic, online alternatives to live theatre – collaborating in isolation[117] – emerge as viable, and potentially sustainable, given the uncertainty of physical engagement with the live theatre space.[118] In turn, power dynamics between creators and technology mediators, with expansive control over production in the digital environment, are magnified even further.[119]

In disruption, there is familiarity, however. Tech companies, like Amazon's entry into the industry, establish seemingly new practices that resemble those of the earliest playbrokers and publishers in the second half of the nineteenth century. Recent mediating developments speak to the rise of the dominant commercial impresarios in the 1890s that still exist in a modified form today. Powerful mediators disrupting

on the study of the Performing Arts" had agreed to terms with BroadwayHD to be its "exclusive educational partner." The "unique partnership between Digital Theatre+ and BroadwayHD comes at a time where, now more than ever, enabling further access to the performing arts is critical." *See* "Digital Theatre+ Partners with BroadwayHD to Be Their Exclusive Education Partner, *Broadway World*, August 5, 2020: www.broadwayworld.com/industry/article/Digital-Theatre-Partners-with-BroadwayHD-to-be-Their-Exclusive-Education-Partner-20200805.

115 Olivia Clement, "How Audible Is Disrupting the Theatre Space – For Good," *Playbill*, September 2, 2019: www.playbill.com/article/how-audible-is-disrupting-the-theatre-spacefor-good.

116 On Audible, *see* Audible Theatre Website at: www.audible.com/ep/theater; *see also* Joshua Barone, "Audible Creates $5 Million Fund for Emerging Playwrights," *New York Times*, May 30, 2017; Andrew Chow, "Audible Moves into the Minetta Lane Theatre," *New York Times*, May 30, 2018; "Audible Announces New Audio Theatre Productions," *American Theatre*, August 20, 2018, www.americantheatre.org/2018/08/20/audible-announces-new-audio-theatre-productions/.

117 *See* Olivia Clement, "2020 Williamstown Theatre Festival to Be Released on Audible," *Playbill*, April 7, 2020: www.playbill.com/article/2020-williamstown-theatre-festival-to-be-released-on-audible. The renowned summer Williamstown Theatre Festival agreed to collaborate with the tech company marking "the first time that a theatrical season of work will be produced on Audible."

118 The transformed live audience experience in South Korea in the aftermath of the first wave of the COVID-19 pandemic is described in this interview: "Every spectator goes through a kind of disinfection shower at the entrance of the theater. You keep your clothes on, of course, but you don't really get wet either. It is a very thin spray. Every visitor has to have their temperature measured, everyone has to wear a protective mask over their mouth and nose for the entire stay in the theater. And the data of every single viewer are registered. After two positive cases occurred in our troupe, the authorities used this data to contact more than 8,000 people who had visited the theater in the days before. As far as we know, no infection was reported. The members of the ensemble, stage workers and other staff were tested. The show was suspended and we were all quarantined, around 120 people." *See* interview: Nico Fried with Rainer Fried, "Through the disinfection shower to the theatre," *Suddeutsche Zeitung*, April 23, 2020, www.sueddeutsche.de/politik/suedkorea-coronavirus-kontrollen-1.4885088?referrer=push (translated).

119 William Deresiewicz writes, "With the destruction that the current crisis is wreaking on brick-and-mortar retail, along with the way the pandemic is shifting even more of our existence onto screens, signs are strong that this upheaval will only serve to strengthen the hegemony of Big Tech in the post-pandemic world." *See* William Deresiewicz, "The Coronavirus Means Curtains for Artists: The loss of revenue from live events is only the start of this particular disaster," *The Nation*, May 7, 2020, www.thenation.com/article/society/coronavirus-artists-culture-impact/.

practices emerged in government agencies during the New Deal period and nonprofit companies proliferated during the first decades of the twentieth century seeking to reconcile financial sustainability with artistic progress.

Until 1976, mediating brokers, publishers, commercial managers, and nonprofit organizations built business models that focused on moving unpublished manuscripts through intimate networks. And the courts developed the law in relation to unpublished scripts and associated performance rights that accommodated mediating interests. Registration systems gave advantages to stakeholders with the skills and resources to turn scripts into publications. The registration system was often defective, allowing mediators to manipulate the process, and creating the illusion of federal copyright protection. Until 1976, many dramatic scripts remained unprotected by federal copyright law, however. The influence of these developments is one reason to begin to scrutinize the effects or absence of effects achieved by the 1976 Copyright Act, which discarded much of the pre-1976 framework.[120] Emboldened with a new statutory framework and unbound by the restrictions of registration,[121] American playwrights presumably had a much clearer path toward control over their written work after 1976.

In post-1976 developments, mediators with abilities to transform intangible rights into material performances continue old, and built new, systems of organization to control the circulation of creative material throughout the theatrical economy. Commercial producers and investors systematically encroach on writer royalties through the transformation of accounting practices, commercial and residential organizations bite into subsidiary streams of revenue, and the residential theatres win their battle to negotiate with playwrights case-by-case. Large studios consolidate their position on Broadway at first contemplating employment-type relationships with writers but settle on a theatre-based author model which could be subject to renegotiation. Mediating brokers and publishers control the gateway into lucrative stock and amateur markets. And looming over all of these post-1976 developments is the unresolved issue of the dramatist's right to enter into a collective agreement with mediating stakeholders while maintaining independent-contractor status. In an interview with producer Ken Davenport in 2015, Ralph Sevush, Executive Director of the Dramatists Guild, echoed the ongoing challenges for the dramatists, framed by the battles with the Shuberts almost eighty years earlier:

> Ken Davenport: It sounds like you are an advocate for opening up the APC [Approved Production Contract] that was written 30 years ago when the business was much different and figuring it out for today.
>
> Ralph Sevush: Absolutely, and we've tried to ask the League to do that with us and they've refused because of what they claim are anti-trust issues, which is just

[120] I am grateful to an anonymous reviewer for suggesting a further examination of differences in legislative frameworks for the period before 1976 and after 1976 in terms of the impact of longer-term practices. As noted, this epilogue is an entry-point into post 1976 developments which requires a deeper investigation.

[121] Unless, for example, a party wanted to commence civil litigation which required registration.

a convenient way of saying, "No, we don't want to talk to you and we don't have to talk to you." And they don't have to talk to us, so why should they?[122]

The overlapping narratives of independence, property ownership, and the preservation of artistic integrity, continue to animate the Guild's position today as they have for the last century.[123] At the same time, courts and legislative bodies have not clarified the issue of whether writers can practice as independent contractors and also negotiate minimum standards as a collective group. Thus, a history of fragile and ambiguous truces continues which could be disassembled if the right opportunities for reform or litigation emerge on either side.[124] Legislators could step in to clarify the ambiguities. The producers could once and for all make the conclusive argument in the courts that contracting dramatists cannot organize as a trade association while also being exempt from competition law. The dramatists could, for example, find a vehicle that allows them to pursue the claim that they can organize like a union, be exempt from antitrust, but still maintain their freedom to contract as independent writers. Playwrights may indeed be found to be a "labor group" party to a "labor dispute" more than sixty years after the proceedings in *Ring* v. *Spina* in a time of more fluid collective organizational structures.[125] But the

[122] Ken Davenport: in conversation with Ralph Sevush, *The Producer's Perspective* (Podcast, Episode 35, August 2015), transcript and audio available at www.theproducersperspective.com/my_weblog/2015/08/podcast-episode-35-ralph-sevush.html.

[123] In defining the work of the Dramatists Guild's Copyright Advocacy Committee in 2020, Georgia Stitt continues to invoke these particular narratives: "Much of the work we do at the Copyright Advocacy committee is in one of two categories. Either we're educating the public about why copyright protection matters so much to the creative integrity and livelihood of artists – how literally an artist's body of work is his/her PROPERTY – or we're educating our own membership base about how best to protect themselves from the inevitable abuses that rob them of their ability to control or monetize the things they have spent their lives building." *See* Doug Wright, "A Message on Copyright from DG President Doug Wright" (citing Georgia Stitt), May 29, 2020: www.dramatistsguild.com/news/message-copyright-dg-president-doug-wright.

[124] And these fragilities for the dramatists will sometimes emerge in moments of particular strain or crisis in the broader industry. *See, for example*, Jonathan Handel, "Broadway's Emergency Relief Deal Doesn't Cover Playwrights," *The Hollywood Reporter*, March 24, 2020, www.hollywoodreporter.com/news/broadway-emergency-relief-deal-doesnt-protect-playwrights-1286258 (in the wake of the COVID-19 pandemic, a deal between a coalition of stage unions and producers to cover wage payments and other benefits did not include dramatists because of the Dramatists Guild's status as a trade association bargaining on behalf of its independent-contracting members); *see also* Michael Paulson, "Straining From Shutdowns, Theaters Ask Playwrights to Return Payments," *New York Times*, March 18, 2020 (claim that "playwrights are reporting that they have been asked to return payments for productions that have been canceled or postponed"). The CARES Act, however, provided potential relief for independent-contracting writers under the Pandemic Unemployment Assistance Program and the Payroll Protection Program. *See also* a range of other internal and external relief programs: Dramatists Guild of America: www.dramatistsguild.com/covid-19-resources.

[125] *See American Federation of Musicians* v. *Carroll*, 391 U.S. 99, 105–106 (1968). I am indebted to ongoing conversations with Catherine Fisk on these issues. *See, for example*, Uber drivers' ongoing dispute with Uber to unionize: http://uberlawsuit.com/ (which includes latest litigation updates across the country). *See also* Dmitri Iglitzin and Jennifer L. Robbins, "The City of Seattle's Ordinance Providing Collective Bargaining Rights to Independent Contractor for-Hire Drivers: An

Dramatists Guild is unlikely to pursue these arguments and indeed views such potential developments as presenting new complications:[126]

> We are often asked, "why do we have to sacrifice one for the other? Can't we own our copyrights and still be a union? After all, choreographers and designers keep their copyrights, yet they are still members of theatrical unions (like the SDC and USA). Why are we different?"
>
> This is a good question, and the answer is complex and legalistic, but it boils down to the fact that the Guild has been the subject of some bad case law over the years and so, after surviving two anti-trust lawsuits, *dramatists are viewed by the law as property owners who license the use of their property, rather than employees entitled to collectively bargain for the conditions of their labor.*
>
> But even if there was a sudden change of heart by the Justice and Labor departments, and dramatists could then somehow attain labor status, it would still not be a panacea. In that event, producers would likely insist on owning your copyrights as a condition of any collectively negotiated contract, just as they have with the writers for film and television. Unlike film and TV, however, where hundreds of feature films and thousands of hours of television are produced every year, providing numerous opportunities for writers to make a living at their craft, there is simply not enough of a volume of theatrical production in America to allow enough dramatists to make enough of a living to justify this trade-off.

This book presents a legal history that looks beyond the intellectual property rights that creators in the American theatre either possess or aspire to possess. Many of the economic and artistic challenges that all creative stakeholders confront – both writer and nonwriter collaborators – can be traced to structures of production more generally, of which the rights of authors of original works are only a part of that larger structure. The focus has been on explaining how a variety of mediating stakeholders established the ways that creation circulated throughout the theatrical economy. It has also been about how creative stakeholders, and especially dramatists, defined the ways they responded to mediating organizational structures, and how areas of law outside of copyright became critical in defining the effectiveness of the response.

Analysis of the Major Legal Hurdles," *Berkeley Journal of Employment and Labor Law* 38, no. 1 (2017): 49; Matthew Bodie, "Lessons from the Dramatists Guild for the Platform Economy," *University of Chicago Legal Forum* 2017 (2017): 17 (describing workers that fall between employees and contractors that provide services in an evolving economy). *See also* ongoing research by Catherine Fisk and Brent Salter, "Assumptions and Fragilities of Labor Relations in the American Theatre," *Ohio State Law Journal* 83 (forthcoming 2022).

126 *See* Dramatists Guild of America, "Authors Should Maintain a Legal Right to Their Work," www.dramatistsguild.com/no-union. At the time of writing, the Guild was also supporting the enactment of the "Protecting the Right to Organize (PRO) Act." The Guild notes in its support: "For far too long, freelancers – including dramatists – have been forced to choose between owning their copyright and organizing with collective bargaining power. Thanks to The PRO Act, it may no longer be necessary to make that difficult choice." *See* Dramatists Guild of America, "ACTION ALERT: Why the Guild Is Pro The PRO Act": www.dramatistsguild.com/news/why-guild-supports-the-pro-act.

The fact that relationships survive and theatre continues to be made under such a fragile framework says something rather profound about the resilience and desire of collaborators to come together and produce theatre – to realize the collaborative endeavor on a stage. But the triumphs of compromise also hide how mediators secure control over production processes through the institutional structures they establish over time. Mediators did not consolidate their extraordinary influence with acts of overt belligerence. Power imbalances evolve gradually through seemingly benign and incremental negotiations in the space between authors and audiences. Unsettled issues at the intersection of labor and competition law encourage these power imbalances to endure.[127]

[127] Kate Andrias's important work on "social bargaining" – occurring in the "public arena" and shifting away from private ordering toward involvement of the state as an "active participant in supporting collective bargaining" – has much to add to ongoing conversations about collective bargaining in the industry. *See* Kate Andrias, "The New Labor Law," *Yale Law Journal* 126, no. 1 (October 2016): 2. For important recent scholarship on labor and antitrust and the need to reframe in terms of the public good, *see also* Sanjukta Paul, "Antitrust as Allocator of Coordination Rights," *UCLA Law Review*, 67, no. 2 (2020): 378. On the concentration of labor market power and anticompetitive employer practices such as the setting of wages below the marginal revenue product, *see* Suresh Naidu, Eric A. Posner, and Glen Weyl, "Antitrust Remedies for Labor Market Power," *Harvard Law Review* 132, no. 2 (December 2018): 536. This scholarship is speaking, or responding, to recent important developments in the Law and Political Economy movement: Jedediah Britton-Purdy, David Singh Grewal, Amy Kapczynski, and K. Sabeel Rahman, "Building a Law-and-Political-Economy Framework: Beyond the Twentieth-Century Synthesis," *Yale Law Journal* 129 (2020): 1784.

# Bibliography

**Notes on References:** In this bibliography, I have not included references to newspaper articles or to archive material which can be found in the body of the book in the footnotes. Throughout the book I spell "theatre" with an "re" but have kept the spelling "theater" with an "er" where a direct quote spells the word with an "er".

## CASES


Aliotti v. R. Dakin & Co., 831 F.2d 898, 901 (9th Cir.1987)
Allen Bradley Co. v. Local Union No. 3, International Brotherhood of Electrical Workers, 325 US 797 (1945)
Am. Fed. of Musicians v. Carroll, 391 U.S. 99 (1968)
Atari, Inc. v. N. Am. Phillips Consumer Elecs. Corp., 672 F.2d 607 (7th Cir. 1982)
Bernstein v. Universal Pictures, Inc., 517 F.2d 976 (2d Cir. 1975)
Bossert v. Dhuy, 221 N.Y. 342 (1917)
Boucicault v. Fox, 3 F. Cas. 977 (C.C.S.D.N.Y. 1862)
Boucicault v. Hart, 3 F. Cas. 983 (C.C.S.D.N.Y. 1875)
Callaghan v. Myers 128 U.S. 617 (1888)
Carillo v. Shook, 5 F. Cas, 68 (C.C.S.D.N.Y. 1876)
Clemens v. Press Pub Co, 122 NYS 206 (1910)
Columbia River Packers Association v. Hinton, 315 U.S. 143 (1942)
Crowe v. Aiken, 2 Biss. 208 (1870)
De Bekker v. Frederick A. Stokes Co., 153 N.Y.S. 1066 (N.Y. App. Div. 1915), modified, 157 N.Y.S. 576 (N.Y. App. Div.), affd, 114 N.E. 1064 (N.Y. 1916)
Donaldson v. Becket (1774) 4 Burr. 2408
Drivers Union v. Lake Valley Co., 311 U.S. 91 (1940)
French v. Conelly, 1 N.Y. Weekly Digest 196 (NY Superior Court 1875)
French v. Maguire, 55 How. Pr. 471 (N.Y. Sup. Ct. 1878)
Gerlach-Barklow Co. v. Morris & Bendien, Inc., 23 F.2d 159 (2d Cir. 1927)
Gilliam v. American Broadcasting 538 F.2d 14 (2d. Cir. 1976)
Grant v. Kellogg Co., 58 F. Supp. 48 (S.D.N.Y. 1944)
H. A. Artists & Assoc., Inc. v. Actors' Equity Ass'n, 451 U.S. 704 (1981)
Hecht Co. v. Bowles, 321 U.S. 321 (1944)
Hervieu v. Ogilvie, 169 F. 978 (1909)
Houghton Mifflin Co. v. Stackpole Sons, Inc., 104 F.2d 306, 311 (2d Cir. 1939)

Hunt v. Washington State Apple Advertising Commission, 432 U.S. 333 (1977)
Jeffreys v. Boosey, 4 H. L. C. 815 (1854)
Jones v. Am. Law Book Co., 109 N.Y.S. 706,710 (N.Y. App. Div. 1908)
Julien v. Society of Stage Directors and Choreographers, Inc., 1975 WL 957 (S.D.N.Y. Oct. 14, 1975)
Keene v. Kimball 82 Mass. (16 Gray) 545 (1860)
Keene v. Wheatley 14 F. Cas. 180 (C.C.E.D. Pa. 1861)
Koppel v. Downing, 11 App. D.C. 93 (1897)
Lawrence v. Dana, 2 Am. L. T. R. n.s. 402; 15 F. Cas. 26, 51 (C.C.D. Mass. 1869)
Little v. Gould, 2 Blatchf. 165 (1852)
Local Union No. 189 v. Jewel Tea Co. 381 U.S. 676 (1965)
Los Angeles Meat and Provision Drivers Union v. United States, 371 U.S. 94 (1962)
MacKaye v. Mallory 79 F. 1 (2d Cir, 1897)
MacKaye v. Mallory and Anor 6 F. 743 (1881)
MacKaye v. Mallory, 80 F. 256 (C.C.S.D.N.Y. 1897)
MacKaye v. Mallory, Mallory v. MacKaye 12 F. 328 (C.C. S.D.N.Y. 1882)
Maisel v. Sigman, 205 N.Y.S. 807
Mallory v. MacKaye, 86 F. 122 (C.C.S.D.N.Y. 1898)
McComb v. Goldblatt Bros., 7 Cir., 166 F.2d 387 (1948)
Murray Hill Publications, Inc. v. Twentieth Century Fox Film Corp., 361 F.3d 312 (6th Cir. 2004)
Nichols v. Universal Pictures Corporation, 45 F.2d 119 (2d Cir. 1930)
N.L.R.B. v. Hearst Publications, Inc., 322 U.S. 111 (1944)
Palmer v. DeWitt, 47 N.Y. 532 (1872)
Parton v. Prang, 18 F. Cas. 1273, 1278 (C.C.D. Mass. 1872)
People v. Klaw, 55 Misc. 72 (1907); 106 N.Y. Supp. 341
Producing Managers' Assn. Inc. v. John Emerson as President of Actors, Lee Shubert et al, 209 App. Div 870 (1924)
Pulte v. Derby, 20 F. Cas. 51,52 (C.C.D. Ohio 1852)
Reardon v. Caton, 18 App. Div. 501(1919)
Richard Barr, Plaintiff, v. The Dramatists Guild, Inc., et al, 573 F. Supp. 555(1983)
Ring v. Authors' League of America Inc et al, 186 F 2d 637 (1951)
Ring v. Spina et al, 148 F 2d. 647 (1945)
Ring v. Spina et al, 166 F 2d 546 (1948)
Ring v. Spina et al, 84 F Supp. 403 (1949)
Ring v. Spina et al, 341 U.S. 935 (1951)
Roberts v. Myers, 20 F. Cas. 898 (C.C.D. Mass. 1860)
Schlesinger v. Quinto (1922) 201 App. Div. 487
Schwartz v. Universal Pictures Co. 85 F. Supp. 270 (S.D. Cal. 1949)
Securities and Exchange Commission v. Torr, 2 Cir., 87 F.2d 446 (1937)
Shook v. Rankin, 21 F. Cas. 1335 (Circuit Court, N.D. Illinois) (1875)
Shook v. Rankin, 21 F. Cas. 1337 (Circuit Court, D. Minnesota) (1875)
Spina et al v. Ring, 335 U.S. 813 (1948)
Taylor v. Local 7, Int'l Union of Journeymen Horseshoers, 353 F.2d 593 (4th Cir. 1965)
Thomson v. Larson, 147 F.3d 195 (2nd Cir. 1998)
Tompkins v. Halleck 133 Mass. 32 (1882)
Turner v. Robinson, 10 Ir. Ch. 121, 510 (1860)
United Mine Workers v. Pennington, 381 U.S. 657 (1965)

United States v. American Federation of Musicians, 318 U.S. 741 (1943)
United States v. Hutcheson 312 U.S. 219 (1941)
United States v. United States Steel Corp., 251 U.S. 417 (1920)
Walling v. Helmerich & Payne, 323 U.S. 37 (1944)
Walling v. T. Buettner & Co., 7 Cir., 133 F.2d 306 (1943)
Walling v. Youngerman-Reynolds Hardwood Co., 325 U.S. 419 (1945)
Wheaton v. Peters 33 U.S. 591 (1834)
Zambito v. Paramount Pictures Corp., 613 F. Supp. 1107 (E.D.N.Y 1985); 788 F.2d 2 (2d Cir. 1985)

## OTHER SOURCES

"A Theatrical Trust for the World," *Current Literature* XLIII (September, 1907): 319–321

Amada, Richard, "Elvis Karaoke Shakespeare and the Search for a Copyrightable Stage Directions," *Arizona Law Review* 43, no. 3 (2001): 677–708

American Bar Association, *Antitrust Healthcare Handbook* (Chicago, IL: American Bar Association, Section of Antitrust Law, 3rd ed., 2004)

"American Stage in Danger, Says William Winter," *The Theatre* 7, no. 80 (October, 1907): 268

Andrias, Kate, "The New Labor Law," *Yale Law Journal* 126, no. 1 (October 2016): 2–101

Areeda, Phillip; Kaplow, Louis; Edlin, Aaron, *Antitrust Analysis: Problems, Text, and Cases* (New York: Wolters Kluwer Law & Business, 7th ed., 2013)

Arewa, Olufunmilayo B, "Copyright on Catfish Row: Musical Borrowing, Porgy and Bess, and Unfair Use," *Rutgers Law Journal* 37, no. 2 (2006): 277–353

Auslander, Philip, *Liveness: Performance in a Mediatized Culture* (London; New York: Routledge, 2008)

Baker, Dorothy G., "Monopoly in the American Theatre: A Study of the Cultural Conflicts Culminating in the Syndicate and Its Successors, the Shuberts" (PhD diss., New York University, 1962)

Balganesh, Shyamkrishna, "Unplanned Coauthorship," *Virginia Law Review* 100, no. 8 (2014): 1683–1756

Balganesh, Shyamkrishna and Zhang, Taisu, "Legal Internalism in Modern Histories of Copyright," *Harvard Law Review* 134 (2021): 1066–1130 (Review Essay)

Bassin, Joel, "The Minimum Basic Agreement of the Dramatists Guild: A History of Inadequate Protection," *The Journal of Arts Management Law and Society* 25, no. 2 (1995): 157–171

Belasco, David "The Theatrical Syndicate: One Side," *Cosmopolitan* 38, no. 2 (1904): 193–198

Bell, John, "Disney's New Time Square: The New American Community Theatre," *The Drama Review* 42, no. 1 (1998): 26–33

Bennett, Susan, "Theatre/Tourism," *Theatre Journal* 57, no. 3 (2005): 407–428

Bernardo, Pedro Jose F., "Transformative Adaptation, Performance, and Fair Use of Literary and Dramatic Works: Delineating the Rights of Playwrights and Adapters," *Ateneo Law Journal* 53, no. 3 (2008): 582–654

Bernheim, Alfred L., *The Business of the Theatre* (New York: Actor's Equity Assoc., 1932)

Bernstein, Lisa, "Opting out of the Legal System: Extralegal Contractual Relations in the Diamond Industry," *Journal of Legal Studies* 21, no. 1 (January 1992): 115–158

Bernstein, Matthew, *Walter Wagner: Hollywood Independent* (St. Paul, Minneapolis: University of Minnesota Press, 2000)

Bianco, Anthony, *Ghosts of 42nd Street: A History of America's Most Infamous Block* (New York: Harper Collins, 2004)

Binns, Archie in collaboration with Kooken, Olive, *Mrs. Fiske and the American Theatre* (New York: Crown Publishers, Inc., 1955)

Blackstone, Sarah, "Alexander Byers, Play Pirate Extraordinaire," *Theatre History Studies* 14 (June 1994): 107–113

Bloom, Ken, *Broadway: Its History, People, and Places: An Encyclopedia* (2nd ed. New York: Routledge, 2004)

Bodie, Matthew T, "Lessons from the Dramatists Guild for the Platform Economy," *University of Chicago Legal Forum* 2017 (2017): 17–34

Boroff, Philip, "'Hamilton' Pays Miranda & Seller Tens of Millions a Year," *Broadway Journal*, April 26, 2018, http://broadwayjournal.com/hamilton-pays-miranda-seller-tens-of-millions-a-year/

Bowrey, Kathy, *Copyright, Creativity, Big Media and Cultural Value: Incorporating the Author* (Abingdon, UK; New York: Routledge Books, 2021)

Bracha, Oren, "Commentary on the U.S. Copyright Act Amendment 1856," in *Primary Sources on Copyright (1450–1900)*, eds. Lionel Bently and Martin Kretschmer (Cambridge, UK: Arts and Humanities Research Council, 2008) available online at www.copyrighthistory.org

Bracha, Oren, "The Ideology of Authorship Revisited: Authors, Markets, and Liberal Values in Early American Copyright," *Yale Law Journal* 118, no. 2 (2008): 186–271

Bracha, Oren, *Owning Ideas: The Intellectual Origins of American Intellectual Property: 1790–1909* (New York: Cambridge University Press, 2016)

Bradley, Edward, *George Henry Boker, Poet and Patriot* (Philadelphia, University of Pennsylvania Press; London, H. Milford, Oxford University Press, 1927)

Brater, Jessica; Del Vecchio, Jessica; and Friedman, Andrew, et al., "'Let Our Freak Flags Fly': Shrek the Musical and the Branding of Diversity," *Theatre Journal* 62, no. 2 (May 2010): 151–172

Braucher, Jean; Kidwell, John; and Whitford William, eds., *Revisiting the Contracts Scholarship of Stewart Macaulay* (Oxford, UK and Portland, OR: Hart Publishing, 2013)

Britton-Purdy, Jedediah; Grewal, David Singh; Kapczynski Amy; and Rahman, K. Sabeel, "Building a Law-and-Political-Economy Framework: Beyond the Twentieth-Century Synthesis," *Yale Law Journal* 129 (2020): 1784–1835

Bronson Howard, *The Autobiography of a Play* (New York: Dramatic Museum of Columbia University, 1914)

Buckalew, Faye, "Joint Authorship in the Second Circuit: A Critique of the Law in the Second Circuit Following Childress v. Taylor and as Exemplified in Thomson v. Larson," *Brooklyn Law Review* 64, no. 2 (1998): 545–584

Burkert, Mattie, *Speculative Enterprise: Public Theaters and Financial Markets in London, 1688–1763* (Charlottesville: University of Virginia Press, 2021)

Campbell, David; and Harris, Donald, "Flexibility in Long-Term Contractual Relationships: The Role of Co-operation," *Journal of Law and Society* 20, no. 2 (Summer 1993): 166–191

Carroll, Michael, "Copyright's Creative Hierarchy in the Performing Arts," *Vanderbilt Journal Entertainment & Technology Law* 14, no. 4 (2012): 797–828

Chach, Maryann, "Behind the Scenes of the New York Review," *The Passing Show* 12, no. 2 (1989): 2–14

Clark, Barrett H., ed., *America's Lost Plays: Vol. 1* (Princeton, NJ: Princeton University Press, 1940–1942)

Corcoran, Kieran, "When Does the Buzzer Sound?: The Nonstatutory Labor Exemption in Professional Sports," *Columbia Law Review* 194, no. 3 (Apr. 1994): 1045–1075

Craig, Carys, *Copyright, Communication and Culture: Towards a Relational Theory of Copyright Law* (Cheltenham, UK: Edward Elgar, 2011)
Curley, Eileen, "A Shot over the Bow: William Gillette and Amateur Play Piracy," *Journal of American Drama and Theatre* 22, no. 3 (2010): 23–41
Curtin, Rebecca Schoff, "The Transactional Origins of Authors' Copyright," *Columbia Journal of Law & the Arts* 40, no. 2 (2016): 175–236
Daly, J. F., *The Life of Augustin Daly* (New York: The Macmillan Company, 1917)
Davenport, Ken: in conversation with Ralph Sevush, *The Producer's Perspective* (Podcast, Episode 35, August 2015) available at www.theproducersperspective.com/my_weblog/2015/08/podcast-episode-35-transcript-ralph-sevush.html
Davis, Andrew, *America's Longest Run: A History of the Walnut Street Theatre* (University Park: The Pennsylvania State University Press, 2010)
Davis, Owen, *I'd Like to Do It Again* (New York: Farrar and Rinehart, 1931)
Davis, Peter A., "The Syndicate/Shubert War," in *Inventing Times Square: Commerce and Culture at the Crossroads of the World*, ed. William R. Taylor (New York: Russell Sage Foundation, 1991)
Davis, Tracy C, *The Economics of the British Stage: 1800–1914* (Cambridge, UK; New York: Cambridge University Press, 2000)
Deazley, Ronan, *On the Origin of the Right to Copy: Charting the Movement of Copyright Law in Eighteenth Century Britain, 1695–1775* (Oxford, UK; Portland, OR: Hart Publishing, 2004)
Dickinson, Thomas, *The Case of the American Drama* (Boston and New York: Houghton Mifflin Company, 1915)
Dramatists Guild of America (website), https://www.dramatistsguild.com/
Drone, Eaton S., *A Treatise on The Law of Property in Intellectual Productions in Great Britain and the United* States (Boston, MA: Little Brown, 1879)
Eaton, Walter P, *At the New Theatre and Others. The American Stage: Its Problems and Performances, 1908–1910* (Boston, MA: Small, Maynard and Company, 1910)
Eaton, Walter P., "Rise and Fall of the Theatrical Syndicate," *American Magazine* 70 (1910): 832–842
Editors, "The Great Theatrical Syndicate: How Six Dictators Control Our Amusements," *Leslie's Monthly Magazine* 59 (1905): 331–334
Edwards, Laura, *The People and Their Peace: Legal Culture and the Transformation of Inequality in the Post-Revolutionary South* (Chapel Hill: University of North Carolina Press, 2009)
Emerson, John (President of Actors Equity), "An Inspiring Address," 28, no.1 *American Federationist* (1921): 233–235
Engle, Sherry, *New Women Dramatists in America, 1890–1920* (New York: Palgrave Macmillan, 2007)
Essin, Christin; and Schweitzer, Marlis, "Communities of Production: A Materialist Reading with an Offstage View," in *A Cultural History of Theatre in the Modern Age*, ed. Kim Solga (London, New York: Bloomsbury, 2017)
Fawkes, Richard, *Dion Boucicault: A Biography* (London; New York: Quartet Books, [1981] 1979)
Fields, Armond, *From the Bowery to Broadway: Lew Fields and the Roots of American Popular Theatre* (New York; Oxford: Oxford University Press, 1993)

Fisk, Catherine, *Working Knowledge: Employee Innovation and the Rise of Corporate Intellectual Property, 1800–1930* (Chapel Hill: University of North Carolina Press, 2009)
Flanagan, Hallie, *Arena: The Story of the Federal Theatre* (New York: Limelight Editions, 1969 ed.)
Ford, Lisa, *Settler Sovereignty Jurisdiction and Indigenous People in America and Australia, 1788–1836* (Cambridge, MA: Harvard University Press, 2010)
Foust, Clement, *The Life and Dramatic Works of Robert Montgomery Bird* (New York: The Knickerbocker Press, 1919)
Fox, Paulette S., "Preserving the Collaborative Spirit of American Theater: The Need for a Joint Authorship Default Rule in Light of the Rent Decision's Unanswered Question," *Cardozo Arts & Entertainment Law Journal* 19, no. 3 (2001): 497–532
Freemal, Beth, "Theatre, Stage Directions & (and) Copyright Law," *Chicago-Kent Law Review* 71, no. 3 (1996): 1017–1042
Frick, John, "A Changing Theatre: New York and Beyond," in *The Cambridge History of American Theatre. Volume 2, 1870–1945*, eds. Wilmeth, Don B.; and Bigsby, Christopher (Cambridge, UK: Cambridge University Press, 1999)
Frohman, Charles, "New Phases of Theatre Management," *Harper's Weekly* 48 (1904): 2022–2024
Gabriel, Ralph, "Foreword," in Oral S. Coad and Edwin Mims, *The American Stage* (Vol. 14, New Haven, CT: Yale University Press, 1929)
Gallia, Carrie Ryan, "To Fix or Not to Fix: Copyright's Fixation Requirement and the Rights of Theatrical Collaborators," *Minnesota Law Review* 92, no. 1 (2007): 231–264
Gassner, John in association with Gassner, Mollie, eds., *Best Plays of the Early American theatre: 1787–1911* (Mineola, NY: Dover Publications, [2000], 1967)
Gervais, Daniel, "The Derivative Right, or Why Copyright Protects Foxes Better Than Hedgehogs," *Vanderbilt Journal of Entertainment and Technology Law* 15 (2013): 785–855
Ginsburg, Jane C. , "'With Untired Spirits and Formal Constancy': Berne Compatibility of Formal Declaratory Measures to Enhance Copyright Title-Searching," *Berkeley Technology Law Journal* 28 (2013): 1583–1622
Goldstein, Malcolm, *George S Kaufman: His Life His Theatre* (New York: Oxford University Press, 1979)
Goldstein, Paul, "Derivative Rights and Derivative Works in Copyright," *Journal of Copyright Society U.S.A.* 30 (1983): 209–252.
Goold, Patrick R., "The Lost Tort of Moral Rights Invasion," *Akron Law Review* 51, no. 4 (2017): 1093–1124
Grau, Robert, *The Business Man in the Amusement World; A Volume of Progress in the Field of the Theatre* (New York: Broadway Pub. Co., 1910)
Greene, K. J. "Intellectual Property at the Intersection of Race and Gender: Lady Sings The Blues," *Journal of Gender, Social Policy & The Law* 16, no. 3 (2008): 365–385
Hapgood, Norman, "The Theatrical Syndicate," *The International Monthly* 1 (1900): 99–122
Hapgood, Norman, *The Stage in America, 1897–1900* (New York: The Macmillan Company, 1901)
Harding, Alfred, "Chapter IV: America," in *Our Theater Today*, ed. Herschel L. Bricker (New York: Samuel French, 1936)
Harding, James; and Rouse, John, *Not the Other Avant-garde: The Transnational Foundations of Avant-garde Performance* (Ann Arbor: University of Michigan Press, 2006)
Harris, Andrew B., *Broadway Theater* (London; New York: Routledge, 1994)
Hays, Arthur G., *City Lawyer* (New York: Simon and Schuster, 1942)
Hodin, Mark, "The Disavowal of Ethnicity: Legitimate Theatre and the Social Construction of Literary Value in Turn-of-the-Century America," *Theatre Journal* 52 (2000): 211–226

Hogan, Robert, *Dion Boucicault* (New York: Twayne Publishers, Inc. 1969)

Holmes, Sean P., *Weavers of Dreams, Unite! Actors' Unionism in Early Twentieth-Century America* (Urbana, Springfield, Chicago: University of Illinois Press, 2013)

Hopkins, Arthur, *Reference Point: Reflections on Creative Ways in General with Special Reference to Creative Ways in the Theatre* (New York: Samuel French, 1948)

Hornblow, Arthur, *A History of the Theatre in America: From Its Beginnings to the Present Time* (Vol. 2, Philadelphia, PA: J. B. Lippincotte and Co., 1919)

Hughes, Glenn, *A History of the American Theatre: 1700–1950* (New York: Samuel French, 1951)

Iglitzin, Dmitri; and Robbins, Jennifer L., "The City of Seattle's Ordinance Providing Collective Bargaining Rights to Independent Contractor for-Hire Drivers: An Analysis of the Major Legal Hurdles," *Berkeley Journal of Employment and Labor Law* 38, no. 1 (2017): 49–72

Johnson, Brandon, "Whitewashing Expression: Using Copyright Law to Protect Racial Identity in Casting," *Northwestern University Law Review* 112, no. 5 (2018): 1137–1170

Kaplan, Carol, "Once More unto the Breach," *Vanderbilt Journal of Entertainment and Technology Law* 16, no. 2 (2014): 297–352

Keller, Susan, "Collaboration in Theater: Problems and Copyright Solutions," *UCLA Law Review* 33, no. 3 (February 1986): 891–939

Kelly, Ashley, "Bargaining Power on Broadway: Why Congress Should Pass the Playwrights Licensing Antitrust Initiative Act in the Era of Hollywood on Broadway," *Journal of Law and Policy* 16, no. 2 (2008): 877–924

Keramidas, Kimon, "The Play's the Thing: Intellectual Property and the Political Economy of Contemporary American Theatrical Production" (PhD diss., City University of New York, 2008)

Khachab, Chihab El, "Current Trends in The Anthropology of Bureaucracy—A Report," https://allegralaboratory.net/current-trends-in-the-anthropology-of-bureaucracy-a-report/

King, Moses, ed., *King's Handbook of New York* (Boston, MA: Moses King, 1892)

Kitts, Thomas, *The Theatrical Life of George Henry Boker* (New York: Peter Lang, 1994)

Klaw, Marc, "The Theatrical Syndicate—the Other Side," *Cosmopolitan* 38 (1904): 199–201

Klein II, William, "Protective Societies for Authors and Creators," in *Copyright Problems Analyzed*, ed. Theodore R Kupferman (New York: Commerce Clearing House, 1953, Vol. 2)

Knapp, Margaret, "Introductory Essay," in *Inventing Times Square: Commerce and Culture at the Crossroads of the World*, ed. William Taylor (Baltimore, MD: The John Hopkins University Press, 1991)

Kraut, Anthea, *Choreographing Copyright: Race, Gender, and Intellectual Property Rights in American Dance* (New York: Oxford University Press, 2016)

Kritzer, Amelia Howe ed., *Plays by Early American Women, 1775–1850* (Ann Arbor: University of Michigan Press, 1995)

Krows, Arthur E., *Play Production in America* (New York: H. Holt and Company, 1916)

Kwall, Roberta Rosenthal, "Author-Stories: Narrative's Implications for Moral Rights and Copyright's Joint Authorship Doctrine," *Southern California Law Review* 75, no. 1 (November 2001): 1–64

LaFrance, Mary, "Authorship, Dominance, and the Captive Collaborator: Preserving the Rights of Joint Authors," *Emory Law Journal* 50, no. 1 (2001): 193–264

Landro, Vincent, "Media Mania: The Demonizing of the Theatrical Syndicate," *Journal of American Drama and Theatre* 13, no. 2 (2001): 23–50

Latour, Bruno, *Reassembling the Social: An Introduction to Actor-Network Theory* (New York: Oxford University Press, 2005)
Leavitt, Michael B., *Fifty Years in Theatrical Management* (New York: Broadway Pub. Co., 1912)
Lee, Ilhyung, "Toward an American Moral Rights in Copyright," *Washington and Lee Law Review* 58 (2001): 795–854
Lee, Jane C, "Upstaging the Playwright: The Joint Authorship Entanglement between Dramaturgs and Playwrights," *Loyola of Los Angeles Entertainment Law Journal* 19, no. 1 (1998): 75–106
Leichtman, David, "Most Unhappy Collaborators: An Argument against the Recognition of Property Ownership in Stage Directions," *Columbia-VLA Journal of Law & the Arts* 20, no. 4 (1996): 683–734
Leonhardt, Nic, "Transatlantic Theatrical Traces: Oceanic Trade Routes and Globe-Trotting Amusement Explorers," *The Passing* Show 30 (2013/2014): 2–23
Leonhardt, Nic; and Scholz-Cionca, Stanca, "Circulation, Theatre Mobility and its Professionalization in the Nineteenth Century," in A *Cultural History of Theatre in the Age of Empire (1800–1920)*, ed. Peter W. Marx (London: Bloomsbury, 2017)
Lippman, Monroe, "The History of the Theatrical Syndicate: its effect upon the theatre in America" (PhD diss., University of Michigan, 1937)
Litman, Jessica, "Copyright in the Stage Direction of a Broadway Musical," *Art & the Law* 7, no. 4 (1982–1983): 309–336
Litman, Jessica, "The Invention of Common Law Play Right," *Berkeley Technology Law Journal* 25 (2010): 1381–1425
Litman, Jessica, "What Notice Did," *Boston University Law Review* 96, no. 3 (2016): 717–744
Litman, Jessica, "What We Don't See When We See Copyright as Property," *Cambridge L.J.* 77, no. 3 (2018): 536–558
Livingston, Margit, "Inspiration or Imitation: Copyright Protection for Stage Directions," *Boston College Law Review* 50, no. 2 (2009): 427–488
London, Todd; with Pesner, Ben; and Voss, Zannie G., *Outrageous Fortune: The Life and Times of the New American Play* (New York: TDF, 2009)
Macaulay, Stewart, "Non-Contractual Relations in Business: A Preliminary Study," *American Sociological Review* 28 (1963): 55–67
Macaulay, Stewart, "Lawyers and Consumer Protection Laws," *Law & Society Review* 14, no. 1 (1979): 115–180
MacKaye, Percy, *Epoch: The Life of Steele MacKaye, Genius of the Theatre, in Relation to His Times & Contemporaries* (New York: Boni and Liveright, 1927)
Marbury, Elisabeth, *My Crystal Ball; Reminiscences* (New York: Boni and Liveright, 1924)
Marker, Lise-Lone, *David Belasco: Naturalism in the American Theatre* (Princeton, NJ: Princeton University Press, 1975)
Marks, Patricia, "A Firestorm of Criticism: Metcalfe and the Theatrical Syndicate, 1904–1905," *American Periodicals*, 1998, 8 (1998), 15–29
Maxwell, Jennifer J., "Making a Federal Case for Copyrighting Stage Directions: Einhorn v. Mergatroyd Productions," *John Marshall Review of Intellectual Property Law* 7, no. 2 (2008): 393–411
McDonald, William F., *Federal Relief Administration and the Arts* (Columbus: Ohio State University Press, 1969)
McLaughlin, Robert, *Broadway and Hollywood: A History of Economic Interaction* (New York: Arno Press, 1974)

Menefee, Larry T., "The Syndicate War in Little Rock," *Arkansas Historical Quarterly* 46 (1987): 27–45

Middleton, George, *The Dramatists Guild: What It Is and Does. How It Happened and Why* (New York: Dramatists Guild, 3rd ed., 1947)

Middleton, George, *The Dramatists' Guild: What It Is and Does, How It Happened and Why* (New York: Dramatists' Guild of the Authors' League of America, 4th ed., 1959)

Middleton, George, *The Dramatists Guild: What It Is and Does . . . How It Happened and Why* (New York: Dramatists Guild, 5th ed., 1966)

Middleton, George, *These Things Are Mine: The Autobiography of a Journeyman Playwright* (New York: The Macmillan Company, 1947)

Miller, Derek, "Performative Performances: A History and Theory of the 'Copyright Performance'," *Theatre Journal* 64, no. 2 (2012): 161–77

Miller, Derek, *Visualizing Broadway* http://visualizingbroadway.com.

Miller, Derek, "Average Broadway," *Theatre Journal*, 68, no. 4 (2016): 529–553

Miller, Derek, *Copyright and the Value of Performance, 1770–1911* (Cambridge, UK: Cambridge University Press, 2018)

Morris, Lloyd, *Curtain Time; The Story of the American Theater* (New York: Random House, 1953)

Morrison, Matthew "Race, Blacksound, and the (Re)Making of Musicological Discourse," *Journal of the American Musicological Society* 72, no. 3 (2019): 781–823

Moses, Montrose J., "The Disintegration of Theatre," *Forum* 45 (1911): 465–471

Murphy, Brenda, ed., *The Cambridge Companion to American Women Playwrights* (Cambridge, UK; New York: Cambridge University Press, 1999)

Naidu, Suresh; Posner, Eric A.; and Weyl, Glen, "Antitrust Remedies for Labor Market Power," *Harvard Law Review* 132, no. 2 (2018): 536–601

Nathan, George Jean, "The Drama Comes into Season," *The Smart Set* 29 (September 1909)

Nelson, Steve, "Broadway and the Beast: Disney Comes to Time Square," *The Drama Review* 39, no. 2 (1995): 71–85

Nevin, Douglas M., "No Business Like Show Business: Copyright Law, the Theatre Industry, and the Dilemma of Rewarding Collaboration," *Emory Law Journal* 53, no. 3 (2004): 1533–1570

Odell, George C., *Annals of the New York Stage* (New York: Columbia University Press, 1927)

Paul, Sanjukta, "Antitrust as Allocator of Coordination Rights," *UCLA Law Review* 67, no. 2 (2020): 378–431

Paul, Sanjukta, "The Enduring Ambiguities of Antitrust Liability for Worker Collective Action," *Loyola University Chicago Law Journal* 47, no. 3 (Spring 2016): 969–1048

Pate, George, *Enter the Undead Author: Intellectual Property, the Ideology of Authorship, and Performance Practices since the 1960s* (Vancouver; Madison: Fairleigh Dickinson University Press; Lanham, MD: The Rowman & Littlefield Publishing Group, Inc., 2019)

Picart, Caroline Joan S., *Critical Race Theory and Copyright in American Dance: Whiteness as Status* Property (New York: Palgrave Macmillan, 2013)

Poggi, Jack, *Theatre in America: The Impact of Economic Forces, 1870–1967* (Ithaca, NY: Cornell University Press, 1968)

Pollock, Channing, "Unmuzzling the Theatrical Season: The Ringmaster," *The Green Book Album* 2 (July 1909): 780–781

Quinn, Arthur H., ed., *Representative American Plays* (New York: The Century Co., 1922)

"Recent Cases," *Harvard Law Review* 112, no. 4 (February 1999): 964–993

Rimmer, Matthew, "Heretic: Copyright Law and Dramatic Works," *Queensland University of Technology Law and Justice Journal* 2, no. 1 (2002): 131–149

Roost, Frank, "Synergy City: How Times Square and Celebration Are Integrated into Disney's Marketing Cycle," in *Rethinking Disney: Private Control, Public Dimensions*, eds. Mike Budd and Max Kirsch (Middletown, CT: Wesleyan University Press, 2005)

Rose, Mark, *Authors and Owners. The Invention of Copyright* (Cambridge, MA: Harvard University Press, 1993)

Rosen, Zvi S., "The Twilight of the Opera Pirates: A Prehistory of the Exclusive Right of Public Performance for Musical Compositions," *Cardozo Arts & Entertainment Law Journal* 24, no. 3 (2007): 1157–1218

Rosen, Zvi S., "Common-Law Copyright," *University of Cincinnati Law Review* 85, no. 4 (2018): 1055–1134

Rosen, Zvi S. and Schwinn, Richard, "An Empirical Study of 225 Years of Copyright Registrations," *Tulane Law Review* 94 (2020): 1003–1083

Rukgaber, Cecile, "The Theatrical Syndicate and Its Effects upon the American Theatre" (MA diss., University of Wyoming, 1955)

Salter, Brent; and Bowrey, Kathy, "Dramatic Copyright and the Disneyfication of Theatre Space," in *Law and Creativity in the Age of the Entertainment Franchise*, eds. Bowrey Kathy; and Handler Michael (Cambridge, UK: Cambridge University Press, 2014)

Salter, Brent, "The Ordinary Authors of the Bureau Of New Plays: Copyright and Reallocating Authority in the American Theatre (1936–1949)," *Cardozo Arts & Entertainment Law Journal* 39, no. 1 (2021): 137–194

Samachson, Dorothy; and Samachson, Joseph, *Let's Meet the Theatre* (New York: Abelard-Schuman, 1954)

Savran, David, *A Queer Sort of Materialism: Recontextualizing American Theatre* (Ann Arbor: The University of Michigan Press, 2003)

Savran, David, *Highbrow/Lowdown: Theater, Jazz, and the Making of the New Middle Class* (Ann Arbor: The University of Michigan Press, 2009)

Schwartz, Michael, *Broadway and Corporate Capitalism: The Rise of the Professional-Managerial Class, 1900–1920* (New York: Palgrave Macmillan, 2009)

Schweitzer, Marlis, "Aggressive, Beleaguered, Commercial, Defiant: Marc Klaw and Abraham Erlanger," in *The Palgrave Handbook of Musical Theatre Producers*, eds. Laura McDonald and William Everett (New York: Palgrave Macmillan US: Imprint: Palgrave Macmillan, 2017)

Schweitzer, Marlis, *Transatlantic Broadway: The Infrastructural Politics of Global Performance* (Houndmills, Basingstoke, Hampshire, UK; New York: Palgrave Macmillan, 2015)

Seville, Catherine, *Literary Copyright Reform in Early Victorian England: The Framing of the 1842 Copyright Act* (Cambridge, UK; New York: Cambridge University Press, 1999)

Simon, David, "Analogies in IP: Moral Rights," *Yale Journal of Law & Technology* 21 (2019): 337–385

Slout, William L., *Theatre in a Tent: The Development of a Provincial Entertainment* (Bowling Green, OH: Bowling Green University Popular Press 1972)

Smith, J. L., "Three Stock Companies: Wallack's, Daly's and Palmer's" (MA diss., University of Iowa, 1927)

Spoo, Robert, *Without Copyrights: Piracy, Publishing, and the Public Domain* (New York: Oxford University Press, 2013)

Stagg, Jerry, *The Brothers' Shubert* (New York: Random House, 1968)

Standish, Burt L., "Dick Merriwell on the Boards; or, Fighting the Theatrical Syndicate," *Tip Top Weekly* 762 (1910): 1–26

Stein, Deana S., "Every Move That She Makes: Copyright Protection for Stage Directions and the Fictional Character Standard," *Cardozo Law Review* 34, no. 4 (2013): 1571–1608

Stewart, Henry T., "The Playbrokers of New York," *Theatre Magazine* 5 (1905): 163–165
Surwillo, Lisa, *Stages of Property: Copyrighting Theatre in Spain* (Toronto: University of Toronto Press, 2007)
Sussman, Mark, "New York's Facelift," *The Drama Review* 42, no. 1(1998): 34–42
Swartz, Mark, *Oz Before the Rainbow: L. Frank Baum's The Wonderful Wizard of Oz on Stage and Screen to* 1939 (Baltimore, MD: Johns Hopkins University Press, 2000)
Talati, Jessica, "Copyrighting Stage Directions & the Constitutional Mandate to Promote the Progress of Science," *Northwestern Journal of Technology and Intellectual Property* 7, no. 2 (2009): 241–260
Tani, Karen, *States of Dependency: Welfare, Rights, and American Governance*, 1935–1972 (New York: Cambridge University Press, 2016)
Teichmann, Howard, *George S Kaufman: An Intimate Portrait* (New York: Atheneum, 1972)
The Jay T. Last Collection of Graphic Arts and Social History, "The Madison Square Theatre Company: Hazel Kirke," Huntington Digital Library: https://hdl.huntington.org/digital/collection/p16003coll4/id/2378/rec/1
Tibbetts, John, *The American Theatrical Film* (Bowling Green, OH: Bowling Green State University Popular Press, 1985)
Train, Arthur, *My Day in Court* (New York: Charles Scribner's Sons, 1939)
Travis, Steve, "The Rise and Fall of the Theatrical Syndicate," *Educational Theatre Journal* 10, no. 1 (1958): 35–40
US Copyright Office website: www.copyright.gov/history/annual_reports.html
Valenzi, Shane, "A Rollicking Band of Pirates: Licensing the Exclusive Right of Public Performance in the Theatre Industry," *Vanderbilt Journal of Entertainment and Technology Law* 14, no. 3 (2012): 759–796
Vickery, Anthony, "The Logistics and Finances of Touring in North America, 1900–1916" (PhD diss., University of Victoria, 2001)
Vickery, Anthony, "Did the Shuberts Save Broadway? The Corporate Producers," in *The Palgrave Handbook of Musical Theatre Producers*, eds. Laura MacDonald and William A. Everett (New York: Palgrave Macmillan, 2017)
Walsh, Thomas, *Playwrights and Power: The Making of the Dramatists Guild* (Hanover, NH: Smith and Kraus, 2016)
Weber, Max, *Economy and Society: An Outline of Interpretive Sociology* (Berkeley: University of California Press, 1978) (edited by Guenther Roth and Claus Wittich; translators, Ephraim Fischoff et al.).
Weidman, John, "Protecting the American Playwright: The Seventh Annual Media and Society Lecture," *Brooklyn Law Review* 72 (2007): 639–653
White, Leslie, "Eugene O'Neill and the Federal Theatre Project" (PhD diss., New York University, 1986)
Wickstrom, Mauyra, "Commodities, Mimesis, and The Lion King: Retail Theatre for the 1990s," *Theatre Journal* 51, no. 3 (1999): 285–298
Wilf, Steven, "Copyright and Social Movements in Late Nineteenth-Century America," *Theoretical Inquiries in Law* 12, no. 1 (January 2011): 123–160
Witham, Barry, *The Federal Theatre Project: A Case Study* (Cambridge, UK; New York: Cambridge University Press, 2003)
Witt, John, *Patriots and Cosmopolitans: Hidden Histories of American Law* (Cambridge, MA: Harvard University Press, 2007)
Wittenberg, Philip, *The Protection and Marketing of Literary Property* (New York: J. Messner, inc., 1937)

Wollman, Elizabeth, "The Economic Development of the 'New' Times Square and Its Impact on the Broadway Musical," *American Music* 20, no. 4 (2002): 445–465

Wollman, Elizabeth, *A Critical Companion to the American Stage Musical* (London; New York: Bloomsbury Methuen Drama, 2017)

Womack, Jennifer, "Big Shop of Horrors: Ownership in Theatrical Design," *Fordham Intellectual Property, Media & Entertainment Law Journal* 18, no. 1 (2007): 225–252

Wright, Doug, "Playwrights and Copyright," *Columbia Journal of Law & the Arts* 38, no. 3 (2015): 301–308

Wright, Doug, "A Message on Copyright from DG President Doug Wright"(citing Georgia Stitt), May 29, 2020: www.dramatistsguild.com/news/message-copyright-dg-president-doug-wright

Yellin, Talia, "New Directions for Copyright: The Property Rights of Stage Directors," *Columbia-VLA Journal of Law & the Arts* 24, no. 3 (2001): 317–348

Zamora, Alison, "The Playwright Licensing Antitrust Initiative Act: Empowering the Starving Artist through the Convergence of Copyright, Labor, and Antitrust Policies," *DePaul-LCA Journal of Art and Entertainment Law* 16, no. 2 (Spring 2006): 395–436

Zecher, Henry, *William Gillette, America's Sherlock Holmes* (Bloomington: Xlibris Corporation, 2011)

# Index

## CAMBRIDGE INTELLECTUAL PROPERTY AND INFORMATION LAW

### Titles in the Series (formerly known as Cambridge Studies in Intellectual Property Rights)

Graeme W. Austin, Andrew F. Christie, Andrew T. Kenyon and Megan Richardson *Across Intellectual Property: Essays in Honour of Sam Ricketson*

Brad Sherman and Lionel Bently *The Making of Modern Intellectual Property Law*

Irini A. Stamatoudi *Copyright and Multimedia Products: A Comparative Analysis*

Pascal Kamina *Film Copyright in the European Union*

Huw Beverley-Smith *The Commercial Appropriation of Personality*

Mark J. Davison *The Legal Protection of Databases*

Robert Burrell and Allison Coleman *Copyright Exceptions: The Digital Impact*

Huw Beverley-Smith, Ansgar Ohly and Agnès Lucas-Schloetter *Privacy, Property and Personality: Civil Law Perspectives on Commercial Appropriation*

Catherine Seville *The Internationalisation of Copyright Law: Books, Buccaneers and the Black Flag in the Nineteenth Century*

Philip Leith *Software and Patents in Europe*

Geertrui van Overwalle *Gene Patents and Clearing Models: Patent Pools, Clearinghouses, Open Source Models and Liability Regimes*

Lionel Bently, Jennifer Davis and Jane C. Ginsburg *Trade Marks and Brands: An Interdisciplinary Critique*

Jonathan Curci *The Protection of Biodiversity and Traditional Knowledge in International Law of Intellectual Property*

Lionel Bently, Jennifer Davis and Jane C. Ginsburg *Copyright and Piracy: An Interdisciplinary Critique*

Megan Richardson and Julian Thomas *Fashioning Intellectual Property: Exhibition, Advertising and the Press, 1789–1918*

Dev Gangjee *Relocating the Law of Geographical Indications*

Andrew Kenyon, Megan Richardson and Ng-Loy Wee-Loon *The Law of Reputation and Brands in the Asia Pacific*

Edson Beas Rodrigues, Jr *The General Exception Clauses of the TRIPS Agreement: Promoting Sustainable Development*

Annabelle Lever *New Frontiers in the Philosophy of Intellectual Property*

Sigrid Sterckx and Julian Cockbain *Exclusions from Patentability: How Far Has the European Patent Office Eroded Boundaries?*

Sebastian Haunss *Conflicts in the Knowledge Society: The Contentious Politics of Intellectual Property*

Helena R. Howe and Jonathan Griffiths *Concepts of Property in Intellectual Property Law*

Rochelle Cooper Dreyfuss and Jane C. Ginsburg *Intellectual Property at the Edge: The Contested Contours of IP*

Normann Witzleb, David Lindsay, Moira Paterson and Sharon Rodrick *Emerging Challenges in Privacy Law: Comparative Perspectives*

Paul Bernal *Internet Privacy Rights: Rights to Protect Autonomy*

Peter Drahos *Intellectual Property, Indigenous People and their Knowledge*

Susy Frankel and Daniel Gervais *The Evolution and Equilibrium of Copyright in the Digital Age*

Edited by Kathy Bowrey and Michael Handler *Law and Creativity in the Age of the Entertainment Franchise*
Sean Bottomley *The British Patent System during the Industrial Revolution 1700–1852: From Privilege to Property*
Susy Frankel *Test Tubes for Global Intellectual Property Issues: Small Market Economies*
Jan Oster *Media Freedom As a Fundamental Right*
Sara Bannerman *International Copyright and Access to Knowledge*
Edited by Andrew T. Kenyon *Comparative Defamation and Privacy Law*
Pascal Kamina *Film Copyright in the European Union* (second edition)
Tim W. Dornis *Trademark and Unfair Competition Conflicts: Historical-Comparative, Doctrinal, and Economic Perspectives*
Ge Chen *Copyright and International Negotiations: An Engine of Free Expression in China?*
David Tan *The Commercial Appropriation of Fame: A Cultural Analysis of the Right of Publicity and Passing Off*
Jay Sanderson *Plants, People and Practices: The Nature and History of the UPOV Convention*
Daniel Benoliel *Patent Intensity and Economic Growth*
Jeffrey A. Maine and Xuan-Thao Nguyen *The Intellectual Property Holding Company: Tax Use and Abuse from Victoria's Secret to Apple*
Megan Richardson *The Right to Privacy: Origins and Influence of a Nineteenth-Century Idea*
Martin Husovec *Injunctions against Intermediaries in the European Union: Accountable but Not Liable?*
Estelle Derclaye *The Copyright/Design Interface: Past, Present and Future*
Magdalena Kolasa *Trade Secrets and Employee Mobility: In Search of an Equilibrium*
Péter Mezei *Copyright Exhaustion: Law and Policy in the United States and the European Union*
Graham Greenleaf and David Lindsay *Public Rights: Copyright's Public Domains*
Ole-Andreas Rognstad *Property Aspects of Intellectual Property*
Elena Cooper *Art and Modern Copyright: The Contested Image*
Paul Bernal *The Internet, Warts and All: Free Speech, Privacy and Truth*
Sebastian Felix Schwemer *Licensing and Access to Content in the European Union: Regulation between Copyright and Competition Law*
Daniela Simone *Copyright and Collective Authorship: Locating the Authors of Collaborative Work*
Emily Hudson *Drafting Copyright Exceptions: From the Law in Books to the Law in Action*
Graeme Gooday and Steven Wilf *Patent Cultures: Diversity and Harmonization in Historical Perspective*
Mark Burdon *Digital Data Collection and Information Privacy Law*
Edited by Niklas Bruun, Graeme B. Dinwoodie, Marianne Levin and Ansgar Ohly *Transition and Coherence in Intellectual Property Law: Essays in Honour of Annette Kur*
Tanya Aplin and Lionel Bently *Global Mandatory Fair Use: The Nature and Scope of the Right to Quote Copyright Works*
Alexander Peukert *A Critique of the Ontology of Intellectual Property Law*
Brent Salter *Negotiating Copyright in the American Theatre: 1856-1951*